Disability and Discourse

Disability and Discourse

Analysing Inclusive Conversation with People with Intellectual Disabilities

Val Williams, Norah Fry Research Centre, University of Bristol

A John Wiley & Sons, Ltd., Publication

Wiley-Blackwell is an imprint of John Wiley & Sons, formed by the merger of Wiley's global Scientific, Technical, and Medical business with Blackwell Publishing.

Registered Office
John Wiley & Sons Ltd, The Atrium, Southern Gate, Chichester, West Sussex, PO19 8SQ, UK

Editorial Offices
The Atrium, Southern Gate, Chichester, West Sussex, PO19 8SQ, UK
9600 Garsington Road, Oxford, OX4 2DQ, UK
350 Main Street, Malden, MA 02148-5020, USA

For details of our global editorial offices, for customer services, and for information about how to apply for permission to reuse the copyright material in this book please see our website at www.wiley.com/wiley-blackwell.

Library of Congress Cataloging-in-Publication Data

Williams, Val.
    Disability and discourse : analysing inclusive conversation with people with intellectual disabilities / by Val Williams.
        p. cm.
    Includes bibliographical references and index.
    ISBN 978-0-470-68266-1 (cloth) – ISBN 978-0-470-68267-8 (pbk.)
    1. People with mental disabilities–Social aspects. 2. People with mental disabilities–Means of communication. 3. Interpersonal communication. 4. Social interaction. I. Title.
    HV3004.W528 2011
    362.3–dc22
                            2010033378

A catalogue record for this book is available from the British Library.

This book is published in the following electronic formats: eBook 9780470977941; Wiley Online Library 9780470977934

Set in 10/12 pt Minion by Toppan Best-set Premedia Limited
Printed in Malaysia by Ho Printing (M) Sdn Bhd

01   2011

Dedication

To my family, Rob, Ben and Naomi, and for everyone at
Norah Fry Research Centre, at the University of Bristol

Contents

About the Author

Val Williams is a researcher at the Norah Fry Research Centre at the University of Bristol, where she has worked since 1997, following previous careers in education. She has always tried to work alongside disabled people and people with intellectual disabilities, in order to make sure they have a voice in matters that concern them. Val has wide-ranging interests in disability studies, as well as conversation analysis, and is an executive editor of the international journal *Disability & Society.*

Preface

by Members of 'The Voice'＊

This book has the title 'intellectual disability'. We know that this is a word used in other countries in the world, and that is why it is in this book. This is just to say that in the UK, we don't understand the word 'intellectual disability'. You need to be quite free-minded to understand all these different words. It's a different way of saying 'learning difficulty'. That's the word we normally use in the UK.

To write this preface (and the prefaces to Parts 1 and 2), we both read a summary of all the chapters in the book. Kerrie read out the summary onto an audio recorder, and Lisa listened and talked about what she thought. We both worked together on this preface. It's really good to have self-advocates involved in a book like this. We are self-advocates ourselves, and we like to do things to help other people.

Most of us don't live in institutions any more. But there are still problems. The social model tells us that there are barriers around. In Chapter 1, Val talks a bit about the social model. If a person uses a wheelchair, and goes to a cinema, and there are steps, how is she going to get up there? That's a barrier. People with learning disabilities face barriers every day. But they can overcome their barriers and fight back. If we want to be independent, we can be. People can help each other, and advise each other.

This book is about talk. Sometimes people can talk, but sometimes they have problems in talking. One of us had a friend who couldn't talk clearly. It's important how people communicate, and you need to find out how they talk. Some people may use sign language. How can people talk to people with intellectual disabilities? They need to talk without being patronising. One of us said that if people are patronising, 'I tell them to push off.'

> This old lady came up to me, and patted me on the head. It made me feel really embarrassed, although I am normally strong about things.

＊ 'The Voice' is the name chosen by a small group of people with learning disabilities who work with staff at Norah Fry Research Centre, where the author is based.

People often talk to our support workers instead of talking to us, and that makes us cross. People also say 'you're doing well', when we're not. That can sound a bit patronising too. We have a voice, and we can speak up when we want to. But there are good times to get feedback, and we often like that. It gives us some sort of praise.

Why should you read this book? If you read the book, it would show you how we feel. Then perhaps you would understand how other 'users' would feel, and how they could have their own voice. And that's the only way you can get through. And you should read this book, because it tells you about us, and it tells you what we want from you. And we want you to read the book carefully. And make sure we've been heard. Don't get this book and just leave it on the shelf!

Acknowledgements

This book has come about because of inclusive research projects, in which people with intellectual disabilities played a central, guiding role. Therefore, their contribution to this book is absolutely vital, and I would first like to acknowledge all the people with intellectual disabilities I have worked with in the past 15 years. Their names appear in credits throughout the book and in their own publications: Julian Goodwin, Neil Palmer, Florence Turner, Brian Vasey, Chris Peacock, Stacey Gramlich, Natasha Snelham, Gordon McBride, Tiffany (Mouse) England, Kerrie Ford and Lisa Ponting. They've all been a fantastic source of inspiration to me. Second, I would like to acknowledge all my colleagues at Norah Fry Research Centre at the University of Bristol, who have supported me while I've been writing this. In particular, a big thank you to Kelley Johnson, who encouraged me to keep at it and to believe it is possible to write a book; also to Jan Walmsley for comments on earlier versions of some of the chapters. Wiley-Blackwell have been very supportive as publishers, and in particular I am indebted to the comments of the anonymous reviewer who had the enthusiasm and interest to read and give incredibly useful feedback on an earlier draft.

The painting on the front cover is by Claude Rimmer, who was an artist with intellectual disabilities, and is in memory of his talents. I am grateful to his family for allowing this to be published. Last, but most importantly, I am very grateful to all the people in self-advocacy groups and the support workers and people with intellectual disabilities who feature throughout the chapters of the book. They are the people who bring it all to life.

Chapter 1

Starting Points

The central interest: communication

This book is about communication. The research reported in these pages is based on recordings of people engaged in social activity. It is a type of research that is fascinating, because it offers a way to understand and change certain patterns in communication, patterns that regularly exclude some groups of people. Every time two or more people interact there is a fresh slate, an opportunity for each person to communicate with the other simply 'as a person' and to be open to new meanings, relationships and ways of interacting. Human communication can sound like something quite emancipatory – a tool for change! As the reader will suspect, it is not quite as easy in practice. In order to move towards more 'empowering' and equal situations in talk, it is vital to explore first the regular, routine power imbalances that affect many people. The chapters in this book therefore trace both problematic as well as positive aspects of communication as they are interwoven in the everyday here-and-now of people's lives.

My central aim in this book is to deliver practical understanding of interactions with people with intellectual disabilities, so that those interactions can be carried out on a basis of equality. People with intellectual disabilities have a right to be included in interactions and have a right to speak out. All those who have an interest in communication, and in working alongside people with intellectual disabilities, will find much in these pages that will support new ways of communicating and working with individuals and groups.

Some readers turning to a book about intellectual disability will expect it to be about communication deficits: most surely, this book is *not*. Rather, it is about the way ordinary resources of social interaction are used in particular contexts by and with people with intellectual disabilities. Rather than offer 'tips for support workers', I aim to capture the complexity and intricate, moment-by-moment contingencies of two-way interaction. The extracts given through the text are detailed transcriptions of audio and video recordings of real-life activities, communication in which more than one participant was involved and where people were engaged in social activities, ranging from checking into a hotel or making a cup of coffee, to planning a research project and chairing a meeting.

Another, equally important starting point was my interest in finding ways to study human communication. Like other analysts, I started doing analysis of interactions because I was drawn to the study of how people understand and communicate with each other. Therefore, a parallel

Disability and Discourse. Analysing Inclusive Conversation with People with Intellectual Disabilities,
1st edition. © Val Williams. Published 2011 by John Wiley & Sons, Ltd.

aim of this book is to interest students, researchers and others who also want to study communication and are searching for inclusive and practical ways of approaching analysis. I use a methodology, described further in Chapter 2, which could be called eclectic, but draws largely on what is called applied 'conversation analysis', referred to as CA throughout (ten Have, 1999). I have taken a position that the tools of CA can be used as a practical methodological resource to explore issues of social concern. Moreover, I have carried out analysis in 'inclusive' contexts of research, involving people with intellectual disabilities themselves in the projects and in the analysis (Williams *et al.*, 2009b). Because there are many conflicting positions and arguments about methodology within discourse analysis, the current book will not presume to side with one set of analysts or another. Instead, it will provide an account of how CA was practised within the current projects. All this is explained further in Chapter 2.

For those unfamiliar with CA methodology, I hope that this book will serve as a taster and a route into a fascinating area of study. Many would-be enthusiasts get put off by the technical and obscure façade of discourse analysis, and also by the seeming irrelevance of some of the findings about how communication is done. I have made a determined attempt to set analysis within a meaningful framework and to explain what I am doing, so that things are more accessible. I have also tried throughout the book to suggest and discuss why analysis matters. By following the analysis and reading some of the texts referred to in each chapter (e.g. Wooffitt, 2005), readers will be able to find out how the tools of CA could suit their own goals.

This book focuses on different social activities that contribute to having a voice in some diverse, lived contexts. It presents actual examples from research studies of what people have said to each other, but not as isolated comments given during interviews or presentations. For instance, the following lines are from a conversation between two people in a living room:

Extract 1.1

45.	Sim	right (.) would you like to help me with the coffee mate
46.	Al	((*smiling*)) if I ha::ve to
47.	Sim	tt th tt ((*LF*))
48.	Al	go on then↓ (0.2) did you take your cup in – you took your cup
49.		in didn't you =
50.	Sim	= yes I put in the sink yeah yes (0.2) ((*gets up and walks to*
51.		*door*))
52.		sorry I've got nothing on my feet and I really should but –
53.	Al	yeah ( ) you know you should but –
54.	Sim	oh that's another story isn't it ((*laughs*))

Transcription conventions used throughout this book are explained further in Chapter 2; significantly the transcription above includes non-verbal noises such as laughter at line 47, indicated by LF. The numbers in brackets relate to the length of pauses in the talk, which are also of interest here.

The two people talking here are Simon and Alan. These are assumed names, like all the names in this book, except where it is acknowledged that people are active contributors and wish their name to be included. In extract 1.1, Simon is a man who has been labelled as having an 'intellectual disability' (or in the UK, where he lives, a 'learning disability'). As they are talking, both men are also doing things – getting up from their seats, walking into the kitchen, and so on. However, there is also a sense in which their talk itself does things. In line 45, for instance, Simon uses talk to instruct his support worker, and at line 52 he accounts for the fact that he has nothing on his feet. All these bits of talk perform actions in that they make it possible for the pair to get to the kitchen and to establish the task of making a cup of coffee. They also perform actions in reinforcing aspects of the relationship between Simon and Alan, whom Simon refers to as 'mate'. A central task for Simon is about 'doing control' and being able to instruct his support worker in a pleasant and friendly way.

The topic of control is an important one in this book. It could be approached (as it often is) via a conventional research interview, by asking people how they feel about the choice and control in their lives. Research participants then reflect on their experiences and talk about how they perceive those experiences. When people like Simon talk about their lives, a researcher can literally give them 'voice' by listening, by giving them a forum and perhaps by publishing their words. I have been committed to all of those things for several years and have supported people with intellectual disabilities to be authors in their own right (Palmer *et al.*, 1999a; Gramlich *et al.*, 2000).

In this book I am more interested in analysing choice and control in action, through the medium of talk. In other words, I am interested to see how these things (such as giving instructions amicably) are done in the ebb and flow of real-life interaction. For instance, an analysis of the above extract could focus on the way in which Simon approaches the instruction which he gives to his support worker in line 45, and also the way that instruction is taken and built into a joke in line 46. It would notice perhaps also how Simon's instruction puts him into a powerful position of control *vis-à-vis* his support worker, a position which then shifts on a line-by-line basis, when for instance Simon apologises for having nothing on his feet at line 52. Taking control of one's life can be seen as a sensitive and subtle task when viewed as real-life interaction.

This book covers two quite contrasting areas of life for people with intellectual disabilities and for those who work with them. Part 1 focuses on communication that happens in everyday life. In particular, the reader will find many conversations with support workers who are working on a one-to-one basis for a person with intellectual disabilities. Part 2 turns to talk in more formal, public situations where people with intellectual disabilities are representing others, speaking up for themselves as a group and campaigning or researching for change. As Goodley (2003) has pointed out, personal and political lives have to be linked: voice and power are central concepts in both these arenas, and one of the central questions throughout this book concerns the links between communication in private life and in collective settings. If I had to pick out one thing I have gained from writing this book, it is a more informed understanding of the massive gulf between what happens in the private lives and the public lives of people with intellectual disabilities, and some of the missed connections between these two arenas.

All the central chapters are based on analysis of communication and feature transcripts from recordings of events that actually happened. That is what discourse analysis, and in particular CA, does, and the methodological tools for this approach will be briefly introduced in Chapter 2. One of the central and most important matters is to do with the stance of the analyst. When faced with a transcript of communication that actually occurred, the trick is to try and see it afresh without making any assumptions about who is who, or about wider issues such as power and equality (see Schegloff, 1998, 1999a & b; and the discussion in Chapter 2). These matters arise from the analysis rather than from any preconceived theories or positions. Therefore, I will try to avoid, in this chapter, any attempt to tell readers everything I know about people with intellectual disabilities. There are many other books which give comprehensive accounts of the field (e.g. Grant *et al.*, 2005). Instead, this chapter merely aims to set some markers relating to identity and the social model of disability. The rest will emerge from the analysis, and the final chapter will serve as a repository for some discussion of the social issues that have arisen from that analysis.

Why does identity matter?

Through studying communication I soon became interested in identity, and would recommend particularly the stance taken by Antaki and Widdicombe (1998b). Their position is that identity is not a given, but is something that can be called on as a resource and reconstructed within talk (see also de Fina *et al.*, 2006). Therefore, there are very close links between communication and identity, and nowhere is this more true than for people with an 'intellectual disability'. The identity of 'intellectual disability' is frequently foregrounded in talk and can affect the way in which conversation is conducted, often with negative implications for people with that label. By the same token, however, it is possible to construct more empowering and meaningful ways of interacting, where people with intellectual disabilities literally 'have a voice', and where they can speak up for themselves. Communication, identity and disability are thus intimately linked.

My initial interest in identity came about because the people I worked with in a research group in 1997–2000 had an interest in labelling. In fact, they rejected strongly the label 'learning difficulty', which was the term used for 'intellectual disability' in the UK in some circles. One of the group members is on record as saying:

> The words 'learning difficulty' were given to us by other people – by those people who diagnosed us. We know we've got this problem, seeing, speaking, understanding – but it doesn't mean we have to have this label on our forehead. I feel like screaming, because people laugh. (Minutes of Self-Advocacy Research Group meeting, 15 January 1997)

The labelling debate itself can easily go off at a tangent, because of the multiplicity of terms. People referred to as having a 'learning disability' or 'learning difficulty' in the UK are labelled in different ways across the globe. 'Intellectual disability' or 'intellectual impairment' are the terms most commonly used now in Australia, New Zealand and at an international level, and there are other terms current in the USA, Canada and some European countries. Most of these terms have been disputed by people to whom the labels are applied, but since the current book aims for clarity internationally, I have chosen to use the term 'intellectual disability'. However, as will be seen from the preface to Part 1, some of the people I have worked with do not relate to that term. Formerly, people in the UK preferred the term 'learning difficulty', as was established in 1994 by researchers who consulted with people in the People First movement (Sutcliffe & Simons, 1994). However, the term 'learning difficulty' has always been a source of some confusion in an international context, where it is often taken as synonymous with 'dyslexia'. This is *not* what is meant here. The people featured in this book all have some kind of enduring and generic impairment, which affects their ability to learn and to manage their lives.

It is relatively easy to follow these debates about which label to use. But the labelling debate is not resolved simply by selecting the appropriate label for the moment. It is also about what is actually meant by the category 'Intellectual Disability'. Many books about intellectual disability start from the presumption that an intellectual disability is something that a person either 'has' or 'does not have', like an illness. However, as Rioux and Bach (1994) pointed out in the title of their book, disability is 'not measles'. Others (see Rapley, 2004) take a social constructionist view, and would argue that 'intellectual disability' is an entirely culturally constructed phenomenon. There are some complex issues to face in working out what 'social constructionism' can mean in the context of the kind of analysis done in this book and these will be picked up again in Chapter 2. For the moment, it is enough to note that a study of communication in action is bound to be interested in the ideas of social constructionism, which would claim that categories such as 'intellectual disability' can literally be talked into being (Rapley, 2004: 1–7) and do not necessarily have any solid existence outside that talk.

Such arguments invariably provoke a reaction, especially in those who live with someone with an intellectual disability. Social constructionism seems to brush aside the problems of an intellectual disability, and indeed the very definition (see the latest edition of the classification manual from the American Association on Intellectual and Developmental Disabilities, 2010). Definitions of 'intellectual disability' are nearly always premised on ideas about an inability to manage one's own life. The current English 'Learning Disability' strategy (Department of Health (DH), 2009) adopts the definition introduced in 2001:

- a significantly reduced ability to understand new or complex information, to learn new skills;
- a reduced ability to cope independently;
- which started before adulthood, and with a lasting effect on development.

(DH, 2001: 14)

These facts about people are not idle abuse, brought about by an arbitrary label. Enduring cognitive differences do of course affect how people live their lives. People with intellectual disabilities across the globe have an assessed need to receive support precisely because they cannot cope independently with their lives; if they did not receive support, they would be in danger or at risk (see Fyson, 2009, for an airing of some of these dilemmas). The discourse of 'incompetence' (Simpson, 1995) underpins and justifies why people need support in the first place. Any description of the lives of people with intellectual disabilities at the start of the twenty-first century has to take into account their needs for social support, as well as their current devalued position in society. What the people included in this book have in common is that someone has decided at some point that they have an 'intellectual disability' – that is their diagnosis, their category or their label, bringing with it many distinct social experiences. For convenience, this book will refer to people with intellectual disabilities, where necessary, by that label.

Nevertheless, it would also be true to say that individuals with the label of intellectual disability do not constitute a homogeneous group, and the fact that they are grouped together under one banner is in many respects a cultural accident, an artificial phenomenon (Beart *et al.*, 2005). There are considerable cognitive and functional differences between the people featured in the following chapters. For instance, at one end of the scale, people with intellectual disabilities may have little or no speech, have multiple or complex physical or sensory problems and perhaps also engage in behaviour which challenges those around them. The term also covers those who are quite independent and would be able to travel to another town or country with little support; they may be able to read, write and speak for themselves. Moreover, it can be appreciated that what counts as an intellectual disability in one society will not necessarily be considered an intellectual disability in another. Functional limitations are relative to the culture, the situation and the goals that people have. For instance, Rao (2006) discusses how Bengali mothers define 'normality' in a family-related way, depending on the achievement of yardsticks in social competence in Bengali culture. This is a quite different perspective from that which prevails in Western cultures, particularly in educational settings (Frederikson & Cline, 2002). Aspis (1999), for instance, describes herself as a 'disabled person who has been labelled by the system as having learning difficulties':

This makes it very clear that the name and the identity 'learning difficulty', have been imposed on me by the system, in particular the education system which pre-defines 'learning ability'. (Aspis, 1999: 174)

There are now global policy goals to afford all citizens greater autonomy and control. The first guiding principle of the UN Convention on the Rights of Disabled People enshrines the notion of individual choice and states that all disabled people should be accorded:

Respect for inherent dignity, individual autonomy including the freedom to make one's own choices, and independence of persons. (UN, 2007: 5)

Some of these issues do not sit happily together. How, for instance, are we to accept that someone can have autonomy in making important life decisions if, at the same time, we know that person needs support to be in control of everyday matters such as budgeting, going to a leisure centre or understanding time? At present, these tensions are seldom transparent in policy, although they are wrestled with in law. In the UK, some of the issues surrounding capacity have been clarified through the 2005 Mental Capacity Act. This legislation attempts to give clear guidance about how an individual can be assessed as capable, or incapable, of making a particular decision on a particular occasion (Jepson, 2008; Myron *et al.*, 2008; Swift, 2008). Although the guidance associated with the Act emphasises the importance of support for individuals to make their own decisions, nevertheless for the first time in the UK, a precise definition of 'incapacity' is formally acknowledged through this legislation. The assessment of incapacity should explicitly be made separately for each context, each person and each decision, and the Act expressly states that blanket assumptions of incapacity should not be made because of a person falling into a particular category.

What does all this mean for people with intellectual disabilities themselves? At one level, the reality is often a life lived as a 'learner', struggling to gain the competence needed for a free and more independent lifestyle:

People with learning difficulties must demonstrate their competence prior to being granted autonomy ... Competence is not liberation, although it may form part of it for some individuals. (Simpson, 1999: 154–5)

It could well be that this tension is becoming yet more marked in the global market of the twenty-first century. For instance, Dowse (2009) explores the increasing impact of neo-liberalisation and market forces on people with intellectual disabilities, and reaches the conclusion that the challenge of 'being competent' is becoming evermore extreme. People in society generally are increasingly valued and rewarded according to their intellectual *abilities*, and this is bound to have a knock-on effect on the position of people who lack those abilities.

Many of the people with intellectual disabilities I have worked with have been caught up in issues relating to their identity (see also Nunkoosing, 2000). They do not want to accept that their 'intellectual disability' defines them, and they would prefer to learn new skills and have recognition for their achievements. For instance, when the people in the research group in the 'Finding Out' project wrote up their work in a chapter for a published book (Palmer *et al.*, 1999a), they described themselves as 'people with intellectual abilities'. Yet they took part in organisations and activities that were defined by the fact that they had 'intellectual disabilities'.

This book will explore in Chapters 3 and 4 in particular, with real examples, how ideas about incompetence inform and underpin the way in which other people talk with people with intellectual disabilities, how their decisions are vetted and how they themselves may seek approval for achievements in their everyday lives. Ideas about incompetence are very pervasive in Intellectual Disability thinking, without necessarily being consciously articulated. That is what is meant by a 'naturalised' discourse; it forms a backdrop to the ways in which people talk with each other, and it is an important job for discourse analysis to unpick and reveal what lies behind the way people communicate.

From this brief exposition I hope that I have given an idea of some of the debates about intellectual disability identity and the tensions underpinning them. Readers who wish to read further about these debates are referred to Beart *et al.* (2005) for a review and also to Finlay and Lyons (1998) and Craig *et al.* (2002). The changing of labels is one part of the battle about identity waged by people with 'intellectual disabilities'; as Eayrs, Ellis and Jones (1993) argued, the word used to refer to people does matter, and people have a right to choose the concept for themselves. However, whatever the latest term adopted for 'intellectual disability' it is also important to acknowledge that it has never been value-neutral in contemporary society. It implies a life set apart, with lesser rights than most citizens in the community (Tideman, 2005), and that separation is visible both in the private and the public encounters which are traced through this book. Through analysing everyday interactions it is possible to unpick some of these matters, and to start to understand how people both draw on a range of identities in order to communicate with each other, and how they reinforce and repackage those identities afresh on each occasion they talk. Approaches to identity using CA are explored further in Chapter 2, pp. 27–30.

The social model of disability

In order to gain a different, and hopefully more productive, perspective on the lives of people with intellectual disabilities, it is essential to take into account ideas that emerged in the 1980s and 1990s from the disabled people's movement. The social model of disability (Oliver, 1990; Barton, 2004; Finkelstein, 2004) was formulated by disabled people because of their concerns about how they were being treated as misfits within a society that is primarily constructed around the needs of non-disabled people. They argued that they were disabled by society rather than by their individual impairments. The enduring contribution of the social model has been to turn attention away from the 'problems' of the individual and towards the barriers created by society. These can range from physical barriers (e.g. steps or lack of physical access to public buildings) to social or attitudinal barriers (lack of understanding or prejudice), and are always about institutional problems that may result in disabled people's rights not being respected.

As Oliver (2004) argues, the social model in itself is a tool – it was originally formulated in order to fight back against the predominant, medicalised view of disability – and it has been profoundly influential precisely because it helps people to see disability in a new light. There have been many concerns, discussions and additions to the ideas at the heart of the social model (see for an example Thomas, 2004). However, the essential strength of the model has not changed, particularly in its application to practice.

It is easy enough to find examples of social barriers in what is known about the lives of people with intellectual disabilities (French, 1999; Abbott & McConkey, 2006). For instance, just as surely as people who use wheelchairs may be physically excluded (by lack of accessible toilets, ramps and lifts) so also people with intellectual disabilities are excluded by a society that is premised on the intellectual ability of all of its citizens (Dowse, 2009). It is still extremely rare for people with an intellectual disability in Western cultures to have paid employment (Beyer *et al.*, 2004) because economies depend on increasing technical skills at work. Social exclusion indices paint a bleak picture for people with intellectual disabilities across the globe (Redley, 2009).

The social barriers faced by people with intellectual disabilities could be viewed as a very high wall, separating them effectively from the ordinary social achievements that make life worth living for most people. Todd and Shearn (1997), for instance, listed marriage, employment and personal relationships as being absent in the lives of most people with intellectual disabilities, and commented that:

> People with intellectual disabilities seem to occupy a marginal social space typically occupied by the sociological form of strangers. (Todd & Shearn, 1997: 343)

The situation has not changed dramatically in the UK in the intervening years, as Welshman and Walmsley (2006) testify and as was borne out by a national survey in 2005 (Emerson *et al.*, 2005).

What do these exclusions have to do with communication? If one thinks of the barriers faced by learning disabled people as macro-level barriers to certain material and physical goods (e.g. a house or a job), then it is hard to see how interaction can matter. Just by talking, people cannot solve every problem. However, as Watson (2003) observes, the exclusion faced by disabled people is enacted on a daily basis in the social practices of everyday life. The larger sociological forms of exclusion are visible in the conduct of individuals:

> Disabling social relations are everywhere, they are part of disabled people's everyday life ... (Watson, 2003: 51)

The social business of the world takes place via communication between individuals. Therefore, when the discourse analyst looks at small chunks of that communication, it is possible to analyse how they both reflect and constitute the barriers faced by disabled people. There are frequent references to disabling communication in the literature and personal biographies of disabled people, for instance critiques of those who implicitly measure 'disability' against measures of what it means to be 'normal' (Swain & Cameron, 1999). To continue the metaphor, the high wall shutting out people with intellectual disabilities is made up of countless smaller bricks and mortar in the communication surrounding them.

An example of the link between discourse and social barriers is found in ideas about independent living. A recent review has found that people with intellectual disabilities throughout Europe are often excluded from policies supporting independent living (Townsley *et al.*, 2009), because of the assumption that they would not be able to choose their own lifestyle responsibly and manage 'independently'. These assumptions are reinforced every time someone talks down to a person with intellectual disabilities, treating them like a child or disbelieving what they say. Assumptions can also be built into higher-level discourses, such as the discourse about independence itself. In the field of intellectual disability, and among professionals in that field, independence is often talked about as 'doing everything on your own'. It follows, therefore, that people with intellectual disabilities are forever learning 'independence skills' so that they can move further on towards that goal. Disabled academics, however, have argued that independence actually means being in control of your own support. Independence can be supported and does not imply that the individual literally has to do everything for himself (Morris, 1993; Office for Disability Issues, 2008). The Disability Rights Commission defined independent living as:

> All disabled people having the same choice, control and freedom as any other citizen – at home, at work, and as members of the community. This does not necessarily mean disabled people 'doing everything for themselves', but it does mean that any practical assistance people need should be based on their own choices and aspirations. (Disability Rights Commission, 2002)

As this new type of discourse surrounding independent living becomes more widespread, it can provide a challenge to assumptions about people with intellectual disabilities and thereby help to change the way people are treated.

Although social model theorists and discourse analysts have not always seen eye to eye (Oliver, 1996; Rapley, 2004), the social model is nevertheless a very useful starting point for a book that is about interaction with others in society. The analytic lens will be focused on those points of contact with other people, and my aim is not to offer insights about presumed brain processes or cognition of people with intellectual disabilities, but rather to unpick the way in which ordinary resources of communication are used by and with people with intellectual disabilities. Social models of disability, as Barton (2004) explains, were created by disabled people and are rooted in self-definition of disablement, by disabled people themselves. This is well expressed by Swain and Cameron in *Disability Discourse* (Corker & French, 1999):

The emergence of a discourse on disability around the social model … has provided disabled people with alternative forms of reference within which to build their own identities. (Swain & Cameron, 1999: 76)

That is why it is appropriate to think about the social model when exploring autonomy and voice. However, as in all discourse analysis, this book takes the position that theories emerge from data, and that the best way to look at real examples of communication is with a 'fresh' eye, unencumbered by theory (Silverman, 1999). That is why any further contribution to ideas and theories will be left until after the analysis, and it is only in the final pages of this book that I return to issues about identity and the social model of disability.

The research context

The two main studies on which this book is based were deliberately set up in ways that challenged and overturned assumptions about power, and in which notions of voice, control and autonomy were paramount. Equally, they provide contexts which become the focus for analysis, particularly in Part 2. The inclusive nature of the projects cannot be taken for granted, and this will be discussed further below. However, the topic and background of each study are also important to note, since this helps to clarify some of the extracts analysed in this book. Therefore, the following sections offer some very brief introductions to the rationale of each research study.

Background to 'Skills for Support'

Part 1 (Chapters 3–8) is entitled 'Individual Voices' and concentrates on examples of conversations from everyday life encounters between people with intellectual disabilities and their support workers. Most of these are taken from a research study called 'Skills for Support' (see also Williams *et al.*, 2009a, 2009b; Ponting *et al.*, 2010). It was funded by the UK Big Lottery and was a partnership project between an academic research centre (the Norah Fry Research Centre, University of Bristol) and a disabled people's organisation (the West of England Centre for Inclusive Living – WECIL). The aim of the research was to analyse, from the point of view of people with intellectual disabilities themselves, what 'good support' constituted. Two people with intellectual disabilities had paid jobs in this project, working with the author in a team based at WECIL, and during the final phase of this study over 20 hours of video data were collected from 14 pairs of support workers and people with intellectual disabilities (Ponting *et al.*, 2010; Williams *et al.*, 2009a, 2009b).

Since 1996, disabled people in the UK have had the opportunity to take a direct payment instead of a direct social service to meet their support needs (DH, 1996), and the philosophy behind direct payments is one of choice, control and empowerment for individual service users. Having previously worked with people with intellectual disabilities to explore the ways in which direct payments could be supported (Gramlich *et al.*, 2002), I was now keen to see how the relationship with support staff played out in practice. Previous research about community engagement for people with intellectual disabilities in residential homes (Felce *et al.*, 2002; Mansell *et al.*, 2002) has emphasised that the single factor that makes a difference to outcomes is staff practices. Further, as will be explored in Chapter 2, discursive work in this area (Antaki *et al.*, 2007a, 2007b) has emphasised the problematic nature of routine communications between staff and residents in care homes. By contrast, the focus in the 'Skills for Support' project was on people who used direct payments and employed their own staff. It seemed to me and to my collaborator, John Kelly, that people would get more personal power because of the type of relationship they had with their support staff. We both hoped as well that this relationship could be turned around through the mechanism of a direct payment. Instead of the staff being in control, now the disabled person could be the 'boss' of their own staff (Gramlich *et al.*, 2002).

More recently, the benefits of choice and control have been embedded in the personalisation agenda of the UK government. The government has set out its universal vision for personalised services for all disabled and older people who need a social service (PMSU, 2005; DH, 2006b). A key mechanism for achieving this control over one's own life is to be the personal budget, defined as:

> A clear, upfront allocation of funding to enable them to make informed choices about how best to meet their needs. (DH, 2008b: 5)

A personal budget is a wider concept than a direct payment; it includes the idea that people will know about the money allocated to them and will be able to get support to plan for themselves how they want that money to be offered. One of their choices may be a direct payment; another may be to hand over the budget to an organisation which provides the services they require. However, even if the service user chooses to pay an organisation or to opt for more traditional services, the goal is that they will still have control over the outcomes for their own life (Daly & Roebuck, 2008).

Will the brave new world of personalised services turn around the lives of people with intellectual disabilities? There are undoubtedly still tensions here, which will be explored throughout this book. I will show in Part 1 that supporting people to be in control of the everyday fabric of their own lives and decisions is not always as straightforward as it sounds. However, I am chiefly interested (as were my colleagues in 'Skills for Support') to gain insight into new, more personalised ways of working, and so Chapters 5–8 in particular will seek to elucidate the shape of more 'equal' interactions between people with intellectual disabilities and those who are employed to support them.

Background to the 'Finding Out' project

The other main research project, which features particularly in Part 2, took place before 'Skills for Support' and was a short study in which a group of people with intellectual disabilities ran their own project, with voluntary support from the author (Palmer *et al.*, 1999a; Williams, 1999). At that point, there had been few examples of similar research involving people with intellectual disabilities, and we wanted to explore, to the limits, what it could mean for these people to actually have research roles. There were four people with intellectual disabilities in the research group, which existed for some two years. During the first few months group members decided to carry out some focus group interviews at other self-advocacy organisations in the area. Their aim, in the words of one of the members, was 'to find out whether other people with learning difficulties are hitting their heads against a brick wall like we are' (Palmer & Turner, 1998). The four research group members compiled a list of questions to talk about in the focus groups, and I helped them to arrange six visits, all of which were recorded on audio and video tape, as were most of the sessions we held on a weekly basis to run the group and learn about research.

In inclusive research nothing can be taken for granted; doing this type of work throws into question both the strategies for inclusion and also the activity called 'research'. The process of carrying out the 'Finding Out' project was also written up in Williams (1999) and provided the basis for a discourse analysis in Williams (2002). It is the latter analysis that informs the current book. Like all social activities (e.g. a criminal trial, a university seminar, a reunion of friends), research is built up from a wealth of communication events. By studying these events, it is possible to gain a better idea of what characterises a particular social activity, and indeed, social research events have been analysed in this vein before (Silverman, 1973). The aim of my own discourse study was essentially to provide an analytical description of the 'Finding Out' project. Instead of assuming that people with intellectual disabilities could automatically step into academic 'research' roles, I set out to analyse the communication events that formed and shaped the research activity. My basic question was 'What actually happens between the people involved in an inclusive research study?' I was interested in what inclusive research actually meant in terms of actual communication practices. It is mainly data from this project which feature in Part 2 (Chapters 9–13), which is entitled 'Collective Voice'. These chapters focus on more public situations, where people with intellectual disabilities are representing others, speaking up through their own organisations or conducting their own research project.

Participation and voice

By claiming to do research, it could be said that people are taking part in collecting and creating their own knowledge. Therefore, a few words are in order here about the background relating to participation generally.

If people with intellectual disabilities are considered to be 'oppressed', then this institutionalised oppression can be challenged. With some support, people with intellectual disabilities, like Black people or women, have set up their own organised movement, which has been called 'self-advocacy' (Sutcliffe & Simons, 1994; Dybwad & Bersani, 1996). Like the idea of 'having a voice', the term self-advocacy is a loaded concept. It is only used at all because the people to whom it refers have not previously been able to advocate for themselves, as Goodley points out:

> The term self-advocacy has been applied to account for the self-determination of minority groups who have historically been denied a 'voice' ... the self-determination of people with learning difficulties is emphasized and members of this labelled group are referred to as self-advocates. (Goodley, 2000: 7)

Goodley's formulation of 'self-advocacy' might sound straightforward, but of course these things are always more complex when they are played out in practice, as I explore particularly in the later chapters of this book. For a start, there are worries about the authenticity of people's 'voice', if this has to be channelled and supported through non-disabled people; this will be explored particularly in Chapters 10 and 12. Another tension exists in relation to the very self-identification of people with intellectual disabilities. One of the major campaigns of self-advocacy groups concerns the battle against categorisation and labelling; but if someone does not even identify as a 'person with intellectual disabilities', how can he or she be part of a movement purportedly owned by people with that label?

Participation in public affairs is associated not only with power, but also with the collective power that people have when they come together and campaign for their own rights (Beresford, 2001; Barnes & Mercer, 2007), challenging the status quo. That element of challenge is the positive point of this book. If it is possible to analyse how social forces of exclusion are re-enacted and constructed in everyday talk, it is also possible to consider ways in which the 'voice' of service users can contribute to changing policy and practice. Instead of being passive recipients of inadequate services, disabled people are now expected to take a full role as active citizens and to determine what types of support they need. These notions of choice and control are at the heart of current Intellectual Disability policy in the UK and across the Western world (Johnson *et al.*, 2010). Consider the following UK policy statement:

> People with intellectual disabilities are amongst the most socially excluded and vulnerable groups in Britain today. Very few have jobs, live in their own homes or have real choice over who cares for them. Many have few friends outside their families and those paid to care for them. Their voices are rarely heard in public. This needs to change. (DH, 2001: 14)

There is an assumption here that the 'voices' of people with intellectual disabilities need to be heard and that this in itself will help to reverse the social exclusion they face. Using the methodology in this book, it is possible to get behind the rhetoric and to analyse how that participation may happen. The extracts in Part 2 focus particularly on 'collective voice', in situations such as meetings, research visits or public events.

This notion of voice is enshrined in the 2007 Convention on the Rights of Disabled Persons, of which one of the guiding principles is: *Full and effective participation and inclusion in society.* The question could be asked, of course, why some people may need a human rights statement in order to participate and 'be included'; the implication is quite clearly that they belong to a category of people who are excluded and that ideas about participation and voice are being marked out as something significant and unusual for them. For instance, the English government's disability policy (DH, 2001; PMSU, 2005; DH, 2006b) uses the following aspirational statement to urge policy-makers, service managers and commissioners to listen to what service users want:

> At the same time as giving people greater choice and control over the services they use, we also need to ensure that everyone in society has a voice that is heard. (DH, 2006b: 7.4)

Does everyone have a voice 'that is heard'? The situation for people with intellectual disabilities in public policy is arguably more problematic than for many other minority groups. In theory, the same injunctions to participate apply to people with intellectual disabilities, just as to other service users. Government disability policy (DH, 2001, 2006b) urges policy-makers, service managers and commissioners to listen to what service users want, and the 'learning disability' strategy, *Valuing People* (DH, 2001), claims that people with intellectual disabilities 'should be fully involved in the decision-making processes that affect their lives' (para. 4.27).

Despite the rhetoric, those of us who have been involved in supporting people with intellectual disabilities in self-advocacy forums, in consultations or in research are generally aware of the tensions and criticisms revolving again around worries about their intellectual capability (see Concannon, 2005, for some useful examples and discussion). Either people are criticised for not participating in a meaningful way or they are criticised for not being representative of the majority of people with intellectual disabilities (Fyson & Fox, 2008). Many people claim that people with intellectual disabilities can only participate in public policy if they are competent and autonomous (Barnes, 2002), and there have therefore been many discussions about the participation of people with intellectual disabilities in the UK and Australia (Frawley, 2008).

Another key concern is the role played by non-disabled supporters. For instance, Redley and Weinberg (2007) found that people with intellectual disabilities were frequently not speaking for themselves in participation forums, but were prompted, guided and moulded by supporters who did not have intellectual disabilities. Like Redley and Weinberg's study, the present book seeks to find direct evidence of interaction in order to gain a deeper understanding of what is going on in the social activities which constitute 'having a voice'. However, unlike Redley and Weinberg (2007), a wider range of social activities, participants and contexts will be sampled – both 'front stage' at meetings or research visits, and 'backstage' during preparation sessions – in order to gain a fuller picture of support strategies and what it means for people with intellectual disabilities to have a voice.

The inclusive research movement

As mentioned above, all the research projects featured in this book have some claim to be 'inclusive', in the sense that they include people with learning disabilities in central roles, beyond that of simply being participants. This is the sense developed in Walmsley and Johnson's (2003) book, *Inclusive Research with People with Intellectual Disabilities*. As explained above, the current book is built on the assumption that social activities, including 'inclusive research', can be analysed via the talk from which they are constituted. Therefore, it is not appropriate here to pre-empt that analysis. However, a few more words about the history of the inclusive research movement, and some of the issues and tensions involved, may be in order for readers new to this area.

Both the main research studies which feature in this book involved people with intellectual disabilities taking up roles as active researchers and were intended to be empowering in their own right (Palmer *et al.*, 1999a; Williams, 1999; Williams *et al.*, 2009a, 2009b; Ponting *et al.*, 2010). That is why I found them both so intriguing and rich, since they contained the seeds of challenge to the status quo about the identity of 'intellectual disability'. They both offered a chance to think about interactions involving people with intellectual disabilities in a new way and in contexts which literally turned things on their head. People with intellectual disabilities, in these pages, are employers (of their own staff), self-advocates in charge of their own organisations and researchers creating their own knowledge. While other discourse work on the subject of Intellectual Disability has concentrated on the way in which people's voices are silenced or manipulated (Antaki *et al.*, 2006; Jingree *et al.*, 2006), the purpose here is to move on and explore how empowerment is played out in interaction, where people with intellectual disabilities not only 'speak up', but also have the right to take on more powerful roles in conversations.

Until comparatively recently, research about disabled people was always commissioned and led by non-disabled people. It was largely about describing the experiences of disabled people, and using this 'objective' evidence (through the filter of the academic researcher) to produce or support theories that might influence policy (Barnes & Mercer, 1997). The roots of criticism about this approach can be traced back to the 1960s, but since the 1990s in particular disabled people and their organisations have expressed their disillusionment with research on disability and with mainstream academic theories and policy approaches (Oliver, 1992). They suggested a clear way forward for disability politics and disability research, a new paradigm which they called emancipatory research, which would be based on the social model of disability referred to above. Oliver's (1992) revolutionary proposal was that disabled people themselves should commission and control research which concerns their lives. Issues of power and control are central to this new paradigm, in which the roles of 'researcher' and 'researched' are essentially flipped over.

How does this new paradigm of emancipatory research apply to people with intellectual disabilities? Until the 1990s, people with intellectual disabilities were often not even considered to be suitable research *respondents*. 'User views' were more frequently collected from parents, carers or professionals than from people with intellectual disabilities themselves (see Goodley, 2001, for a discussion). That is still the case in much social research. However, there have been many developments and ground travelled in recent years, with publications written primarily by people with intellectual disabilities about their own point of view as researchers (March *et al.*, 1997). Funders such as the UK Department of Health now recognise that people with intellectual disabilities can have an involvement in research studies, and the research which followed the *Valuing*

People strategy (DH, 2001), for instance, was monitored by a group of people with intellectual disabilities, who checked on the user involvement in those projects. They wrote a report called *Let Me in, I'm a Researcher* (DH, 2006a).

There are many well-discussed issues and tensions when people with intellectual disabilities take part in research. Because they invariably have supporters or do partnership work, this type of research has been referred to as participatory (Zarb, 1992), where it is assumed that full power does *not* lie in the hands of the disabled person. As Walmsley (2001) pointed out, research with people with intellectual disabilities started from the self-advocacy movement and has generally been carried out with 'allies' or supporters. She points out that much of what has gone under the title of 'inclusive research' has been about advocacy, where non-disabled allies help people with intellectual disabilities to fill more powerful and valued social roles (Walmsley, 2001: 193–5). The issue of power is very central to these debates; the concept of 'emancipatory research' implied that full power lay in the hands of disabled people themselves, and indeed that the research was initiated by them (Oliver, 1997). Many commentators have questioned whether this is ever possible with people with intellectual disabilities (Chappell, 2000; Walmsley, 2001).

Some of the early inclusive research projects were evaluations and were based firmly on notions developed by non-disabled academics. However, more recently people with intellectual disabilities have been involved in many different types of research, including, for instance, life-story research (Johnson *et al.*, 2001; Meininger, 2006), surveys (Emerson *et al.*, 2005) and the current video interaction analysis (Williams *et al.*, 2009c; Ponting *et al.*, 2010).

There is also a strong link between inclusive research and the action associated with campaigning, undertaken by people within their own representative movement. This trend also raises eyebrows in some quarters, since this type of 'action research' may not count as objective, systematic or unbiased. Nevertheless, action research clearly has a role to play as a tool for change within communities, and inclusive research by people with intellectual disabilities can likewise lay claim to be about change. This was one of Oliver's (1992) central insights, and is taken up again by Walmsley (2001):

> The implications of the emancipatory model are that the conditions of research production are changed so that theory and action emerge together, and out of one another. (Walmsley, 2001: 198)

In order to avoid unwarranted assumptions about the emancipatory or participatory status of any particular project, the current book follows Walmsley (2001), who coined the term 'inclusive research' for that reason. The last few years have seen an increase in the number of research projects that have adopted an inclusive approach with people with intellectual disabilities, and they have contributed to our knowledge about how best to design and support such work. We know, for instance, how important and sensitive the roles of supporters are (Swain, 1995; Rodgers, 1999) and how central the self-advocacy movement is for inclusive research (McClimens, 1999; Chapman & McNulty, 2004; Abell *et al.*, 2007). Many different models and levels of inclusion are possible (Stalker, 1998; Ward & Simons, 1998). The projects on which this book is based have also contributed to that literature, by descriptions and analysis of inclusive research projects from the point of view of disabled researchers (Palmer & Turner, 1998; Tarleton *et al.*, 2004; Williams & England, 2005) and non-disabled supporters (Williams, 1999; Williams *et al.*, 2005). The themes emphasised in our own body of literature are very much to do with the definition of roles within teams and the somewhat problematic nature of research skills training within inclusive projects. Others have also written about particular practices to include people in analysis (Richardson, 2002), as was also attempted in Williams *et al.* (2005).

The current book, as explained above, aims to describe social activities as 'emergent': they only come into being by virtue of the talk or other communication that goes on within them.

Therefore, no assumptions should be made about the status of any activity as constituting research, as being 'participatory', 'inclusive' or indeed powerful. However, in order to index some of the data throughout the book, the two main research studies in this book will now be summarised in a factual format so that readers can refer back to these thumbnail sketches.

Thumbnail sketches of the two main research studies in this book

The 'Finding Out' project

In 1997, four people with intellectual disabilities set out to form their own research group. They had previously been members of a movement known as 'Europe People First' and I knew them from that movement and also from the fact that some of them had been students in a college where I had worked. Two of the group were already members of the local People First organisation as well, and that is where we had our group meetings.

From the time we started on this project, we made audio recordings of nearly all our sessions together and so had a considerable collection of data about what we were doing. After some group sessions in which the members discussed what they wanted to do, they decided that their main aim was 'to find out whether other people with intellectual disabilities were hitting their heads against a brick wall like we are'. Supported by myself in a voluntary capacity, the group decided to contact six other self-advocacy organisations in the south-west of England and to carry out group interviews there (see Table 1.1). They wrote their own research questions and were largely unencumbered by any requirements from research funders, although they did obtain a small grant from the Regional Lottery Fund, which covered expenses.

One of the group members and I attended a disability studies conference in Leeds, UK, during 1997, which was about disabled people's research. Through contacts at that conference, the group was offered the opportunity to write a chapter based on their research for a published book (Palmer *et al.*, 1999a). All the data from the group interviews were recorded in audio and video format, and group members found it useful to look at the videos in order to decide on their own points for their report. They subsequently wrote an accessible report of their findings (Palmer *et al.*, 1999b) as well as some journal articles (Palmer & Turner, 1998).

Following the practical data collection and the group's own analysis and publications, I approached them to ask if I could look at the tapes myself as part of my PhD. Not only did they

Table 1.1 Research visits carried out by research group in the 'Finding Out' project

Visit	Type of group visited	How many people (in addition to four in the research group plus author)
1	Self-advocacy group in day centre	Six people in group visited plus one support worker
2	Network meeting for several independent self-advocacy groups; in sports centre	Approximately 20 people in group visited, plus two support workers
3	Independent self-advocacy group	Four people in group plus one support worker
4	Independent self-advocacy group	Six people in group visited plus one support worker
5	Independent self-advocacy group	Approximately 12 people in group visited, plus two support workers
6	Relationships support group	Four people in group, plus one support worker

give consent, but two of them in particular wanted to carry on being involved in my PhD research. My aim was to look back at the process of our 'inclusive' project and to offer an analytic description of 'inclusive research' as a social activity. The continued involvement of group members meant that I could discuss with them my analytic conclusions and include their insights about self-advocacy, campaigning and research in my thesis (Williams, 2002). Our journey together ended when the Open University agreed to offer the group members diplomas at the same time as I gained my PhD, and we had a joint ceremony at the regional office of the Open University in our home town of Bristol.

'Skills for Support' project

The initial idea for the second project, 'Skills for Support', originated from discussions in 2002 with people with intellectual disabilities who were members of a People First organisation in Swindon. Following previous research about direct payments (Gramlich *et al.*, 2002), it seemed to all of us that people with intellectual disabilities would only be in charge of their lives with the right support. I wrote a research proposal based on these ideas and submitted it unsuccessfully for funding. However, the proposal was later discussed further with WECIL (a disabled people's organisation) who were also interested in the relationship between disabled people and personal assistants. A partnership between WECIL and my university research centre (Norah Fry) ensued, and we were successful in obtaining funding for a 30-month research study from the UK Big Lottery.

'Skills for Support' was planned from the start as an inclusive project and employed two people with intellectual disabilities, Kerrie Ford and Lisa Ponting, who both had jobs for two days a week. The aim of the study was to find out what people with intellectual disabilities themselves valued in their one-to-one support workers, and there were several stages of the project, as had been planned in the original proposal. First, a UK-wide survey examined the employment conditions and perspectives of personal assistants (PAs) who were employed by people with intellectual disabilities; second, interviews were held with people with intellectual disabilities, PAs and managers of direct payments schemes. This book, however, focuses on the third and final stage of the project, when videos were made (20.5 hours of recording) with 14 support workers and the people with intellectual disabilities they worked with (see Table 1.2).

The roles Lisa and Kerrie played in the project were central at all stages; the project office was within WECIL and Lisa and Kerrie were both managed and supervised by WECIL staff. The actual research team consisted of me, as lead researcher; a research supporter employed by the project; the two researchers, whom we referred to as 'self-advocate researchers'; and a personal assistant employed by one of them.

By contrast with the 'Finding Out' project, 'Skills for Support' was a major, national project, and was fully funded. In certain respects, this meant that we had less freedom to follow the lead set by Lisa and Kerrie, since there was a research plan to follow and we were accountable to our funders. However, in other respects, we had the time and resources to carry out research training and for Lisa and Kerrie to have full support to take part in interviews, data analysis, design of outputs and particularly in the collection of video data. When we interviewed people at stage 2 of the project, we discussed the possibility of taking part in a video, and each pair of participants (the person with intellectual disabilities and the support worker) explained what they would normally do together and suggested in broad outline what activity we could record. However, when we finally went to do the filming, we simply recorded what was happening at that time, which often went far beyond the initial discussions. For example, one person with intellectual disabilities told us about going to a football match with his support worker. However, most of our recording took place in his kitchen before they set out for the match.

Table 1.2   Background details of participants in 'Skills for Support' videos

Video	Context of activities filmed	Support and living arrangements of the person with learning disabilities
V1	Cleaning up in the house; chatting together	Rented flat; support worker employed through direct payment
V2	Visit to a public café	Ditto (same pair as in V1)
V3	A dance class for people with learning disabilities	Lives in own house, through shared ownership arrangement; employs support staff through a direct payment, with support from family and others.
V4	Sensory relaxation group	Ditto (same person as in V2)
V5	Supper time at home	Ditto (same person as in V2)
V6	Going to the supermarket	Ditto (same person as in V2)
V7	Visiting local youth club	Ditto (same person as in V2)
V8	Visit to leisure centre; pub visit	Lives with elderly parents; has small direct payment, which funds someone from an organisation to visit and go out
V9	Arrival at train station, taxi journey and checking into hotel	Rented flat, support worker employed through direct payment
V10	At home, making coffee, socialising, cleaning up	Rented flat, support worker employed through direct payment
V11	Personal care: preparing for a shower, socialising	Rented flat, support worker from an agency
V12	Arts group for people with learning disabilities	Lives in parents' home; support worker from day centre
V13	Preparing for supper at home	Lives in parents' home, same person as V12, different support worker: employed by direct payment while parents away
V14	Writing shopping list and going shopping	Rented flat, support worker through an organisation
V15	Checking emails at home; going to bank, then to pay for support worker time	Own house, support worker through an organisation
V16	Composing a letter; preparing supper at home	Rented flat, support worker through an organisation
V17	Writing shopping list, socialising; going shopping	Rented flat, support worker employed through direct payment
V18	Visit to football stadium; visit to public library	Lives in 'family placement'; employs support workers through direct payment
V19	Preparing for rugby; travel to rugby match	Temporary group home; employs support worker through direct payment

In the final months of the project, Lisa and Kerrie took part in analysis of the video data, by watching the tapes we had made. They used accessible record sheets to note down the parts of the videos they found interesting and comment on them. I myself created a full, rough transcript of all the video data, but I was then able to use their insights to select extracts for close transcription and analysis. While the technical side of the analysis was my job, nevertheless I was able to take back points about the analysis and discuss them with Lisa and Kerrie. Moreover, Lisa and

Kerrie both had extensive experience of presenting their findings to other people at conferences and training events.

A final output of the project was a resource pack (Ponting *et al.*, 2010) to help people with intellectual disabilities train their own support staff. This pack includes a DVD with extracts from the original project data, interspersed with comments from Lisa and Kerrie about the significance of the videos. Their skills in commenting on and analysing the data are thus visible to those who buy the pack. Both the resource pack and the main project report were organised around five aspects of 'good support' identified by the whole team after the interview stage of the project, which were: 1) giving respect; 2) enabling choices; 3) being friendly; 4) giving good advice; 5) supporting people to speak up.

Structure of the book

This chapter has raised questions about 'voice' and what this might mean, within the context of the social problems faced by people with intellectual disabilities, both in the UK but also internationally. The whole argument about voice has to be seen in the context of policy moves towards participation, inclusion and autonomy. Next Chapter 2 offers an introduction to some of the basic principles of analysis and introduces some of the tools of conversation analysis (CA) and the debates in this area, with some examples from short extracts of conversations involving people with intellectual disabilities. Finally, Chapter 2 examines what other discourse analysts have outlined about interactions involving people with intellectual disabilities.

Following these first two chapters, all the central chapters in this book are 'data chapters', containing real-life examples of communication involving people with intellectual disabilities and those around them. They are divided into two parts: 'Individual Voices' (Chapters 3–8) and 'Collective Voice' (Chapters 9–13). The reasons for this division are explained further in the preface to each part. It suffices to point out here that the conversations in Part 1 are nearly all from people's 'home life' context, while they go about their business, do things in the house or engage in activities outside the house. Most of these conversations are taken from the 'Skills for Support' project, which targeted people who mostly lived in their own individual flat and who employed support workers through a direct payment. Part 2, by contrast, features conversations set in more public arenas, such as self-advocacy meetings and research projects. These are situations which are premised on the idea of 'collective voice' where people are communicating for and on behalf of others.

Finally, Chapters 14 and 15 summarise and explore the implications of the analysis of communication given in this book. Each analyst's methodological stance is subtly different, and there are divisions between those who practise CA (Schegloff, 2007), critical discourse analysis (Fairclough, 1989, 1992, 1995) and discursive psychology (Wetherell, 1998), to name but a few. As this book has taken an eclectic position within an inclusive research context, it is important to return to the journey of analysis undertaken here. In Chapter 14, I therefore explore my own experience as a qualitative researcher in carrying out applied CA in inclusive contexts with people with intellectual disabilities.

The last chapter returns to the issues and questions raised in the current chapter in order to explore the social explanations and implications of what has been analysed. This type of wider theorising is left to the end so that it does not clutter up any insights that come directly from the way in which communication is constructed. Inevitably, the central themes of identity, competence and power will be explored further. However, these are not seen as broad, theoretical concepts, but as positions to be produced, enacted and played out in real interactions, as Simon and Alan did in extract 1.1 in this chapter, when Simon directed his support worker's activities. Understanding how power is both undermined and achieved, across a wide range of situations, enabled me to gain insight into what 'having a voice' really can mean and how people with intellectual disabilities can be enabled to have a say in matters that concern them.

Chapter 2

Some Building Blocks for Analysis

Conversation analysis

Given the considerable social problems faced by people with intellectual disabilities outlined in Chapter 1, why should the reader want to look in detail at their interactions with other people? What is to be gained from conversation analysis (CA) as it is presented and applied through the current text? Discourse analysts apply themselves to the study of communication because most of the world's business is managed, reflected and achieved through social interaction (Atkinson & Heritage, 1984; Schegloff, 1992). However, as I indicated in Chapter 1, by setting out to do this type of analysis, it does not mean that I believe everything can be solved by getting interaction 'right'. Not all the ambitions of people with intellectual disabilities can be attained through improving communication. Financial resources, housing, sex, relationships – all matters of vital concern to people with intellectual disabilities – are not *just* about talk, although they may involve talk. In particular, they may not be achievable by having a voice in policy forums, as the following oft-quoted remark implies:

> How's all that stuff on politics going to get me a girlfriend and a job? (Tiger Harris, cited in Armstrong, 2002: 341)

In this book, I use the tools of CA (Pomerantz & Fehr, 1997; Silverman, 1998; ten Have, 1999), and in common with CA analysts, I am interested in how talk *does* things; the focus is not on a description of the formal language system or the grammar of a language. Instead, like other CA analysts, I consider each utterance as an action, something that can and does achieve something in the flow of communication, a view originally expounded by linguistic philosophers such as Searle (1969) and Dore (1977). They proposed a study of communication events which focused on the pragmatic or functional aspects – what words 'do' in social life – and this focus was one of the driving forces in the development of discourse and conversation analysis (Wooffitt, 2005: 8). Many discourse analysts in fact use the word 'discourse' to refer to that same view of language, something that is used by people to perform social actions; for instance, according to Taylor (2001: 5), discourse is 'the close study of language in use'. Pomerantz and Fehr make it clear that CA is less concerned with language *per se,* but rather with the way in which people in society

Disability and Discourse. Analysing Inclusive Conversation with People with Intellectual Disabilities,
1st edition. © Val Williams. Published 2011 by John Wiley & Sons, Ltd.

'produce their activities and make sense of the world around them' (1997: 65). The activities on which analysts focus can range from the everyday, mundane acts of meeting and greeting (Sacks *et al.*, 1974); selling items in market trading (Clark & Pinch, 1988, discussed in Wooffitt, 2005: 187–93) to the unusual activities involved in conducting a séance (Wooffitt, 2001). In the current book, the activities in Part 1 are to do with the management of ordinary, everyday life, and people are engaged in shopping, planning and budgeting, as well as socialising and making cups of coffee. By contrast, in Part 2, the talk examined is mostly between groups of people, and features both meetings and research encounters. Although these are less familiar territories for CA analysts, the focus here is on *how* these social activities are accomplished, and this has been a driving motive behind other broadly CA work in this area (Silverman, 1973; Myers, 1998; Roberts & Sarangi, 2005).

One of my main aims in this book is to show that the end results of this type of study can contribute to practical, social goals, as Bloor (1997) discusses in relation to qualitative methodologies more generally. Like Silverman (1999) and Wetherell (1998) I have tried to carry out an analysis that is detailed and grounded in the detail of what actually happens in communication, but I am then concerned to look beyond those details in order to draw out the relevance and practical value of the analysis, in a similar way to the stance taken by those who conduct **institutional conversation analysis** (Drew & Heritage, 1992), where the goal is to analyse the patterns which differentiate various institutional or work-related roles (see Argaman, 2009, for a recent example of this approach). Unusually for discourse analysis, I also worked in various ways with people with intellectual disabilities themselves, who helped to pinpoint important aspects of communication as they related to their own lives (Williams *et al.*, 2009a). For all these reasons, I do not want to assume that I fit neatly into one approach or another and would not want to give birth to a new type of methodology, since there are already quite enough of those! However, I hope in the following pages to show how a very fine-grained analysis of short extracts of communication can lead to wider and practical insights. Communication does matter.

This is not a CA textbook, nor is it a comprehensive guide to discourse analysis. It aims instead to give a glimpse into how the tools of CA can be used and how exciting and relevant the results can be. Readers who want to pursue discourse methodology further are recommended to follow through the details that are offered in each chapter, together with the texts on methodology in the reference list. A good introduction and overview is provided in Wooffitt (2005), and a more technical and detailed methodological blueprint for CA is given by ten Have (1999), while readers wishing to gain an overall flavour of CA and other discourse methodologies are recommended to flick through some papers in *Discourse Studies* or (for critical methodologies) *Discourse and Society* or van Dijk's edited collection (1997b). Additionally, the twin volumes produced by Wetherell and her colleagues at the Open University are very informative and cover a wide range of viewpoints and approaches (Wetherell *et al.*, 2001a, 2001b). The following paragraphs attempt to offer a very quick tour of some points that are fundamental to the CA approach and other forms of discourse analysis, in order to inform the analysis in this book.

The nature of data

The fundamental data of CA is **naturally occurring transcribed talk**. All of these terms warrant further explanation. First, why does CA use the word 'talk', instead of interaction, for instance, or discourse? In this book, the word 'communication' is used to refer to what goes on between people when they engage in communicative events, but the word 'talk' is also used on occasions. This is for three reasons:

- 'Discourse' can also refer to philosophies or bodies of ideas, and so has some ambiguity (McHoul & Grace, 1993).
- 'Talk' aligns what this book proposes to do with the methodologists who want to study as closely as possible naturally occurring interactive data; because of the emphasis on talk in real situations of use, the term **talk-in-interaction** is also frequently found.
- The word 'talk' is simply shorter and easier to use with people with intellectual disabilities themselves.

It should be noted that 'talk' is not intended to refer solely to verbal activity. In this book, several people are introduced who do not communicate verbally, and the analysis takes into account body language as a universal means of communication. In order to avoid confusion, I will make an attempt to keep to the word 'communication' wherever possible.

The acknowledged pioneer of CA is Harvey Sacks (1995). In the early 1970s, Sacks started to discuss the possibility of examining how social life actually works, and to get access to it, he turned towards **naturally occurring data**, in the form of tape-recorded episodes of talk. As Silverman (1998) points out in his discussion of Sacks' work, what attracted Sacks to talk was the fact that it could be recorded, transcribed and studied. It was one of the few aspects of social life that was amenable to being preserved and re-examined. Sacks wrote: 'We are trying to find the machinery. In order to do so, we have to get access to its products' (1984: 26–7). The data of other related disciplines, such as ethnography or anthropology, were simply not as revealing, depending as they did on fieldworkers' memory and retrospective note-taking, while theoretical linguists at the time (Chomsky, 1966) almost universally used invented examples of language to illustrate their points. The reliance on naturally occurring data, what has *actually* been said, heard or seen, is one of the most refreshing and attractive aspects of CA.

Since then, discourse analysts such as Speer (2002) have questioned whether analysts can ever collect data that would have happened exactly in the same way without them being there. It is undoubtedly true that some interactions are more 'contrived' than others. For instance, an interview or a 'set conversation' with a group is arranged specifically for a research project. However, Speer argues that this does not, in the end, matter too much:

> Naturalness is not some thing that resides in certain types of data, and our data collection practices are not intrinsically natural or contrived. (Speer, 2002: 519)

What matters, according to Speer, is the stance taken by the analyst. For instance, an interview or a focus group can be analysed with an eye to unpicking what is happening in the talk between participants (Baker, 1997; Myers, 1998; van den Berg *et al.*, 2003b), and this is what is done in Part 2. The transcripts through this book are taken from data collected with full knowledge of the participants, and indeed, often in the face of an amateur camera crew. Of course, even if we wanted to, it is ethically impossible to collect data without the knowledge of the participants, and so the researcher is inevitably one of the audiences for the talk. The nature and effects of this involvement can be incorporated into the analysis, and that is what I set out to do.

Once data are collected onto audio or video tape, they still have to be **transcribed**. The reader will notice throughout the book extracts of talk that have some unfamiliar punctuation marks, such as ↑ and =. These are all explained in the Appendix. The level of detail included in the transcription is a vital part of the analysis, both reflecting and helping to formulate the analytic assumptions. For instance, a transcription system in CA takes care to reflect not only *what* is said, but also *how* it is said, including overlaps between speakers' turns, interruptions and pauses. Consider the following extract as an example:

Extract 2.1

16.	Ang	do you <u>like</u> going to a training centre every day or do you find it – or
17.		do you find it BORING
18.	Har	no I think Marland is in our area because (.) [cause I get the –
19.	Ang	[no no what I'm saying to you
20.		do you like going every day five days a week↑
21.	Har	five days a week yeah
22.	Ang	do you find it bo::ring
23.	Har	no (.) what I - well I <u>like</u> going to work

Explanation of symbols used in above extract

↑ upward intonation
- word concludes abruptly
CAPITALS segment of talk that is louder than surrounding talk
<u>Emphasis</u> marked by underlining
[the beginning of overlapped speech
(.) short pause
:: elongated vowel sound
Line numbers refer to the original full transcript.

   One speaker here dislikes the idea of a training centre, while the other says he likes it. Without the transcript, that is perhaps all the reader would retain from this bit of talk. However, by being able to examine the detail of the talk, it is possible to learn far more. I noticed, for instance, how Angela herself constructs the object of 'training centre' in lines 16–17, by her emphasised contrast of two words 'like' and 'boring'. This is a loaded question! The slight hesitation Harry makes in his response in line 18 gives Angela a place to get back in and overlap with what he is saying. This is a strong way of getting back a turn and shows what Angela thinks of Harry's response. She then pursues the question until he admits at line 23: 'I <u>like</u> going to work', his use of the word 'work' contrasting with her use of 'boring'. Much more could be said, even about this short extract; however, just from these few comments one can appreciate how transcription conventions are linked with analysis, since they reveal and mark out features that may turn out to be important.

Talk as social construction

One of the debates in discourse analysis, and indeed in other forms of qualitative research, relates to the view of reality that informs the researcher's perspective. As Wetherell (2001: 392) points out, most discourse analysis proceeds 'through a questioning of simple realist assumptions'. In other words, communication, as studied in various forms of discourse analysis, is *not* seen as a window on some objective truth. First, this stance towards reality has to be distinguished from the debate between positivist and non-positivist research more broadly in social science. In non-discursive forms of qualitative research, the term 'social constructionism' is also used (Charmaz, 2006), where it is broadly taken to mean the opposite of 'positivism'. A positivist researcher assumes that she or he is pursuing truths that are objectively knowable: indeed, in quantitative methodologies researchers have to assume they already know how to define and delineate the categories they are counting or measuring (Bryman, 2008). By contrast, a social constructionist researcher is interested to discover how participants frame their own realities and does not assume that these matters can be defined in advance. Social constructionism in this sense has led to a raft of qualitative methodologies, such as grounded theory (Glaser, 1992), interpretative phenomenological analysis (Smith *et al.*, 2009), and so on. All these methods purport to 'get behind' what people say in some way and to harvest themes and ideas from the views expressed by research participants.

When discourse analysts talk about 'social construction' however, they are not claiming an interest in the psychological or social underpinnings of what people say; what they are more interested in is the actual process of construction. As Wetherell (2001: 392) argues, 'reality is a collective social product', in which discourse and communication take centre stage. This version of social constructionism is more radical than that more commonly found in qualitative methodology textbooks. For instance, Wetherell and Potter (1992) show how a cultural phenomenon such as racism is actively formed and sustained through discourse: it is not something that could ever exist independently of discursive practices, and it is the job of the discourse analyst to unpick and reveal aspects of *how* those discourses work. In a subsequent book (van den Berg *et al.*, 2003b), Wetherell gave her original 1992 data to a range of analysts from different traditions, to explore how the same data could be analysed from subtly different discursive perspectives, and demonstrated clearly that the significance of what is going on in data relies as much on the analyst's perspective and interests as on anything residing within the data *per se*.

Moving back to the territory of CA, these ideas about social constructionism sometimes appear to contradict, or at least to jar with, the central motives of CA, which are essentially empirical and driven by real, hard data of recorded naturally occurring interactions. The original aim of CA, as developed first by Sacks and his associates in the 1960s–1970s, was to discover the way that social interaction works – the machinery of talk. Sacks died early and so his lectures and his legacy have been reconstructed by students and followers, and are contained in Sacks (1995). As will be appreciated from Sacks' very engaging lectures, pure CA starts and ends with what was actually said, and is concerned to understand better the structures and hidden rules underlying what people do when they interact with each other. It is value-neutral. As ten Have states, 'the ultimate "results" of CA are a set of formulated "rules" or "principles"' (1999: 135).

This might seem to be a very different endeavour from the stated goal of the current book, which is to gain some understanding about changing patterns of talk involving people with intellectual disabilities. Nevertheless, CA provides a systematic way to study what is going on in the text and some tools for starting to look at this in detail. It is not a cold, mechanical type of analysis, but returns continually to what the participants themselves were doing at the time and their demonstrated understandings. Schegloff (2007) is the most authoritative recent text to offer a comprehensive tour of the building blocks of interaction, and ten Have's (1999: 101–28) guide to doing CA was particularly useful in developing the analysis used in these pages. He recommends four basic stages in examining a text:

- Turn-taking organisation: the analyst looks at the way in which members take turns or allocate turns to each other.
- Sequence organisation: the analyst notices the way in which utterances are linked – for instance, one turn is frequently linked to another in a pair, where the first turn provides the slot for the second. An example is 'Hello, how are you?' 'Hi, fine thanks'.
- Repair organisation: much can be gained from analysing where members correct what they are saying, rephrase or help each other.
- Organisation of turn construction: the analyst looks at the choices speakers have made, how they have shaped their turn and what effects these choices have in the subsequent talk.

All these matters will be returned to throughout the book so that analytical points can be understood more clearly in the context of actual data and discussion. For the moment, however, I would like to explain how a social constructionist approach can usefully be pursued via CA analysis.

Analysing social activities by using the tools of CA

As shown above, the interests of CA from its beginnings have been in the technicalities and rules that underpin the observable patterns of talk: for instance, questions driving analysis have included 'How does one person get a turn when another one is speaking? What do simple greetings tell us about the rules governing social interaction?' However, analysts within CA traditions also claim that they are interested in the social construction of categories such as 'intellectual disability' (Rapley, 2004). How can these matters be reconciled?

The clue lies in the analytic focus of the research, which can be different for each CA researcher and for each study. If the focus (as in 'pure' CA: Schegloff, 2007) is to add to cumulative knowledge of patterns of social interaction, then there is not much room for speculation about what is being socially constructed. Matters like that are simply irrelevant. However, if the focus moves to larger social activities (such as negotiating a relationship; conducting a doctor–patient appointment; or even asking someone to make a cup of coffee as in Chapter 1), then it is possible to examine how these activities are accomplished by the fine detail of talk.

A social constructionist would say that these activities simply do not exist outside the talk which makes them up; they are **emergent** (Wetherell, 2001: 396). Every time two or more people interact they are not only enacting social activities, but also reconstructing and repackaging them. That is the sense in which Sarangi (2003) explores activity types, not as fixed, rule-governed frameworks, but as activities that literally emerge from, and are made up by, talk. It is also the stance that informs **institutional CA,** as mentioned above (Drew & Heritage, 1992; Heritage & Clayman, 2010), which aims to uncover the patterns of talk that typify and construct a range of work-related activities.

A wide range of social activities can be analysed in this way by focusing on the fine detail of interactions, and these include research activities themselves, among them focus groups (Myers, 1998) and interview accounts (van den Berg *et al.*, 2003b). Taking a CA perspective, the analyst is not so much interested in the outcomes of the research, but in the ways in which research encounters can be analysed as social activities. In Part 1, and indeed throughout this book, I am interested in how support is carried out, how supporting a person with intellectual disabilities is actually done. In Part 2, my main focus is to explore in this way how the social activity of 'inclusive research' emerges from both public and more private encounters. In this book, then, I am interested in talk precisely because it has the power to construct afresh what is happening whenever people communicate:

> Social objects are not given 'in the world' but constructed, negotiated, reformed, fashioned and organized by human beings in their efforts to make sense of happenings in the world. (Sarbin & Kitsuse, 1994: 3)

The attraction of studying the details of real talk is that they both reflect and constitute social realities. Looking back at extract 2.1, the social reality constructed by Harry is very different from that constructed by Angela, and by doing this bit of talk, they add to the possible meanings and stances about training centres. As Heritage puts it: 'Social worlds are evoked and made actionable in and through talk' (1997: 161).

A good example of what this stance means in practice can be seen in extract 1.1, in Chapter 1. It is a brief exchange between two participants, prior to their main activity of making coffee together. In most forms of analysis, it would be totally overlooked and probably not even transcribed. However, if the reader were to analyse that extract in a traditional, qualitative way, they might pick out the health-related implications of Simon going barefoot when he has circulation problems in his legs, or possibly his own knowledge that he should have something on his feet. Much would depend on the focus of the analysis: if the analyst were interested in how to help people learn new independence skills, then they may pick out the fact that Simon and Alan go to make coffee together, at Simon's request.

However, the type of analysis done in these pages is more interested in the way in which the relationship between the two men is negotiated in the talk; the CA analyst could take into account the laughter occasioned by Alan's mock reluctance to go and make coffee and look at the role played by this laughter in the talk, noticing how it is carried on by Simon into his mention of his bare feet. This might lead to observations about the smoothness and fluency of their talk and the way in which the speakers are supporting each other in that short extract, to produce joint action. Discourse analysts in general, like ethnomethodologists (Garfinkel, 1967), aim to take a fresh view of what is going on, unhindered by previous theory and looking beyond 'common-sense' explanations. In other words, the fine-grained analysis of that extract, as well as others, may contribute to an understanding of how the relationship between two people can be constructed through talk, or how the task of making coffee can be carried out alongside displays of social intimacy.

CA and identity

If CA is interested in social activities and how they are 'socially constructed', there is equally an interest in how certain psychological or social phenomena are constructed through interactions. Antaki and Widdicombe (1998), for instance, set out to explore how identity categories are *used* in talk and how they emerge from the moment-by-moment contingencies of conversation. Equally, this version of social constructionism is expounded in Rapley (2004), who is interested in how the category of 'intellectual disability' is constructed through talk. This stance also informs the current book. Rather than assume that Simon (in Chapter 1) simply 'has an intellectual disability', the analyst is interested in how that category emerges from the talk. When Simon, for instance, effectively apologises to Alan for not wearing shoes, and Alan accepts the apology as something unremarkable, the analyst can start to show something about the way in which 'intellectual disability' emerges from interactions between powerful, knowledgeable support workers and people who are assumed to need guidance and direction to manage their lives.

This version of social constructionism is a very concrete, situated and local one. The way in which a particular identity is constructed on one occasion may work out quite differently on another occasion. By working with transcribed data of detailed conversations, the analyst is enabled to situate the talk in that particular occasion, as it unfolds. Antaki and Widdicombe (1998a) refer to this as **occasionedness**:

A good part of the meaning of an utterance … is to be found in the occasion of its production – in the local state of affairs that was operative at that exact moment of interactional time. (Antaki & Widdicombe, 1998a: 4)

This might not seem remarkable, until one considers that much analysis in social research proceeds by taking quotations, out of context, as illustrations of an argument. The word **local** is often used to refer to this aspect of discourse analytic research. The analyst is not interested in talk as an exemplar of a worldview or general philosophy of life, but in how this particular bit of talk was produced in this particular situation. This is true even when the analyst is ultimately concerned with ideology (see van Dijk, 1997a: 1–35).

This does not mean that each communicative event is totally fresh and has nothing to do with any other such event. As communicators, we draw on resources of languages (systems of rules, vocabulary and speech sounds), as well as knowledge (bodies of ideas and information). Any single communicative event is a site to which speakers and listeners bring their own resources and simultaneously recreate a new version of reality. Understanding these issues is important, because it turns out that they are really useful tools for getting into analysis. As Fairclough and Wodak put it: 'Discourse is socially *constitutive* as well as socially shaped' (1997: 258).

The wider context of talk

Academic discussion over the relationship between CA and society has been vigorously pursued, since the original conversation analysis 'project' was in effect to discover the rules by which social interaction works. Therefore, analysts who start with ideological commitments about human rights or inequalities are often criticised by the purists, since they approach the business of analysis with pre-conceived theories. A published exchange between Wetherell (1998), Billig (1999) and Schegloff (1998, 1999a, 1999b) is probably the best known and clearest in its exposition of the issues, and interested readers are referred to those articles.

According to Schegloff (1998), CA must remain faithful to the evidence in the text (i.e. the evidence of what people in the data were heard or seen to be doing, evidence which is transcribed into 'text'). He claims that analysis must not go beyond the text; the analyst is simply drawing on the interpretations that ordinary participants in conversation themselves make apparent. Billig (1999), on the other hand, looks towards discourse analysis to reveal underlying truths and both social and political realities that are mirrored in talk, while Wetherell (1998) argues for some reconciliation and that the analyst's work should be concerned not only with empirical demonstrability, but also with 'the social and political consequences of discursive patterning'. She goes on to demonstrate what such an approach looks like in practice.

The question of how much context to use in analysis may seem like a very academic one to some readers. Again, an example may make the point more clearly. Extract 2.1, with Angela and Harry, was simply a conversation between two people. That is all that a CA analyst needs to know. Or is it? Does it add anything to the analysis if the reader knows that Harry goes to a day centre for people with intellectual disabilities? Equally, does it add anything if the analyst is aware that day centres can be stigmatising and are recognised as such in current UK government policy? Most readers, as well as students, would probably argue that this background knowledge *does* influence the analysis. They may therefore side with Billig, who claims that 'an implicit sociological understanding … is the precondition for the analysis' (1999: 574).

A useful handle on this issue is to be found in **discursive psychology** (Potter, 2003; Edwards, 2003, 2005). In this approach, the analyst can and does draw on issues, such as power, identity or social change, that go beyond the talk. However, the reason for doing this is to analyse how these issues are put to work in particular, situated conversations. In effect, they become a tool for the analyst and also provide wider sociological or political points to the analysis. The analyst can be concerned with the local unfolding of the talk, and also with the various discursive positions open to members, which go beyond the talk. Staying with extract 2.1, the analyst would be interested in how the controversy over day centres is reflected in the conversation between Angela and Harry. Angela in effect draws on the **repertoire** (Wetherell, 1998) of the stigma associated with day centres, to downplay their value and to throw scorn on the fact that anyone may regularly attend a day centre. If the social debate about day centres is taken into account, it then becomes clear that Harry is resisting the discourse related to day centres by using the word 'work'. In claiming that he 'likes his work', he is associating the day centre with a quite different repertoire. Not only, then, do these wider social themes enable the analyst to situate aspects of the talk, they also provide a route into a wider social critique that can emerge from the analysis. In the late twentieth century, in the UK, it could be said that conflicting positions were available about segregated day centres for people with intellectual disabilities. For some, they were a part of the government's work agenda; for others, they were a stigmatised form of collective inactivity. That type of commentary may in fact sound much closer to **critical discourse analysis** (CDA) as practised by van Dijk (2001), Fairclough (1995) and others.

Like Wetherell (1998: 205), this book adopts an eclectic approach, bringing together the insights from text-based methodologies (in the above sense of text, meaning a faithful transcript) and from wider, critical traditions. A very similar position can be found in Silverman (1999), who argues that a fine-grained approach to analysis of text can be followed productively by an exploration of the wider social issues revealed by that analysis. Another example will illustrate this approach. It is taken from a video recording in the home of Janet, a person with intellectual disabilities, who is at this point sitting and talking with her support worker, Meg.

Extract 2.2

341.	Meg	right (0.5) ((*puts down paper work and looks up at Jenny, leaning*
342.		*forward and smiling*)) have you got anything planned for the
343.		weekend↑
344.	Jan	yes my coffee morning
345.	Meg	you've got your coffee morning tomorrow morning↑
346.	Jan	yes
347.	Meg	a::h is it in aid of [anything↑
348.	Jan	[yes the Hilary House hospice
349.	Meg	oh right↓ do you know anyone at Hilary House↑
350.	Jan	no but I know it's a good cause↑ that's why I wanted to do it
351.	Meg	oh

Looking carefully at this extract, one can see how important turn organisation is. Meg has the opening turn at line 341, which she issues to deliver a general opener for Janet to talk. Together with the word 'right' and the fact that she puts down her paperwork, this is a way of marking a new phase of the talk. Meg appears to be in control here, while Janet simply says something in the turns that are offered to her. CA analysts would call these places **turn slots**, and would say that Meg has **allocated turns** to Janet. One could also notice here the overlap at lines 347 and 348, and the structure of Meg's turns, in which she tends to respond minimally (ah, oh) and then follows up with a renewed query to Janet. Her turns are also designed to focus on Janet's owner-ship of her own activities – 'have *you* got anything planned', '*your* coffee morning', and Janet takes up the opportunity to discuss not only what she is planning, but to justify why she is doing the coffee morning (in order to support a good cause).

This level of analysis can reveal something about the way this conversation is handled, the strategies for enabling someone to speak and how a speaker can express interest in the other person by an 'oh right' or an 'ah'. However, once that is done, the analyst can move beyond what has been noticed and make some wider observations. For instance, it seems here that Meg has the **interactional right** (Ochs & Taylor, 1992; Shakespeare, 1998) to ask Janet about her activities, while Janet does not reciprocate by asking about Meg's plans. Further, both Janet and Meg immediately mention not only the coffee morning, but also the fact that it is in aid of something.

They are both drawing on an understanding that Janet is likely to do something useful, something charitable in fact, and this is presumably based on prior experience they both have of Janet's 'coffee mornings'. The identity being built up for Janet appears to be one of a voluntary charitable supporter. However, at line 349, Meg offers an alternative identity for Janet, that of someone who might 'know someone at Hilary House'. This threatens to highlight Janet's identity as a person with intellectual disabilities, someone who receives care and who is likely to know others who receive care at Hilary House, and this interpretation is strengthened by the fact that Janet immediately claims she does *not* know anyone there, but simply wants to support 'a good cause'. Close textual analysis thus seeks evidence from what is there in the video or on the page. The analyst's task is to point out what is happening and show 'that the parties are oriented to it in doing whatever they do' (Schegloff, 1999a: 570).

Much depends on what has already been said and what comes next. In analysing naturally occurring data, it is always a problem to know where to start and where to stop, since everything in fact is interconnected. The above extract, for instance, continues with Janet talking about a course she has done about 'death' and a conference she is going to attend. As she does this, she paints her own identity in different ways, as a conference attender, a serious person and a delegate. CA analysts call this 'identity work'. However, she then mentions to Meg a colleague of Meg's who is also going to attend and give Janet care and support while she is there, helping her with her shower. Meg, however, chooses to focus on the activity of the conference and asks Janet, 'Are you going to give a speech?' It is evident here how identity categories can be worked up through talk. However, communication can be a very shifting and blurred activity at times, and people can and do move from one aspect of their identity to another, according to what is happening in the conversation at the time. It should be noted that this approach to analysis does not assume that certain institutional roles, such as supporter or self-advocate, bring with them corresponding rights, nor that particular verbal practices are **category-bound** (exclusively part of certain roles). Instead, the aim of institutional CA is to analyse the 'verbal practices and arrangements' through which such institutional roles are 'talked into being' (Arminen, 2000: 436). Even categories as seemingly obvious as girl and boy have to be worked up in the talk, as Mean (2002) showed in relation to 'doing gender' on the football pitch. As mentioned in Chapter 1, readers interested in this way of approaching identity should look at Antaki and Widdicombe (1998b) and de Fina *et al.* (2006).

Finally, a discussion of these issues will enable the analyst to stand even further back from the text. The above example may, for instance, raise the issue of what it means to be a person with intellectual disabilities, to be in a category that has traditionally been the object of charity. Janet is arguably challenging that categorisation by becoming a charity worker, and one might also observe that Meg is enabling her to talk about Janet-as-charity-worker, an important function for the support worker. This could be an example of personalised support and could be linked with disability policy in the UK in the early twenty-first century.

CA and change

If analysis can provide insights into wider social issues based on the detail of talk, can it also then be useful? I claimed in the opening paragraphs of this chapter that I was seeking an approach that would provide clues to change. Like Oliver (1992), I have always worked in a tradition where research is linked with practice and with the opportunity to understand social barriers, to challenge them and to change things for the better.

If wider social issues can be controversial matters in CA, then using CA for change can lead to even deeper waters. How can a neutral, objective enterprise like CA be used for social goals? However, Sarangi and Roberts (1999) and colleagues have developed a strong tradition in medical communication in which the analysis of the researcher can be offered back to the practitioner, in order to develop and actually improve practice (Sarangi & Roberts, 1999). There are several ways in which researchers can interact with practical knowledge, and indeed with actual practice, and these are well explored in Perakyla and Vehvilainen (2003). These authors propose, with examples from counselling and medical practices, that CA research can adopt a critical and complementary role in relation to professional knowledge. They claim that:

> Accomplishing these tasks does not compromise the strictly empirical stance of CA studies, but it may be vital for the wider social relevance of the CA enterprise. (Perakyla & Vehvilainen, 2003: 747)

In the present book, the central aim, as stated in Chapter 1, is to deliver practical understanding of interactions with people with intellectual disabilities so that those interactions can be carried out on a basis of equality. However, CA does not *automatically* deliver that practical understanding: for instance, a fine-grained analysis can simply reveal how one speaker's turn follows from the previous one, or how identity categories are used in talk. None of this is about identifying 'good' and 'bad' practice, and throughout the book, an attempt is made to avoid any simplistic classifications of support practices. Indeed, the analysis leads to an appreciation that talk is always (at least) two-way: not only is it about support practices, it is also about the contributions and work done by people with intellectual disabilities themselves.

CA can never feed into a practice manual in any easy way: as Sarangi and Roberts state, as discourse analysts, they do not position practical problems as 'something out there, which needs expert solutions from discourse analysts' (1999: 473). Instead, they see their work with professionals as forming 'joint problematization', and that is exactly the stance here. There is no cookbook approach, for instance, to how to provide good support. However, in Part 1, by exploring examples of talk between support workers and the people they support, some patterns emerge that may be useful in understanding how it is that people with intellectual disabilities are treated like children, what might help in ensuring they can take a turn in a conversation and how the relationship between support workers and their clients can be shaped within social chat. Some of this has been touched on elsewhere (Williams *et al.*, 2009a, 2009b, 2009c) and has formed the basis of a training pack which uses video material to promote discussion (Ponting *et al.*, 2010). The current exploration, however, digs further into CA analysis and aims to show how that in itself can be of practical value.

Similarly, in Part 2 I explore inclusive research encounters, including some which take place 'backstage' and involve supporters talking with people with intellectual disabilities. There is no straightforward link between any of this and 'good (or bad) practice': each encounter is multifaceted and emerges from the local context of talk. Nevertheless, by analysing data in this way, professional practice and CA analysis can form a type of dialogue, as Perakyla and Vehvilainen (2003) and Sarangi and Roberts (1999) suggest.

The aim of this book, then, is first to analyse in a detailed way the unfolding organisation of talk, and then to move back and relate this to the wider issues of identity and positions taken by each participant. This is not a dry, technical analysis, but has practical as well as social and political consequences. The way in which people communicate really can reveal the social reality in which they live.

Intellectual disability and CA

Although it is unusual to approach issues about intellectual disability through the lens of discourse analysis, the research featured in this book is not without its precedents. What has other discursive work revealed about communication with people with intellectual disabilities?

One of the first social situations that fuelled discourse analysis in this field was the research interview itself, the point at which researchers usually come face to face with people with intellectual disabilities. Sigelman *et al.* (1981), in the first of a series of papers, established an interactional concept that has had very wide currency in the research community ever since, namely the idea of 'acquiescence bias'. According to Sigelman, this bias consists of a strong tendency on the part of the person with intellectual disabilities to agree with the interviewer, and in fact often to echo the final item that has been suggested.

> Because mentally retarded persons [*sic*] asked yes or no questions tend to acquiesce, their answers are likely to be invalid. (Sigelman *et al.*, 1981: 57)

The influence of this conclusion has been widespread and, in the extreme, has meant that people with intellectual disabilities have been excluded as direct participants in research, as they are considered to be unreliable interviewees, even when speaking about their own lives. As Rapley (2004) points out, however, Sigelman's original work was not based on a pragmatic analysis of data, although there have been some useful and more data-driven summaries of the evidence since then (Finlay & Lyons, 1998). For instance, Rapley *et al.* (1998), examining a set of 'quality of life' interviews with people with intellectual disabilities, analyse how interviewees oriented to the social situation of the interview, treating it as a 'test' situation. Moreover, discourse analysts will pay attention not only to what the interviewee does, but also to the precise way in which interviewers handle the talk. Antaki (2002) and Antaki *et al.* (2002), for instance, show how interviewers shape and 'edit' official questions in an interview schedule in order to elicit agreements. Given the complexities of the talk in these interviews, acquiescence on the part of the person with intellectual disabilities may be a 'smart interactional strategy' (Rapley, 2004: 109).

Another important theme that has driven discourse work in this field, as mentioned above, is the matter of identity. Again, early work here was motivated by a reaction to influential non-discursive work (Davies & Jenkins, 1997; Todd & Shearn, 1997). These papers argued that people with intellectual disabilities were 'invisible' to themselves, as they did not accept or even understand the category to which they belonged. Further, parents and family members were seen to be part of a conspiracy of silence, shielding people with intellectual disabilities from knowledge about their own identity. These matters were taken up in an important paper by Finlay and Lyons (1998) who re-analysed Davies and Jenkins' (1997) data and showed, for instance, how denial of an intellectually disabled identity could be a matter of face work. In other words, when an interviewer questions someone about their 'intellectual disability', this could be seen as both rude and threatening to that person's self-respect. Denial, avoidance of the topic and several other related strategies could be seen as appropriate responses in that situation.

One of the most substantial pieces of work in this vein about people with intellectual disabilities is Rapley's book *The Social Construction of Intellectual Disability* (2004). As well as a discussion of some of the issues mentioned above, Rapley presents data from Australian people with intellectual disabilities who live in residential homes, in conversation with their support staff. Rapley's analysis brings out very clearly the institutional asymmetry of the interactions between staff and residents, with staff, for instance, having the right to determine the agenda and what constitutes a relevant answer. He also notes many instances of infantilising talk, in which people with intellectual disabilities are treated like children and in which their *incompetence* is highlighted. This work goes on to consider the detail of some strategies that can be used in talk in order for staff and people with intellectual disabilities to start interacting on a more equal basis. For instance, 'collaborative pedagogic talk' (Rapley, 2004: 177–9) is illustrated by a sequence in which the support worker formulates the problem, the person with intellectual disabilities responds and the support worker confirms. However, the data given here still sound very much like instructional work, and it is interesting to see how the person with intellectual disabilities (William, in the extract below) is thus put into the position of pupil or learner, with the limited interactional rights that may entail:

Gerald	So (1) (clears throat) (2.5) what do you reckon we should <u>do</u>
	with it (.) to thaw it ↓ out
Will	Mm put it in the micro↓wave
Gerald	↑yep (.) good think↓ing

(Rapley, 2004: 179)

The identity issues inherent in supporter talk are taken up again in a body of work by Antaki, Finlay and others (Jingree *et al.*, 2006; Antaki *et al.*, 2007a, 2007b; Finlay *et al.*, 2008a, 2008b). These researchers draw on data collected in English residential homes for people with intellectual disabilities, with a particular interest in interactions that display identity tensions. Their work gets to the very heart of issues in the current book.

'Choice' may be a driving theme in English Intellectual Disability policy, as has been pointed out above, but the jobs of support workers are not only to deliver choices. They also have institutional responsibilities relating to safety and to regulating the lives of the people they support. Therefore, CA can be useful in determining what strategies might be, and are, used to resolve those identity conflicts. Jingree *et al.* (2006), for instance, show how power can manifest in subtle ways during staff–resident interactions, and in particular via staff failing to acknowledge what residents were saying, and by producing affirmations of service philosophy through the talk.

Antaki *et al.* (2007a) discuss how staff use the strategy of personalising the choices they offer people with intellectual disabilities by mentioning *people* associated with certain events and activities. Further, strategies intended to be 'empowering' can misfire. For instance, Antaki *et al.* (2008) analyse small stretches of interaction when staff in group homes respond to residents' choices by offering them a further choice. This can have the effect of implying to the resident that their original choice was wrong. When people say 'no', this is not always accepted (Finlay *et al.*, 2008b). For instance, support staff can take on the powerful role of pointing out health or safety issues, while exercising power over the choices people with intellectual disabilities actually have.

Like Rapley (2004), Antaki *et al.* (2007b) analyse how staff routinely highlight the incompetence of the people with intellectual disabilities, by controlling the structure of the conversation:

> It might be argued that here we see the bald operation of power: it is the staff who control the interaction and its outcome, and judge whether an utterance is adequate or not, even though the agenda item they are following mandates them to find out the residents' views. The content of the discussion is almost irrelevant here – it is in the process that relationships and identities are enacted. (Antaki *et al.*, 2007b: 12)

Staff can also subtly undermine the identity choices and positions of residents, by suggesting to them during a discussion of friendship that 'staff can be their friends'. It is the staff members who seem to have the key to understanding how the social world is organised.

It is essential to understand these interactions, since the issues raised seem to be very pervasive in Intellectual Disability support services. However, Antaki's group collected data within residential settings, which in the UK are acknowledged to operate generally according to a more traditional model of care: home managers own the home; residential staff are employed by them; people with intellectual disabilities may not have many real choices about where they live, and certainly not with whom. Emerson and Robertson (2008) report that one third of people with intellectual disabilities in residential care are sent out of their home area, and the majority of these are people with 'challenging behaviour' or complex needs.

By contrast, the chapters in Part 1 are based on interactions involving people with intellectual disabilities who employ their own support staff, or who have one-to-one support from a chosen supporter (Gramlich *et al.*, 2002; Williams & Holman, 2006). The move towards 'personalised' support discussed earlier is a reaction against the type of interactions premised on assumptions that the support worker has to be in control. By analysing in detail how these interactions unfold in real time, it is possible to understand better how to achieve more equal interactions. The current book thus takes these themes and explores them in two contexts which deliberately set out to be empowering, namely the 'Finding Out' project (Williams, 1999, 2002) and 'Skills for Support' (Williams *et al.*, 2009a). (Outlines of both projects are given at the end of Chapter 1.) Data were collected in both projects using audio and video recording devices, and recordings were made at 'front stage' events such as meetings and routine daily life activities, as well as during 'backstage' events, such as preparation meetings for researchers or at analysis sessions. The 'Finding Out' project also showcases some self-advocacy contexts, since the research interviews were carried out in self-advocacy organisations.

This kind of analysis does not rely on representative sampling procedures. No claim is made in either project that the data to be analysed in some way represent the spread of interactions with people with intellectual disabilities in general. The selection of extracts in both projects was determined largely by what the researchers with intellectual disabilities found interesting, but also by analytic considerations. I was attempting essentially to find insights that go beyond the immediate example and to notice patterns, regularities and 'social orders' that appear to be routine, both for people with intellectual disabilities and in interaction generally. Particularly in the 'Skills for Support' project, I had the privilege of being able to discuss the selection of extracts with the people with intellectual disabilities who had been involved in collecting the data. Thus what is of interest to me is based on what is of interest to people with intellectual disabilities themselves. That is why the term 'inclusive' has been used about the analysis.

In bringing together data from these two projects, it is possible to explore the organisation of talk that goes on in both personal and public life. The platform on which people with intellectual disabilities stand in public arenas is one that is built on a wealth of private, personal experiences, and one of the problems may be that there is often a disjunction between these two areas of life. This book will attempt to question what it means to have a voice, within a wide range of individual, personal and public interactions. It will aim to demystify the analytical processes I have followed in conducting analysis and show how we can all learn to be sensitive to the detailed patterns of talk and to be part of changing those patterns.

Part 1

Individual Voices

Preface to Part 1 by members of 'The Voice'[1]

The first part of the book is mostly based on research that we did in the 'Skills for Support' team. It's about how people with learning difficulties get treated. People do get treated differently if they have a 'learning difficulty' or an intellectual disability. They get patted on the head, and people say 'Do you feel all right? Are you OK, love?' We don't want to be treated in a patronising way; we want to be treated with respect. That's the thing that goes right through this part of the book.

In Chapter 3, we meet someone called Henry. Henry's story tells us something. It tells us that Henry is not believed, even when he does speak up. We think that's wrong. That happens to us too. It will make Henry feel that he can't talk to anyone, and he must find his own way of coping.

> Sometimes I can say things till I'm blue in the face. It makes me angry when I'm not believed, and I'd then do things like self-harming or being challenging. People need to have belief in me, otherwise I won't have belief in myself. (Kerrie Ford)

If people don't want to speak, the other person should respect their wishes. It doesn't often happen to us, but it does happen to other people. If they wanted to do that to us, we would say 'shut up!'

Chapter 4 is about how sometimes people get bossed about, and they get used to it. It may be the only way they understand. Support workers should understand that we are in control of our money, and in control of our decisions. And in control of our lives. We like to feel that we can be the boss.

---

[1] Like the other prefaces by The Voice members, these comments were recorded and written after reading through an easy-read summary of Part 1.

> When I'm working with other colleagues in The Voice group, I can feel like I'm
> the boss, and I've got to look after the team. In ordinary conversation, I can also
> feel that I've got a voice. People need to treat me as if I've got a right to be
> around. (Lisa Ponting)

All the chapters here are about people talking with support workers, and Chapter 5
shows how support workers help people to get a word in edgeways.

Chapter 6 is about people being friendly. But people don't always get much social life.
They want people around, just to see them and spend time with them. That's not
about support, it's just about seeing people and being friendly. We don't like other
people always thinking 'that's Lisa, and there's her support worker' – it's just about
an ordinary relationship and having a laugh together. It's friendship, not supporting.
Support workers can also be friendly, and it all depends on the person. Someone who
gets paid is a professional and they support you in a different way to how a friend
would support you. Friends can be supportive, and support workers can be friendly.

Some people have been institutionalised and have lived in long-stay hospitals. There
are people like that in this book. One of us was institutionalised. It's a bit like being
locked up, in a padded cell, a bit like prison. A woman we know, Sarah, was 45 years
in an institution, and she didn't have her mum and dad. People were punished and
put in straitjackets. They used to punish us if we didn't do our job well enough.

People find it hard, after being in an institution, to think that where they live is their
own home. People find it hard to adapt, even after a long time. For instance, in
Chapter 7, people are making choices. But some people feel that others are going to
make the choice for them or tell them what is good to choose. That's like living in an
institution.

One of us has a problem with balance. Often, when she falls over, people may ask her
if she can get up and see if they can help. It's not very good how some people in the
street treat you. Someone couldn't remember the bus number the other day, and the
person in the bus queue said, 'People like you shouldn't be out'. So one of the important things is to look at how people get treated out on the street. That's what Val looks
at in Chapter 8.

If we work together as a team, we could change society. Sometimes change happens
from the way people talk to each other, but not all the time. We think we can change
things, but it could be improved a lot more. People with intellectual disabilities should
be given chances to do different things like teaching, training. Just by doing different
things, people will be talking with us in different ways.

Chapter 3

Challenging Disempowering Patterns of Talk

Background

The chapters in Part 1 are bound together by the fact that they draw mainly on contexts from people's everyday, routine lives. In particular, many of the conversations take place on a one-to-one basis, as people with intellectual disabilities interact with their support staff. Most of those conversations are drawn from the 'Skills for Support' project. It will be recalled that this research study deliberately sought out people who were employing a support worker through a direct payment or had one-to-one support from an organisation. However, the deeper reason for naming Part 1 'Individual Voices' is that the analytic focus will be on how individuals negotiate their encounters on their own behalf and how their support workers enable them to do that.

All the conversations in this book involve people like you and me, whose identities shift and change according to each shift within the interaction. At one moment, a person can speak as if they are a friend, and at the next, their identity as a housekeeper, a mother, a support worker or a teacher can be highlighted. All this depends on the context, on how the other person responds and what is happening in the talk on a moment-by-moment basis. Although nothing is fixed, analysts have noticed how inequalities in society can be reflected and re-enacted on a regular basis through certain patterns of talk. For people who have the label 'intellectual disability', an imbalance of power almost defines their very identity. The later chapters in Part 1 examine some more empowering personal strategies in everyday talk, and Part 2 shows how those inequalities can be challenged by people taking back that power into their own hands. However, first it is important to analyse how *dis*empowerment actually happens in talk, so that it can be challenged and changed. That is the goal of the current chapter.

There are certain mechanisms that routinely exclude people with intellectual disabilities from taking a full part in communication. Based on an understanding of how exclusion works, change can happen. Since the aim of this book is that people with intellectual disabilities will take up more 'equal' positions in conversation, this chapter will therefore look at three specific patterns of talk which are 'disempowering', when:

- your chance to speak literally gets usurped by someone else;
- you do say something, but others do not trust what you say;
- you are pushed into speaking up when you do not want to.

Disability and Discourse. Analysing Inclusive Conversation with People with Intellectual Disabilities, 1st edition. © Val Williams. Published 2011 by John Wiley & Sons, Ltd.

Supporters and people with intellectual disabilities have a role both in avoiding these patterns and in challenging them when they occur.

This chapter introduces two conversations with different groups of people, one from each of the research projects mentioned in Chapter 1. Both conversations take place in living rooms, which are the home/living space of people with intellectual disabilities, and both conversations include people who are paid to be there in order to provide support for the person (or people) with intellectual disabilities.

Barry: Filling out a form for employment support

The setting for the first extract is the front room of an ordinary house in the centre of a small town. It was the home of a person with intellectual disabilities (Barry) who lived with his carers in a 'home placement', and occurred one evening when his support worker (Naomi) had come to accompany him on a trip out. Naomi was employed to come occasionally during the week, while the carers actually lived with Barry. Naomi had explained that normally she would call at the house and talk with Barry's carers, whom we refer to here as Fred and Ann, and that she fulfilled a role in supporting them as well. Thus we agreed to start filming Naomi and Barry while they were all still sitting and discussing a form which Barry needed to fill in so that he could apply for employment support. Barry is sitting in an armchair to Naomi's left, while Ann is beside Naomi on the sofa and Fred is opposite.

Extract 3.1[1]

62.	Nao	what about (.) JOBS Barry↑ what other jobs did you have apart
63.		from apart from the one you're doing now (.) in reception↑
64.		((looking up at Barry, eyebrows raised))
65.	Fred	Wooffit's ((Naomi looks towards Fred))
66.	Ann	Wooffit's Garage cleaning cars ((Naomi writes on form))

Getting a turn and losing it

A useful way to start noticing what is happening in an extract of conversation is to look at how people take turns in the talk, or how turns are allocated. There are two basic ways for anyone to get into any conversation. One is that they are **selected by another speaker**; the other is that they **self-select**. The short exchange in extract 3.1 illustrates a very typical structure in conversations with people with intellectual disabilities, which only becomes remarkable when set against an understanding of how turn-taking works in general (Sacks *et al.*, 1974: 717). People generally take turns in conversation in an orderly way, with the second speaker selected by the first, and so on. In extract 3.1 Naomi **selects** Barry as the next speaker by looking up at him and raising her eyebrows, and actually using his name: 'What about JOBS Barry'. However, immediately after Naomi's turn is delivered, instead of Barry filling the slot for his turn, first Fred and then Ann jointly take his turn for him. They clearly self-select, and in quite a forceful way. What happens next? Naomi immediately turns her gaze from Barry to Fred, and then writes the information given by Barry's carers on her form.

It would be clear to any casual observer that Barry is being cut out of the talk. However, by understanding some of the basics of CA, it is possible to show how this kind of pattern flouts the rules of ordinary conversation. The first thing to mention is the basic principle of sequential

---

[1] See the Appendix for a list of transcription conventions used in this and all other extracts in this book.

organisation illustrated in this short extract; one thing leads to another, and what matters in conversation is what comes next.

> When we talk, we produce utterances which perform actions, which in turn invite particular next kinds of actions (or which at least limit the range of actions which can come next without seeming unusual). In this sense, verbal interaction exhibits a structure: the shape and form of the ways in which contributions to interaction form a connected series of actions. (Wooffitt, 2005: 8)

The 'slot' for what comes next is not just a neutral, empty space, open for anyone to say anything. One turn opens up the space for another turn, not in a neutral way, but in a way that sets the scene for what can be said next. Another basic pattern in conversation must be introduced here and will thread throughout this book. It is the **two-part structure**, or **adjacency pair** (Schegloff & Sacks, 1973; Sacks *et al.*, 1974; Heritage, 1984; Schegloff, 2007: 13–14). This is a basic unit of conversation, which operates across different cultures, in which the first part sets up the ground for the second. Naomi's 'What about (.) JOBS Barry?' is a good example of a first part.

Therefore, when Fred comes in with the name of the place Barry worked, and when Ann takes up and expands on this, they are both jumping in and filling the expected 'second part', which Naomi had set up for Barry. This is more than simply giving information on Barry's behalf – they are usurping Barry's slot in the pattern of talk and supplying a second part that clearly satisfies Naomi. She shows this by turning back to her paperwork and writing down what Fred and Ann have told her. It is worth here just introducing another term, **preferred response** (ten Have, 1999: 120). Every first part of a two-part sequence has a corresponding second part, which fits with the function of the first part. In other words, it is what the speaker wants to hear. This is precisely what Fred and Ann give Naomi, with their response about Barry's workplace. By doing this, they effectively block the opportunity for Barry to come in and say something more at that point.

After a very short pause, the talk continues, as shown in extract 3.2:

Extract 3.2

67.	Ann	((clears throat)) very good ↑at that↓ (4)
68.	Nao	was it just cleaning cars there or did he have any more =
69.		((Ann turns towards Barry as he starts to speak))
70.	Bar→	= cleaning cars (.) and sweeping up in the gar – in er (.) Wooffit's
71.	Nao	yeah ((writing this down all the time)) sweeping up –
72.		((Ann does circular gesture with right hand towards Barry, as Naomi
73.		says 'sweeping up'))
74.	Nao→	((looks towards B)) so it was just generally it was just tidying up =
75.	Bar	= yeah tidying
76.	Nao	and helping the people out
77.	Bar	yeah
78.	Nao	OK ((looks back to paperwork))

Figure 3.1, like all the figures in this book, is a drawing based on a still frame from the video, exactly at line 74, and shows how Naomi looks up towards Barry as he speaks. The precise timing of eye gaze is significant here. It effectively marks the point where Barry comes back into the conversation in his own right.

In line 67, Ann says that he is 'very good at that', assuming the right to evaluate Barry's performance in the garage job; and then an exchange begins in which Barry performs a very strong

Figure 3.1　Naomi's direct eye gaze acknowledges Barry's turn. (This line drawing, like others in various chapters, is a tracing of a still shot on the video.)

piece of conversational work in order to have a voice in this exchange for the first time. As has been seen, turn sequence is a very basic underlying structure in conversations. In this case, the new first part which Naomi delivers at line 68 ('was it just cleaning cars there or did he have any more ='') is directed to Barry's carer, Ann, and opens up a slot for her to respond. Note that Naomi now uses 'he' about Barry, instead of directing herself to him and saying 'you'. However, this time it is Ann who loses her slot and Barry at last gets a chance to respond, as he does in line 70.

Again, a short detour into CA territory may help to explain what is happening here. If a turn comes to a natural conclusion, without being interrupted, then there is naturally a point at which someone else can start speaking. CA analysts refer to this as a **transition relevance place** (TRP) (Wooffitt, 2005: 27), and it can be recognised by a range of clues, including the intonation pattern, the speaker looking directly at the other person and by the sense of what they are saying reaching completion. However, in this case, Naomi's first part about the detail of Barry's job does not get a chance to come to that natural conclusion – in fact, she is interrupted, not by the person she is addressing (Ann) but by Barry himself. That is why Barry's turn at line 70 is marked with an arrow, to show its significance. Note that the equals sign = is a 'latching sign', indicating that one turn jumps in immediately on the tail end of another. Timing is of the essence here for Barry. If he had hesitated, he might have lost his chance. In effect, he attaches his turn to the end of Naomi's question, even before it has reached the TRP.

A two-part sequence is often completed with some kind of **third part**, a slot which is often filled by an acknowledgement, as it is here at line 71 with Naomi's 'yeah'. This has the effect of telling Barry that his response has been accepted; she then opens up another sequence by checking: 'was it just tidying up', this time looking directly at Barry. In other words, the main participants are now Naomi and Barry. Barry seems to take his cue from Naomi by repeating the word 'tidying' in line 75, and he affirms what Naomi suggests about 'helping the people out' in line 77.

It is clear how important Barry's sense of timing is, so that he becomes the main recipient of Naomi's talk. However, even as he starts to talk, it is worth noticing exactly what Barry's carer does. She turns her face to him as soon as he opens his mouth and also prompts him with a gesture at lines 72–3. In fact, if her gesture referred to sweeping, it comes too late, as Barry has already said the word before the prompt! However, her observation of Barry and her gesture seem to be incipient prompts; his entry into the conversation is not accepted as a natural, unremarkable event. Prompting is very common and will be returned to throughout this book.

There then follow some 10 or so turns, which are not given here, in which Barry does not say a word. The topic of a farming job which Barry had done is brought up by Naomi, and his carer immediately offers her opinion that 'that was nasty'. This part of the conversation includes a summary evaluation by Ann that: 'they took advantage of him because of his being like he is'. In saying this, she nods in Barry's direction, then turns back to Naomi who is attending to her.

Naomi then asks how long this job lasted and where it was. Again, Barry's carers respond immediately on both counts. At this point, the grandfather clock in the hall starts chiming and Naomi glances at it, while the other participants ignore it. The following extract (3.3) then ensues.

Not believing what someone says

Extract 3.3

99.	Nao	and on the Wooffitt's garage how long did you work there for Barry↑
100.		((*looking directly at Barry*))
101.	Ann	° quite a long time °
102.	Bar	quite a long time
103.	Nao	how long is a long time ↑((*still looking directly at H*))
104.	Bar	about three weeks [er six weeks-
105.	Ann	[no no
106.	Bar	eight eight weeks
107.	Ann	he was there over a year (1) [about twelve months↑]
108.	Bar	[over a year] twelve months↓ I
109.		think Tim er Tim Tim got me the job I think
110.	Nao	OK
111.	Bar	from the er resource centre
112.	Nao	OK so would it be over a year – less than a year and a half↑
113.		((*looking directly at Barry*))
114.	Bar	over a year I think
115.	Nao	just over a year↓ I'll just write this down now
116.		((*turns back to paperwork*))
117.	Ann	I don't think Tim was there actually [when you worked at Wooffitt's
118.		((*turns to H, shaking her head*))
119.	Bar	[he was
120.	Ann	I'm sure he wasn't
121.	Nao	well that's all right I've got quite a – quite lot of information there
122.		already I can fill that out at work↓

At the start of this extract, Naomi introduces a new sequence with her question 'how long did you work there for Barry?' As at line 62 when she had asked Barry about his 'other jobs', this turn is addressed to Barry by looking up directly at him, and also in this case by using Barry's name and by using the pronoun 'you' (instead of 'he' as in extract 3.2, when Naomi had got drawn into a sequence with Barry's carer). This is a clear indication that Barry is selected as the next speaker. However, again his carer quickly takes the next turn, with a rapid, muttered response 'quite a long time', which Barry picks up and repeats. This time, the interruption by a carer is dealt with differently as Naomi carries on looking directly at Barry, expecting him to speak next. However, she takes what Ann has said ('a long time') and redirects the question back to Barry with 'how long is a long time?' She thus manages to acknowledge that the carer's response is appropriate and has been heard, while using it to make a renewed attempt to bring Barry himself into the conversation. This strategy works well, and finally Barry answers for himself, providing the information 'about three weeks – er six weeks' at line 104.

It is clear from this section how very difficult it is for Barry to get into the turn structure. He is given plenty of slots, but his turns are so frequently usurped that it appears as if he is jointly constructing turns with his carer's assistance. For instance, at line 108 Barry overlaps with his carer's turn and echoes what she is saying, thus taking back the turn for himself. Despite Naomi's best attempts, Barry's right to take his own turn in the conversation is continually violated.

However, there is something else happening in this conversation, beyond the actual turn structure. CA analysts are interested in what happens when speakers hesitate, interrupt, self-correct, and so on, since this can give a clue as to what is happening and how each speaker is contributing to the conversation. This is sometimes called **interactional trouble** (ten Have, 1999: 116), and it is easy to see the trouble in this talk. When Barry does have his say and provides a response to Naomi's question, he is immediately interrupted and contradicted by his carer, at line 105, with 'no no'. This is a challenge which is stated baldly and could come over as quite rude: Ann could, for instance, have designed her turn more sensitively to express her doubts about Barry's response, by saying something like 'Did you?' or 'Is that right?' There is no particular comment from anyone present about this 'no no'. Ann thus establishes not only the factual truth about Barry's job history, but also her right as his carer to correct him and to have the final say. Her concern is to provide factual accuracy for Naomi's form rather than to 'save face' for Barry.

The challenges to Barry's version of events continue. Barry's 'eight weeks' is turned into 'twelve months' by his carer at line 107, and she switches to the pronoun 'he', thus addressing Naomi directly and casting Barry into the third person. It is interesting that Barry does persist at this stage. Despite the doubts cast over his reliability, he now has the floor and gets a turn at line 108 by echoing his carer's 'twelve months', actually overlapping with her turn. This is a quick way of getting in again to the conversation and ensuring that Ann does not take the next turn. Once he has the floor, he expands his turn by introducing another topic, quickly switching to 'I think Tim' and then hesitating. Because he has started speaking, it is easier now for him to continue. He can take his time and give Naomi other background information:

Bar	think Tim er Tim Tim got me the job I think	
Nao	OK	(lines 109–10)

Thus despite his supposed unreliability as an informant, Barry appears again to be fighting his way back into the conversation. The new topic at line 109 functions as a first part and Naomi again acknowledges this with 'OK'. She then asks Barry for his confirmation of the timespan of the job as she writes it down on the form, and again she looks up directly at Barry. However, once more it is Ann who comes in to challenge his account at line 117. This time, Barry directly counters his carer's challenge and defends his own account. In view of how the turn structure has proceeded thus far, Barry's challenge is a very marked action.

Trying to get accurate information

What are we to make of this? Barry appears, after this conversation, to be someone who does not know the factual details about his own life. Although the form which Naomi is filling in is about Barry himself, the answers tend to be given by his two carers. Because they know so much about Barry, they clearly consider it their right – and possibly their duty – to provide factual responses, even though this is to the detriment of treating Barry as an adult who can reliably speak up for himself.

People with intellectual disabilities may often have difficulties in coming over as 'reliable witnesses' (Williams, 2005) and this is in some ways naturalised and accepted. It is interesting that Naomi makes many concerted efforts to speak directly to Barry. Despite her acceptance of the factual accuracy of his carer's interventions about the timing, she does check this information with Barry at line 112 with 'OK so would it be over a year – less than a year and a half↑' She does *not* return to Barry's original formulation of 'about three weeks', thus clearly indicating that his attempts were inadequate. In CA analysis, the accumulation of several possible responses in a conversation is referred to as **candidate responses**, a useful way of reminding us as analysts that any of these responses could be chosen as acceptable by the speaker who has posed the question. Wetherell (1998), for instance, uses this idea in analysing how young men answered questions about their behaviour. In the present case, the candidate responses to the question 'How long did you work there?' are:

a)   three weeks;
b)   six weeks;
c)   eight weeks;
d)   over a year;
e)   about 12 months;
f)   less than a year and a half.

Of all these, the version that finally gets written on the form is 'over a year', which is interesting since this is in fact the formulation eventually agreed by Barry himself.

When the final disagreement between Barry and Ann ensues, Naomi winds it up with her turn:

| 121. | Nao | well that's all right I've got quite a – quite lot of information there |
| 122. | | already I can fill that out at work↓ |

This turn brings the sequence to a close and so stops the counter-talk between Barry and his carer: 'She was', 'no she wasn't'. However, Naomi still does not establish that Barry could be right about what he is recounting. Naomi's final turn merely shifts the relevance of the whole exchange to another occasion, with the justification that she has enough information.

Barry's competence to remember and recount factual details about his own life is called into question during this conversation. Yet Barry clearly has a good enough level of speech to answer and to take part in conversation; he also has recall of the particular job which they were talking about. It could be concluded that the questions about timing were simply too difficult for him and that he would be unlikely to be able to reply accurately. The reader may also wonder whether it actually matters whether or not he had worked in a place for six weeks or 18 months. However, professionals in employment support would know that basic CV information about the length of a job might well be important in establishing the fact that Barry is able to stay in a particular workplace for a certain amount of time. This information might be crucial in enabling him to appear a reliable employee and thus gain another job. There seems to be some trade-off here for Barry between being a 'reliable employee' and a 'reliable account-teller': in order to appear as a reliable employee, he becomes an unreliable account-teller. Clearly, his carers and support worker all feel that his identity as a reliable employee who kept a job for over a year was more important than his reliability in recalling details for a form. However, to some extent Naomi has started in extract 3.3 to illustrate ways in which she can save Barry's face by giving him a way to change his version of events and to introduce other topics relating to his work. Above all, she has shown the value of talking directly to Barry himself, even when listening to his carers.

Brendan: Prompting or forcing someone to speak

Where Barry's voice was silenced by others speaking for him, unequal structures of conversation can disadvantage people with intellectual disabilities in other ways, even when they are being 'encouraged' to speak out.

The next extract is from a seemingly different context, during the research described as the 'Finding Out' project. It is taken from the sixth and final visit carried out by the four people in the Bristol Self Advocacy Research Group, with me in a support role (Williams, 1999; and Chapter 1, pp. 15–16). The research group had arranged visits to ask what they described as research questions. Many of those visits had been to organisations of people with intellectual disabilities or to day centre groups. The physical location of this particular visit was slightly different. The participants in the extract below were part of a group of people who were taking part in a relationships project and the talk took place in the front room of a house they used for meetings. It can be noted here that Jack was a paid member of staff in the host group and Brendan was one of the members who had not spoken at all at this stage. Mark, Angela and Harry are Bristol research group members. The research group members had a sheet of their own written questions and their routine was to take turns in asking their prepared questions, but to support each other with other follow-up remarks and questions. Earlier on in the talk, there had been several hitches – silences in response to questions, fill-ins by research group members and supporters being called in to rescue the talk. At this point, the third question had been posed some 30 lines previously: 'What do you think about jobs?' and one of the host group, Kathy, had just mentioned her job at a pet shop, which appears to be the lead-in for more animal talk in the following extract.

Extract 3.4

212.	Jack	what about <u>your</u> animals Brendan↑ (0.5)
213.	Bren	mm↑
214.	Jack	your <u>animals</u> at your house↑
215.	Bren	° yeah mm °
216.	Jack	you ought to tell people what – what you've got at your house↓(0.5)
217.	Bren	° shoes and socks °
218.	Kath	shoes and [socks↑ ((LF))
219.	Jack	[animals yeah animals (.) you've got an interesting animal
220.		haven't you↑ well not an animal↓ what is it↑ your PETS↑↓
221.	Kath	[like YOUR name↓ begin with F
222.	Bren	[yeah I know (3)
223.	Kath	with F isn't it↑ (2)
224.	Val	((LF))
225.	Jack	what do you have that's interesting at [home↑
226.	Ang	[what a dog↑ ((LF))
227.	Jack	maybe you don't think it's interesting↓ ((LF))

The right to be silent

What is all this about? A quick gloss is that one person, Brendan, is prompted to talk by at least two other participants (Jack and Kathy). It is the detail, however, that is interesting. As with Barry, a good place to start is with the turn structure. Brendan appears to be the focus of the talk here and is most frequently selected by other speakers, most often by Jack who tries to bring Brendan in to the conversation five times, though also by Kathy twice and Angela once. Consider the first four lines:

212.	Jack	what about <u>your</u> animals Brendan↑ (0.5)
213.	Bren	mm↑
214.	Jack	your <u>animals</u> at your house↑
215.	Bren	° yeah mm °

Lines 212 and 214 are straightforward examples of 'first parts', as illustrated above with Barry in extracts 3.1 and 3.2. In this case, Jack's initial 'What about your animals Brendan?' gives a strong framework into which Brendan should slot his turn. Brendan does not fail in this – he produces a questioning noise, which could indicate that he has not heard or understood. Certainly, Jack takes it as an indication that Brendan needs some clarification, since he rephrases and slightly expands his original remark, with 'your animals at your house?' (The underlining indicates that the word is stressed or emphasised.) Again, Brendan fills his slot at line 215, but only with a 'yeah mm'. This is sometimes called a **minimal response** in CA. Throughout this extract, Brendan very rarely comes in with something which is not prompted by another speaker's turn. However, all the other speakers self-select during this extract. Jack has more turns than anyone else and appears to be leading the conversation, certainly towards the beginning. Jack both self-selects and seems intent on selecting Brendan for the next turn, while Angela's and Kathy's turns seem to support the work that Jack is doing:

| Jack | what do you have that's interesting at [home↑ | |
| Ang | | [what a dog↑ LF | (lines 225–6) |

As for Brendan, his turns are noticeably shorter than others and often consist of minimal responses that simply fill the slot, like: 'mm ↑'(213). There is also a considerable degree of over-lapping, hesitation and pausing, indicating that the interaction is not running smoothly, and it is not always clear who is selecting whom – one turn does not necessarily lead to the next. This is very different from some of the talk during other research visits the group had organised.

Prompting or forcing a person to speak

Talk is not just an empty framework of turns. Each turn does something in the conversation, and it does so in a particular way which is designed by each speaker. Going back to Brendan's dilemma, we can see that nearly all of the turns selecting Brendan are in the form of initiations, requiring a response from him. The whole purpose of the sequence seems to be to prompt Brendan to produce a particular response, and each of the other participants has a go at doing this work in a slightly different manner. For instance, Jack's initiations could nearly all be heard as **display questions** (Stubbs, 1983), such as a teacher in a classroom would use. These are questions to which the speaker already knows the answer. Jack's formulations can be heard as prompts or even guided invitations for Brendan to speak, and we also have the evidence from the talk that Kathy hears these remarks in this way. Jack tries different formulations:

what about your animals Brendan↑ (212)
your animals at your house↑ (214)
you ought to tell people what – what you've got at your house↓ (216)
animals yeah animals you've got an interesting animal haven't you↑ well not an animal↓ what
   is it↑ (219–20)
what do you have that's interesting at home↑ (225)
maybe you don't think it's interesting ↓ ((LF)) (227)

No two of Jack's initiations are identical. Each time he adds another bit of information. He starts with an open invitation, but to talk about a specific topic, which relates to Kathy's talk about her work placement in a pet shop. At 214, he adds the prompt 'at your house', then the purpose of getting Brendan to talk is made more explicit ('you ought to tell people': 216), and in 219 and 225 he focuses Brendan on the word 'interesting'. Finally, line 227, 'maybe you don't think it's interesting ↓, can be heard as a laughing admission of defeat, or a meta-comment on how this conversation is going, intended for the company at large and to save his own face. Although Jack knows the answer that he is searching for, he does not give Brendan the answer and ask him to confirm it. It later turns out that Jack knew about the fact that Brendan had a goldfish and wanted him to answer with the word 'fish'.

Throughout all this, Brendan does not give the preferred response. In this case, the prompt question from Jack sets up the expectation that Brendan (preferably) will deliver a fuller response than he actually does. When Brendan does respond, with 'shoes and socks' (line 217), he produces a literal response to the immediately preceding initiation, but ignores the topic of animals proposed by Jack. Doing literal answers can sometimes be a way of making a joke and it certainly leads to laughter here, which then persists throughout the extract. Just after extract 3.4, Brendan does finally comply, although not in the way that was expected, by saying 'I'm a fish, I'm a fish'. Looking back at lines 221–3, it becomes evident what Kathy is getting at when she says that Brendan's name begins with 'F'. As Kathy had hinted, Brendan's surname is actually 'Fisher', and so the conversation may have been both confusing and sensitive for him.

Jack's remarks all appear to be designed according to one underlying rule: 'It is important for Brendan to speak, and it would be good if he said something relevant.' Defining what is relevant in a conversation is a powerful move and one that again is reminiscent of teacher talk. It is a particularly strong move here, since arguably the research group had made bids for this right, by asking their research questions. Although Jack links his prompts topically with what *Kathy* had been saying, in fact the topic of 'animals' is not part of the research group's agenda. Jack seems determined to keep giving as open an initiation as possible, to lead Brendan to give a response that could mark him as a contributor to the conversation.

So what happens when Kathy (one of the people with intellectual disabilities in the house) and Angela (a research group member) join in? These are their attempts to get Brendan to respond :

Kath	like YOUR name↓ begin with F (line 221)
Kath	with F isn't it↑ (line 223)
Ang	what a dog↑ LF (line 226)

Kathy's technique, it will be noticed, is far more direct than Jack's. At line 221, her introduction of the letter F sounds like the start of a riddle. By providing this frame, she is acknowledging the game that Jack has been playing: it is as if she is giving a clue to Brendan about what is going on here, which is something like: 'Jack is trying to get you to say a particular word. I will give you a clue, then you might get the right answer.' This riddle-making seems though to contribute to something else which the reader will have noticed – the talk is sounding more and more like something involving children rather than adults.

Conversations that make others see people as incompetent

Having looked in some detail at how this bit of talk is organised, it is now possible to see what it does to the people involved in it. For instance, what happens for Brendan? In this extract, despite his failures to reply, Brendan is still expected to display his experience and to contribute something to the talk. He is expected to say something appropriate, and almost seems to be pursued by other speakers until he does. Kathy, another group member with intellectual disabilities, as has been noted above, takes on the role of go-between. She effectively tries to explain to Brendan what is going on and she later takes on the task of explaining to others (and in particular to Jack) the reason for Brendan's reticence.

It should also be noted that the exchange between Jack, Brendan and Kathy can only take place because they share knowledge of the personal details of Brendan's life: that he has fish at home. They pursue him with a question to which they already know the answer, again reminiscent of teacher talk. These three players all create a group identity by making relevant their common knowledge. In some places, this group identity is mirrored in joint work within the talk – Kathy with Brendan (answering for/with him) and Jack with Kathy (when they are both pursuing Brendan with questions). Angela and the other members of the research group do not share the knowledge that Brendan has fish at home. They (and the author, who it will be recalled is also present in the role of research supporter) are the genuine audience for the performance that is conducted by the Kathy/Jack/Brendan trio. In a way, it is being done for our benefit; if we had not been there, then this bit of talk would not have happened.

In many ways, then, Jack usurps the identity of researcher. He persists in framing questions, or prompts, in ways that he hopes will produce a response from a particular individual. All this provides a good example of how someone can make the other person appear incompetent. This is not just about one 'bad' support worker hounding Brendan into saying something. Brendan himself collaborates in creating an impression of himself as an incompetent conversational partner, by answering minimally and giving **dispreferred** responses (Schegloff, 2007: 58–9). He has difficulty remaining relevant, and moreover has seemingly idiosyncratic reasons for not wanting to say certain words. He appears rather like a child. It is revealing to see how quickly this identity, which is rooted in the unfolding discourse, can then be transferred to assumptions about the kind of person Brendan is outside this situation. It is easy to think we know what he is like because he has not been able to take on a full role in the conversation. I will pick up this theme again in Chapter 4 to see the ways that different layers of identity are connected. It is important to say clearly here that I am not thinking of identity as something that is set in stone, but something that emerges because of the way people talk together. So much depends on how a conversation goes:

> For a person to 'have an identity' – whether he or she is the person speaking, being spoken to, or being spoken about – is to be cast into a 'category with associated characteristics or features' … People work up and resist identities in indexical, creative and unpredictable ways. (Antaki & Widdicombe, 1998a: 3, 14)

Implications for practice

One of the main points of discourse analysis is that it can reveal and unpick how power structures are re-enacted through everyday interactions. The conversations in this chapter show how the ordinary resources of talk, such as turn-taking and the like, can be used in rather 'special' ways. Each of the extracts examined here has shown how inequalities can be reflected and also created by talk. Both the conversations discussed in this chapter are typical of many I have collected, and of those analysed by Rapley (2004) and Antaki and his colleagues (Antaki *et al.*, 2007b). They will be familiar to many readers who work with or know someone with an intellectual disability. However, by analysing what happens in these extracts, change can start to happen. That is why paying attention to the way communication works can be very important to those in support roles, and this section now draws out some of those implications.

The situation for Barry, for instance, is very common for people with intellectual disabilities when a third party is present. Their right to speak is often weakened by the presence of others, and in particular by the presence of others who are very familiar with them. It is a regular occurrence for a response to be given by the person who is accompanying the person with intellectual disabilities, even when the first part is very clearly directed towards them. This happens on other occasions, for instance, when Barry himself goes out with Naomi to a café, and also very clearly in many other videos that were made of people with intellectual disabilities going out with their support workers.

There are many other similarities in the conversational patterns which emerge. One, for instance, is that other speakers tend to deliver joint responses with the person with intellectual disabilities, just as Ann did with Barry. The analysis in this book shows how often people with intellectual disabilities find themselves in situations like this, in which another person either supports them to speak or answers for them. It can of course be done in a more 'open' way by offering people a prompt, and this theme will be taken up again in Chapter 5. There is a very narrow dividing line between providing support to the talk and threatening to take it over, and so much depends on the surrounding context of the talk – exactly what has happened before and how each turn is slotted into the whole pattern. A key implication for practice is therefore for those surrounding a person with intellectual disabilities to say less, to step back and to let a person speak.

Barry himself does fight his way back into the conversation during extract 3.2, despite the disadvantages he clearly faces: he is sitting in his carers' living room, with their possessions around (viz. the grandfather clock); he is with people who patently have shared knowledge and better recollection of the details of his own affairs than he does; he is being asked for factual knowledge which could actually matter in terms of accuracy. Furthermore, however, despite his fight-back attempts, he does buy into the identity which is being ascribed to him as an unreliable account-giver. He immediately accepts his carer's 'twelve months' as accurate and abandons his previous attempts at answering Naomi's question. In fact, it could be said that the answer to Naomi's question about the length of time is given jointly by Barry and his carer.

Elsewhere in the videos, there are many places where people rely on each other to produce an acceptable response. However, it is possible to do this by introducing a light-hearted note into the conversation and by making jokes, as will be demonstrated in Chapter 6. Barry's carer had no such concern for delicacy! In other words, the same thing can be done in different ways. In this case, the same result (i.e. filling in an employment form) can be achieved by doing things in ways that either include or exclude people with intellectual disabilities. There are many situations in which someone may come over as incompetent or simply ignorant of the correct answer, and in many areas of life, the person talking with them would be concerned to 'save their face' or avoid embarrassment. One way would have been to ask Barry if it is all right to give the information or perhaps to give the information but then reframe the question so that it is one which Barry could have answered. This would have kept Barry in the conversation and given him a chance to rephrase what he had said. Naomi in fact tried to take Barry's words seriously, while also accepting the factual detail given by his carers. She did this by looking directly at Barry when she spoke and by reframing the question, while Barry clearly played his part in producing answers for Naomi. This was also true in the extract with Brendan, where Kathy rephrased the question being asked of Brendan. All these things are joint achievements, in which each person plays their part.

CA analysts assume that talk continually constructs social situations. That means that a situation such as filling in an employment form or carrying out a research interview only takes on that shape by virtue of what people actually say to each other and how they conduct themselves. However, in both cases given above, the social situation became quite blurred and shifting. In the first extract, one could say that the social situation was about filling in an official form to apply for employment support and that Naomi took on the role of form-filler, with Barry as the obvious respondent. However, the presence and the part played by Barry's carers changed this situation, at one point, almost into a personal dispute. One possible way of challenging that shift would be to remind them politely about what was going on, but this was difficult to do, as discussed, since Naomi did need factually correct information from Barry. What she actually did was to move things on by slightly changing the subject, and that tactic worked.

What about Brendan? He was in the opposite situation to Barry, as he was not cut out of the conversation. Instead, he was pestered with questions until he gave some response, very much as children are sometimes treated. Hutchby (2002) showed how children use strategies to resist the incitement to talk, just as Brendan used silence. What can a support worker do to start talking with Brendan on a more equal basis? Clearly, the first implication is to think about how important it was for Brendan to speak or not to speak. Perhaps in that situation it did not matter and the support worker could have left him in peace. However, there are more open-ended ways of offering him a chance to get into the talk, as Kathy demonstrated by starting the riddle with the letter 'F'. She could have gone further, by giving him the clue with the word 'fish', and then asking him if he *wanted* to say something about fish. Note that Kathy was another person with intellectual disabilities, in the same group as Brendan. The strategies for supporting someone in a conversation do not just belong to those in the role of support worker.

Finally, in all the conversations under discussion, it has been observed how all parties contribute to what is happening. It is not just about one person 'oppressing' another; the patterns of talk which have been discussed are naturalised into conversation with people with intellectual disabilities and, to a greater or lesser extent, all the participants contribute to the framework of that talk. This naturalisation makes it all the more difficult to challenge and change the rights of people with intellectual disabilities in interactions, which is why this chapter is an important prelude to some of the other, more positive analyses of empowering talk. Nevertheless, it is important to remember the routine, regular nature of this type of disempowering talk, since it is the backcloth for efforts by people with intellectual disabilities and their support workers to move into new types of conversations, where people engage with each other on more equal terms.

How conversation works: summary points

- Analysts who are interested in discourse or conversation look at what actually happens when two or more people interact. The words 'naturally occurring' are used, which mean that the researcher records data from real-life situations (see Silverman, 1998: 60–2; Speer, 2002).

- This type of analysis focuses on interaction in real-time sequences. It is about an understanding of one turn as linked with the context, and in relation to what has gone before and what will come next. This is the local context for any particular turn in any conversation (see van Dijk, 1997b: 11 and 15; Antaki & Widdicombe, 1998a: 5–6).

- A fundamental starting point for analysis based on CA is to understand the structure of conversation, which is composed of functional units, or 'turns', in conversation. A turn is simply a slot in a conversation, and all talk is composed of this to-and-fro between speakers (see Wooffitt, 2005: 8–9).

- Speakers in a conversation can select themselves for the next turn – i.e. they may break in on another person's turn, or they may simply fill a silence or start a new sequence. Speakers can also be selected by someone else in the conversation (see Wooffitt, 2005: 29–30).

- Sequences of turns often occur in pairs. Adjacency pairs are a fundamental unit in CA: a first part opens up a slot for a second-pair part (Schegloff, 2007: 13–14).

Inclusive approaches to communication: summary points

- People with intellectual disabilities often get sidelined in conversations. The way people look towards each other, or look away, is very significant in ensuring that each person gets equal turns at talk.
- People with intellectual disabilities are often disbelieved by others. Good supporters will trust the person's word, but also will make sure that the information is within the grasp of the person with intellectual disabilities.
- People may want to keep silent or not answer. Pursuing someone for an answer can be counterproductive, and is more like a conversation with a child than with an adult.

Chapter 4

Supporting Someone to be Competent

Background

When we set out with a camcorder in the 'Skills for Support' project, we felt confident we would be filming empowering interactions. We had found great people to take part in our research, all of whom had individual support and most of whom felt they were 'in control' of their lives. In the jumble of real-life interactions, though, we found the good and the bad, the empowering and the disempowering, side by side. We do not wish in the least to say that these particular individuals were 'bad' or 'good' communicators. This is simply how communication works.

Chapter 3 showed how people may get sidelined in conversations, prompted or forced into responding, and they were not always believed when they did respond.

This chapter turns to even more difficult and sensitive areas and explores social activities which could be glossed as 'advice-giving' or 'behaviour control', common tasks for support workers interacting with people with intellectual disabilities. In our project we called these the 'grey areas' – neither good nor bad, but just plain difficult. People with intellectual disabilities are assessed as needing funded support services precisely because of their 'inability' to manage certain aspects of their own lives, as was explored in Chapter 1 (p. 5). Thus the support worker's job is at least partly to help people manage risk, to give advice and to protect people from harm. What is of interest here is how these matters are played out in the day-to-day interactions between disabled people, their support workers and others in their lives.

This chapter explores these difficulties and sensitivities, but also the positive ways in which supporters can:

a) give advice and keep someone on task, while allowing them to have a voice and to 'own' their own affairs;
b) include the person with intellectual disabilities in understanding their own support needs;
c) treat a person with high support needs as an active agent in conversation, even while helping them to manage difficult behaviour.

Disability and Discourse. Analysing Inclusive Conversation with People with Intellectual Disabilities,
1st edition. © Val Williams. Published 2011 by John Wiley & Sons, Ltd.

Ellie: Budgeting for a shopping trip

In order to find an activity involving advice-giving, the 'Skills for Support' team chose to focus on discussions about money, since this was frequently mentioned as a sensitive area by participants in that project. Ellie was in her thirties and had her own tenancy in a flat. She was supported by an organisation that supplied her with support workers, and the worker with her in our video (Jenny) was someone whom she knew well.

The following extract occurs in Ellie's flat, prior to a shopping trip. Jenny and Ellie had explained beforehand that the activity of budgeting was very important to Ellie, since she wanted to go to the shops every day. This was more than a 'want', it was part of her daily routine and she depended on it. However, in order to be able to afford that, she and her support worker regularly constructed a shopping list of intricate detail and precision, so that her daily budget did not exceed £15. Throughout this extract, Jenny is sitting with a calculator and a list on her lap, while Ellie has been squatting down beside her, or getting up to check what items she may need from the shop. When extract 4.1 occurs, the list has already been added up and has gone over the £15 limit. The task facing Ellie and Jenny is therefore to reduce the list, and several items (including tissues and butter) have been struck off, when the following exchange occurs. Both Ellie and Jenny are looking at the list with concentration on their faces:

Extract 4.1

54.	Jen	right you've still got a bit of change up to fifteen pound er
55.	Ell	but how much [would I have
56.	Jen	[because we've kno:cked (0.5) hang on let me just
57.		check (.) let's say 9.30 =
58.	Ell	=ooh you'd rather me keep it wouldn't you say don't spend it
59.		((laugh voice)) ((standing up and leaning over Jenny))
60.	Jen	((smiles)) plus (.) four – hang on ((laugh)) – 48 right 9.80↓ right
61.		because we've knocked off that dear one (.) you can now afford to
62.		have your butter back on ((looks at Ellie)) (.) if you want
63.	Ell	maybe it's good to give the tissues a miss =
64.	Jen	= we're going to give the tissues a miss
65.		[because we can't afford em] ((looks at Ellie))
66.	Ell	[because because tomorrow] because what Bob can do is get two lots
67.		of tissues in to last me the month [do you know what I mean used to
68.		buy two lots =
69.	Jen	[do you want the butter back on↑
70.	Ell	= to last me (.) often then I don't have to buy them so much maybe
71.		buy a big – a big packet of them
72.	Jen	ye::ah so do you want to have the butter back on↑ because you can
73.		afford to have the butter back on
74.	Ell	yeah go on then – if you – if I can afford it that is [if I can
75.	Jen	[that's 14.80 – so
76.		you've got 20 p left
77.	Ell→	yeah (1) knock it on then I suppose (.) HAH
78.	Jen	yeah so that'll be 14.80
79.	Ell	yeah
80.	Jen	right (.) and we're going to stick to that yeah↑
81.	Ell	yeah because that has been crossed off for tomorrow that's 86 isn't it
82.	Jen	yeah tissues I'll write that one down

Keeping someone on task

When approaching CA analysis it is often necessary to do some pre-work on simply noticing what is there. For instance, it is sometimes important to notice not just *who* takes a turn and what they do with it, but also *how* the conversation sounds and looks. Extract 4.1 is a very fluent bit of talk and has a chatty feel to it. This is shown in the fact that turns follow on fast, one after another. This is called 'latching' in CA, and is marked on the transcript by the equals sign (=). There are frequent **overlaps,** points where two people are talking together, marked by [square brackets], and occasions on which one speaker comes in with something quickly right in the middle of the other's turn (see line 58), without seeming to disturb the flow. These interruptions do not seem to cause any problems for the speakers. They just carry on with writing the shopping list. There is scarcely a hesitation, except when Jenny is waiting to see the result of the calculation she has typed in.

However, there is one pause that appears to be significant in the context of all this fluent chat. It is Ellie's one-second pause at line 77, and possibly the most interesting point of this extract is marked by that pause. If the pause is so central, what the analyst needs to do is to show in some way what 'work' it does in the talk. This is slightly different from asking 'why did Ellie pause?' It is about analysis of how a pause, in this particular context, could make a difference to how the conversation is interpreted. In order to get to that point, however, it is necessary first (as it often is) to provide an overview, a kind of gloss, of what is happening.

The goal behind the talk between Jenny and Ellie is to add up prices and construct a shopping list for Ellie. This is Ellie's shopping and so Jenny is quite explicitly performing a support function in helping Ellie with the task. However, Jenny does some work to achieve this and it's worth investigating that first. The first question that seems to stand out is about ownership and the mismatch between the personal pronouns used by Ellie and Jenny. It is interesting to see how Jenny switches with some ease between the pronouns 'you' and 'we'. Of 12 instances, she uses 'we' five times, at line 80 in a highlighted position after a forcible (emphasised) 'right':

Jen right (.) and we're going to stick to that yeah↑

That was actually the line that was picked out by Kerrie and Lisa, the self-advocate researchers in this project. They thought it was important to notice how a support worker can keep someone on track. Ellie, however, refers throughout to 'I' and 'my' shopping: she only once drifts into 'you' at line 74, immediately self-correcting with 'I'. If this really is Ellie's shopping, then Jenny is simply there to help her with the technical aspects of adding up the prices. That interpretation of Jenny-as-calculator could be an accurate depiction of what is happening during the first half of this extract, with Ellie self-selecting (i.e. choosing to take up a turn) at lines 55, 58 and 63. In two of those turns, she introduces a new topic and so initiates a new sequence, for instance at line 55 with: 'how much would I have'. Jenny responds with 'hang on let me just check', and then proceeds to do exactly that. However, at line 63, Ellie introduces another topic and potential shopping item: 'maybe it's good to give the tissues a miss'. Jenny then simply repeats this and reminds Ellie of the reason 'because we can't afford em'.

As Jenny is saying this she looks at Ellie, and this seems to be significant. The pair had previously been through the conversation about tissues, Ellie had discovered she still had enough tissues to last and that decision had already been made. Jenny's look could be seen as a way of getting Ellie to stop talking about an item they had already decided on. That look has the force of saying 'Let's move on'. Instead of tissues, Jenny is concerned that Ellie should decide whether to buy butter today. The choice becomes framed as 'butter on' or 'butter off', rather than 'butter or tissues'. Jenny poses this decision for Ellie three times, at lines 61, 69 and 72, and some of her financial arguments sound quite persuasive:

because we've knocked off that dear one (.) you can now afford to have your butter back on
  (*looks at Ellie*) (.) if you want (line 61)
do you want the butter back on↑ (line 69)
so do you want to have the butter back on↑ because you can afford to have the butter back on
  (line 72)

Therefore, the three main strategies that Jenny has deployed are: a) the use of 'we/our', which positions them together in the budgeting endeavour; b) use of directed gaze; c) persuasive argumentation relying on financial economy. It is in this context that Ellie's pause at line 77 has to be viewed.

The sequence structure from line 69 onwards becomes rather confused, because Ellie carries on talking about the decision about whether to buy a 'big packet' of tissues rather than responding to Jenny's questions about butter. Instead of responding immediately to Jenny's request, she carries on pursuing her own agenda; moreover, it is an agenda which makes her out to be an astute shopper: 'two lots of tissues … will last me the month … then I don't have to buy them so much, maybe … a big packet of them'. This in itself is a way of taking back control of the whole activity – this is *Ellie's* shopping, and it has to be her decision about what she wants to buy. As she does this, she significantly leans forward with a hand gesture.

Only when she has dealt with tissues to her satisfaction does Ellie turn to the butter decision. At line 74, she responds with: 'yeah go on then', but then introduces the proviso 'if I can afford it that is'. This prolongs the sequence, with Jenny confirming the new total as '£14.80' with '20 p left'. It is at this point that Ellie finally confirms her decision at line 77 with 'yeah', but then significantly pauses for a whole second, before saying 'knock it back on then I suppose'. It is that pause which tells Jenny, and the reader, that Ellie is in control. She is stopping to think about her own shopping decision and she finishes with a flourish of satisfaction 'hah'. The technical devices that Ellie has used to keep her stake in the shopping (and in the conversation) are:

- sticking to the first-person possessive 'my' in the face of the 'our' from Jenny;
- resisting the completion of the two-part structure introduced by Jenny;
- developing a logical argument around the purchase of tissues;
- using devices such as that pause followed by an emphasised word, which have the effect of establishing her talk as decisive.

It is interesting that none of this is actually about Ellie insisting on buying tissues. She is quite happy to drop her shopping item from the list, but she manages (through conversational devices) to redress the control of the conversation which Jenny could have had. The idea of a **repertoire** is useful here (Wetherell, 1998), in the sense of a familiar set of arguments and/or way of talking. People habitually draw on various systems of thought within which they can persuade others about the truthfulness or 'rightness' of a set of propositions (see Rapley, 2004: 11). It is possible to see how Ellie draws on a repertoire of shopping, which brings with it a whole understanding of what it takes to be a good shopper, buying wisely and planning ahead. One could also say that Ellie does **identity work**, since she talks in such a way that the listener starts to see her in a different way.

Incidentally, none of this is taken very seriously. Jenny and Ellie have a laugh and smile together, as is shown by the laughter at lines 59–60, and this is very typical of this pair. In fact, at line 58 Ellie even delivers what amounts to a teasing comment, or a taunt:

= ooh you'd rather me keep it wouldn't you say don't spend it *((LF voice))*
  ((standing up and leaning down over Jenny))

The joke hinges on what Ellie thinks of Jenny's personality – a cautious and penny-pinching adviser! Jenny takes this comment light-heartedly, as she shows by her smile as she carries on with her calculations. Ellie is laughing at Jenny's concerns and poking fun at her in a gentle way, and the fact that she can bring off this teasing shows us something about the rights Ellie assumes in the interaction. As it turns out, this joking style appears quite typical of the relationship between these two; later on when they are in the shop, Ellie turns to Jenny and puts her arm around her, saying 'don't worry woman, you're a worrier'. Making a personal comment, even in jest, is quite a powerful move and perhaps not something one expects a person with intellectual disabilities to do to her support worker. The nice thing here is that Ellie chooses to do this exactly at the point when she could be 'dominated' by a support worker who is guiding her through her budgeting. The support worker could have ignored this joke and continued to pull Ellie back to the task in hand. The fact that Jenny accepts and appears to enjoy this interaction (as evidenced by her laughter) is significant. The result is that the task of writing the shopping list comes over as a joint effort, within a relationship that appears to be harmonious and friendly.

Enabling someone to talk about their own support needs

In extract 4.2, Ellie continues with identity work in quite an explicit way, this time displaying her identity as a person with Asperger's syndrome, and she does this deliberately 'for the camera'. Readers might have noticed that the precise shopping planning in extract 4.1 was unusual, and might suspect that it is specific to an intellectual disability setting, or at least that it is something pre-planned and driven by Ellie's particular needs. Most of us do not plan our shopping trips so precisely, even if we have to stay within tight spending limits. The way that Ellie receives support on these issues is in fact part of an agreed plan between her and her support workers, and this is alluded to by Ellie herself in the following extract, which occurs immediately after the lines given above. At this point, one of the researchers with intellectual disabilities (Kerrie) speaks up and asks Ellie a direct question:

Extract 4.2

83.	Ker	do you just stick to what you've got in your pocket then Ellie
84.	Ell	I try to ( ) it's a frustrating thing for me because I've got – you knew
85.		that I had autism already didn't you *((sits down on floor))* aut-
86.		aspergers syndrome didn't you aspergers syndrome *((circular gesture*
87.		*with index finger))*aut – asperg mild one I- I – I find routine quite er
88.		good I do I'll look at the camera find routine quite quite um um I'm
89.		sometimes find everyday life a bit of a struggle *((looks towards*
90.		*camera))* but I try to get through everything I find it hard don't I Jenny
91.		but it -
92.	Jen	yeah but it's priority isn't it and you're doing very well↑↓ you really
93.		are doing well on this scheme
94.	Ell	yeah
95.	Jen	( )
96.	Ell	Anns going to look at things – just to let you know Anns going to look at my finances in late November

The very fact that Kerrie speaks here is significant. Kerrie was one of the research team and had been behind camera until that point and was in fact under instruction not to say anything. Therefore, her turn at line 83 can be described as a very 'strong' self-selection. Ellie responds without hesitation; however, she goes beyond a literal response. She could have just answered with 'I try to' and stopped there, offering Kerrie the opportunity to get back in at that point with another turn. Instead, she carries on without pausing, and her turn at line 84 becomes a justification or account for the whole way in which she budgets her money and for the activity Kerrie had just witnessed. She explains it by resorting to the medical labels for her condition, 'autism' and 'aspergers', and the consequent need for 'routine' in her life.

When a speaker does something with a turn, he can choose to **design the turn** (ten Have, 1999: 119–23) in different ways, which will have different outcomes. Here, Ellie is addressing an audience wider than just Kerrie: she makes this clear with 'I'll look at the camera'. Part of turn design is visible in the way speakers shift their gaze or change their body posture. Exactly at the phrase 'I find routine quite good', Ellie looks away from Kerrie, as if about to say something more. This is a classic way of keeping the floor (Goodwin, 1984, 2007), and here it is an even stronger move, since Ellie explicitly turns to deliver the rest of her turn to the camera. This enables her to go on without a pause into something much longer. She designs a turn which shows concern to put the whole activity of budgeting in context and to explain her position as someone who is being supported to manage her shopping behaviour. Having answered Kerrie's literal question with 'I try to', she then says: 'It's a frustrating thing for me'. This in effect links the literal answer with what comes next. One can see now that she has understood Kerrie's underlying meaning to be something like 'why is it so difficult for you?' and that is the question she is answering. She then carries on to relate her frustration to aspects of her wider identity, which she draws on quite explicitly here as autism and Asperger's syndrome. It is interesting that there is a slight hesitation and stutter in bringing out these phrases. It is the first time in this discussion that anyone has referred directly to her impairment, and it is a sensitive but powerful thing to do in this context. In doing so, Ellie is telling 'the camera' (and thereby the outside audience) not only that she has particular impairment-related needs for support, but also that she is aware of them. Because of this impairment, her argument goes, she needs 'routine'. This is a deep-level answer to a question which is only very vaguely implied by Kerrie's question. It is an answer to something which Ellie herself realises could appear odd to an outside observer, the routine of budgeting in detail and constructing a shopping list to match an exact sum of money. Ellie's turn is thus designed to justify what has been happening and to ensure that she herself appears both sensible and rational.

All this is sophisticated talk which shows a good deal of awareness of both self and the situation. Ellie at this point makes relevant aspects of her identity which relate to her support needs – she apologises for herself and effectively does face work about her own wider identity as someone with autism. This is reminiscent of how Naomi saved face for Barry in Chapter 3 (p. 43). Zimmerman (1998) suggests that one can analyse identity in talk at three levels: the **discourse level;** the **situational level**; and the **level of transportable identity** (the identity that people take away from a situation and which stays with them). In other words, people take on particular identities simply by the things they do in conversation (discourse identity); by virtue of those things, they then take on particular social roles (situational identity) and also bring to the conversation their wider identity as a man, a woman, a person with intellectual disabilities or a support worker (transportable identity). These three levels are interrelated, which is clearly illustrated here. As Ellie talks about her transportable identity as someone with Asperger's, she is at the same time taking on a new situational identity. Instead of appearing as a woman with intellectual disabilities who is having support with her shopping, she now becomes the analyst of her own needs and situation, capable of explaining it on camera. It ought to be noted here that Ellie can only do all this because of the ways in which her support team have included her in discussions about her needs in the past, as becomes clear from what happens next, at line 92 onwards.

In attending to the sequence of conversation, it is not enough just to note down which turn comes after which. Sequence is also about the way each speaker hears and interprets the previous turn, as is very obvious at line 92:

> Jen   yeah but it's priority isn't it and you're doing very well↑↓ you really are
>   doing well on this scheme

The first interesting thing Jenny does here is with her 'yeah but'. Speakers often preface, or even announce, what they have to say in various ways. This 'yeah but' is an example of a common conversational device to introduce something – a **pre-sequence**. However, this is a particular type of pre-sequence, a type of mitigation; Schegloff (2007: 64) suggests that it is a way of introducing a 'dispreferred' response (see Chapter 3, p. 47), something that the other speaker may not want to hear. What it seems to do in this case is to acknowledge, but then brush aside, Ellie's claim that she 'found it hard'. Although Ellie finds it hard, Jenny says, 'it's priority'. This is an example of what has been called an **extreme case formulation** (Pomerantz, 1986), chosen here to add some persuasive force to the argument about the need for budgeting. Jenny uses the occasion to remind Ellie, in effect, that her effort is worthwhile.

Jenny then goes straight on to a positive evaluation: 'you really are doing well on this scheme'. Praise like this can always be read in more than one way. In some sense, Ellie's appeal to Jenny at the end of her turn in 91 strongly opens up a slot for this praise. Ellie seems to expect it. Both parties seem to buy in to a routine where Jenny is expected to 'encourage' Ellie or to praise her efforts. However, praising another person's efforts can be part of a way of exercising power over that person. The result is that Ellie runs the risk of appearing like a child, someone who needs encouragement and praise. It is interesting also that Jenny uses the word 'scheme' to describe what Ellie is doing with her money: this is an institutional word, even an educational word (as in 'schemes of work'). It is drawn from a repertoire of 'schemes' which are planned and probably written down. This scheme is designed to solve problems precisely relating to Ellie's lack of competence with shopping, with reasonable behaviour and with budgeting. However, it may well be the word that Ellie herself uses when discussing her needs, and thus it is a way of reminding her of the things she has agreed to do.

From this brief example it can be seen how the relationship between support worker and person with intellectual disabilities can change moment by moment, from an empowering, professional relationship to one that could threaten the autonomy of the person with intellectual disabilities. The reader may justifiably feel some unease that Jenny is 'giving control' to Ellie, rather than Ellie actually taking control. The whole problem hinges around Ellie's competence and her need to have direction from her support worker. What Jenny does is to make sure that Ellie herself can explain her own needs and has a say over the type of support she needs. She then backs her up with some praise and encouragement, but it can be seen how easy it would be to go too far. Giving advice in an empowering way is a rather sensitive matter.

Keeping someone safe

Budgeting constituted one of the most frequent grey areas that people with intellectual disabilities and their support workers talked about in the 'Skills for Support' project. However, an even more sensitive area is the issue of advice relating to health or safety. People told us about incidents relating to drinking and the problems that can arise when a support worker feels they have to give advice or guidance on drinking. However, we did not manage to capture any of that on video. What we did manage to film was one incident where a supporter intervened in a situation where damage to the home, or even damage to people, could have occurred. Extract 4.3 takes place in Ben's home. He is a young man of about 20, with no verbal communication, but is physically active and communicates with a variety of non-verbal actions and signs. Colin is his support worker. The camera was not on when Ben, briefly alone in the living room, picked up a candle-holder to bang against the window. It ought to be mentioned here that Ben has a known concern to look out of the window and to see who is coming. He is also very anxious to make contact with people and would be likely to communicate with anyone outside the house by knocking on the window.

Extract 4.3

1.	Col	put that down that's the thing for carrying the candle
2.		((Col walks towards Ben, who has picked up the candle holder and is
3.		starting to use it to bang on the window. Col takes candle holder from
4.		Ben, turns away and puts it down. Ben holds arms out at his side. Col
5.		walks past Ben towards window, pauses, and juts out his hand towards
6.		Ben, making a mock fist))
7.	Col	((whistles, picking up the tune from the TV that is on.
8.		Then turns back towards Ben, puts one arm round his back and holds
9.		his other hand, as if waltzing.))
10.	Ben	he-huh
11.		((Both dance out of the door, turn and come back in.))
12.	Ben	((points towards far wall, upwards))
13.	Col	((Still resting his hand on B's shoulder, but breaks away with his right
14.		hand. Pats Ben's back)).
15.		er you're looking for Harry are you↑
16.	Ben	eeh ↑
17.	Col	I think he's probably having his tea now mate (2) alright↑
18.		((Looks round to face Ben.))
19.	Ben	((Touches Col with right hand, then moves hand down, palm open.))
20.	Col	fish and chips
21.	Ben	((Repeats same gesture))
22.	Col	e:::r um apple pie and custard
23.	Ben	((Repeats same gesture))
24.	Col	and a cup of tea (.) then put his feet up
25.	Ben	((Repeats same gesture))
26.	Col	and watch TV
27.		((Takes hand off Ben's back during this, then slaps him gently on
28.		back.))
29.		think it's football on tonight↑
30.	Ben	((moves hand out again, palm open. Then pulls away from Colin and
31.		walks towards TV))
32.	Col	shall I have a look↑

The underlying structure of adjacency pairs is a strong foundation for conversation, and also for CA. What is interesting here is that the adjacency pair structure can be so imperative that it is also adhered to with great precision by two speakers, one of whom is not in fact able to speak. In line 1, Colin responds to Ben's banging by telling him in a serious tone of voice not to do that and to put down the candle-holder. Given that the window is a large one, the candle-holder a heavy object and Ben a very strong young man, the combination could of course have led to problems. Colin follows through by taking the object away from Ben without any further words. There is then a brief pause in which Colin looks out of the window and makes a mock fist at Ben, but he then starts to whistle. At line 7, it is Colin, the support worker, who initiates the next sequence by starting the whistling and pulling Ben into a dance. The pair dance out of the door at the end of line 9 and back in again at line 11, when there is a smooth flow into the final part where Ben and Colin stand together, with Ben putting questions to Colin in the form of gestures.

The first point to note is that the turns are almost evenly distributed between these two partners. Colin has 10 turns (if his whistling is counted as a turn) and Ben has seven, of which five are delivered with his gesture language. Although Ben is 'non-verbal', he in fact selects Colin for next turn on six occasions. Five of these are with gestures and one is with an insistent 'eeh' sound, on a rising tone (line 16). On each occasion, Colin responds verbally and often with an action as well.

The overall impression is of conversational partners who are well in tune with each other. There is one hesitation at the start of line 22, in Colin's turn: 'e:::r um apple pie and custard', and pauses occur without any noticeable trouble during activity in which the two drift away from each other. There is also one significant pause in line 17, during which Colin watches Ben's face, and then asks him 'all right?' Colin's eye gaze is in fact constantly on Ben. The extent of looking done by any communicator varies; however, in this case, it seems to be an essential part of the feedback loop between Ben and Colin.

In transcribing these sequences, I have tried to show how physical actions form a part of the total flow of communication, on an equal basis to words. For instance, Colin's pretend gesture towards Ben when he makes a fist at him is a communicative act and is taken as such by Ben. There is clear evidence that he takes the dance itself as a communicative act, as he comes back into the room smiling broadly. Ben's gestures at this point seem to be a continuation of a conversation, not just an initiation, and perhaps follow on from the contact that they have both had through the dancing.

Figure 4.1 Colin watches Ben's face as he responds to Ben's gesture.

The dance thus flows directly into the sequence where Ben is asking questions with hand gestures, from line 12 onwards. To any outside observer, the intention of the gestures would be quite obscure. At the most, they would all be interpreted as a 'where?' question, with palms up. However, Colin interprets these gestures quite precisely, as requests to know about what Ben's brother Harry is doing and eating (his brother does not live with him, but is local and has frequent contact). All this depends on intimate knowledge of the context and of what Ben is likely to be talking about. It is also clear from the video that Ben himself takes Colin's responses as 'adequate' or correct. (By contrast, on other occasions, when Ben performs a gesture which is misunderstood, he will always persist and often become frustrated at lack of understanding.) The fact that he accepts the flow of the talk here shows that Colin has understood well what Ben wanted to talk about.

In all this the physical timing seems to be very important. The sequence has a coordination of action and counteraction, with great sensitivity to the flow and position of the other partner. In fact, there is almost a slapstick approach to the interaction, initiated by Colin. The most obvious features of this sequence are the physical contact and the jokes. It would seem that Colin is using the jokey-dance routine with Ben as a way of distracting his attention away from hitting the window. Thus, instead of focusing on Ben's potentially difficult behaviour, Colin downplays it, and the incident with the candle-holder becomes just another activity in a whole flow of mutual responsiveness. It seems particularly appropriate that this emerges as a dance, since the whole sequence has many properties of a coordinated dance, with gesture, posture and movement all playing a role.

The interaction between Colin and Ben depends on intimate knowledge and trust between the two, comparable perhaps to that which would exist between a couple in a longstanding relationship. In the same vein, the atmosphere of shared jokes, the routine conversations and the physical humour are all more reminiscent of intimate personal relationships than professional support relationships.

Implications for practice

The job that a support worker does with a person with intellectual disabilities can easily move into some very sensitive areas, some of which have been sampled and analysed in this chapter. Telling someone else what to do, preventing harmful actions and helping people organise their life – all these are aspects of what was referred to as 'advice-giving' in the 'Skills for Support' project, and it is a social activity which almost unavoidably brings with it an imbalance of power. It is very difficult to give or receive advice without buying into this power imbalance, where the advice-giver is a knowledgeable and controlling figure. There are inherent tensions in establishing equal rights in a conversation where there is an element of control or advice.

For instance, Colin's task was to maintain a good relationship based on intimate knowledge of Ben, while also helping him to control aspects of his behaviour. When Jenny was advising and encouraging Ellie in her budgeting, and when Colin was controlling Ben's behaviour by distraction, it was very hard to conceive of the person with intellectual disabilities as having 'equal conversational rights'. The support worker can advise or guide the person with intellectual disabilities as part of their institutional work; however, there were very few cases in the 'Skills for Support' data of the person with intellectual disabilities advising or guiding their support worker. It is important to note that this does not mean that people with intellectual disabilities cannot give advice and guidance themselves, and later chapters will show how they can take on important roles as researchers and self-advocates, supporting each other and those around them. However, the particular job of the support worker, as illustrated in this chapter, is based on the assumption that the support worker is 'right' and the person with intellectual disabilities is 'incompetent' in certain aspects of life. That is the reason the support worker is there.

What was noticeable, however, in both the examples given here was that the person with intellectual disabilities did take a full and active role in the conversation. In Ellie and Jenny's case, it was Ellie who led the conversation, initiating sequences, asking Jenny to calculate items for her. She also made a strong bid for holding on to the 'agenda' and defining what she was going to talk about. In extract 4.1, for instance, she actually resisted or delayed providing a direct answer to Jenny's question about the butter, while finishing her own preferred discussion about the tissues. As pointed out, the discussion about tissues put her in the role of astute shopper, planning ahead to get a bulk packet.

In the final extract, Ben also maintained an active and leading role in the conversation, as was noted above. He initiated sequences, filled his own slot in the conversation and responded by body language to the initiations of his support worker. However, compared with Ellie, Ben had fewer verbal resources. It was therefore harder for him to deliberately put himself over in a certain way, to do 'identity work' or to account for his actions, as Ellie had done. A parallel statement to Ellie's account of her autism, delivered by Ben, would be something like: 'I am active and lively – that is why I like banging on windows. But I know that my support worker has to distract me from this, and I do enjoy dancing with him as well.' These are in fact precisely the sort of statements that appear in written form in Ben's person-centred plan, which has been constructed with his family and friends in order to guide his support. However, Ben could not produce that statement in the here-and-now. That is why it was important for Colin to know exactly the type of support strategies that worked with him. The very fact that support is delivered on the terms of the person with intellectual disabilities means that, to some extent, that person is in control of things. It is up to those around Ben to make sure that his person-centred plan does express these precise needs for communication, and it is extremely important that those who come into his life understand, work with and contribute to his person-centred plan (Coulson, 2007).

In the ebb and flow of the conversations above, it is interesting to trace the identity issues which occurred. These are sometimes about the 'labels' or the diagnoses that have been applied to Ellie and to Ben. In Ellie's case, the label was expressed as 'autism … asperger's. A mild form'. In Ben's case, the label is not openly expressed, but if it were, it would be 'challenging behaviour'. Both these are what Zimmerman (1998) refers to as 'transportable identity'. As Zimmerman demonstrates, each person's transportable identity is reformulated and shaped afresh on each occasion they take part in an interaction. For instance, Jenny became someone who is 'good at calculating' because this was what she was doing with Ellie. Ellie herself, as she described and accounted for her own support needs, became someone who was self-aware and capable of explaining Asperger's to other people. She became a commentator on her own condition. Clearly, if the support worker can help someone to understand, plan and articulate their own support, this will give them far more control over how they are treated by support workers and others.

Despite this understanding, it is important to remember that the labels of 'autism' and 'challenging behaviour' are very strong and difficult identity labels to live with (Gillman *et al.*, 2000). A key to providing good support is often to forget about the 'label' and talk directly to the person, and the examples given in this chapter clearly illustrated how both parties could 'soften' the interaction with laughter and jokes, even during instructional sequences. Discourse analysts have often studied what laughter and joking can do (Jefferson, 1979) and, in a parallel case to the present study, Ryoo (2005) found that jokes could form the basis of a friendly approach between shopkeepers and customers of different races, where there was a need to 'equalize' the relationship.

Through small choices in the way that interaction is managed, this chapter has shown how each speaker can shift the conversation into and out of the frame of 'giving advice' or 'controlling behaviour'. For instance, in extract 4.1, it was noticeable that Jenny used the pronoun 'we' and 'our' in referring to Ellie's shopping. This could be a way of taking joint responsibility for the budgeting and the shopping, but it could also detract from Ellie's sense of ownership of her own shopping, money and her life. She herself referred to 'my shopping', and 'my money', rather than 'our'. In making that shift, it could be said that Ellie was actually making a bid to own her affairs and to make her own decisions about shopping. Jenny was simply the pair of hands operating the calculator! Similarly, there were small details in the extract with Ben that were key to the social activity going on. It was very noticeable how Colin curtailed the matter of the window with a slight hint at a joke and then moved on to something quite different. This ended in his responses to Ben's questions, which had the effect of changing the social activity into a chat about Ben's family. Ben started to ask questions (his discourse identity changes) as he led the conversation; at the same time, Colin reminded us that Ben was a 'brother' rather than a person with challenging behaviour. Colin's sensitivity to these shifts marked him out also as someone who knew the family situation and someone who knew intimately what Ben's gestures and initiations were likely to mean. As in Chapter 3, it is vital to remember that this is not just about the non-disabled person's strategies. Each conversation takes shape because of the way in which both people contribute turns and respond to the other. Both Colin and Ben had active roles in the talk and in establishing their own terms for interaction.

In providing empowering contexts for talk, therefore, this chapter has emphasised how difficult and sensitive a matter it is for a person with the label of 'intellectual disability' to have equal rights in an interaction. High on a support worker's job list will be interactions that are precisely about advising, educating, changing or controlling the person with intellectual disabilities. However, we have also seen how these interactions can be successfully managed by both parties. Because of the skills of the support worker, Ben and Ellie are given:

a)   the power to define the agenda,
b)   an opportunity to account for their actions, to explain and justify what is happening,
c)   a chance to initiate interaction through gestures.

How conversation works: summary points

•   Body language and non-verbal features are important parts of an interaction. Some gestures have the force of a 'sign', as in a formal sign language. However, when analysing what is happening, it is also important to notice the coordinated nature of actions, facial expressions and even where each person directs their gaze (see Kendon, 1990).

•   The type of analysis that has been demonstrated starts from the particular, the very fine detail about what is happening for the speakers and what can be demonstrated from the data about the speakers' own understandings. Only then does the analyst move on to the wider issues about social position, identity and so on (see Silverman, 1999; Wooffitt, 2005: 186–210). This avoids empty theoretical statements, and offers an analysis grounded in the data.

•   Identity is not something that is 'given'. In CA, the analyst looks for ways in which participants themselves make relevant certain identities, or do 'identity work' (Antaki & Widdicombe, 1998a: 1–2; de Fina *et al.*, 2006). They do this within the flow of the talk and to some extent by the way in which they manage the talk.

Approaches to inclusive communication: summary points

- Giving advice and guidance about behaviour is a sensitive thing to do. It is important to find ways for the person with intellectual disabilities to take control of their support plan, and if possible to know and agree to the reasons for that plan.
- Taking the time to listen is important when a person with intellectual disabilities wants to talk things through. This gives them a chance to 'own' their issues and to take control of their life.
- Distraction can work if there is a potential crisis. But the best way is to know the person with intellectual disabilities in great detail and depth. Those who know that person best will understand how to communicate successfully, and they will be able to forget the 'label' and talk directly with the person.

Chapter 5

Opening up Conversation

Chapters 3 and 4 have focused on some problematic issues that occur routinely in conversations with people with intellectual disabilities. In this chapter I now turn to what promise to be more positive situations. First, though, a 'health warning' is in order: the reader seeking an ideal, cookbook approach to empowering support will always be disappointed. Analysis of what happens in real-life encounters is always more complex and nuanced. In the 'Skills for Support' project, as we watched the videos, we noticed many occasions on which the support worker seemed deliberately to try to encourage the person they were supporting to communicate. That is why this chapter explores what happens when people 'open up a conversation', following in the tradition of early CA studies (Schegloff, 1968). However, conversational strategies by one party are deployed in response to what the other person has just done. It is important for supporters to be able to facilitate conversations and to encourage the person they are supporting to speak up, but of course a good social chat depends on the contributions of both conversational partners.

This chapter considers first some ways of opening up channels for someone else to speak at all, and then looks at how conversations are kept going in the context of shared interests and relationships. Specifically, the chapter deals with:

a) Offering and taking up an open invitation to speak, which is not always successfully achieved;
b) A pattern that seems to work better, where a specific question is followed up by a more open invitation to say more;
c) Ways in which people keep conversations going by expanding and expressing interest in specific bits of information;
d) Times when someone has been reminded about a shared experience or interest, to lead them into the conversation.

Alice: A woman who keeps quiet

Alice was a woman who took part in the videos for the 'Skills for Support' project. She lived with her mother and had two support workers, employed to help her to go out and enjoy activities that she liked, which included rugby, going to fairs, going out for meals and a walking group.

Disability and Discourse. Analysing Inclusive Conversation with People with Intellectual Disabilities, 1st edition. © Val Williams. Published 2011 by John Wiley & Sons, Ltd.

The first part of our video with Alice was made in her home, where she sat at a table with her mother and both the support workers. The main activity they were doing was planning the rota for the support workers. All the arrangements over the next two weeks for Alice had to be talked through and planned. Over 12 minutes of conversation went on *about* Alice's activities, in which her own contributions amounted to three turns. However, Alice was not completely disengaged. She was attending to what was going on, as shown by the following incident. Her mother had lost a letter about Alice's new work placement and Alice had just found it. At this point, her mother has the letter in her hand and the following exchange takes place:

Extract 5.1

98.	Mum	anything you want to say now Alice↑
		((holding letter, and looking at it))
99.	Ali	no:: ((smiles, looking at letter))
100.	Mum	no↑(.) ((shaking head slightly)) sure now↑↓
101.	Ali	no
102.	Jud	any questions you want to ask↑
103.	Ali	no

Giving someone an opener

At line 98, Alice's mother offers her a very general opening question to bring her into the conversation: 'Is there anything you want to say Alice?' It is certainly an invitation to speak, but could be followed by practically any comment on Alice's part. For instance, she could have said 'I don't like going to rugby', or 'I don't like the way I've been left out of this conversation'. Neither of those comments would be what her mother wanted to hear, but they would have been conversationally appropriate. Instead, Alice chooses to ignore the 'invitation' aspect of the opener and to respond literally to the 'Is there anything?' part of the question, with a 'no'. Effectively, in this situation it is a refusal to speak. Note that the precise phrasing of such openers can have profound effects on the subsequent conversation. Heritage *et al.* (2007), for instance, demonstrate how the phrasing of a question in a doctor's surgery ('Do you have some other concerns?' as opposed to 'Do you have any other concerns?') can lead to totally different outcomes. While 'any' holds within it the possibility of a negative response and often receives one, the word 'some' has a positive presumption.

It is impossible to know here if the word 'something' would have had a better outcome. Whatever the case, what Alice does is very much a dispreferred response (see Chapter 3, p. 47), and Alice's elongation of the 'no::', together with her smile, might indicate that she is aware of this to some extent. Her mum then gives her another chance with 'sure now', delivered with a sing-song intonation pattern, and this time Alice simply repeats her original response (note that a literal response to 'sure now' would have been 'yes I am sure'). One of her support workers, Jude, then self-selects at line 102 to give her a third opener in a slightly different form: 'any questions you want to ask'. This opener could conceivably have met with more success, as it suggests something specific that Alice might want to do – she might want to ask questions about any of the activities or details that had just been arranged. However, again Alice repeats her 'no'.

Why are all these invitations to speak unsuccessful? Coming where they do in the conversation, after 12 minutes of silence from Alice, they could be heard as an acknowledgement that Alice has not said anything – and perhaps they come over almost as a rebuke to her. In other words, there is an implication that Alice should have said *something*. Yet throughout the conversation, Alice's mother's eye gaze, her body language and her specific questions had all been directed at Rachel and Jude, the two support workers. Therefore, Alice's refusal to take up the invitation to speak could well be heard as an admission of defeat – 'I have not been given a chance to speak all this time, and now you expect me to say something? Well I'm not going to.'

After that exchange, the reader might think that Alice is simply a very quiet person or that she does not have the verbal skills to participate. However, in other contexts, neither of these things is the case. Later that same day, Alice walks to the library with Rachel. The following conversation occurs:

Extract 5.2

212.	Rac	that's what you did the last time↑
213.	Ali	yeah
214.	Rac	what did you – did you research
215.	Ali	I do the er – double double dot er er rugby
216.		*((Rachel turns her head to look at Alice, smiles, eyebrows raised))*
217.	Rac	oh↑ you (want to) look at rugby↑
218.	Ali	yeah
219.	Rac	any rugby teams↑ or just Herons
220.	Ali	uh er writing the n- names up on the pa – the sheets and that
221.	Rac	oh right right (2) printing them out then
222.		*((Rachel moves ahead as they reach the edge of the pavement, and*
223.		*puts one arm back towards Alice. Alice stops behind Rachel.))*
224.	Ali	yeah

What makes this interaction so different from what had happened in Alice's house? Why does Alice start talking here when she didn't before? The answer could lie at least partly in the sequencing of the turns, the way that one thing follows after another. As has been seen several times (see Chapter 3, p. 39), turns are often organised in pairs, but the first part of each pair does not simply offer a neutral or open space for a second part. Instead, the first turn in a pair will open up a limited range of options for the second speaker. For instance, a question opens up the frame for an answer; a greeting for a return greeting.

At line 212, Rachel asks a simple yes/no question, 'that's what you did the last time?', which is a request for confirmation of what Alice has previously said. Such a question is appropriately answered with the short forms 'yes' or 'no', and at line 213 Alice does simply confirm what she had previously said. But Rachel's next turn does not let the matter drop. At line 214, she follows up the confirmation by asking a more specific question, 'What did you research?', which cannot be answered by yes/no.

This is successful in eliciting slightly more detail from Alice, who becomes quite animated in her body language, gesturing with one hand to show how she would key in 'www.rugby' on the computer in the library. Rachel then immediately follows that up with a reference to what Alice wants to do today at the library: 'Oh you want to look at rugby'. Again, Alice only has to answer 'yes', which she does. The cycle is then repeated from line 219 to line 224, with another more specific question ('any rugby teams or just Herons') provoking a specific answer.

In effect, what Rachel has done here, in two repeated rounds, is first to ask for a simple yes/no confirmation and then to follow that up with a more specific question. Asking for confirmation is sometimes done to find out what the previous speaker has said, although here Rachel uses it to check her understanding (in CA terms, a **candidate understanding** is offered). Rachel's question serves the function of providing a staged framework for bringing Alice into the talk.

The rule would be

1. First, offer an easy question with an easy answer; then,
2. Once Alice has responded minimally, ask her something which requires a more elaborate answer.

Further evidence of that underlying pattern would be that in fact Alice's answer at line 220 does not literally provide a preferred response to Rachel's question about which rugby teams Alice is interested in. Rachel however accepts Alice's response as fine with 'right right', and confirms what they will do in 'printing them out'. In other words, Rachel demonstrates here that her question at line 219 was not simply a question to get some information. It was in effect an opener, an invitation to speak, and that is how Alice takes it.

Showing attention to the other person

The researchers with intellectual disabilities in the 'Skills for Support' project picked out the video clip between Rachel and Alice as 'good practice'. They noticed many other features of this clip, which add to the way in which Rachel brings Alice into the conversation. For instance, Rachel is lively in her body language, she turns her head round to look at Alice, she smiles and she takes Alice's remarks seriously, by responding to her with a raise of the eyebrows. By turning to look at Alice (e.g. at line 216) Rachel can see when Alice herself becomes animated and is engaging with the conversation. Rachel's timing is therefore finely matched with what she observes.

Rachel and Alice move on to the library, and there is some filmed interaction between the pair as they access the computer and search for the website they want. Rachel and Alice appear to be people who share a common interest. What is interesting here is to unpick *how* this impression is put over. There are some obvious strategies – for instance, Rachel and Alice sit beside each other, Rachel gazes constantly at the screen, just like Alice does, and both show pleasure when the right website appears on screen. Much of what Rachel does is about timing: she is prepared to wait, to let Alice take the lead and to show by her tone of voice and facial expression that she is genuinely interested in Alice's contributions. All this made us aware, as we watched them, that they are sharing their interests in rugby. Perhaps it is this 'sharing' that matters most and encourages Alice to speak up. In the research team we became interested therefore in how support workers shared interests with the person they were supporting, and in order to explore this with another pair, this chapter will turn next to Sam and Len.

Sam: Preparing to go to a football match

Unlike Alice, Sam had been quite talkative on each occasion the 'Skills for Support' team met him. The DVD we made with Sam and his support worker, Len, starts with a chat in the kitchen, prior to heading off to a football match together. The conversation in extract 5.3 takes place with both Len and Sam holding open bottles in their hands, from which both of them sometimes take a drink. Both are wearing football shirts, showing that they are football enthusiasts. CA analysts might call this **making relevant** (Antaki & Widdicombe, 1998a: 4–5), or perhaps 'making visually relevant', since they are openly displaying their identity as football fans. They even adopt the same body posture – they are both leaning back against the kitchen cupboards, and both appear relaxed. All of this could also be called 'identity work', as seen in Chapter 4

(p. 54): both identify as people who have a common interest, just as Alice and Rachel did in the library.

How does that work out in the talk? There are many points in this long stretch of talk at which Sam says something about the football which could close down the conversation – in other words, he is tending not to ask questions which could bring Len back into the talk. Len therefore has to self-select many times. For instance, in the following extract, Sam has been mentioning that Princess Anne might be visiting the football ground.

Extract 5.3

45.	Sam	she might be down there – see the match↓
46.	Len	possibly
47.	Sam	yeah (.) in the royal box↓
48.	Len	in the royal box yeah (.) have they got a royal box↑
49.	Sam	by the – where the players come out
50.	Len	oo:h up at the top↑
51.	Sam	yeah
52.	Len	yeah that's right (.) yeah – who knows she might be there

Keeping the talk going

Line 45 finishes off something that had been said previously about a visit by Princess Anne – the 'she' in Sam's turn at 45 refers to the Princess. Sam hopes that she might be there tonight, at the match they are about to visit. Thus Sam's turn at line 45 actually closes down the conversation rather than opening it up. The conversation could easily finish at that point.

Instead of just closing the topic, however, Len picks up with 'possibly' at line 46. This could be heard either as a way of throwing into doubt the likelihood of this visit or of offering a rather 'hedged' agreement. In any case, Sam responds with a minimal 'yeah', but after a slight pause, he chooses to continue with some more detail. The term 'royal box' is well chosen by Sam, as it could add credibility to the fact that Princess Anne will be there. Len picks this up and echoes the term at line 48, by confirming 'in the royal box yeah'. Just like Sam, instead of leaving the discussion there, he retakes and asks 'have they got a royal box↑' This final remark has the effect of eliciting a lot more detail from Sam, and so the conversation continues, with Sam able to display his expert knowledge of the layout of the football ground.

What seems to be happening here is that both Sam and Len are prolonging the conversation, and their joint strategy is to expand on the obvious, to offer more detail than is strictly necessary. This is a **joint accomplishment** – they are doing this together – although it can be noticed that in Sam's case the mention of the 'royal box' gives him the status of an expert about the football ground and about the likelihood of the royal visit. Len's expansion ('Have they got a royal box↑') in the following line does something slightly different. In questioning the existence of the royal box, he could be throwing doubt on the truth of Sam's account; but another way of looking at this is that the remark also serves to defer to Sam's greater knowledge. Len in effect claims that he himself is ignorant of the layout of the football ground. The remark works as a challenge to Sam to say more – to explain what he means by 'royal box' and where it is. We can see how both Sam and Len keep up a conversation with each other by expanding and encouraging each other to say more. Every time the conversation could end, one or other of them comes up with a new 'opener', an offer to the other person to say something more.

Using shared memories

Further on in the same conversation, Len and Sam start to use another strategy which was very common in the data from the 'Skills for Support' project – the strategy of referring to shared past knowledge or drawing on shared memory.

Extract 5.4

59.	Sam	that's what I'd like to do meet the players ↑ all the players
60.	Len→	you've met a lot of them haven't you↑
61.	Sam	yeah
62.	Len	cause they've come over to see you in work↑
63.	Sam	yeah Darren has
64.	Len	Darren – now which one is Darren↑
65.	Sam	tall one
66.	Len	and does he wear anything↑ specific↑
67.	Sam	he wears a blue hat

Again, it is Sam who leads on the topic by expressing his wish to meet the football players, but at line 60 Len expands on Sam's remark in a different way this time, with a reminder: 'You've met a lot of them, haven't you?' As with Len's previous expansion, this could be heard as a rejoinder to Sam, a way of saying, 'Well, why do you want to meet them again? Remember, you've already met them.' However, Sam takes it as an opener to talk about particular players he has met. 'Darren' is introduced, and Len immediately seizes on this detail to ask for more information. Very much as in extract 5.3, Len claims ignorance of the players, which works as a way of asking the other person for more information, and in so doing he draws on two aspects of Sam's identity. The listener now knows that Sam is not only a 'football enthusiast', but also a worker – he met players 'at his work'. None of this detail would have been talked about had Len and Sam not drawn on some common knowledge – in this case, Len's knowledge of what has happened in Sam's life.

It should be noted here that the support worker, Len, is the person who asks the questions. Sam, like Alice in the previous examples, tends to deliver **second part** turns, as in:

1. have they got a royal box↑
2. by the – where the players come out

1. you've met a lot of them haven't you↑
2. yeah

1. does he wear anything↑ specific↑
2. he wears a blue hat

Each sequence is typical of many two-part sequences (or adjacency pairs) throughout the recordings in the 'Skills for Support' project, in which the support worker says something and the person with intellectual disabilities fills the slot for 'second part', often in fact providing a response to a question. As observed, some of these initiations are more successful than others in keeping the conversation going. However, all of them place the person with intellectual disabilities into the role of 'respondent'. Interestingly, the supporter then often comes in with another turn, evaluating or confirming what their conversational partner has said. After Sam's explanation about the royal box, Len says 'oh up at the top↑' and Sam confirms this, with Len then adding 'yeah that's right'.

These small remarks or 'third parts' (sometimes referred to as **post-expansions**) (Schegloff, 2007: 118–27) tend to serve the purpose of giving feedback, telling the other person that their remark is acceptable – that it was a relevant part of the conversation.

Talk like this can reveal and indeed enact power structures. Speakers take turns in conversation, as has been seen. Clearly, these turns do not all fulfil the same function; a speaker can use his or her turn to ask a question, to probe, to answer, to give information or to celebrate someone's achievement, among many other things. However, it is a powerful thing to have the interactional right to ask the question, to initiate and then to evaluate whether something is 'right' or appropriate, and conversely, it is a less powerful position to be the respondent and to be speaking on someone else's terms, and with someone else's prompts. CA has developed a whole branch of analysis, called institutional CA (Drew & Heritage, 1992; Wooffitt, 2005: 56; Heritage & Clayman, 2010), which is based on noticing the inequalities between different categories of speaker.

Although support workers may be trying to encourage someone to talk, in so doing they position that person in a less powerful respondent role. This is a dilemma that relates again to identities: a support worker in some respects actually becomes a support worker *because of* and *through* the ways in which she or he encourages the person with intellectual disabilities to speak. Similarly, the 'intellectual disability' identity is reinforced as the person responds to their support worker's prompts. The particular relationship of a staff member with a person with intellectual disabilities will often veer into an adult–child framework, a supportive and therapeutic relationship in which the support worker is in control of the conversation. This is not typical of professional relationships in general – one only has to think of a professional relationship one might have with an employee who is coming into the house to carry out a job (e.g. a plumber; a piano tuner) to realise that the conversations in this chapter are very specifically designed to 'draw out' the person who needs support. In these conversations, a casual observer would not have much difficulty in distinguishing who was the person with intellectual disabilities and who was the member of staff.

Drawing on shared past experiences

Remembering can be used to achieve different things in a conversation. In both the projects discussed in this book, people very often remind each other about something that happened in the past. In exploring collective voice, Chapter 10 will explore further the way in which supporters remind people with intellectual disabilities of aspects of their life to help them think of what they'd like to say in a meeting. However, there is another way that shared knowledge is used as a basis for conversation, and this is where the experience has literally been shared by both people who are talking. This happens slightly further on in the conversation between Sam and Len.

Extract 5.5

72.	Len	and who else – number 10↑
73.	Sam	number 10 Mark Taylor
74.	Len	Mark Taylor↑(.) yeah↑(1) we saw him in Bath didn't we after the match↑
75.	Sam	yeah match↓man of the match
76.	Len	he was man of the match↓ we had a good day in Bath
77.	Sam	yeah we had a good day
78.	Len	fantastic
79.	Sam	yeah – we saw it on the web didn't we with the fan

Again, a similar pattern can be seen in line 74 as previously, a pause and expansion, typical of this pair and their shared way of keeping the talk going. Len draws on shared knowledge, something he knows about Sam. But in this case, it is more than that – he refers to something he and Sam have done together: 'We saw him in Bath didn't we after the match↑' Using common, shared experience enables Len to use the shared pronoun 'we', and in so doing, he offers a very strong framework for Sam to continue the conversation. Once a speaker has implicated himself directly in a shared memory, it would be very hard for the other person to ignore the opener offered. Even if Sam did not remember, he would have had to account for this in some way, perhaps by saying 'Did we? Are you sure?' In the event, Sam is enabled to carry on with more detail – both echoing Len's 'we had a good day' and then remembering that they had seen the whole event represented on the football fan club website.

Sharing their memory of a football match is just one of a range of strategies Len and Sam use in this conversation. Their concern to keep the talk going has been analysed in terms of some quite precise, and seemingly technical, strategies they adopt; however, they are simply the kind of things we all do to carry on a conversation with another person. In using these strategies, both partners draw on a wider repertoire. This has to do with identity work, the way people put themselves over. Sam and Len both draw on the identity they have in common (the football enthusiast), and actually construct that identity through their talk (Antaki & Widdicombe, 1998a). The fact that they show their identity as football fans (or 'make it relevant') prior to going to a match together helps to mark the fact that they are going as fellow enthusiasts, rather than as a person with intellectual disabilities and their paid support worker. As was shown earlier, their demeanour, their clothing and their body language all feed into this shared identity, and it is one that clearly underpins the conversation and enables it to keep going.

Implications for practice

When one conversational partner is quieter than the other, the more vocal partner may well have some particular work to do in encouraging the other person into the conversation. This happens routinely in everyday conversation, not just with people with intellectual disabilities: the measures and strategies analysed in this chapter are not specific, 'special' ways of interacting with a person with intellectual disabilities. Any non-responsive conversational partner could, for instance, force the other person into being over-talkative because they feel they have to 'fill the gap'. They could also create long silences in conversation. The more sensitive strategies that have been described in this chapter could easily be witnessed in many conversations, for instance, when two people are first meeting; when they are intent on impressing each other; when they have a common interest in prolonging the talk (for instance, at a party or a chance meeting at a conference).

There were certain aspects of the current conversations, however, that seemed to indicate a 'supportive' relationship, rather than just any relationship in which two people were talking. Both Len and Rachel used the tactic of 'shared knowledge' to remind their partner of something, to introduce or extend a topic and to place it within a framework of something that is already known and shared. Rachel, for instance, knew that Alice's favourite rugby team was 'Herons' and so she was able to ask 'any rugby teams, or just Herons?' Len reminded Sam that the football players had in fact visited to 'see him in work'. Details relating to the past life of the person with intellectual disabilities were brought into the conversation – they were in effect used as part of an ongoing narrative about that person's life, a narrative on which the person could draw in order to contribute to the present conversation.

However, there is an asymmetry here. Neither Len nor Rachel introduced details about their own lives. The 'prompting' was done *by* the support workers, and the person who was 'prompted' was the person with intellectual disabilities. In that sense, this strategy could be seen as a one-sided affair, certainly an indication that Len and Rachel saw it as part of their duties to help the person with intellectual disabilities to speak. This is of course a valid part of the job; in other videos we made, the support worker deliberately and explicitly sat down to chat with the person with intellectual disabilities, explaining that this was a very normal part of their routine. On one occasion, this was done by a personal assistant who had come in to help someone take their shower; on another, it was done by two people before some other domestic activities; and on a third it was done before a shopping trip. In all these cases, the supporter displayed similar tactics – searching for things to ask about and things which might be relevant and memorable from the experience of the person with intellectual disabilities (see also Antaki *et al.*, 2007c).

The often debated practice question here is whether the supporter should reveal things about their own personal life or whether they should retain a professional distance. As with all matters of communication, there is no one 'right' answer. The relationship we each have with each other is different, and that is also so for support relationships. However, this chapter has shown how patterns of talk are directly affected by that professional distance. A small amount of 'loosening up' can go a long way, as long as it is on the terms of the person with intellectual disabilities.

In this chapter there has been discussion about 'rights' in conversation. Of course, these are not like legal or human rights – they are simply the things that certain people regularly do as they talk with each other. According to the way people position themselves (or get positioned) in a conversation, they have certain 'rights' associated with that position. In this case, the 'right' to prompt the other person seems to be associated with being a support worker. It is important to understand this concept of 'interactional rights', as it seems to be fundamental to change. Part 2 will explore how it is possible for people with intellectual disabilities to have a wider range of interactional rights, by taking up lead roles in research or in self-advocacy meetings.

Finally, wider identity issues emerge from the very topics that are introduced in the conversation. For instance, Len refers to Sam's work and to the fact that football players have visited him. The status of Sam's work is not known, but it would seem odd at first sight that football players would visit a workplace. However, those who are familiar with the world of 'intellectual disability' would understand immediately that football players, of course, might well visit a sheltered work-shop or day centre as part of their charitable activities. As the support workers are referring to small details like this, they are showing that they know all about what it is like in the world of intellectual disability. Perhaps it is useful to enter into this world, as Len and Rachel both do, in order to start up a successful conversation with the person they are supporting.

How conversation works: summary points

- When something is not understood or not heard, then speakers may ask for confirmation or clarification. This is called '**repair**' in CA (see ten Have, 1999: 116–19). As explored in this chapter, these things can also serve the purpose of encouraging the other person to speak.

- Turns at talk often come in pairs (adjacency pairs), as has been noted. This pattern is often followed by a 'third part', or post-expansion (Schegloff, 2007: 118), which can take the form of acknowledgement or feedback.

- Different types of turns perform different actions. Some of the social actions seen in this chapter were 'prompting', 'encouraging' and 'recalling' and some are associated with particular roles or identities. This type of association is sometimes called an interactional right (Ochs & Taylor, 1992) and the unequal distribution of these 'rights' can result in institutional asymmetry (see Sarangi & Roberts, 1999: 62–5).

Inclusive approaches to communication: summary points

- A supporter is sometimes like a counsellor or therapist. The job is about encouraging people to speak, giving openers for conversation and showing an interest in what people say.
- Much depends on how the conversation develops. Someone who has been excluded from a conversation for a long time will not necessarily respond to an open invitation to speak. It is often more successful to follow up what the other person has said, to ask something quite specific, and then to follow up with a more open question. This is what Rachel did when talking with Alice.
- Shared interests and experiences can be a good basis for encouraging someone to speak. Supporters often demonstrate that they share an interest by the way they dress, as with Len and Sam, and by their non-verbal behaviour. Reminding people about something they have done or referring to a shared past activity is often a good way of keeping a conversation alive.
- When encouraging someone to speak up, it is hard to avoid differences in power. The person who puts the question and says 'well done' often has the power to direct how the conversation goes. Much depends on being sensitive to what the person with intellectual disabilities may want to say, and when they may be able to take the lead. The person who is drawn into a conversation about football one day may be leading a group discussion the next month.

Chapter 6

Equalising Talk and Friendliness

Many of the social problems for people with intellectual disabilities are to do with inequalities of various kinds. In this chapter I consider how inequalities can be tackled simply by being friendly. The idea of a paid support worker becoming a 'friend' is controversial, since a reliance on relationships with paid staff can conceal the paucity of social relationships for many people with intellectual disabilities (Forrester-Jones *et al.*, 2006). Antaki *et al.* (2007b) revealed through CA how support workers tended to promote themselves as friends of the people they work with. Although this seemed to be routinely accepted by the participants Antaki *et al.* studied, these authors discussed the problematic aspects of friendliness in support workers:

> If staff are constructed as acting on the basis of friendship, then their motivations, and loyalties, are not brought into question. (Antaki *et al.*, 2007b: 13)

Conversely, it has also been noted by research studies in Australia and in the UK that staff can fail to recognise the true feelings and the sexuality of the people they support (Johnson *et al.*, 2001; Abbott & Howarth, 2007).

Even more than other, more formalised relationships, friendship is something that implies a deep, emotional connection between two people. Therefore, there is some tension and unease about 'doing friendliness', as if that may be deceptive. Nevertheless, friendship is clearly something that is socially constructed and contingent on particular cultural and contextual settings: what is accepted as friendship in one social circle may not count as friendship in another. Being a friend in a British boarding school may be quite a different relationship from friendship in Japan or in China; in some settings, friendship is about loyalty and belonging, in others it may be more about social niceties. However, in Western cultures, most would agree that relationships tend to be called 'friendship' when they are dyadic, voluntary and equal (Newcomb & Bagwell, 1995).

How do these ideas of friendship measure up to the friendliness offered by paid members of staff? In the 'Skills for Support' project, our team worked on a day-to-day basis within an organisation of disabled people, an inclusive living centre. That gave us the opportunity to have frequent chats about what 'friendship' with support workers means. Most disabled people who did not have intellectual disabilities were wary about the friendship issue and talked about professional boundaries. However, the co-researchers in 'Skills for Support' were quite clear that they wanted their supporters to be friendly. We set out therefore to try to analyse what this might

Disability and Discourse. Analysing Inclusive Conversation with People with Intellectual Disabilities,
1st edition. © Val Williams. Published 2011 by John Wiley & Sons, Ltd.

mean. Just as with other activities, such as budgeting or advice-giving, it is possible to look more closely to see how friendliness is 'done'. That is what this chapter sets out to do.

A striking feature of the videos recorded for the 'Skills for Support' research is that they show two people who appear to like each other and who make this visible in a number of ways in their interaction. For instance, as we watched the videos in the research team, we noticed how people with intellectual disabilities and their support workers fine-tuned their body movements to each other, how fluent they were in taking turns in the conversation and how they smiled at each other and made eye contact. Friendship carries with it ideas about mutuality and is associated with casual, informal relationships and equality, rather than with institutional power. However, the interesting point is that the interactions in this chapter are not between friends who have been freely chosen. At least one of the participants in each interaction is someone who is paid to be there or has an official role of some kind. Therefore, the relationship must be both professional and personal at the same time.

Friendliness in interaction is important for two reasons. One is that people with intellectual disabilities themselves often say they want support workers to be friendly. The co-researchers in 'Skills for Support', for instance, spoke of 'trust' and 'valuing' when they made their comments for the training DVD from the research material, and picked out the factors in friendliness that were important for them:

> I also think Lisa, when you value somebody. If we look at it there's a bit of common ground, Lisa. There's no pressure, sort of 'you must do this, you must do that'. There's no pressure on it, which is very good. (Ponting *et al.*, 2010)

The second reason is that friendliness seems to loosen up the situation, so that the person with intellectual disabilities is more likely to be able to have a say. Chapter 5 showed how support workers could use past experience, or shared knowledge, in their everyday interaction, in order to prompt people with intellectual disabilities to speak. The current chapter takes that strategy a step further and shows how people bring in their shared experiences as a way of signalling a close relationship.

Ruth: Having a joke about housework

The first extract in this chapter is chosen because it appeared to our team to be an example of two people engaged in an ordinary activity as friends. It was also interesting because the topic they were discussing was the sensitive area of encouraging and negotiating housework – to be carried out by the person with intellectual disabilities. The extract takes place in a café (where there is considerable background noise). Two people are seen sitting at a table, one facing the camera and the other at a 90 degree angle. One has a cup of coffee in front of her and the other has a salad roll and a drink.

Extract 6.1

1.	Nor	housework↑ we were going to clean your bedroom out (weren't
2.		we) ((*looks at Ruth, smiles*))
3.	Rut	yes
4.	Nor	we were going to sort that out↑
5.	Rut	yeah ((*Nora looks away*))
6.	Nor	do you want to have a go at doing that ((*N smiles at Ruth*))

7.	Rut	yeah I might do ((*smiles*)) ((*Nora looks away*))
8.	Nor	yeah↑((*R and N make eye contact*))
9.	Rut	yeah ((*smiles*))
10.	Nor	that took us all day ((*LF + eye contact*))
11.	Rut	yeah ((*LF + eye contact*))
12.	Nor	yeah we'll do that (.) you'll have to make sure you have
13.		some black bags and a pile for the charity
14.	Rut	just been doing – chucking out leaflets today
15.	Nor	leaflets↑
16.	Rut	yeah

Showing that you are friendly

When people are being friendly with each other, one would perhaps expect them to have equal rights to speak. This appears to be true in the extract above, as Ruth and Nora have an equal number of turns, one coming in after the other. However, it does seem as though Nora (the support worker) has some control over the way the conversation progresses. Ruth is nearly always deliberately selected by Nora to contribute the next turn: furthermore, Ruth's first 12 responses are minimal ('yeah' or 'yes'). Nora, by contrast, quite clearly self-selects in many of her turns:

> housework (1)
> we were going to clean out the bedroom, weren't we (1)
> we were going to sort that out (4)

It could be argued of course that, in a two-way conversation, there is only one possible next speaker and both simply follow that rule: when one person has stopped speaking, it is all right for the other one to start. However, it is often Nora who introduces a new topic and it is not until line 14 that Ruth expands on Nora's query and offers new information:

> just been doing – chucking out leaflets today (14)

Ruth does however have a role in keeping the conversation going. The video shows that she continually looks at Nora, smiling and inviting her to carry on with the conversation. For instance, the sequence from lines 6–7 is a typical two-part sequence, with Nora initiating and Ruth responding with 'yeah I might do'. In effect, Nora is inviting Ruth to plan for some domestic activity in her flat, and this is arguably part of Nora's responsibility as a support worker. However, Ruth's response clearly does not match Nora's expectation; in some respects it is a 'dispreferred' response, and the observer understands that by the way it is taken. Instead of a simple third-part acknowledgement, Nora comes back with a teasing 'yeah↑'. The force of that is to ask Ruth for a definite confirmation of her plan to clear up her flat. Ruth's previous equivocal 'I might do' is seen as not good enough. Ruth too seems to hear Nora's 'yeah' in that way, since she simply responds with an agreement, 'yeah'.

All this sounds quite controlling. Ruth is pursued until she agrees to a definite plan for how to spend her time in her own flat. However, that is not how the episode comes across, since the whole turn pattern appears to be very smooth and well coordinated. There are many non-verbal markers here of an ordinary friendship and indeed of conversational partners who are finely tuned to each other's moods and needs. On several occasions in this short extract Nora breaks gaze with Ruth with a smile or a giggle. On each occasion, the moment at which their gaze reconnects seems very significant. On some occasions, this is done with a smile and even with mutual laughter (between lines 10 and 11); on other occasions, Ruth seems to control the decision about whether to laugh, smile or be serious. As with Ellie and Jenny in Chapter 4, Nora and Ruth are very responsive to each other and they notice what the other person is doing, often mirroring each other's facial expressions.

The timing of the smiles and laughter is not left to chance: it is no coincidence that they occur precisely when Nora is pursuing her agenda to instruct Ruth about her domestic life. Perhaps they play a mitigating or softening role in this particular interaction. They also imply a wealth of personal knowledge between Nora and Ruth, who clearly have something that they can laugh about together. However, softening an instructional sequence may make it more 'friendly'; it clearly does not imply a friendship in the sense in which it was discussed in the introduction to this chapter.

Frank: Social chat while making a cup of coffee

Next is a sequence in which Frank is making a cup of coffee with his support worker, Adam. Frank is the man who asked his support worker in Chapter 1 to make a cup of coffee. As well as his intellectual disability, Frank has a considerable physical impairment and a visual impairment.

Extract 6.2

31.	Ada	right coffee pot is that one there ((*Frank's hand reaching out*))
32.	Fra	that one=
33.	Ada	= yeah ((*Adam moves back and to one side*))
34.	Fra	can't tell nowadays because it's – cause it's powder and I used
35.		to get granules =((*unscrews lid on coffee pot*))
36.	Ada	= yeah
37.	Fra	thought it was sugar at first and had – had to stick my finger in
38.		to find =
39.	Ada	= oh god
40.	Fra	and that's terrible
41.	Ada	that is terrible ((*LF*))
42.	Fra	I hate this stuff↓ I don't hate it but (.) but it's just powder=
43.	Ada	= you see I don't drink coffee so
44.	Fra	you don't↑
45.	Ada	no
46.	Fra	all right
47.	Ada	not at all
48.	Fra	oh I didn't know that↓ so you just like tea↑
49.	Ada	I don't even drink that much tea to be [honest]
		((*Adam walks to fridge, bends down, opens fridge door*))

Doing something together in a coordinated way

Extract 6.2 is part of an episode in which the support worker, Adam, appears to be entirely focused on successfully making a cup of coffee. He does not make the coffee himself, but instead is supporting Frank to use his own kitchen. The turn structure is very neat, with alternate turns throughout and only short pauses (the longest silence lasts about six seconds) while Frank is doing specific tasks. Frank and Adam tend to finish each other's remarks, as is recorded in the transcript by the latching marks (=). There is very little misunderstanding or hesitation in the conversation, and both Frank and Adam appear to be fluent conversational partners – as well as fluent coffee makers! The video shows that Adam is continually moving around behind and to the side of Frank. They had previously been sitting in the living room, when Frank asked Adam to help him make a cup of coffee. From the moment they get up from their armchairs to go into the kitchen, Adam waits and watches, stepping back for Frank to go into the kitchen first. Frank then starts things off by bending down to get cups out of the cupboard and Adam again stands behind him. It looks like Adam is there as a servant, waiting to see what he should do; each of his actions is determined by Frank's previous action.

It is interesting to observe where Frank and Adam put themselves in relation to each other. Their movements around the kitchen are determined largely by the activity of making a cup of coffee (getting the milk, pouring out the water, washing up the cups), but each time it is Frank who moves to do the task. Adam often moves back physically, which enables Frank to move around without bumping into him. They appear to be very finely tuned to each other, and this is seen in the way they move around each other. Frank is the one who takes the lead. Although he cannot see Adam, he does look accurately towards him at several points in response to noises Adam makes. Adam watches carefully, and when he does perform an action or point something out, it is done exactly at the moment when it is needed. For instance, his verbal offer of 'coffee-pot, that one there' is done exactly at the point when Frank's hand reaches out for it.

Having a social chat about things you both know

In addition to being the ever-observant butler, Adam performs another role while the two are in the kitchen, and that is to provide a partner for social conversation and jokes. There are many points at which the two of them move into 'off-task' talk. As with the physical activities, Frank also appears to lead the social conversation. Much of the talk is related to making the drinks – but in a way that extends the present activity into other scenarios, introducing other characters or reflecting on stories relating to Frank himself. Both Frank and Adam often bring in material that is only understandable to the other because of their shared history, as in the following example.

Extract 6.3

50.	Fra	my stockings actually come on the third of July
51.		unfortunately
52.	Ada	ah so you'll be wearing them then for the er – night club
53.		((smiles))
54.	Fra	no – no I don't have to wear them

It is Frank who brings up the topic of his support stockings (see Figure 6.1), which he is supposed to wear for medical reasons. He also mentions the date on which they are being delivered and expresses his reaction to the support stockings with the word 'unfortunately'. This is something he is not looking forward to, and Adam acknowledges this with 'so you'll be wearing them then for the er'. This, as it turns out, is a reference to a planned visit to a night club, and Frank's 'no no' at line 54 relates not to the accuracy of Adam's reference, but to the fact that he actually does not want to wear the stockings at the club. The smile on Adam's face in line 53 quickly fades, as can be seen in Figure 6.2.

Figure 6.1   Alan and Frank match their smiles and head turns to start a joke (line 50).

Figure 6.2   Alan follows Frank in dropping the smile to close off the joke (line 54).

Only once in the extended sequence does Adam reveal something which is actually about himself, and that occurs in extract 6.1, when he says that he does not like coffee or tea. Frank reacts to this information with surprise, implying that he would and should know personal details about his support worker.

43.	Ada	= you see I don't drink coffee so
44.	Fra	you don't↑
45.	Ada	no
46.	Fra	all right
47.	Ada	not at all
48.	Fra	oh I didn't know that↓ so you just like tea↑
49.	Ada	I don't even drink that much tea to be [honest

By contrast, Adam is allowed to know, and is in fact expected to share, a fund of stories about *Frank's* personal life and he uses these on occasions to make jokes or poke fun at aspects of Frank's character. Here is an instance, at the point when Frank had asked where the milk was:

Extract 6.4

67.	Ada	it's just there . just on the (.) fridge top
68.	Fra	just up here
69.	Ada	yeah ((*reaches to pick up the milk and almost drops it*))
70.	Fra	eeeh tssss ((*LF*))
71.	Ada	you're really not a morning person are you↑

Taken by itself, Adam's comment about Frank at line 71 might appear to be rather rude: 'you're really not a morning person are you'. However, there is evidence that this is a bit of a routine joke between the two. It is matched elsewhere in the extended sequence by other mentions of being 'not a morning person' and being 'hopeless'. There are also frequent occurrences of laughter from Frank or Adam while the other one is talking, which appear to be a marker of the way they are receiving that utterance. The repertoire on which they draw is one in which Frank's actions and words foreground an identity of being clumsy or half-asleep. This of course does some identity work for Frank, as it enables others to see how he presents himself as a person. Instead of his problems being put down to his impairments, they are seen as a natural occurrence for someone who might have been out late or who may even have a hangover.

Joking

The laughter and the jokes in this extended sequence could be interpreted as an indication that both Frank and Adam are intent on 'doing friendship' and creating a sense of being mates. They could also be seen as a way of glossing over the fact that Frank is receiving paid support precisely because of his particular impairments. Frank often uses the word 'mate' when he is asking Adam for something and seems to be intent on creating a friendly relationship, rather than a professional one.

However, there are important ways in which Frank remains in control of this developing relationship. The slight 'tss' sounds Adam makes quite often seem to be like testing the water before proper laughter, and he often waits for Frank to take up a joke before continuing with it. For instance, in extract 6.3 Adam quickly drops his smile and incipient joke when Frank takes the question of his support stockings seriously. Adam also watches Frank carefully in the following extract:

Extract 6.5

125.	Ada	((*LF*))
126.	Fra	oh I must tell em that story that's a good story to tell actually
127.	Ada	((*LF*))
128.	Fra	tell em about my foot as well↑ and there's me still standing
129.		there with you know the erm slippers I've got↑
130.	Ada	yeah=
131.	Fra	= really difficult to walk in
132.	Ada	are they↑
133.	Fra	mm
134.	Ada	I'll put some er cold water in there for you↓

This extract immediately follows another joke about blocked toilets, which Adam had initiated. Frank then uses this cue to move into a 'good story to tell', which he introduces at line 126. This is punctuated by Adam's laughter. But at line 131 Frank seems to drop the story suddenly and reverts to serious information about his slippers. Adam's tone of voice immediately becomes serious with 'yeah' and 'are they↑'. At line 134 Adam then introduces a functional comment about what they should do with the coffee ('I'll put some cold water in there for you'), moving the conversation away from story-telling and back to the present. Adam's concern is always to know exactly how Frank is taking something, and at the same time to let Frank know how he is taking his remarks.

Friendliness within new institutional relationships

What frame of reference are Adam and Frank using? Is this the 'institutional' frame in which Adam is a 'controlling' member of staff or is Adam actually behaving as an employee? It is interesting that Frank steps outside both of those frames and often treats him as a friend with 'yeah mate', 'that's it mate'. These almost seem like exaggerated markers of friendship, a way of indicating that the relationship is being moulded into something explicitly different from that of support staff–disabled person.

This interpretation is borne out at the end of the extract, when Frank is about to go back into the living room. Adam has just added the cold water to his coffee and offered the cup to Frank to test for temperature. It is at that moment that Adam brings in his own identity as 'new employee' in the joke-aside 'I'm getting better', and Frank caps this with an evaluation:

Extract 6.6

150.	Fra	that's just fine↓ cheers (.) just how I like it actually
151.	Ada	cool↓ I'm getting better
152.	Fra	((LF)) you're not bad at all mate

The right to deliver an evaluation of someone's progress is an important marker of status; institutionally, a teacher, a parent or someone in authority might reserve the right to judge someone else's actions and progress and to deliver remarks of praise or rebuke. It is that remark ('you're not bad at all mate') more than anything that reinforces Frank's role as 'employer', and by contrast underlines Adam's role as employee. Interestingly, not only is Frank in control of the activity of coffee-making and in control of his support, but he also shows that he can be in control of the frame of reference between himself and Adam. The relationship is on Frank's terms. Adam is not there to care for Frank, to take responsibility for his safety or to take charge of his affairs. There is an institutional frame here on which both Frank and Adam are drawing, but it is Frank who is the institutionally more powerful person.

Being friendly colleagues

The interactions highlighted in this chapter so far have all been in the context of domestic activities. It could be observed that the physical context of the home (or, in extract 6.1, the café) is conducive to a relaxed, friendly relationship, in which participants take on more equal roles. However, equality can also be observed in other contexts, where one might expect particular patterns of institutional talk. One such context is the classroom, or indeed any learning context. The following example is taken from a group session at the very beginning of the 'Finding Out' project, where people with intellectual disabilities are preparing for their own research project, by learning and practising their skills. I am present with the group, very much in the role of a tutor (I had in fact previously been the tutor for several of the group members in a further education college) and I had assisted the group in planning a learning activity related to interviewing. At this point, they have prepared interview questions and asked each other a question on tape. Angela and Harry then decide to practise their interviewing skills on me, and this is what ensues.

Extract 6.7

42.	Ang→	I will – I thought YOU had retired (.) since you left south
43.		bristol tech college↓ why are you – why are you still
44.		working for ↑ (1)
45.	Val	um I didn't retire when I left south bristol college↑(.) I
46.		took – I became redundant that means I took redundancy
47.		and I left my job <u>there</u>
48.	Jam	(…) job
49.	Val	and I didn't work for a bit (.) but then I got interested to do
50.		other things (.) and so (.) I managed to get another job↑=
51.	Ang→	=>I thought you retired (you weren't going to work any
52.		more)<
53.	Val	(1) right
54.	Har	why you decided you said you work at Norah Fry is it
55.		Norman Fry↑
56.	Val	it's called Norah Fry (.) research centre
57.	Har	so where's that to roughly er
58.	Val	that's in –um in Clifton
59.	Har	on Clifton
60.	Val	well it's in the university (.) of Bristol so it's in a place
61.		called Priory Road
62.	Har	yeah

The turn structure of this extract follows exactly the pattern of an interview, with Angela, Harry and James posing the questions, and Val providing the answers. It could be divided into a series of two-part sequences, which are almost all question–answer pairs. By and large, I deliver 'preferred responses', as can be seen from the flow of the conversation. For instance, at line 56 I answer what Harry has asked to clarify the name of my workplace:

Har	why you decided you said you work at Norah Fry is it
	Norman Fry↑
Val	it's called Norah Fry (.) research centre (lines 54–6)

That is taken as an adequate response to the question, as is evident from the fact that Harry then expands with a question about the geographical location of the centre:

| Har | so where's that to roughly er |
| Val | that's in –um in Clifton (lines 57–8) |

The achievement of this turn structure is in fact very significant, given that the purpose of the session was to learn about interviewing; the previous attempts had been rather hesitant and the idea of being the questioner appeared quite daunting to the research group members. However, in the extract above, the members suddenly become very fluent with their questions, and so the talk here fits well with the underlying educational aim of the session, which is that the group members should practise interviewing.

What identity am I taking on, then, in answering these questions? At one level, I am playing the role of interviewee, but this is done very precisely so that the members will learn how to be interviewers. In other words, there is an element of role-play here. At another level, then, through supporting the role-play, I am emphasising my identity as a tutor or facilitator to the group – certainly as an educator of some kind. In analysing these sessions, it is hard to find examples where the agenda, at some level, is not in my hands. By limiting my turns to responses, I am modelling for the group what a 'good' interviewee might do and hence what their work as interviewers might entail. Setting the agenda as a research skills session is a powerful move, however it is enacted. Therefore, despite the initial appearance of an equal turn structure, there is a deeper level at which the power remains with me and not with the group members.

Despite this arguably institutional purpose for the conversation, however, the members challenge that frame on more than one occasion. The points at which these challenges occur are marked with an arrow ($\rightarrow$). In her first turn, Angela loads her question with her personal evaluation of the situation:

42.	Ang	$\rightarrow$ I will – I thought YOU had retired (.) since you left South
		Bristol Tech College why are you – why are you still
		working for ↑ (1)

This is by no means a neutral question, but is designed more as a challenge or a demand to justify something. It also touches on aspects of my personal life and motivation, and (like the conversations between Frank and his support worker) draws on shared knowledge about what Angela thought about my actions. Following my attempt at drawing a distinction between 'retirement' and 'redundancy', which is probably far from clear, Angela provides a third part. This is the prerogative of the person who has asked the question and a way of summing up what she thinks of it:

| 51. | Ang | $\rightarrow$ = I thought you retired (you weren't going to work any more) |

Angela is certainly blurring the boundaries here between a friendly person-to-person chat and a research interview. If we had been talking as friends, line 51 would probably have led to more talk. For instance, I might have responded and perhaps enlarged on my feelings about retirement and about work. However, I merely pause at that point and then finish the sequence with a 'right'.

Having responded to the next round of questions, about the name and location of my new place of work, I myself then initiate a shift out of the role-play of interviewer–interviewee in the following extract, which follows on immediately after the previous talk.

Extract 6.8

63.	Val→	(.) and it's just an ordinary building↓ you'll have to come up there and see it
		sometime all of you
64.	Har	right er er (.) is that is that in Clifton did you say
65.	Val	well it it depends what you call Clifton it's the other side of um Habitat and
		the Victoria Rooms and the BBC↑
66.	Har	yeah
67.	Val	it's just behind where the BBC is
68.	Har	yeah
69.	Jam→	Ken Simons works there don't he↓ (.) do you know him↑
70.	Har	er so what sort of work do you do at Norman Fry↑

71.	Val	um I do <u>research</u> work at Norah Fry (2)
72.	Har	yeah
73.	Val	(2) ((LF))
74.	Ang	do you like doing it↑
75.	Val	yes ((LF)) it's very very interesting

As with Angela's initial questions, at line 63 I start to do some personal talk. The phrase 'it's just an ordinary building' is interesting, since it seems to shift the workplace talk into something to do with everyday life, something the group members might relate to. There is then a complete move into a personal invitation to the group to come up to Norah Fry and see the new workplace. This is definitely not something one would expect of a good interviewee, and by doing it, I shift identity to being, in some ways, a friend who is inviting friends to visit her. The conversation then continues with the questions about specifying the geographical location, but instead of being simply 'interviewing' this could now be heard as Harry checking out exactly where he is going to go when he does in fact visit. Again, it could be noted how much these details also depend on shared knowledge of the area and of each other. James then brings in yet another personal detail by making a link between his own life and the topic under discussion:

> Jam   → Ken Simons works there don't he↓ (.) do you know him↑ (line 69)

It turns out later in the conversation that James knows Ken Simons, a former colleague at the Norah Fry Research Centre, from the People First group, and that he has heard of 'Norah Fry' before through Ken. That linkage of social relations is very much the type of opening ploy someone might make when talking to a new acquaintance at a party or any social gathering. Through establishing a third party known to both interlocutors, there is an implied claim of common ground from which a new relationship could be built.

What social activity is being carried out by this talk? Are we doing an interview, practising doing an interview by means of a role-play or chatting as friends about personal, and sometimes shared, information? The talk certainly moves in and out of a type of educational frame of reference, and this shifting is very much a joint achievement of all the participants. Although the underlying purpose of learning research skills might have been at the centre of my agenda, the group members are at points using this frame in order to bring in their own, more personal concerns and questions. The conversation becomes more equalised in three ways. First, at the level of the turn sequencing, the group members both ask questions and evaluate answers. Compared with Brendan, in Chapter 3, they have much fuller interactional rights (see Chapter 2, p. 29). Second, the talk turns on many personal aspects by bringing in 'real-life' concerns, both of myself and of the group members. Unlike a typical supporter, I am prepared to reveal aspects of my real life and indeed lay myself open to the group members' questioning on this. This stretch of talk would not have occurred between people who did not previously know something about each other, and all the speakers have a role to play in drawing on personal knowledge about the topics. Finally, the conversation becomes more equal at a deeper level, since the very definition of the activity we are carrying out is at stake. Not only does the supporter have a lead role in defining the agenda, but the group members successfully challenge and almost subvert, this agenda, using the frame of the interview to open up personal talk with me.

Implications for practice

This chapter has started to explore some of the ways in which people with intellectual disabilities achieve a more equal status with their supporters; I have explored how personal assistants achieved a friendly tone to the interaction by calling on their knowledge and shared background with the person they were supporting (Williams *et al.*, 2009a). This is similar to the observation of Georgakopoulou (2006: 102), drawing on data from young people in Greece, where the 'co-experienced ... shared interactional history and assumptions' were shown to be central to identity construction in narratives. Georgakopoulou refers to this as the 'long conversation'. As Gergen (2001) points out, social life is a chance for people to narrate their own identities or to rearrange those identities.

Body language and movements were also key to the ways in which personal assistants were able to follow the lead of the person with intellectual disabilities they supported, and both partners signalled their close relationship through jokes and laughter. However, as in all the interactions examined in this book, things are never totally straightforward. These were not actually relationships between friends, which as mentioned above would be defined as mutual, reciprocal and voluntary relationships, since the personal assistants had a paid job to do in their dealings with the person they were supporting. Therefore, to a certain extent the markers of friendliness were simply ways that both parties had for signalling a more 'ordinary' relationship, one that pulls away from the institutional frame in which support staff have powerful roles.

In traditional ways of working with people with intellectual disabilities, Adam would be in control of what is going on. Instead, this chapter has shown how the person with intellectual disabilities (Frank) was in control. He decided what was being talked about, and also how the talk and the laughter were to proceed. A joke was only a joke with this pair if Frank showed that it was. As a support worker, then, it is important to work at achieving a friendly tone, and this is part of the skill required. However, the person with intellectual disabilities can also give a message to their support worker about how they see their relationship, perhaps by using words like 'mate' as Frank did.

Friendly and jokey relationships may depend on the context. Are they essential for 'equalising' the talk and ensuring that people with intellectual disabilities have a wider range of rights to do things in conversation? This chapter has also explored an example from 'behind the scenes' talk in the 'Finding Out' project, where people with intellectual disabilities were preparing for their own research study. The talk in this chapter all occurred during sessions in which I was working with group members to prepare for their research roles. As discussed, the dominant frame was a pedagogic one, in which the people with intellectual disabilities were cast as learners. Such frames can create inequalities, since the teacher is a powerful person. However, the talk can be managed by all parties to create a greater sense of equality.

One of the important points to note is that this is not a one-sided effort: all the participants are responsible and take part in the shifting nature of this talk. For instance, in extract 6.7, I thought at the time that we had started off on a practice interview. However, the group members used that context to ask me some personal questions and to reflect their own views about my career move. This in turn pushed me into some talk in which I was no longer the person being interviewed, but became more like a friend. Our personal and shared knowledge threaded through this talk, as it was the backdrop for our understanding of each other. In fact, during the course of doing this exercise about interviewing, the group members actually learned more about my own background and circumstances, and this would then help them to talk to me on a more equal, personal basis in the future.

Working relationships between colleagues on a project, like relationships between people with intellectual disabilities and supporters, can move towards a type of equality. Nevertheless they remain relationships between people playing out certain roles or categories. In the 'Finding Out' project, I considered myself a supporter or facilitator and I often took on the right to 'teach' the group members about research. In fact, I did not refer to myself as a group member at all and was concerned that the group appeared and was felt to be something that belonged to the members themselves. It is not possible to escape entirely from roles and identities in talk: they are an important part of the way that all human interaction works, as Sacks (1995) pointed out. Not only are membership categories an important basis for organising talk, but also certain institutional contexts are characterised by distinct patterns of talk which adhere to particular roles; indeed institutional conversation analysis (Atkinson & Heritage, 1992) was built on the basis of that point.

When people with intellectual disabilities and others achieve greater equality, then, it is not a matter of ridding the talk of roles, labels or identities. It would be impossible to have a conversation without in some ways referring to different roles for each other. However, what the extracts in this chapter have illustrated are ways in which the rigid boundaries of institutional roles can be shifted and moulded. At the same time as a supporter or enabler moves into a more fluid role, people with intellectual disabilities are enabled to take up interactional rights which are often denied to them. Compared with Barry, for instance, in Chapter 3, the people in this chapter did a far greater variety of things in the conversation. They asked questions, they told other people to do things, they characterised and found out information about another person and to some extent they defined the situation – for instance, Frank defined the situation with his PA as a friendly relationship between employer and employee, and Angela and the others in the research group defined the mock interview as a way for them to discover more personal information about me. Setting out to do a new social activity such as interviewing is all about doing new things with talk. This is why group members experience it as so powerful: it is through creating these new types of social activity that people with intellectual disabilities can become freed from the traditional assumptions about their contributions to talk. These new contexts for talk will be explored further through the rest of this book.

How conversation works: summary points

- By doing different things in the conversation, people take on a range of different 'situational identities' (Zimmerman, 1998). For instance, Frank becomes a narrator and a story-teller about himself. He is also a joker with a good deal of self-humour, and he is the 'boss' of his support worker.

- Sacks (1995) talked about '**membership categorization**' in relation to roles and identities (see Silverman, 1998: 74–97). When a particular membership category is invoked (here, 'supporter' or 'enabler' or 'facilitator'), this brings with it a bundle of role-related assumptions and assumptions about the interactional rights of all parties. It is not possible to escape entirely from roles and identities in talk, because they are one of the bedrocks of communication.

- Talk often draws on repertoires (Wetherell, 1998) or frames of reference, which bring with them a range of assumptions. For instance, speakers can choose certain phrases or words (like Frank's 'mate') which draw on particular repertoires – in this case, the repertoire of friendship.

Inclusive approaches to communication: summary points

- People with intellectual disabilities generally do want their support workers to be 'friendly', and this may mean that the support worker has to step out of a strictly 'professional' role when talking with the person they support.

- People can show that they are friendly through their body language by smiling and relaxing together.
- Social chat is important, if the person with intellectual disabilities wants it. It is easy to strike up a social conversation if the support worker shares some interests or experience with the person they are supporting.
- Support workers and people with intellectual disabilities often share jokes, but this should always be on the terms of the person with intellectual disabilities.
- Support workers have to watch closely, and follow the lead of the person they are supporting. In learning contexts (e.g. sessions preparing for a research project), people can also interact in a friendly way.
- Being more friendly is about being more 'equal'. This means that people with intellectual disabilities have more chances to do different things in the conversation and to take the lead in organising their own support.

Chapter 7

Doing Autonomy

'It's entirely up to you'

Having a choice is a vital part of having a life. Chapter 7 is therefore a central point in the book, as well as a central part of policy and practice. This is what current English policy about health and social care has to say about control:

> Our society is based on the belief that everyone has a contribution to make and has the right to control their own lives. This value drives our society and will also drive the way in which we provide social care. (DH, 2006b: 204)

'Choice' is also a central concept in Intellectual Disability policy and has been associated very strongly with 'control' and the right to make decisions about one's own life. For instance, choice and control were among the leading principles of *Valuing People* (DH, 2001) and figure prominently also in the renewed policy statement about English Intellectual Disability services, *Valuing People Now* (DH, 2009).

> All people with learning disabilities and their families will have greater choice and control over their lives and have support to develop person centred plans. (DH, 2009: 17)

Decision-making has also recently been brought to further prominence with the Mental Capacity Act (MCA) 2005 in the UK. The MCA seeks to draw a clear dividing line between situations in which an individual can give informed consent and those in which she or he *cannot* understand and make an autonomous choice. One of the guiding principles of the MCA is that every individual should be assumed to be capable of any particular decision, unless proved otherwise. However, if an individual is deemed to be incapable of making a decision about some matter in their lives, the MCA lays out the principles which should guide good practice in making a best interests decision on behalf of that individual. Recent work about the MCA (Jepson, 2010), shows that most decisions are made jointly (Williams *et al.*, 2008a), and this is also true for decision-making in general (Jenkinson, 1993; Edge, 2001).

Antaki *et al.* (2008), using similar CA methodology to the current book, points out that support workers are often concerned to offer alternatives to people with intellectual disabilities. This practice may have some perverse results, since the person being supported could presume that a follow-up offer of alternatives implies that their original choice was wrong. Additionally, some practitioners have questioned whether the rhetoric of choice matches the reality for some

Disability and Discourse. Analysing Inclusive Conversation with People with Intellectual Disabilities, 1st edition. © Val Williams. Published 2011 by John Wiley & Sons, Ltd.

people, who may have complex needs or autism. Schelly (2008), for instance, writing from the point of view of a personal assistant, presents an ethnography of his activities with the young man he supports in Canada whose choices are often determined by others.

Many of the extracts and strategies that have been discussed in preceding chapters have involved choices: opening up conversation with Alice, in Chapter 5, for example, involved asking her what she intended to do in the library. Similarly, Ellie, in Chapter 4, the woman who was constructing a shopping list, had some choices to make, although they were tightly constrained by the necessity of budgeting, and her support worker essentially talked her through those choices.

As with other chapters in this book, the focus here is not on presumed mental constructs or achievements, such as 'individual autonomy'. Instead, the focus is on interaction – how decisions are achieved in the to-and-fro of communication, what strategies and patterns emerge and what these imply for the presumed autonomy of people with intellectual disabilities. Put another way, it is not 'autonomy' itself which is in question, but the way in which the concept of autonomy is produced (or negated) through actual interactions. This chapter will consider how choices are achieved in everyday interaction.

Henry, Penny and Charles: Deciding on what to do next

In the small things of everyday life, choices are continually being made by individuals. For instance, throughout the video data in 'Skills for Support', there are moments when people with intellectual disabilities and their support workers have to organise themselves around what to do next. These are the day-to-day, routine matters that make up their time together. Watching the videos, it is often very hard to work out exactly who does make the choice about the next activity. In the case of Frank in the previous chapter, who was making a cup of coffee in his kitchen, there were clear indications that he was able to decide and tell his support worker what he wanted him to do. At the beginning of the coffee-making sequence, as mentioned in Chapter 1, Frank started the activity with: 'Right, would you like to help me with the coffee, mate?' This, however, is rare. On most occasions, activities are carried out as part of a generally understood routine, and there are very few points at which people say 'let's do this next'. The first extract here features Pippa and Henry, who are walking from the leisure centre to the pub.

Extract 7.1

91.	Pip	which one do you want to go to Henry↑
92.	Hen	King's Arms
93.	Pip	the King's Arms↑ ((turns to look at Henry))
94.	Hen	yeah
95.	Pip	why is that↓ is it because of the pool table↑
96.	Hen	yeah ((smile))
97.	Pip	by any chance↑ is it↑ ((LF voice))
98.	Hen	yes

Clearly, Henry has one easy answer to Pippa's question about which pub he wants to go to, there is no hesitation in his response and he only produces minimal responses ('yeah') once he has named that establishment. Since there has been some discussion previously between Henry, Pippa and me about how decisions were made, it could be that the exchange in 7.1 is partly for the sake of the camera; nevertheless, it does show that the matter of choosing a pub is not ordinarily worth much talk. They always go to the same pub and normally do not discuss the issue.

The two-part adjacency pair which starts this sequence (lines 91–2) is initiated by Pippa, with a second part duly given by Henry. Although this may be heard as a preferred response, nevertheless Pippa does not just give an evaluative third part (e.g. 'good'). Instead, she repeats what Henry has said with a questioning intonation. This is a **request for confirmation** (see Chapter 5, p. 73, on repair), something one might do if the item had not been heard or understood, and this gives rise to Henry's 'yeah' in line 94. However, Pippa extends the sequence yet again:

> Pip   why is that↓ is it because of the pool table↑ (line 95)

It now seems that something else is going on beyond simply clarifying Henry's choice of pub. Asking someone why they have made a choice could be heard as a challenge, a criticism of the original choice; however, Pippa does not leave it at that. She immediately answers her own query by suggesting to Henry the reason for his choice. Note that this strategy not only feeds Henry his answer, it also tells Henry and the listener that both parties (Henry and Pippa) are well aware of the preference for pool tables in pubs. In other words, Henry knows already that Pippa has this information, and so the conversational 'why' is in many respects redundant. It could simply be an attempt to prolong the talk about choices.

This interpretation is borne out by Henry's minimal responses throughout, and he concludes with a 'yes'. The laugh voice at line 97 indicates an incipient attempt to make a joke of this: the joke is perhaps not so much that Henry likes pool tables, but refers more to the unnecessary airtime spent in discussing the matter! Following this exchange, the pair do in fact go into the pub and Henry does go straight to the pool table, once he has got his drink. Therefore, their course of action is evidently determined by Henry's prior choice and his preference.

In other cases, the choice of what to do next is determined to some extent by the logic of what *needs* to happen next. For instance, in another video a woman called Penny goes into the bedroom to sort out her clothes, prior to taking a shower. The clothes have to be selected and taken into the bathroom, and the object of having a shower is fixed by the fact that the support worker, Beth, has come to Penny's flat specifically to assist with it. Therefore, the room for manoeuvre about 'what to do next' is very limited.

Extract 7.2

1.	Bet	right OK (.) we're going to sort out your clothes first↑
2.		shall we do that↑
3.	Pen	yes yep
4.	Bet	let's do that first then↓

The 'right OK' is a type of boundary marker, also noted with Jenny and Ellie at the start of Chapter 4 (extract 4.1). On both occasions it does the work of focusing the attention of the person they are supporting. What Beth does here is to articulate, or describe, what the next step is. Before having a shower, 'we're going to sort out your clothes first'. Just as with Ellie and Jenny in Chapter 4, this support worker uses the pronoun 'we', somehow including herself in the activity, but stopping short of claiming ownership of the clothes (they are 'your clothes').

As the person with intellectual disability does the action, the support worker describes or pre-empts it with an implied instruction. It may be worth here recalling how Simon did the same thing with his support worker in Chapter 1, as they were both getting up to go into the kitchen:

Right do you want to help me with the coffee, mate.

This type of punctuation of activity is very typical of the talk by support workers, but rare (and 'marked') when done by someone with an intellectual disability. Here, Penny simply accepts the instruction sequence with 'yes yep' and this appears to be part of the normal routine of her interaction with Beth.

The routine nature of support workers introducing activities in this way is evident throughout the data; for instance, in the next extract Charles is searching through his emails for a message from his mother. Much of the interaction with Pat, his support worker, during this activity consists of what might be termed instructional sequences:

Extract 7.3

15.	Pat	right so which one have you got to go on first↑
16.	Cha	this one ((*puts right hand on mouse*))
17.	Pat	that's right

Charles is sitting behind his computer during this extract, and Pat is sitting at a slight distance behind him and to one side. The structure of the sequence is a classic adjacency pair, with a 'third part' or evaluation at line 17. Although Pat's first part, 'which one have you got to go on first', is framed as a question, it is not heard as a request for information, but rather as an instruction, telling Charles what to do. The second part that Charles performs consists of his verbal response 'this one' together with his action of clicking on the mouse button, and Pat then produces the third part evaluation 'that's right'.

Both Penny, in extract 7.2, and Charles, in extract 7.3, have choices to make. These are the simple choices about what to do next, which activity to engage in, what part of the computer screen to double-click. They are also demonstrating their autonomy by choosing the actual activity: it is actually by his own choice that Charles has gone to his computer to check his emails. The support worker's contribution in both cases does not dictate the choice, but could be seen as facilitative. Once the choice has been made, the support worker is providing instruction, or commentary, in order to guide the person to the correct next step. However, the form in which this commentary is given makes the interaction sound very much like a pedagogic conversation in which instruction is followed by response, and then a short evaluation or affirmation by the support worker. It seems that choices are fine as long as they are the right ones!

Penny: Seeking approval

It is noticeable how a support worker can almost unwittingly have power over choices through some very subtle means. Examples of showing approval could be given from many points in the data. The following comes from Penny, the woman in extract 7.2 who was sorting out her clothes prior to her shower. In the following extract, she is choosing her clothes for the day and passing them to her support worker to put on a pile prior to moving into the bathroom.

Extract 7.4

17.	Pen	I'm going to wear this (0.5) spotted um looks good
18.		that will look alright won't it↑
19.	Bet	mm hm that's lovely that's lovely (…)
20.	Pen	what socks do you think↑ ((*holding blue socks*))
21.	Bet	blue ones (.) they're pretty↑ we'll have those

The act of choosing clothes here is part of a social routine, consisting again of a series of two-part sequences or adjacency pairs. In the first part, Penny makes a tentative choice and mentions it (either by saying the name of it, or by showing it physically). In technical CA terms, she simultaneously creates a slot for her support worker to comment on the choice. Having already chosen the item, Penny is presumably not really expecting any counter-arguments. She seems to accept as very natural what the support worker in fact does, which is to praise and reinforce Penny's choice with 'that's lovely' and 'they're pretty'. Timing and sequence are important here. During line 19, Penny is already picking up the blue socks. Therefore, her question at line 20 does not have the force of an open-choice question. It is heard by Beth as another request for confirmation and praise, which she duly gives at line 21. Note also how the support worker moves to make the choice at line 21 a 'joint' one: 'we'll have those', as if the pair of them were choosing Penny's clothes together.

In fact, it is not remarkable when a choice like this receives praise. What is more noticeable with people with intellectual disabilities is when they choose something and it is not praised. When there is silence, Penny could understand this to mean that her choice was wrong in some respect. There are a couple of points in the video when the support worker makes a comment or asks a question which Penny immediately appears to take as an implied criticism (of her clothes or of her competence to care for her own clothes). For instance, the first item Penny picks up is a bra and the following exchange occurs.

Extract 7.5

5.	Pen	you said have I got a clean – ((*holding a bra*))
6.	Bet	well yes is that clean↑
7.	Pen	yes it is clean it's just that they – it got put with something
8.	Bet	yes I can see that right right

This time, it is Penny who does the first part of the adjacency pair. As she picks up the bra, she accompanies the action by 'you said have I got a clean –', which effectively brings Beth in to the conversation; Penny is referring to something the support worker, Beth, has previously said. In fact, the conversation had presumably turned on the availability of clean underwear in Penny's cupboard. Beth gives a second part in this adjacency pair, but instead of just acknowledging what she had previously said, she uses this slot to question whether the particular bra that Penny is holding is in fact clean. At line 7, Penny then gives an account for the fact that the bra was taken from a pile of less-than-clean clothes: 'it got put with something'. Effectively, she is defending her actions, and the support worker accepts this explanation and finally gives her approval at line 8.

What can be made of this? It would seem that the support worker is exercising some powerful rights here – the right to judge Penny's actions against standards of cleanliness and the right to determine Penny's standards of hygiene. This power dynamic between the two is played out in the talk and it could be observed that the support worker, Beth, is drawing on some strong interactional rights (see Chapter 5, p. 71) to judge and to question Penny's actions against standards of cleanliness. For her part, Penny appears to accept this pattern as quite natural and shows no frustration or anger in having to defend her actions in choosing the bra. This is all part of the way that she and her support worker regularly interact.

Another telling point, towards the end of this sequence, is when Beth herself decides to rearrange the outfit Penny had previously hung up on a hanger. This is a decision she makes herself; it is not something Penny has asked her to do.

Extract 7.6

42.	Bet	there we are we'll take that off there (.) just put it up the
43.		right way round
44.	Pen	((*laughing*)) yes I didn't realise it was the wrong way round actually

Penny has a smile and looks embarrassed at line 44, as she accounts for the fact that she has made a mistake in hanging up her outfit. Like many people with intellectual disabilities, Penny is perhaps used to being in situations where other people have to approve or disapprove of what she is choosing. It is clear from the sequence of turns in extract 7.6 that Penny has heard Beth's turn (lines 42–3) as a criticism, something which leads into her laughter and then her acknowledgement of being in the wrong. These interactions with her support worker sound as though they come from a schoolroom rather than a bedroom where someone is having some assistance to get dressed and choose her own clothes. Penny not only seeks to do things 'right', but also seeks reassurance from Beth that her choices are correct; she in fact gives accounts and justifications of her own mistakes. Like many people with intellectual disabilities, Penny comes over as a continual learner, trying to meet the expectations of others – a construction of her identity reinforced and shaped by the interactions she engages in with her support worker (see Zimmerman's (1998) idea of three levels of identity, referred to in Chapter 4, p. 56). What Penny does in the talk (her discourse identity) continually affects her wider, 'transportable' identity.

Telling people they can choose

It is interesting to find ways in which the support worker can resist and begin to challenge these assumptions. There is a good example later in the same sequence with Beth and Penny. Penny continues to choose her clothes, and after her outfit, she moves on to a t-shirt. In choosing a t-shirt, she pursues the alternatives until she gets a positive reaction from Beth. At first she suggests 'white', but there is a long pause of about 14 seconds while she is hanging her outfit on a hanger. She then goes to her drawer again and looks at the alternatives of pink or navy blue t-shirts, before asking Beth's advice:

Extract 7.7

135.	Pen	navy blue – would that go↑
136.	Bet	what do YOU think would that look alright↑
137.	Pen	yes
138.	Bet	yes I think

What Beth does here is interesting. Instead of continuing to praise every choice Penny makes, she responds with a second question at line 136. This is a dispreferred way of responding (see Chapter 3, p. 47). She does not answer Penny's question, but returns it to her, thus effectively doing some work in establishing who should be making the aesthetic judgement on clothes and colours. 'What do you think' is not a neutral way of asking for an opinion; in this context (after Penny's seeking of approval) it is a way of reminding Penny that it is *her* business and her right to decide for herself. It is through these small conversational ploys that the support worker can help a person with intellectual disabilities to be confident in thinking and deciding for herself.

   These examples of approval-seeking, praise and withholding praise are very common patterns in all the data, from both projects. For instance, Neil spent some three of four minutes at the opening of a video sequence in tying his shoelaces, and he then showed his shoe to his support worker, accepting her 'well done' as natural. The same pair were later seen crossing the car park towards the supermarket, having been chatting about a possible pub visit in the car, on which there was a question about which support worker might be on duty, to help out with this visit.

Extract 7.8

34.	Jan	but if you wanted to go with Larry that's your choice yeah↑
35.	Nei	I don't want him getting drunk down there
36.	Jan	((LF)) you don't need Larry to get you drunk
37.		you can get drunk by yourself

Although quite a short, throwaway sequence, this extract is rich in inference. In order to understand how speakers display their understanding of each other, it is often necessary to unravel some of these inferences. They are the backdrop to the talk.

Prior to extract 7.8, Neil had been trying to organise or find out about the support rota in order to see if a supporter would be able to come with him and his friend to the pub. Therefore, Jan's reminder at line 34, starting as it does with a contrastive 'but', carries the force that the decision on the pub visit should *not* be dependent on support staff. It is 'your choice' and, by implication, your (Neil's) responsibility. Why does Neil then counter with 'I don't want him getting drunk'. The implication here is that if he goes on his own with Larry, Larry may get drunk and by contrast the inference is that the presence of a support worker may stop Larry from getting drunk.

However, Jan then fills the slot for the third part (line 36), not with a simple praise or encouragement line, but with a joking comment on Neil's own tendency to get drunk. In this context, not only does this signal something about Jan's relationship and her assumed right to discuss Neil's drinking habits, but it also perhaps underlines the ordinariness of this pub visit. In fact, what it does is to counter the inference underpinning Neil's request for a support worker; a support worker is not needed to stop Larry getting drunk, because Neil himself might want to get drunk. Further, Jan pulls the talk away from the institutional assumptions about support workers and their responsibilities. This situation, she suggests, is not about support workers, rotas and responsibility for Larry; it is simply about two men going out and both potentially having a good time.

The choice Neil has to make for himself is set within the frame of an ordinary, man-to-man relationship, and he is effectively given a hint or a prompt about how to handle his choice on the pub visit. Note that Jan does not tell him whether or not to go to the pub, but simply removes some of the worrying barriers about potential drunkenness and responsibility for Larry.

In these encounters, then, both parties seem routinely to draw on repertoires which include:

- seeking approval;
- asking for advice;
- shelving responsibility onto support staff.

Just as Penny asked for approval on her choice of clothes, so Neil here is asking his support work team to take some responsibility for a projected visit to the pub. In all these cases, the issue of 'whose choice is it?' becomes a talked-about issue, something explicitly raised by support workers and others. Some of the strategies for facilitating choices, then, are far more subtle than simply presenting alternatives. They are about at least:

- giving information on the pros and cons of alternatives;
- using persuasive devices to present alternatives in a favourable light;

- withholding praise or failing to fill the expected third-part slot with a 'well done' or a 'good';
- stripping away some of the institutional barriers that restrict people's choices.

Brian and Colin: Joking about choices

As was explored at the beginning of this chapter, it is often hard to find the precise point at which a choice is made or discussed. Additionally, there may be many factors that people have to consider when making choices, even for something as straightforward as a shopping list. In Chapter 4, Ellie constructed her shopping list with considerable support in order to calculate the bill to keep within her budgetary limit. As Ellie herself pointed out, the very way in which her shopping and budgeting are supported is something that has been the topic of negotiation and which she has (at least) agreed with, something that she feels is helping her.

Another video shows Brian, who is also engaged in making a shopping list and who has a different system for doing this, one that he explicitly has 'made his own'. This is a laminated checklist which he can use to keep a tally on what he has in his cupboards and what he might need to buy. In the following extract, he has the laminated list in his hands as he stands in the kitchen, reading from the list, and his support worker, Emma, goes through his cupboards checking for the contents. He reads out what he wants, she goes to look and tells him what he has already got. There are some longish pauses in this sequence as Emma waits for Brian to read out the next item. Brian has just put his checklist back in the drawer when the following short sequence occurs:

Extract 7.9

62.	Bri	I might look at DVDs but I won't <u>buy</u> em though
63.		((*Brian has his back to Emma, and is moving out of the door. He is*
64.		*smiling*))
65.	Emm	((*laughs*))
66.	Bri	I'm getting addicted to them at the minute (1) DVDs
67.	Emm	((*giggle*)) you've got a collection haven't you↑ you could start a
68.		business
69.	Bri	I could yes =
70.	Emm	= start renting them out =
71.	Bri	on e-bay yeah ((*general laughter*))

Line 62 does not sound like a first part; in the context of the shopping list Brian has just been constructing, it is one more thing to talk about in relation to the proposed shopping trip. The way in which a turn is placed in the sequence structure can only be known by the way it is taken, and in this case, Emma uses her slot simply with a giggling noise. This shows Brian that he has been heard, but does not necessarily require him to carry on with another turn. The fact that he does carry on is therefore quite a 'marked' thing:

> I'm getting quite addicted to them at the minute (1) DVDs (line 66)

This is an extreme case formulation (see Chapter 4, p. 57; Pomerantz, 1986), but in this case mitigated by a smile on his face, and used within a kind of joke against himself.

All this choice talk, and the justification for his choice and self-critique, has been done exclusively by Brian so far. There is quite a long pause in line 66, but Emma does not use it to get in with her next turn. Therefore, when she finally does take a turn, it seems as if Brian really has completed what he had to say and she then picks up the topic of DVDs. Instead of taking Brian's joke further, she changes it slightly:

> Emm   (*giggle*) you've got a collection haven't you↑ you could start a business
> (line 67)

By using the words 'collection' and 'business', Emma turns the whole topic of DVDs into something that sounds potentially professional. Brian responds with 'I could yes', and the pair start finishing off each other's sentences. Emma smiles as she suggests that Brian could rent them out, and Brian shows that he is well up for this joke by his mention of 'e-bay'. In some ways, what Emma is doing is also an 'extreme case formulation', responding to Brian's use of that device against himself. She makes her point by exaggerating and emphasising the large number of DVDs Brian already has: this is surely a way of telling him that he has no need to buy any more. However, the extreme formulation is done in the guise of a joke, and it is a joke which gives Brian a slot to come in and show how sophisticated he can be with self-humour.

This jointly constructed joke thus frames Brian as an autonomous actor, someone who can make the decisions both about his own immediate food requirements and also about the allocation of his budget to DVDs. However, it does so in a way that emphasises his superior judgement, and indeed his ability to laugh at himself, in relation to what he might buy. Instead of negating his decision, the matter of DVD purchases becomes an occasion for a joke in which Brian has a lead role.

Ben and Karen: Deciding without words

Brian, along with Penny and Henry in this chapter, are people who can speak for themselves and articulate their decisions. Therefore, supporting their autonomy may be largely a matter of listening and responding. However, autonomy and choices were also highlighted by other participants in our data, those who did not use words. For instance, Ben (the lively, engaged young man in Chapter 4 who uses signs to communicate) appeared to have a preoccupation with knowing what was happening next. Much of the conversation in response to his gestures focused precisely on that point, and when he was revisited at the end of the project, he was wearing a t-shirt with the inscription: 'What's happening? What are we doing? What's next?' This says as clearly as anything that his support workers felt these were Ben's concerns.

On a previous video, when coming out of a shop with a trolley full of goods, Ben taps his support worker on the shoulder and does his open-hand 'where' sign, and this is immediately interpreted as talk about what he wants to do next. 'Go swimming' is one alternative that his support worker suggests, and later as they put the shopping into the car, he asks Ben what he might want for lunch. Ben, however, does not respond to this and his attention wanders as he watches other cars in the car park. However, 'choice' is very much on the agenda and Ben's status as an autonomous human being is often emphasised by this type of talk.

When discussing this video with the research team, it was felt that it might be most important for Ben's support worker to watch what he likes and help him to relax into each activity, whether or not it is something he has chosen:

> we need to think of a way – what Ben likes doing, and get him to focus on the things he likes doing, whether it's music, whether it's exercise, or shopping.

With people in Ben's position, the importance of a formal system for choices is reflected in the idea of a 'person-centred plan'. This is effectively a method for those around the individual to build up a picture of what works for that individual and to record that picture so that others will know in general what choices that person may want to make. Therefore, people around Ben who know him well will know that he enjoys eating his lunch, that he likes to talk about what will be happening next and that he is intensely interested in other people. Therefore, his choices in different situations can be inferred to some extent from this prior knowledge. This is very evident both with Ben and also with a young woman in our data, Karen, who had profound physical, sensory and speech impairments. In the following extract, the support worker Laura was starting to arrange Karen on the mat in order to put her in the sling for her hoist:

Extract 7.10

34.	Lau	oh well done Karen↓ right going to get your sling on (…) where you're
35.		going a minute *((puts sling around Karen))* sorry- it's in your face sorry
36.		(0.5) right come over here a bit (.) I know it's not comfortable at the
37.		moment Karen↓ right (1) going to roll you on your back – are you ready↑
38.		*((L rolls K over))*

What is interesting in this sort of monologue, as with Ben, is that Laura talks to Karen as if she were able to respond. She treats her throughout as an autonomous human being, although her knowledge of what Karen likes and does not like cannot possibly be built on anything Karen might say to her at that point. Laura's use of 'sorry' and also her continuous talking through what she is doing for Karen ('roll you over on your back') are reminiscent of the way a parent might speak to their infant when carrying out a routine task. In effect, there is an assumption of agency here, challenging the visible fact that Karen does not have much choice about what is going to happen next. However, as with Ben, the support worker here had some very precise knowledge of what might work – what Karen in other circumstances had shown that she liked and disliked. In Karen's case, this knowledge is reflected in the fine detail of what positions she likes to lie in and the tenseness of her body as something touches her face. All this is part of what may be termed 'person-centred knowledge' and person-centred support, at the very fine level of body movements and responses.

Charles and Rachel: Discussing pros and cons of a choice

Many of the choices talked about in this chapter have been about everyday actions, small issues relating to what to do next or planning of domestic routine. They are the sort of things that many people would simply carry on and do without articulating their reasons or justifying their preferences. The very fact that these matters are routinely talked about with people with intellectual disabilities is worth considering. Maybe their choice-making ability is continually, by implication, called into question. That is the backdrop to the talk. This final section of this chapter about choices moves on to consider a slightly wider decision which needs to be made about the future, something that any of us may want to talk about – where to hold a birthday party. What I am interested in here are the interactional strategies used to do this.

Charles is the man who was seen earlier checking his emails. Here he is seen later the same day, in the office of a service manager. Charles both works for this service as a part-time cleaner, and also buys his assistance from the service. He has just gone to the office to pay his bill and he is now in the manager's office to talk about work-related matters. They have just finished discussing these issues when the following extract occurs.

Extract 7.11

76.	Sue	fantastic Charles ((*thumbs up gesture*))
77.	Cha	you know that thing (ka) we were talking about↑
78.	Sue	((*sits back, folds arms, mouth open*)) party
79.	Cha	a party right (.) well it might er might cost a bit of money um I was
80.		asking in the sports ha::ll the man the manager called Marty a::nd it might
81.		gonna cost six pounds a head ↓ (0.5)
82.	Sue	((*nods head slightly*))
83.	Cha	so if I have thirty it would come to hundred and eight
84.	Sue	eighty
85.	Cha	hundred and eight that's
86.	Sue	hundred and eighty↓
87.	Cha	no it's not hundred and eight
88.	Sue	if you have 30 and it's six pounds each it's six 3's
89.	Cha	that's 180
90.	Sue	equally I've spoken to um Bob Jepson
91.	Cha	yeah↑
92.	Sue	and he'd run a disco for you↓ so that'll only cost probably if you give him
93.		twenty quid↓ (0.5) ((*pauses, arms open gesture*))
94.	Cha	yeah
95.	Sue	which he'd be more than happy to do↓
96.	Cha	yeah
97.	Sue	and then all the food and stuff like that we can go out and buy (.)
98.		((*arms open, palms together gesture*))
99.	Cha	yeah
100.	Sue	or you and Patricia can go out and buy
101.	Cha	yeah
102.	Sue	then we can come back and prepare it all ready for the evening↓
103.	Cha	yup
104.	Sue	and you can use the hall over there for nothing – our hall over there for
105.		nothing anyway ((*hand gesture, raising arm to the left*))
106.	Cha	we'll see what happens (.) that chap is going to ring up Patricia so he
107.		can have a
108.	Sue	yeah
109.	Cha	if it isn't going to be expensive – I think it is a bit cheaper (.) and if it isn't
110.		I'll let you know
111.	Sue	ye::ah I think you know -
112.	Cha	also the sports hall is a bit nearer to the house
113.	Sue	yeah but
114.	Cha	you're not near at all
115.	Sue	yes but you've got a lot of friends in this area as well Charles ((*hand gesture*))
116.	Cha	I'll see I'll see I 'll let you know
117.	Sue	as I say you could use that hall free over there anyway (.) and if we all
118.		give you a hand to do the food and the erm and the um disco's going to
119.		be about £20 cos the chap does it as a hobby
120.	Cha	yes
121.	Sue	um you know you're probably talking about 50 or 60 [pounds all in so –
122.	Cha	[yes OK yeah
123.	Sue	that's a lot cheaper
124.	Cha	alright

125.	Sue	I'll leave it entirely up to you
126.	Cha	OK I'll see what happens and I'll let you know↓ any changes I'll let you
127.		know
128.	Sue	all right Charles
129.	Cha	nothing to it is it↑
130.	Sue	absolutely right Charles ((shakes head, smiling))

This extract has been given in full so that readers can appreciate the structure and overall arrangement of the sequences. It can be divided into four main sections, which can be glossed as follows:

a) lines 77–89: Charles tells about his plans for hiring the sports hall;
b) lines 90–105: The manager offers her counter-plan for Charles' party;
c) lines 106–24: They both reiterate the plans and their advantages;
d) lines 125–9: Charles' right to decide is reinforced and agreed.

This exchange happens immediately at the end of a work-related discussion about Charles' cleaning job. The manager has been acting very much like the 'boss' and listing tasks to Charles (e.g. cleaning the carpet in her office), as well as some plans for the next time Charles comes in. Thus at the start of this extract the manager is formally marking the end of a discussion in which Charles was in the position of employee, receiving instructions. The fact that Charles chooses to start a new exchange at line 77, with a new first part, is thus a very strong action. He is standing in front of the manager and he visibly marks the new topic by relaxing, slightly moving around and shuffling. He becomes, in other words, much more animated in his body language, while the manager sits back, arms folded.

In CA terms, what Charles does in line 77 is a pre-sequence ('you know that thing (ka) we were talking about'), something to get the manager's attention and ensure that they both know and agree on what is being talked about. Schegloff (2007: 37) calls this a **pre-announcement**, serving the function of ensuring that the 'news' – i.e. the main focus of the upcoming talk – is heard and responded to without any trouble. This is a particularly good way of introducing the new topic, but it would seem as if Charles is doing slightly more than that. His whole performance, with pre-announcement, his foot shuffling, smiling and his sudden initiation of a new sequence in conversation, possibly marks out what he has to say next as something he is prepared to lead on. This is *his* news, *his* affair.

This first sequence, initiated by Charles, carries on for some 10 lines, down to line 89. Sue's turns are all either clarifications (party↑) or corrections (hundred and eighty). Charles, however, does not accept these corrections, or repair turns. Twice he insists on his original formulation of 'hundred and eight'. This provides the context for Sue's eventual explanation of her calculation at line 88, which Charles finally agrees with.

Why is Charles' booking of the hall something worth talking about? Having established the party as the topic, Charles then mentions what he needs to say about it. It seems as if the cost of the sports hall is what Charles is focusing on in lines 79–81 – he is recounting his discussion with Marty at the sports hall solely so that he can comment on the expense: that is the point of the turn. Indeed, he repeats the issue of the expense twice during what he says. Hence, the manager's correction of the figures does not actually go against what Charles is saying; it reinforces the point – one hundred and eighty, considerably more even than Charles has calculated before. In this context, the next sequence about the alternative venue is a logical next move.

90.	Sue	equally I've spoken to um Bob Jepson
91.	Cha	yeah↑
92.	Sue	and he'd run a disco for you↓ so that'll only cost probably if you give him twenty quid↓ (0.5)

Building on the idea of the sports hall being expensive, Sue suggests an alternative. She expounds on what she claims to be a cheaper option, to use the hall in the centre belonging to the company for which she works. The disco is cheap, the food comes at cost value and the hall comes free. This sounds like the perfect answer to Charles' problems. However, Charles in the meantime has established himself as someone who can think for himself, who can talk about his own decisions and actions – he has found out information and he is now able to discuss this matter about his plans. At this point, he is a strong, autonomous individual.

Resisting persuasion

The way in which Sue's counter-plan is introduced is interesting. At line 90, she moves decisively away from the discussion about the calculation (£108 or £180) as if to wrap that up. This discussion is not about mathematics, nor is it the 'main issue'. The way in which she does this is with a link word, or marker: 'equally'. This could be a shorthand for 'You may want to consider this as an equally good option'; it has the force of introducing her new proposal as an alternative, something that matches up to Charles' plan in many ways, something that is worth listening to. She then follows up by reporting on what she has already done – she has 'spoken to Bob Jepson'. Not only does she have a counter-plan, but she has actually taken action on it and has some information to give Charles. All this is persuasive talk and is designed so that it is actually quite hard for Charles to resist. It is accompanied (e.g. at lines 93 and 98) by 'offering' gesture displays – possibly the two-handed, symmetrical gestures also signal 'this is manageable'. What does Charles do? During this section he listens, and the manager frequently gives him turn allocation points where he could say something. However, Charles sticks to the minimal response 'yeah'. In this context, his failure to take up the alternative proposal is a marked act, a resistance to the persuasive argumentation being used.

The third section is then introduced by Charles himself – with a very neat move to delay the decision and to keep the ball in his camp:

we'll see what happens (line 106)

'We'll see' is a formulation which puts off the decision to a later date, and the choice of 'we' instead of 'I' fudges the issue about who is going to make that decision. It is a successful way for Charles to keep the next move for himself without being rude to the manager and doing an outright rejection of her suggestion. This is sensitive work. He proceeds to set up a scenario in which Marty from the sports hall is going to phone Charles' support worker, Patricia. If this call does not result in a price reduction, then Charles concedes that he will 'let you know'. Charles seems to be not only a strong and autonomous decision-maker, but is able to marshal conversational resources very effectively so that he does not appear overbearing or rude. This is what might be called 'mitigation'.

Nevertheless, this section continues with some more persuasive turns in which both parties compare the relative advantages of the two possible party venues. First, Charles himself introduces the disadvantage of option 2 (the manager's offer), since the sports hall is nearer his house.

However, that reasoning is countered immediately by: 'but you've got a lot of friends in this area as well Charles' (115). Charles does not deny this, but returns to his former stance, ensuring that he has the next move. This time, however, he moves from the 'we' to 'I', and repeats:

> I'll see I'll see I'll let you know (line 116)

This strengthens his position and rights in the discussion. Even so, there is still another move to go. The manager then decides to repeat and summarise the offer she is making.

117.	Sue	as I say you could use that hall free over there anyway (.) and if we all
118.		give you a hand to do the food and the erm and the um disco's going to
119.		be about £20 cos the chap does it as a hobby

This not only runs through the elements of option 2, but the attractiveness of that offer is emphasised by a choice of vocabulary and phrasing. The salience of the word 'free', the offer that 'we all give you a hand' and the 'chap' who 'does it as a hobby': all these devices serve to frame option 2 as a friendly, easy and above all a cheap option. That economic aspect is then emphasised in the summing up – 'about 50 or 60 pounds all in'.

All the sections of this long extract thus demonstrate a build-up of argumentation and counter-arguments, or resistance. As the persuasion escalates, Charles' refusal to get drawn in appears more and more to be a decisive interactional strategy. In view of the entire thrust of his arguments throughout, Sue's introduction of the final sequence could sound like an empty rhetorical device:

> Sue   I'll leave it entirely up to you (line 125)

However, Charles immediately moves to accept this and to reiterate that he will 'get back to' the manager and the sequence ends with a slight shift, where they first seem to reach agreement and secondly reinforce and encourage Charles' right to make his own decision:

> Cha   nothing to it is it↑ (lines 129–30)
> Sue   absolutely right Charles

What has been agreed, then, is not the actual option Charles is going to choose for his party, but the right that he has to make the decision 'entirely' by himself.

This extract is unusual for our data, mainly because of Charles' resistance strategies, which seem mainly to consist of giving minimal response to keep everyone happy, be polite, but stick to his guns. From the point of view of support strategies, Sue does have a good try by introducing an alternative, explaining the advantages of that alternative and summing up some of the things that Charles needed to consider – the price and also the whereabouts of his friends and the likelihood of a friendly, relaxed event. She also recognises explicitly and highlights Charles' right to autonomy at the end of the extract. All these points would very much count as good practice; for instance the Code of Practice for the MCA (Department for Constitutional Affairs, 2007) repeatedly promotes the importance of providing appropriate information for decision-making. What this analysis has shown, however, is that the very activity of providing information, if coupled with persuasive devices, could make it very hard for the other person to stick to their own decision.

The reader might wonder why Charles introduces the topic at all; a discussion about how expensive his birthday party is going to be would seem to have nothing to do with the manager for his support service who is also his employer. It can only be assumed that the naturalised discussion of Charles' money issues (neither Charles nor Sue seems to be embarrassed by talking about Charles' money) draws on a repertoire where this manager does in fact have some kind of overview or responsibility for Charles' budgeting. This issue will be returned to in the final section of this chapter. For the moment, it is worth noting that there are elements of approval-seeking, both in Charles' initial introduction of the topic and in his final plea at line 129: 'nothing to it is it↑' Whenever people with intellectual disabilities talk about choices, as seen earlier with Penny and Beth, they often seem to be simultaneously seeking approval for the choice they've made.

Negotiating from a position of strength

Charles came over as decisive and in charge of his own plans, by virtue of presenting his independent actions and also by resisting persuasive counter-arguments. In other cases, however, people with intellectual disabilities came over as active decision-makers in the context of organising their own support. With a direct payment, some of the participants in 'Skills for Support' engaged in talk with their support worker which hinged on the organisation of that person's work. The reader has seen in Chapter 6 how Frank took on the role of employer with his support worker, reserving the right to instruct the support worker and also to evaluate his performance. In some of these pairs, however, the topic of employment and shift-work was frequently discussed, as in the following extract from Ruth and Norah, recorded in the car on their way to a café:

Extract 7.12

1.	Rut	can you do double time↑
2.	Nor	is that all day↑
3.	Rut	yeah
4.	Nor	I will have to check (.) it depends if Robert's working (.) because my
5.		dad can't really have Jake all day↓(0.5) but it is on the 8th↑
6.	Rut	yeah
7.	Nor	I'd better write it down then (5) ((stops at traffic lights)) my dad can't
8.		really cope with Jake all day ((LF voice)) it stresses him out for a
9.		couple of hours ((laughs, turns to Ruth))

Ruth's turn at line 1 marks the introduction of this new topic, one she had mentioned earlier, namely the possibility of Norah covering an extra shift for support work in order to accompany Ruth to a special meeting. There are two matters here which probably deserve a mention. One is that Ruth frames her request to Norah as a 'positive' – by taking this extra piece of work she will earn 'double time'. Norah is thus put into the position of an employee, someone who receives an offer of work and has to ask for further details of what this might entail. Ruth is operating very much from a position of power: she has the money and she can afford to allow Norah to do 'double time' for this piece of work.

At line 4, Norah starts on some hedging and excuses. There are several pauses in this section (not least because Norah is driving at the same time). However, she is hesitant and does not commit herself to Ruth's plan. The possible factors that she introduces against doing extra work are all, it should be noted, personal ones. She talks about her young son, Jake, and the fact that her husband, Robert, might not be able to look after Jake for an extra day. She also mentions her father, explaining that Jake 'stresses him out' after a couple of hours. All this is accepted by Ruth; the personal details about Norah's family are known to her and she sympathises with Ruth's position. In fact, they share a smile and a laugh about this. The unusual aspect of this conversation is that Ruth is in the 'professional' position of being able to offer a choice; Norah, by contrast, introduces personal topics. Although the decision about whether to do the extra work lies with Norah, both parties orient to the strong position of Ruth-as-employer, who has the power to offer work and to pay for it.

Essentially, every decision is about more than one person, and it is a process of negotiation which often includes contingencies which have to be taken into account. Here, in fact, Ruth had already made her decision. She knows that she wants to go to the meeting and she has made a decision to ask Norah to do extra work and pay her 'double'. That is all she can do. It is now Norah's turn to claim her right to make her own decision about accepting the extra work, based on contingencies that she does not know about yet. Not every choice is really a free one and often the choice the person with intellectual disabilities makes will depend on others' choices. We are all interdependent.

Implications for practice

This chapter has offered a tour of some different contexts in which decision-making and autonomy are matters for discussion, or where choices are being made and supported. The extracts in this chapter are all ones in which the social activity at hand is actually about choice (e.g. choice of some next activity, choice of how to accomplish something) or where choice and decision-making are highlighted in the talk.

Conventional wisdom about facilitating choices for people with intellectual disabilities tends to focus on offering alternatives. Although the offering of alternatives may be one strategy, this was not frequent and as seen in this chapter it may be accompanied by other interactional work, for instance to persuade and convince people of the benefits of an alternative. Antaki *et al.* (2007a, 2008) explored this dilemma as it played out in residential homes, and they showed neatly how attention to 'choice' can have the paradoxical effect of undermining the autonomy of the person with intellectual disabilities. The actual act of offering a choice implies institutional power, something which distances the wisdom of the support worker from the supposed incompetence of the person they are supporting.

The opposite of choice facilitation may be identified as bossing people about, or instructing people, and in some respects therefore the positive mode of support is to desist from this type of activity: making a virtue out of *absence*. However, as was noted at the beginning of this chapter, choice-making is not generally something which happens simply inside people's heads. Individual autonomy is built, for most of us, on interaction with others. Decisions are often joint accomplishments, and the feeling we have of 'making our own decision' is seldom done in total isolation. That is no different for people with intellectual disabilities.

What is evident in these data is the extent to which the choices people with intellectual disabilities make become noticeable and a talked-about phenomenon. For instance, the manager says to Charles 'I'll leave it entirely up to you'; Penny is asked 'what do you think' about her clothes; and Jan tells Neil 'that's your choice' when discussing his visit to the pub. There are repeated occasions on which the conversation foregrounds the agency of a person with intellectual disabilities. It is interesting to reflect on what this does in the communication. In ordinary circumstances, people's decisions are not necessarily prompted by others telling them 'it's your choice'. One can imagine several circumstances in which that phrase might come over as rude or imply that the other person does *not* want to get involved in his choice, as when a wife may ask her husband:

| Wife | Do you fancy going to the cinema tonight? There's a new movie I'd like to see. |
| Husband | It's your choice. |

Therefore, although support workers are often advised to 'give people choices', it is worthwhile to reflect on the distinctive ways in which choices are talked about with people with intellectual disabilities.

Why is choice so often a remarkable matter in talk involving people with intellectual disabilities? The repertoire on which all parties are drawing in these conversations is the background of intellectual disability talk, in which people have traditionally not been treated as autonomous. There is a certain self-awareness therefore about 'choice' and the importance of people making their *own* decisions, instead of being influenced or instructed by others in their lives. Both supporters and people with intellectual disabilities in these data subscribe to this 'choice talk': it is very rare for someone with an intellectual disability to turn to a supporter and say 'it's your choice', and this is why Ruth's negotiation with her support worker, Norah, is so unusual. People often think of offering choices as empowering; however, the examples in this chapter show that sometimes it is a powerful position to be able to offer choices, and not necessarily as powerful to be able to make a choice.

As seen in this chapter, the business of making choices is something that people with intellectual disabilities have to work at. They often frame interactions with other people (in particular here with support workers) as attempts to display their achievements. Penny, for instance, sought praise from her support worker for her care and choice of clothes, and this was not unusual. After all the discussion of choices for his party booking, Charles turned to his manager for approval of what had gone on right then and there: effectively, the final sequence of extract 7.11 had the function of supporting and praising Charles' attempts to run his own life and make his decisions. People with intellectual disabilities often sought praise for their choices.

Conversely, a large part of the support worker's job seemed to be about building confidence and helping people to have a positive self-image as a decision-maker. This is very much what Emma did in joking with Brian about his DVDs, and many other examples could be given throughout the data. Can autonomy be learnt? Choice-making and autonomy could be viewed here as constructs which emerge out of the joint work in talk, by all parties. How successfully autonomy is achieved depends very much on the ebb and flow of talk and small details in interaction, such as the tone of voice with which a 'well done' is delivered. Making your own choice is about being trusted and being able to trust yourself, to say what *you* want. Autonomy does not mean simply 'doing things that you might choose, at this moment'; the ability to reflect on constraints and outcomes is of course part of the whole business of being 'capable' of a decision, and indeed the ability to give informed consent is something which has to be assessed in England under the Mental Capacity Act. Perhaps 'autonomy' is best achieved by appearing to be wise about a decision (as Ruth and Charles were) rather than by simply making a choice and sticking to it. The talk about choices certainly includes much which is about these constraints and outcomes. A support worker's job is in some ways to coach people about those outcomes so that they can make wise decisions for themselves.

Nowhere was this clearer, perhaps, than in the extract with Charles and his manager when they were discussing the relative costs and other benefits and drawbacks of bookings for his party. However, when someone gives detailed information about alternatives, it is easy to be influenced by the views and feelings of the person giving that information. There is nothing unusual in that. These matters have also been noted by other commentators. Antaki *et al.* (2007a) highlight a strategy commonly adopted in their data by residential support workers of people with intellectual disabilities, which consisted of mentioning a name associated with a suggested activity. This seems also to be a persuasive device, something someone might use to familiarise the other person with a particular option, to make it into something which they would want to choose. In their body of work, Antaki *et al.* (2007c) have illustrated clearly some routine patterns, which are also evident in the current chapter. In conversation with people with intellectual disabilities, it is all too easy to imply that their choice was wrong, to advise and suggest better alternatives and to use persuasive devices to bring the person round to the institutionally correct choice. As with all the conversations in this book, there are some fine lines to tread between offering constructive support and becoming too overbearing.

Supporting choices is about enabling the person's confidence in their own autonomy; it is also about giving clear information about the possible pros and cons of alternatives (as, arguably, Charles' manager tries to do in extract 7.11). However, it is hard to establish a good balance between ensuring the 'right choice' and ensuring the 'right to make a choice'. It is precisely that fine distinction which is captured in the MCA, with the principle that people have a right to make an 'unwise decision'. There is a moment to offer advice, a moment to go with and accept a seemingly unwise choice, and there are strategies such as humour and self-disclosure that support workers can use to soften people's self-critique and to boost their confidence. Getting this 'right' is all about the local context, what has happened in the talk before and how things are taken in the unfolding sequence of interaction. By looking at their own interactions on video, support workers and others can learn more about how to sensitively manage these interactions and really enable people with intellectual disabilities to 'do autonomy'.

How conversation works: summary points

- Talk is action, and can accomplish actions – like making choices. However, actions are not always verbalised, and sometimes analysis can take account of what is *not* said, as well as what is said. Choices may not be verbalised. In all cases, the analyst is looking for the evidence of how speakers themselves understand each other (Pomerantz & Fehr, 1997: 72–3; Silverman, 1998: 120–7).

- The types of conversational ploys analysed in this chapter are very common and happen with everyone. For instance, anyone may ask for approval for a choice they have made. However, it can often be revealing to look at a particular bit of conversation and ask how it would be heard by people outside the intellectual disability world. That stance of 'standing back' is essential to the ethnographer also (Garfinkel, 1967).

- Conversations offer us opportunities to take on particular identities, by virtue of what we are saying. We have seen how this can relate to 'discourse' and to 'situational' identity (Zimmerman, 1998). However, through doing these things in conversation, people can then change the way they see themselves more widely, and how others see them. By making choices, people become known as more competent choice-makers. This is sometimes known as their 'transportable identity'.

Approaches to inclusive support: summary points

- People with intellectual disabilities often seek approval for a choice they have made. This could be seen as a sign of lack of confidence. This is very much a matter of knowing the individual and what they need at each stage in their life; however, there is certainly some value in trying to 'wean people off' the constant need for approval, by reminding them that they can think things through for themselves.

- A good support worker will support someone to be in control. This often means treating the person with respect, and following his own questions and thoughts about the choices he is making, without worrying too much about the institutionally correct choice.
- Even people who don't use words can make choices for themselves, and support workers can talk to people about their choices.
- Sometimes choices have consequences which are difficult to foresee, and support workers have to talk through what might happen, the pros and cons. People are entitled to have good information about their choices.
- It is hard to do this without showing what you yourself think and persuading the person with intellectual disabilities to do something you think is good. But people have a right to listen, to resist persuasion and to make their own choice, even if someone else thinks it is the wrong one.

Chapter 8

Public Encounters

The previous chapters have shown how support workers and people with intellectual disabilities could make interactions friendly, with both parties orienting towards familiar, shared experiences, and Chapter 7 followed the way choice-making is done and talked about between people with intellectual disabilities and those around them. All these things are essential groundwork for more public situations, where support workers and people with intellectual disabilities may come across other people – third parties. Engagement with ordinary community settings is a key theme in UK policy (DH, 2006b, 2009) and was identified by Williams *et al.* (2008) as a major research priority in intellectual disability. Hall and Hewson (2006) followed up the same group of 60 people with intellectual disabilities in the UK who had been part of a study in 1995. They lived in 11 community-based houses staffed and run by a local NHS Trust. These authors found that there was no improvement on any measure between 1995 and 2002, that 88% of the residents went out less than once a day and that 55% had no 'personal visitors' at all during the four weeks of the study. These results were unequivocal and bleak. The lives of many people with intellectual disabilities are isolated and uneventful. De-institutionalisation is associated with greater community contact, but the 'community use' and activities of people in group homes are still low by comparison with others in the general population in England (Baker, 2007) and in other countries as diverse as Iceland and Australia (Johnson & Traustadottir, 2005).

Despite this lack of community presence, there have been some attempts to investigate and develop more positive practice (Cole *et al.*, 2006; Swift & Mattingly, 2008), whereby people with intellectual disabilities are offered one-to-one support to engage with community activities. These initiatives are thus specifically premised on the idea that support workers will in some way be able to 'facilitate' and provide a good interface between the person they are supporting and others in the community. In 'Skills for Support' we were very fortunate in finding several people with intellectual disabilities and support workers who were happy to take us (and a video camera) on trips to pubs, banks, shops and even rugby matches. In fact, going out to ordinary community settings was one of the most frequent activities that people with intellectual disabilities in our project had support workers for. This chapter therefore moves on to data from occasions on which people with intellectual disabilities interact with others who are relatively unknown to them at a personal level. This mainly occurs in situations where there is a third party who may have a professional role, perhaps as a shopkeeper or librarian. However, it also occurs when people meet up with an acquaintance or friend.

Disability and Discourse. Analysing Inclusive Conversation with People with Intellectual Disabilities,
1st edition. © Val Williams. Published 2011 by John Wiley & Sons, Ltd.

In general, CA looks at patterns in talk which occur routinely and which are simply part of the way the social fabric of interaction happens. When CA refers to 'strategies' in talk, these are not generally conscious, deliberate strategies that people implement. Thus we all conduct friendly conversations at times, based on a history of shared experiences, as the people in Chapter 6 did. However, in the type of inclusive analysis conducted in 'Skills for Support', we were interested in certain skills that may typify and define the role of the support worker. The current chapter starts to pick out some of these activities which are not obvious and which may have to be pointed out and learnt.

The nice thing about studying these types of situation is that they occur all the time all around us, and the reader can easily see how things happen in public encounters, just by keeping their eyes and ears open. One can observe how interactions unfold and start noticing things about the patterns. Three-way conversations are always interesting, since it requires a special effort on the part of a speaker to include two people as listeners. For instance, eye gaze becomes crucial, and the precise sequencing and co-occurrence of different body postures, eye gaze and tone of voice may all be necessary to indicate who is talking to whom (see Kendon, 1983, 2004; Goodwin, 2007). In the case of people with intellectual disabilities, however, there may be specific issues: it is possible that they will get left out of the conversation and that the third party will engage only with their carer or support worker. It is here that the support worker's role becomes very sensitive in indicating who should be the recipient of the talk.

The extracts in this chapter all depict three-way encounters in which support workers also have a voice. The social activity we start with in this chapter is a very general one, which occurs in many different encounters, both casual and formal, and it echoes the original interests of CA pioneers (Schegloff, 1968). This is the activity of greeting. Since a greeting is usually the first activity in a social exchange, it has some importance in setting what will happen next.

Colin and Ben: Meeting and greeting an acquaintance

One of the most straightforward and routine occurrences in social life is simply meeting and greeting a friend or acquaintance. However, doing a successful, casual greeting is not necessarily routine for a person with intellectual disabilities. Among people with intellectual disabilities in the UK, social contacts, as we know, are frequently limited (Robertson *et al.*, 2001; Emerson, Malam *et al.*, 2005). Furthermore, their social networks are less durable and diverse and mainly comprise staff, families and other people with intellectual disabilities (Forrester-Jones *et al.*, 2006). A person with intellectual disabilities might seldom have the chance to be out on the street on their own. One of the things the 'Skills for Support' team particularly objected to was the situation where a support worker or family member answered for them, or even talked about them, in their presence. Our research team was therefore surprised that, on the two occasions on which we filmed people casually meeting an acquaintance on the street, that 'third party' spoke directly to the person with intellectual disabilities. Extract 8.1 gives an example.

Extract 8.1

85.	Man	((*shakes hands with Ben*)) hi (0.5) OK↑ ((*walks past Ben*))
86.		((*Ben stands for 2 seconds, staring after the man, smiling, one hand in*
87.		*the air*))
88.	Col	((*Catches Ben up, walking up from behind him. Ben catches Col's*
89.		*arm*))
90.	Ben	uh uh uh
91.	Col	I'm ignoring you↑

Ben is the young man from Chapter 4 who is very 'people-centred', but generally uses signs rather than words to communicate. In extract 8.1, he is walking along the pavement with Colin, his support worker, who had been playing a joke with Ben by keeping out of sight. In both this extract and the following one the third party is presumably an acquaintance, although not well known enough to stop and talk for long. In both cases, of course, there is a video camera present, and no prior permission had been sought from the people who stopped in the street. Therefore, their choice of stopping and saying hello implies a certain amount of implicit understanding of what was going on – and their role in it. For this analysis, I refer to these people as 'passers-by', as nothing else is known about them.

In extract 8.1, the offer of a greeting is initiated by the passer-by, who approaches, smiles, holds out a hand and says 'hello'. Ben responds appropriately by shaking hands. Therefore, at the level of a routine greeting sequence there are no interactional troubles (ten Have, 1999: 116). On this occasion, this is as far as it goes. The man walks on, having shaken hands with Ben. Ben is left with his right arm in the air, staring with an expectant look at the man who has just greeted him. Perhaps he wants more interaction or perhaps he is looking at the man (as anyone might do) to ask himself who that could have been.

Whatever the case, the remainder of the extract shows Ben's reaction and possibly his attempt to communicate that to Colin, his supporter. Just prior to this extract, Colin had been playing a joke with Ben, hiding behind the corner of the road and letting Ben walk on unaccompanied. Thus as he returns there could have been a continuation of the joke – or even the punch-line: 'Here I am!' However, this is replaced by Ben first touching his supporter's arm, a gesture that regularly helps him to get attention and to indicate 'I've got something to tell you'. He then delivers 'uh uh uh' at line 90. It is unclear from the video evidence whether Colin had witnessed the encounter, or indeed whether he knew the identity of the passer-by. However, he chooses to continue with the theme of the practical joke he had been playing, and his response at line 91 ('I'm ignoring you↑') is in the form of a question, accounting for a possible reason for Ben's approach and arm-touching, a reason that would have linked this gesture with the joke sequence.

It is impossible to go any further than this from the evidence of the video. However, it looks very much as if there could have been two agendas here, with Ben trying to signal to Colin that he had just shaken hands with someone and Colin intent on concluding a practical joke with him. What can be said is that the practical joke (hiding behind the corner) in fact does facilitate the independent greeting sequence. Because Ben is on his own at that particular point, the encounter with the passer-by is entirely in Ben's hands.

Alice and Rachel: Expanding on a greeting

Another example of a casual encounter occurs in Alice's video, as she is walking to the library with Rachel, her support worker. Alice was the woman seen in Chapter 5.

Extract 8.2

1.	Wom	((*shaking hands with Alice*))
2.		hello (.) you're not going to watch any rugby then↑
3.	Ali	no
4.	Rac	no not yet↓ we've just been down the stadium though to buy
5.		her tickets
6.	Wom	oh↑((*smiles directly at Alice*)) see (…) have you↑ then (.) see
7.		you Alice
8.	Ali	yeah ((*smiles, walks on*))

Figure 8.1   Passerby listens to Rachel, but looks at Alice.

In extract 8.2, the greeting sequence moves straight into a social question about rugby. Evidently, the passer-by for some reason expects Alice to be watching rugby, since possibly there is a match on the television at that point. The question also indicates that the woman knows Alice and her interest in rugby, and is drawing on that personal information to open a social encounter. What she does is to point out as 'remarkable' the fact that Alice is out walking and not watching rugby – it is something that has to be accounted for. This is clearly a way to give Alice a lead-in to the conversation. Instead of taking up this invitation to account for what she is doing, however, Alice simply replies with a literal 'no': she is not going to watch rugby.

It is at this point that her support worker, Rachel, intervenes with an expansion on what Alice has said: 'No not yet↓ we've just been down the stadium though to buy her tickets'. The fact that an expansion is thought necessary here does some work in the conversation. It effectively implies that Alice's short 'no' is not an adequate response to the enquiry about rugby. There is an implication that Alice should say more about her destination or activity at that point. This kind of simple expansion on information given by a person with intellectual disabilities seems to be a very common occurrence. The pattern is that the person speaks directly for himself or herself first, and then any subsequent detail is supplied by the person accompanying them. What is remarkable here is the work done by this expanded information from the point of view of the passer-by, who accepts the added information offered by Rachel, but then responds directly to Alice as if Alice had uttered this herself. This is shown by her gaze direction and smile on line 6, which is shown in Figure 8.1. In this case, the conversation does not then continue, nor does it involve Alice in any further substantive turns.

Henry and Pippa: Requesting a service

Many more examples of greetings from data in 'Skills for Support' could be given from public places other than the street. Here is one in which the greeting is the precursor to a more extended social activity, and it occurs when Henry goes to get his leisure card with Pippa, his personal assistant.

Extract 8.3

1.	Pip	last time we were here the lady told us that we need to renew his card
2.	Man	right
3.	Pip	and in order to do that I'd need a letter from the Benefits Agency
4.	Man	have you got the card↑
5.	Hen	yes ((*Henry hands over the card*))
6.	Pip	Henry's on benefits and that's the letter that you asked us to bring
7.		((*hands over letter*))

As the pair go to the counter, there is an expectant look of greeting from the man behind the counter. It is Pippa who leads the way, in line 1, by giving an account for why they are here. It is interesting that the man at first ignores the issue about the letter from the benefits agency and asks Henry directly for his leisure card. Henry is clearly listening to what is going on, as he hands over the old leisure card when it is needed, which could have prompted a continued interaction between him and the leisure centre official. However, Pippa raises again the reason they are there. It is not simply to exchange the card, but to bring in a specific letter which they have been asked to do. Her talk makes sure that the purpose for their visit is fulfilled and she herself hands over the letter to the man. In doing so, she marks herself as the person who has the important document (although Henry is in possession of the leisure card itself). Referring to a previous conversation is a strategic way of introducing an official encounter. By doing this, Pippa is ensuring that the exchange continues on the terms set by 'the lady' who had seen them last time. She performs the role of linking the two conversations – the previous visit they had made and the current one. This is a powerful move and arguably one that is essential to the successful conclusion of their transaction over the leisure card. However, it clearly has the effect of moving Pippa into the role of primary spokesperson. Line 6 underlines this move: Henry is referred to as a third party – 'Henry's on benefits' – and is then bracketed with Pippa: 'that's the letter that you asked *us* to bring'.

This particular exchange proceeds for a further seven minutes, with many long pauses and infrequent questions as the man looks up from his computer screen. On each occasion it is Pippa who is addressed, and Henry's attention starts to wander from the matter in hand. He looks round at the camera and seems ready to sit down. Finally, the paperwork is complete and the exchange terminates in the following way.

Extract 8.4

24.	Pip	OK brilliant ((*Pippa takes paperwork from man; goes to*
25.		*give it to Henry*))
26.	Pip	OK you didn't bring your bag did you↑
27.	Hen	no
28.	Pip	that's fine ((*takes card from man*))
29.	Man	you can use this now
30.	Pip	that's absolutely fine↓ there's your card ((*Pippa gives card to Henry*))

It is interesting to see how Pippa takes on the function of go-between, or channel, for the talk. At line 28, it is Pippa who takes the card from the leisure centre man, and he then addresses her (not Henry), saying 'you can use this now'. Therefore, the final line (30) involves Pippa responding to the man with 'that's absolutely fine' and then turning to Henry to give him the card. Henry is a quiet man and does not generally talk a lot. However, he appears to have been completely sidelined in the leisure centre transaction, despite Pippa's attempts to bring him into the conversation and to ensure that he takes his leisure card. As observed in extract 8.3, the opening greeting has a key position and could determine how the rest of the transaction goes. Here we have a classic scenario of a third party, official person, talking directly to a support worker rather than to the person with intellectual disabilities about his own affairs. However, it is fascinating to see what comes next, in extract 8.5.

The importance of being first speaker

Henry and Pippa move on from the leisure centre, and the video follows them back along the high street to the pub. As they go into the pub, a very different scene happens. This time, Henry approaches the bar first and the barmaid looks directly at him, as he says:

Extract 8.5

55.	Hen	can I have lemonade please↑
56.	Hen	lemonade↑ want ice in that↑
57.	Hen	no
58.	Hen	no

Things have got off to a different start here and Pippa comes second, as she asks for her 'usual', which is coffee. Following a brief intervening conversation between Pippa and the barmaid about someone in the other bar, Henry turns to the camera and offers me (Val) a drink. Henry repeats Val's order to the barmaid, and Pippa turns to find a table in the corner by the pool table, leaving Henry to complete the drinks order. Henry ends up by handing over the money for all the drinks, and the barmaid thanks him and offers to bring all the drinks over to the table.

What makes extract 8.5 so different from extract 8.4? The most obvious difference is that Henry speaks first – he knows that in a pub it is not necessary to wait to be asked, nor is it necessary to wait for a polite greeting sequence, although both those things would be possible. His 'Can I have a lemonade please' is accompanied by him holding out some money to the barmaid, and this in itself might be sufficient to identify him as the main customer here. Whatever the case, once he is in direct interaction with the barmaid, Pippa is the one who is sidelined. She does not need to do the ordering, and indeed, it is evident that Henry is going to pay, so she goes to get the table. This is a straightforward pattern which Henry clearly knows well and from which none of the parties deviates. There is no additional question, for instance, about Henry's status of being on benefits (as in the leisure centre) or about his ability to pay or indeed to drink. It could be observed that this is simply a set pattern which Henry knows well and has learnt. As has been seen in other conversation with him and Pippa, visits to this pub are a part of his ordinary routine. Like any other interactional pattern, though, it is not something that can be assumed to be universal: ordering a drink in a British pub, as is well known, is very different from the business of ordering a drink in Germany or France, say, where Henry's approach to the barmaid would have been considered quite inappropriate. Like any of us, Henry has to learn patterns of culturally acceptable social action, and practice makes perfect.

Michael and Teresa: Rescuing someone from trouble

I now turn to a different situation, where someone with intellectual disabilities is accomplishing a routine 'service' encounter. Michael, who features in the following extract, is checking into a hotel with his support worker Teresa, and he starts by confidently initiating the exchange, just as Henry had done in the pub. Michael is the first to walk through the hotel door, ahead of Teresa. Further, just as Henry has money, Michael is holding a credit card and directly addresses the receptionist, who is facing him and attending to him visually. Michael begins the interaction confidently:

> Mic   Two rooms for Michael Cutlass and Teresa Beech. (line 110)

Just as with Henry in the pub, it may seem unremarkable, but the simple fact of going first and not having a support worker speak on his behalf is a marked, or unexpected, activity for someone with the label 'intellectual disability'. Similarly, Teresa's action in holding back is also a marked activity. By doing it, she is contributing strongly to the message that Michael is taking on the role of hotel guest in his own right.

Following this initial interaction between the receptionist and Michael himself, the talk goes on with some joking references to keys and room numbers – Teresa in fact (as a guest in her own right) plays a leading role in the talk at this point. The receptionist then produces two forms for each of the guests to fill out, and Michael is standing beside Teresa at the reception desk, filling out his form by consulting his diary at the point when the following exchange starts:

Extract 8.6

121.	Mic	phone number↑
122.	Rec	yes any number home number or mobile number
123.		((*Mic opens his diary and looks in it*)) (5)
124.	Rec	that's fine if you leave something we can (.) give you a call↑ (7) and
125.		just if you need some early morning call in the morning↑ (2) or a
126.		newspaper↑ (2)
127.		((*Teresa looks directly at Michael, then at receptionist*))
128.	Ter	are we allowed a newspaper↑ can we – can I pay for that separately if I
129.		have one↑
129.	Rec	yes of course you can
130.	Ter	great
131.	Rec	I've got a price list as well actually (.) and what newspapers we can
132.		get you↓ that's fine then (1) ah-ha

The first thing to notice is the relatively long pauses around lines 123–6. Pauses often mean that things are not going smoothly; however, in the above exchange the pauses are filled for Michael by the time-consuming business of finding the page in his diary with his own phone number and copying this onto the form. From line 122 onwards, he is totally engaged with this task and there are some long silences. Watching him fill in the form, the receptionist partially fills some of the gaps in the talk with her remarks about why the phone number is needed in:

> that's fine if you leave something we can (.) give you a call↑ (lines 124–5)

The slight pause and rising intonation, together with a soft tone of voice, mean that these remarks really do seem to be gap-fillers. No one is expected to respond, so Michael can get on with the task in hand.

However, the receptionist's next remark (lines 125–6) opens a slot for a response of some kind. As she asks about the 'early morning call' and the newspaper, there is again a pause. Figure 8.2 shows how gazes and glances are exchanged precisely at this point, offering Michael

Figure 8.2 Looking towards Michael and waiting can signal to a third party that it is Michael's turn to talk.

a potential slot. Michael does not respond, as he is still busy with his task of form-filling. Teresa, however, has looked up towards Michael, and when he doesn't respond she is the next to fill the gap with: 'are we allowed a newspaper'. This is an interesting formulation, very clearly orienting to Michael's position as being in charge of the hotel visit and placing herself in the position of a subsidiary – someone who is there on Michael's terms. Michael glances up towards her, but then immediately turns back to his form. At this, Teresa raises the possibility of paying for her own newspaper and carries on the conversation about the newspaper for the next couple of turns with the receptionist, in her own right.

Just as the receptionist was filling a gap from line 124 onwards, now Teresa's talk with the receptionist could be seen as having the function of buying Michael some time. Instead of him having to respond to every detail, he can concentrate on the task he has started in completing his form and leave the chat to Teresa. This type of support activity has to be sensitive to the very personal and individual needs of the person being supported. Because Teresa knows that Michael will need time she moves fairly rapidly into taking over some of the talk in order to allow him the concentration he needs.

Narrowing down choices

If it can be said that Teresa is 'rescuing' Michael at this point and allowing him to manage the situation, there is also a danger that she will become the focal point for the rest of the exchange and Michael will be sidelined, just as Henry was in the leisure centre (extracts 8.3 and 8.4). However, this does not happen. Extract 8.7 shows what happens next.

Extract 8.7

133.	Ter	what shall I get↑ which paper shall I get ((*looks at M, and touches his arm*))
134.		because you can have a look at it as well
135.	Mic	(let you look…) (5) ((*Michael looks up at Teresa, then back at form*))
136.	Rec	aha (1) there you go ((*puts written list in front of Teresa*))
137.		there's the ones we do that's what I was looking for there you go and that's
138.		the prices for Monday to Friday↑

138.	Ter	what shall I get↑ we can see the news in the morning can't we↑
139.		((*turning to Michael*))
140.	Mic	((*leaning forward, looking at computer screen*)) (6) oh we'll have the er
141.		(4)
142.	Ter	mm↑(3)
143.	Rec	((*LF*)) there's too many to choose from
144.	Ter	any one (3)
145.	Mic	hang on (2) there's too many t- (.) which is your favourite paper↑
146.	Ter	out of those↑
147.	Mic	yeah
148.	Ter	well I think just for easy simple news something like the
149.		Express or the Mail↓or the Mirror or just one of those
150.		just basic stuff what do you reckon↑ [so we know what's
151.		going on
152.	Mic	[yeah Express
153.	Ter	Express↑
154.	Mic	get the Express yeah
155.	Rec	yeah
156.	Ter	yeah I'll pay for that that's no problem
157.	Rec	OK you can pay that on checking out if you like
158.	Ter	that's it isn't it ((*finishing her form*))
159.	Rec	and just a signature at the bottom would be brilliant↑

At line 133, Teresa explicitly asks Michael to join the discussion about newspapers, but he rejects this, saying 'let you look'. Following that, the receptionist carries on trying to find the information about newspapers on her computer monitor. At line 136, she finds the screen she has been looking for and turns back to Teresa. Again, instead of answering directly, Teresa attempts to bring Michael into the conversation by turning towards him and asking him for advice: 'what shall I get', again correcting to a 'we can see the news in the morning', foregrounding the fact that this newspaper and the decision about the newspaper is for both of them.

This attempt finally draws Michael's attention away from his form, and he leans over the counter at line 140, squinting at the computer screen for some six seconds, following which he starts to respond 'oh we'll have the er-'. Just like with the pauses, when someone interrupts themselves like this, there is clearly some trouble going on. Teresa seems to be aware she again needs to do some repair work. She first simply looks towards Michael and gives an encouraging noise ('mm↑') waiting for him to come up with a choice. Following another pause, the receptionist also does some face-saving work for Michael, filling the gap with a laugh and 'there's too many to choose from'. This effectively accounts for Michael's pause and his indecision in a light-hearted way.

Eventually, however, after several attempts to give Michael the next turn and the choice of newspaper, he himself gives up and asks Teresa what would be her preferred choice. It is unclear whether in fact he could see the screen or whether the difficulty lay in the fact that he could not read the words on the screen. Alternatively, he could simply have been indecisive. Whatever the case, Teresa only moves back into a more active role in the talk at Michael's own invitation. However, even then, she does not simply move in and take over. She effectively narrows down Michael's choice by naming three different possible newspapers at line 149, the *Express*, the *Mail* and the *Mirror*. This tactic is immediately successful. Michael comes in straightaway with his choice of the *Express* and the talk moves on without further pauses.

From this example, it is clear that assisting someone to talk to other people is not always simply a matter of 'stepping back'. Teresa does some subtle conversational work to ensure that

Michael can check himself into the hotel, while providing his own responses to the receptionist. Because she is aware of Michael's dilemmas and his need for time, she is prepared to enter into the talk in her own right. Essentially, she talks like a friend or companion, someone who is also going to stay in the hotel and has her own needs and wishes. However, she looks towards Michael throughout the exchange, she narrows down the choices so that Michael has some actual names of newspapers to choose from and she looks to him for a final decision about the newspaper: 'what do you reckon?'

Karen and Joan: Scripting and ventriloquism

Trouble in the talk can occur for many reasons. With Michael, it evidently was to do both with the time he needed for certain tasks and possibly also to compensate for his indecision and to ensure that he kept up an active role in the conversation with the hotel receptionist. However, there are other non-responses which are due more centrally to the lack of verbal ability of the individual. Here again, support workers seem to play a very important role in interacting with third parties. The following exchanges take place in a drama group which is attended by a young woman, Karen. This is the same woman who was seen in Chapter 7 with her support worker, Laura. At this point, she is with a different supporter, Joan. Both Joan and Karen are on the stage, in a semi-circle with about 12 other participants, and Alan is leading the group. Karen uses a wheelchair, she is visually impaired and does not use speech to communicate.

The drama sequences being rehearsed are various short scenes, some consisting more of scripted dance to music and others which have a topic and story. In the dance sequences, Joan can be seen moving Karen's wheelchair to the front of the stage, into the same spot where others have performed. Her particular movement is a kind of arm-flinging self-presentation, which Joan literally does for Karen, leaning over her wheelchair and flinging one arm at a time out to each side. Similarly, when the group members are expected to perform a particular movement in the warm-up, Joan simply does this for Karen, manipulating her arms.

> Joan holds Karen's right elbow, and sways her body to the music. Immediately looks up towards others. She is adapting the movement everyone else is making. Looks towards Karen. Karen turns her head away.

It is interesting on these occasions to see how Joan glances back and forwards from Karen to the group facilitator, almost as if she was checking that her response was in fact what Karen wanted to do. Together, Karen and Joan perform many of these joint movements or responses, with Joan becoming the hands, arms and voice for Karen. There is then a very lively piece, featuring one man who dances to a pop tune, and each member of the group has to go up to him. Again, Karen achieves this with total support, Joan pushing her chair forwards and speaking for her ('Hello:::') and neatly turning her and going back to the original position. At this point, it could seem as though Karen is simply a puppet, with Joan manipulating her physically and answering for her.

The group then moves on to several short pieces they have been rehearsing, including a play which involves a social worker who fails to come up with the goods for his various clients. The group facilitator plays the social worker. When he comes to Karen, Joan is again standing beside her and moves to take on the role of Karen's support worker. The following occurs:

Extract 8.8

| 33. | Joan | Karen and I would love to go on holiday together |
| 34. | | ((holding out a pretend map in front of Karen)) |

35.	Alan	no problem you can↓ how long are you going for↑
36.	Joan	couple of weeks↑
37.	Alan	no problem spending money↑
38.	Joan	yeah
39.	Alan	24 hour support↑
40.	Jan	yeah
41.	Alan	no problem *((John turns to Karen, holding his arms out*
42.		*Kar looks up towards John))*
43.	Karen	(.) take the money *((touches K's hands))*
44.		listen make sure you send me a postcard (.) have a really
45.		good time
46.	Joan	yeah we will do
47.	Alan	all right then see you later

Clearly, in this exchange Joan is taking a role in the drama in her own right. By playing Karen's support worker, she is enabled to speak in her own voice, as she ordinarily would, to represent Karen's needs. Of interest here are the strategies she uses to animate Karen and to articulate her voice. This is done partly through the reference to Karen as an active agent who can behave intentionally ('Karen and I would love to go on holiday') and partly through the mime with the map. Joan jumps between these animation strategies and speaking in her own role, as Karen's support worker (e.g. answering Alan's question about 'how's it going' with 'not too bad'). What is very remarkable on the video, and hard to transcribe, is that each time Alan approaches Karen she shows some alertness in her facial expression by looking up towards his voice, mouth open (see line 42). Thus, although it is Joan who speaks, Karen herself is starting to take a more active direct part in this drama.

It might seem that this scripting activity is specific to the drama situation. However, on another occasion Karen was with a different personal assistant, Laura, in her own home. The boy in the extract is Laura's young son.

Extract 8.9

54.	Lau	eh↑ you going to tell Val what you did when I painted your toenails↑
55.		*((leans down and looks directly into Karen's face))*
56.		you going to tell Val what you did when I painted your toenails↑
57.	Boy	eeeh, bump *((walks round to Laura and puts his hand on her head))*
58.	Lau	eh↑*((boy climbs on L's back))* oh you showing off as well↑ this is
59.		what he used – sometimes used to do with Karen (.) didn't it↑ didn't he
60.		used to clamber all over you *((to Karen))*

The past shared experience of painting toenails is used by Laura as a way of attributing intentionality to Karen and also a way of 'scripting' Karen's talk ('you going to tell Val': line 56). This is similar in many ways to the talk that goes on between parents and infants, in which the infant is attributed a conversational role way beyond their developmental age (Pine, 1994). It also, however, serves a function in underlining the close and continued relationship between Laura and Karen. Painting her toenails is portrayed more than once as something Karen had enjoyed. Earlier on, Laura had told the video crew that Karen had rolled over and rubbed the nail varnish on the grass:

Laura	And she – I said 'Karen!' and she just burst out laughing she knew exactly what she had done it was so funny

Laura continually peppers her talk with references to past shared experience with Karen and highlights Karen's intentionality. Karen is no longer simply a woman in her twenties with very little movement, no speech and total dependency. She is now a young woman who has something to say through Laura's articulation of her voice.

Preparation talk

Instructions and scripts can also be used as preparation talk. This happens with Ben, the young man who featured at the beginning of this chapter, greeting a passer-by on his way to the youth club. Immediately after that extract (8.1), the following occurs:

Extract 8.10

90.	Col	we'll get you paying your money when you get in
91.	Ben	HAH (.) eh↑
92.	Col	I'll give it to you now look ((*turns and offers Ben some money to hold.*
93.		*Ben takes the money*))
94.		that's – you've got to pay 50p to get in haven't you (0.5)
95.		don't lose it ((*Ben has stayed still, holding money in one hand. Colin turns*
96.		*round, looks at him*))
97.		you've got to give that to Mary haven't you ((*points to money*))
98.		Mary or Olly or whoever's on there (.) or if any of the girls
99.		are there (0.5) don't drop it
100.	Ben	hey hey eeh ((*points to shoes*))
101.	Col	((*goes back to look*)) that's OK it's not undone↓ I did a double
102.		knot↓you keep hold of that quid
103.	Ben	hey

The way in which Colin prepares Ben for a future encounter is exact. First he gives Ben the money to hold and tells him what it's for. He then makes sure he mentions the name of anyone who might be there to receive the money, and he reminds Ben at line 102 'you keep hold of that quid'. There are many pauses in the extract, during which Ben is standing in the road behind Colin. However, Colin frequently turns round, glances at Ben and, on those occasions, Ben shows every sign of communicating with Colin – through his eyes, his alert posture and sometimes with noises (as at line 100). Colin's remarks about the money are delivered in short bursts, timed exactly to match the moments of non-verbal communication between Ben and himself.

   One minute later Ben and Colin are in the youth club, and Colin is standing at the opposite end of the room from Ben. He reminds him 'you've got to pay your dues' and points at Mary. Ben then goes straight over to Mary, who is behind the counter, and gives her the money, without any intervention at all from Colin. Again, as with Henry in the pub, it is possible for Ben to initiate this sequence independently. However, his social and verbal ability are not like Henry's: the fact that Ben is able to manage this encounter is no doubt due to his rehearsal with Colin. In the event, Ben takes his change from Mary and then stands by the counter, watching one of the girls climb up to check a fitting on the ceiling. What is clear here is that the supporter's role in a public three-way encounter can be minimal, but in order to achieve this, it may require careful preparation.

Scripting and ventriloquism as story-telling devices

Talking about shared past events also provides a continuous articulation or narration of a person's life, and this may be important for people who cannot speak for themselves. The following extract is typical of the way in which Colin and Ben interact; in this case, Colin is sitting on a stool opposite Ben, helping Ben put on his trainers. Here is one part of that verbal exchange:

Extract 8.11

7.	Ben	ma maba
8.	Col	no (.) do you want to give her a ring↑
9.		going to give her a ring later are you after you've had a bath↑ (2) and ask her
10.		what she's been doing↑ think
11.		she's been out today (3) in her car (2) you can tell her
12.		we got on the bus (1) and we saw the bus driver that
13.		beeped the horn didn't he↑(2) and the bus driver that
14.		knew you he knew you didn't he

In this extract Colin shows his knowledge of one of the only verbal utterances which Ben uses (maba = mother) and because of Colin's familiarity with the family, he can talk to Ben about the possible events in his mother's life that day. In effect, he does a very 'rich' interpretation of Ben's contribution and uses it as an anchor point for weaving his story. He builds up this conversation on many levels of shared knowledge, including his knowledge of Ben's utterance 'maba' and their recent shared experience on the bus. This incident is related as something which they were both involved in and Colin uses 'we' throughout ('we got on the bus … we saw the bus driver').

Just as Laura 'scripted' Karen's talk, Colin uses the device of the future telephone conversation with Ben's mother as a way to script Ben and to go back over the things they'd been doing that day. It is notable that he allows pauses and **turn allocation points** at the end of each phrase, as if Ben would and could take his turn in the conversation. Neither Ben nor Karen in the previous examples could speak for themselves. However, both are a part of conversations in which their contribution is sometimes spoken *for* them, on their behalf, and even more interestingly, in which they appear to be *prepared* or rehearsed for future conversation.

Implications for practice

This chapter has highlighted an area of communication which is very central to this book. Inclusive communication for people with intellectual disabilities is not just about talking with support workers. It is about going out and meeting people, and being part of the community.

First, it should be acknowledged that the episodes in this chapter were all relatively 'benign', and of course all parties were aware of the camera. Therefore, it was not likely that we would observe any hostility or name-calling. These public acts are increasingly known as 'hate crime' (Perry, 2004) and it is a vital task for a support worker to counter and challenge them. However, even a simple greeting in the street from a passer-by involved some intervention from the support worker, although it was also apparent how important and effective it was for the supporter to step back in order for a direct two-way interaction to take place between a person with intellectual disabilities and the third party. This happened with Ben, when his supporter happened to be carrying out a practical joke and hiding behind the corner as he walked along the street. This gave Ben the seemingly rare opportunity to interact with someone in his own right, without any intervention by anyone else around him. By contrast, Alice's greeting from a passer-by resulted in an interaction that was judged to be slightly inadequate by her support worker, who expanded on Alice's contribution. This may have done some face-saving work with the passer-by concerned, but it did nothing for Alice's autonomy as a speaker in her own right. Sometimes, it is a matter of getting the balance right and weighing up whether it is more important to speak for someone or to let them manage their own affairs, even when this may result in a very short encounter.

In Henry's case (extract 8.3), exchanging a leisure card proved to be a complicated activity and one about which his support worker had to do some explanation and scene-setting. However, as the support worker took over the initial explanation, this seemed to have catastrophic effects on the ensuing interaction. Instead of Henry and the leisure centre official communicating directly, the support worker, Pippa, became the main party in the exchange. Henry was totally sidelined. Nevertheless, some 10 minutes later, Henry appeared to be much more in control and in fact initiated an interaction with a barmaid at the local pub. Well-rehearsed sequences were obviously within his repertoire and he was able to manage a pub interaction without any intervention from Pippa. Clearly, the type of talk needed is closely linked to the location and context. In a British pub, there are some very precise, though unwritten, rules of conduct. Henry had some years of experience in pubs and was able to carry out his role in the interaction fluently, while the leisure centre transaction was slightly more complicated and perhaps also less familiar to him.

What is of interest here, though, is not just Henry's cognitive and experiential skills in community situations. Given that some people with intellectual disabilities, like Henry, will be inexperienced and tongue-tied in certain situations, what can support workers do to ensure that people do have a voice? Pippa's support talk was clearly not successful in redirecting the leisure centre man towards Henry. What could Pippa have done in this situation? Sometimes simply holding back, waiting for Henry to speak first or redirecting her eye gaze to Henry would have had the desired effect. By contrast, Teresa does some of these things when supporting Michael to check into the hotel. For instance, although she responds in her own right to some of the enquiries from the hotel receptionist, there are key moments at which she redirects the talk to Michael, simply by looking at him, by including his interests in the talk and by ensuring that he says what *he* wants and that he speaks in his own right to the receptionist.

Both Teresa and Pippa are there, to some extent, as go-betweens. There are often things which are said in these public encounters that the PA feels she or he has to 'translate' for the person with intellectual disabilities. Instead of Henry, for instance, communicating directly about the future use of his leisure card with the man behind the counter, Pippa hands his card to him and virtually repeats what the man has said. Similarly, Teresa picks up questions posed by the receptionist, for instance on the topic of newspapers, and redirects them to Michael by articulating in different ways what the receptionist has said. It is at times almost as if a person with intellectual disabilities is a foreign-language speaker accompanied by a translator, someone who will interpret the outside world and its strange meanings for them.

So much depends on the way in which that support is done, and indeed the attention given both to preparation and to rehearsal. In the end, if a person with intellectual disabilities is going to manage a particular public situation unaided, then learning has got to occur. The tactics of giving support, prompting, even speaking for someone – and then stepping back – are typical teaching or mentoring strategies. In educational jargon they are referred to as 'scaffolding', a concept based on the Vygotskian model that, 'what the child is able to do in collaboration today he will be able to do independently tomorrow' (Vygotsky, 1987: 211). The support worker's role frequently has educational and developmental overtones.

The last few extracts in this chapter were taken from videos of people who do not use words to communicate. Even more than with other participants, these people needed considerable support to meet and respond to third parties. Not only did the support workers in question speak for the individual, but they often spoke *as if* they actually were the person with intellectual disabilities. When Joan was on stage with Karen, it was almost like a masked performance or puppetry. She literally enabled Karen to interact with others, moving her into the right position, engaging with her by touch, moving her arms, and so on. All this appeared to be effective. Karen was normally quite unresponsive and passive, but eventually she reacted, smiled, made noises and started to interact with those around her. What does this ventriloquism imply? In child-directed speech, parents or caregivers may do something very similar when interacting with an infant. For instance, they may talk at length about things the infant cannot understand, they may attribute intentionality to the infant and base their conversation on an assumption that the infant has actually said something (Pine, 1994). Beth's talk with Karen at home was very much in this mode. She switched between recounting events from their shared past and talking about these events *as if* Karen herself were remembering and recounting them.

At one level, all these devices could be seen as ways to keep the talk going and to fill the gaps. They are ways of ensuring that people have a narrative of their own past and preparation for their future social life. When Ben's support worker talks him through a telephone conversation with his mother, not only is he preparing him for what he should 'say' to his mother, but he is also using this occasion as a way of recounting and going over the events they both experienced on the bus. Ben is literally surrounded by the narrative structure his support worker creates; through this conversation, he becomes a narrator in his own right, someone who can tell a tale – albeit with considerable support. Note that the tale is entirely Ben's; the support worker does not start recounting something from his own life of which Ben would have no memory or part. This is something which is about Ben's own life, a story which is 'tellable' and which both he and the support worker can recount – now for the camera, but perhaps later also for Ben's mother.

To speak up with a third party, particularly with someone who may not be so familiar, people with intellectual disabilities often have considerable support. Some of this is *in situ*, with the support worker by their side enabling them to understand, to play their role and to respond. However, at other times the support worker's role is to ensure that the person they are supporting has good preparation. By giving Ben that coin and setting him off towards the youth club door with a mission to pay his fees, the support worker was enabled literally to take a back seat – to step back so that Ben could manage the transaction with minimal assistance. This was a simple transaction and one that did not have too many possible loopholes where it could go wrong. However, other transactions too may have been possible for other people with intellectual disabilities in this chapter, with a little forward thinking.

The current chapter has showcased some very ordinary, everyday encounters – many in public places – and all involving 'third parties', people who are not there directly to support that particular person with intellectual disabilities. We have seen how the intervention of the support worker can be essential to the successful completion of these transactions. What does this say about the autonomy of the person with intellectual disabilities? Can one say that Henry, Michael or Ben are actually managing their own life, engaging directly with their own communities in their own right? All of us, of course, at various points in our life, have been in situations where others have spoken for us. We may be trying to purchase something, for instance, which the person with us has more experience of (perhaps a computer, a tool or even some clothes). We may also choose not to be the person who 'speaks up': in an encounter with a passer-by, we may sometimes stand back and let a partner or a friend speak instead. The social position of people with intellectual disabilities is therefore not entirely of a different nature from the ordinary position of any two people who go out together and meet other people. The same kind of strategies are used by support workers as are used by all of us in everyday life – translation of information, attempts to bring someone back into the conversation and even preparation talk are things we all do at times. Ventriloquism and scripting are perhaps more associated with talk to very young children, but they are not unheard of as social practices. What is clear from our data, however, is that these situations are simply more frequent for people with intellectual disabilities, many of whom seldom go out of their house on their own.

It is important to bear in mind the backcloth of these patterns and repertoires, which dominate the lives of people with intellectual disabilities. Seldom without someone at their side to speak with them and for them, they are very used to having some kind of support in ordinary activities, particularly when the activity becomes slightly challenging. This experience will no doubt shape the strategies they may have available in more formal encounters and in events where they are expected to 'speak up' or to participate meaningfully.

How conversation works: summary points

- Turn allocation points (also known as transition relevance places or TRPs: see p. 40) are the points when one person's talk has come to a natural end (see Wooffitt, 2005: 26–30) and this is often marked by a pause, by downward intonation or by eye gaze. Noticing these points can be useful when looking at how people talk 'for' a person who does not use words.

- Eye gaze, body posture and orientation will show who a person is addressing. The analyst can also see who is being addressed by noticing who talks next (Kendon, 1990).

- It is sometimes necessary to look at the whole structural map of a conversation in order to understand the work done by particular features. For instance, repair work, laughter or repeating can all be devices for filling gaps, enabling someone else to manage a social situation (see Roberts & Sarangi, 2005, for interactional mapping).

Inclusive approaches to communication: summary points

- Stepping back is extremely important in three-way encounters. But it is not the only thing that has been noticed in this chapter. Sometimes, the support worker can only step back and let the person with intellectual disabilities manage the situation when there has been good preparation beforehand.
- A support worker can give good support by being natural and having a voice at times. This is very useful when someone with intellectual disabilities may need more time to do something or may need some hints about how to manage a social encounter.
- People who do not use words to communicate can also have support to 'speak up'. In some instances the support worker actually acts as their voice, just like a ventriloquist.

Part 2

Collective Voice

Preface to Part 2 by Members of 'The Voice'[1]

I think I've got a strong voice. (Lisa Ponting)

But when you don't have a voice, it's like being trapped, you've got nowhere to go. It helps to get people's support. I think it helps if you're currently with a group of disabled people, in doing the same thing that you are. I think it worked with me, being in People First, and actually doing some work with them and coming out to join in research. It helped me tremendously. We need to get people to understand us and often it's one to one. Maybe sometimes we need an advocate. It's about trust and instincts. Having friends is important. There are friends I do trust. When we're all together, we share things, without other people listening.

In Chapters 9 and 10, you will see what it's like inside a People First group. That's where we have our power, and we run things ourselves.

Most of the other chapters (11–13) are about research projects. We (Kerrie Ford and Lisa Ponting) were researchers and we made a pack after our 'Skills for Support' project. It was for people with intellectual disabilities to train their own support workers. People may say that we don't have power, because we need support to do research. But people who have support can have power. They just need support to exercise that power in the right way. People should have support when they need it, and it's up to them if they want support and how they want it. It's important that the support doesn't tell you what to say and how to do the research. We all need support in some ways, everyone does. When we come to Norah Fry Research Centre, we are colleagues and friends. Everyone, whether or not they have a learning difficulty or an intellectual disability, needs support.

---

[1] Like the other prefaces by The Voice members, these comments were written and recorded after reading through a summary of Part 2 of the book.

What we do in our projects is real research for us. We get paid for it, and that's a bonus. Norah Fry gives me an opportunity to do research. It puts the point across about what we're trying to say. If we turn the tables round, then other people can have a go and tell us if it's hard. For us, just the fact that we're out here doing it makes it research. If people are given the opportunity, then they could come and learn from us. If the research is about our lives, then we are the experts. We should have the ideas about what needs to be done.

It's a good idea to tell people about us doing research. When you're doing research, people think 'What is it?' They need to be clear about what research is, and there needs to be a bit more work about what research is and what it means to people. We have done research that is made easy for us, but other people may find it difficult. Research could be reading a book or writing stories. We can show people that this is what we mean when we say we're doing research.

The thing about what we did in research is that we did it together. We had a good laugh. Now we do teaching as well. All these things are good ways of mixing with other people and meeting friends. It's different when you're in work; when you go home it's a different story, and that leaves a gap between it. My mind is saying 'research' but I say 'no', I need to relax. It's easy to get like a workaholic.

We hope you enjoy reading about our strong voices.

Chapter 9

Self-Advocacy Talk

The personal to the political

Moving from individual to collective voice

The data and analysis presented so far in this book have been drawn from everyday encounters that involve individual people with the label 'learning disability'. By contrast, the following chapters focus on more formal situations, in which people with learning disabilities participate and have a voice, as well as exercise some sense of collective ownership. These are activities such as meetings, research sessions or interviews, which are premised on the voice of people with learning disabilities *as representatives* of others and which only take shape as people participate and speak up. In other words, it is the voices of people with learning disabilities that construct and define these social activities.

However, in case the contrast between collective and individual voice should raise false expectations, this preamble should also point out the vagueness, overlaps and blurred edges of all the talk featured in this book. When people speak up in everyday life contexts, the functions they fulfil and the verbal and non-verbal practices in which they engage are very general ones. For instance, in Chapter 5 when Alice met an acquaintance with a two-part greeting exchange, this could happen in any context. In Chapter 8, when Pippa went to sit down in the pub and left Henry to order their drinks, she could be doing a similar thing when supporting Henry in a conference. There are therefore many overlaps between the practices already highlighted and those to be seen in the following few chapters. However, the reason for taking a specific look at these more formal, collective situations is threefold:

1. Social activities such as self-advocacy discussions, consultations and research are premised on the ownership and voice of people with learning disabilities. It is vital that they are constructed around this ownership, since otherwise many would argue that they become tokenistic and insincere.
2. As will be seen, there are many tensions between the kind of talk in formal, collective situations and that which occurs in private, everyday life situations for people with learning disabilities. However, there is a direct sense in which people with intellectual disabilities bring their individual, private experiences into the pubic arena of self-advocacy.
3. By analysing occasions which are successful in giving people with learning disabilities ownership and autonomy, there may be lessons to be learnt for interactional practices more generally.

Disability and Discourse. Analysing Inclusive Conversation with People with Intellectual Disabilities, 1st edition. © Val Williams. Published 2011 by John Wiley & Sons, Ltd.

Emergence of the term 'self-advocacy'

This chapter has the title 'self-advocacy talk', and so a brief explanation is in order for those who may be new to the field. In the early 1990s, the concept of an organisation run by people with intellectual disabilities spread from the USA to the UK. People came together in objecting to the labels they were given, and so they called their own organisation 'People First', emphasising their right to be considered primarily as individual human beings. The title 'People First' is now often used across the globe (e.g. in Germany and in Japan), but the generic title given by those outside the groups is often 'self-advocacy groups', marking their purpose as one that is intimately connected with having a voice. This is the opening statement on the English national People First website:

> People First is an organization run by and for people with learning difficulties to raise awareness
> of and campaign for the rights of people with learning difficulties and to support self advocacy
> groups across the country. (People First, 2009)

Self-advocacy groups are brought together precisely for people with intellectual disabilities to become stronger, to support each other and to speak up (Sutcliffe & Simons, 1994; Goodley, 2000). These organisations have members with the label 'intellectual disability' and they often obtain support from people who are paid members of staff. Day centres and other 'service' settings may also have their own self-advocacy group.

One of the founder members of People First in the UK was Gary Bourlet, who provided the inspiration and leadership for a movement called 'Europe People First' in 1995–6. It was through that movement that I became involved, as a voluntary supporter to Gary, and started a European interest group in the college where I worked at the time: it was members of that European group who set out to form their own research group in 1997 and carried out the project referred to in this book as the 'Finding Out' project. It can be appreciated therefore that this project had a direct historical link with the self-advocacy movement and was deeply embedded in ideas about self-advocacy. Moreover, their project involved the research group members in talking with people who were members of other self-advocacy groups. The extracts in this chapter all come from research group visits (essentially focus group discussions) with various self-advocacy groups in the south-west of England during 'Finding Out'.

Having given that brief historical overview, my approach to self-advocacy in this book is to stand back from any assumptions which could emerge from the public statements or history of the movement. Instead, I am interested in how 'self-advocacy' is done, in the same way as Chapter 7 explored how autonomy was done, and Chapter 6 'friendliness'. However, the social activities explored in those chapters included everyday, chance events such as social chats or going shopping. The current chapter focuses on the social activity of formal meetings, in which many people are involved and in which turn-taking strategies and chairing rights are at stake. Meeting talk, or indeed self-advocacy talk, could be considered as a hybrid **genre** (Bakhtin, 1986): as Fairclough (2001) explains, a genre in Bakhtin's sense is a type of 'text' (or talk) available in a culture, such as an interview, a formal speech, but also a casual conversation.

> [Bakthin] claimed that while any text is necessarily shaped by the socially available repertoire
> of genres, it may also creatively mix genres. (Fairclough, 2001: 233)

The goal of this chapter is to follow people with intellectual disabilities into their own self-advocacy forums, where people are speaking up for themselves and conducting their own business. This is arguably a 'collective' setting, drawing on genres of meetings and of minority campaign groups, where people speak up in order to represent others and to express a view on behalf of a wider constituency of people with intellectual disabilities. I was particularly interested to analyse *how* that was achieved, but the analysis here goes beyond the technical construction of turns and counter-turns typical of CA. This is not just about how people manage a meeting; it is also about how talk can be designed to move from the 'personal' goals of individuals to the collective goals of a movement.

Darren: Moving between the personal and the political

The data in this chapter are taken from the 'Finding Out' project, in which group discussions were held between the central 'research group' and the various groups they visited. The focus here is not on the construction of research, however. That will be dealt with in greater detail in Chapters 11–13. For now, the point of interest is how people can use group discussions to move between personal and political positions. Extract 9.1 occurs some 45 minutes into the first visit, which involved a day centre self-advocacy group. There are 10 people with intellectual disabilities sitting round a table, with one member of staff, June. I am also in the room, operating recording equipment and occasionally assisting when asked to do so. The main speaker in extract 9.1 is Darren, whose speech is slow and difficult for newcomers to understand at times. That explains the repair and checking turns, which are in the main initiated by me. The question which had preceded this chunk of the discussion was 'What services or transport do you go on?' and the extract given here occurs immediately after some talk about the needs of wheelchair users for a minibus with a tail lift.

Extract 9.1

44.	Dar	I like to say that we should be able -ab – not we – I or people like
45.		me↑ (.) that are in wheelchairs↑(0.5) should be able to go out
46.		anywhere ((*gaze directly to camera*))
47.	Mar	yes
48.	Dar	if we got a life (0.5) no↑(1)
49.	Mar	I see your point there (0.5)
50.	Dar	but can you tell me why not↑
51.	Mar	uuhh (.)
52.	Dar	no you can't↓
53.	Ang	> hard question that to answer isn't it that one <
54.	Ian	yeah
55.	Dar	aahhh ((*scowls*)) (2)

The first thing to notice is that Darren appears to be the focus of attention because of his self-identification as a wheelchair user; he is taking the floor on behalf of others, 'people like me↑ (.) that are in wheelchairs', and he moves between 'I' and 'we', speaking as a representative. In effect, he is using his ordinary, everyday experience as a wheelchair user in order to make some political points here. Since wheelchair users had already been under discussion, the relevance of his identity as sole wheelchair user present was important. It could be that members expected him to have something to say on this subject, and this is why the slot for first turn is left open for him, with everyone looking towards him. His first turn is delivered directly to camera. He is addressing everyone and commands everyone's attention. There are no sub-conversations here, no overlaps nor interruptions.

What I explore first is how membership categorisation (Sacks, 1995; see Chapter 6, p. 87) is used here. People often speak in certain roles, for instance, as a researcher, as an MP or as a day centre user. When they do this, they automatically put others who are talking with them into roles that are complementary. Two roles go together: customer and shop assistant; doctor and patient. In extract 9.1 Darren starts to manipulate membership categories, and, I shall argue, thereby pulls the talk into a more political arena.

Following his opening gambit that people 'like me' should be able to go out, Mark does a conventional third-part feedback, providing confirmation with 'yes' and again with 'you've got a point there'. Darren then delivers a rhetorical question to the whole group at line 50: 'can you tell me why not↑' This is the type of challenge someone may throw at an official who has the power to change the built environment. One could imagine it being said to a planning department official or a local councillor. Since none of these people is in fact present, what ensues is a definite sense of trouble in the replies. Mark hesitates at line 51 and Angela voices the trouble with: 'hard question that to answer isn't it that one' (line 53). Mark and his colleagues clearly hear the question as challenging or perhaps unexpected. At this point, Darren is not including the other members in the same category as himself (people with a common cause), but is posing the arguments on behalf of the category to which he has assigned himself ('people like me that are in a wheelchair'). It is this act of splitting into two camps – wheelchair users and non-wheelchair users – that provides the real challenge, and it is one that Darren orchestrates in expert fashion.

Darren's first turn is a statement of a general right ('should be able to go out anywhere'), while his second turn at line 48 ('if we got a life (0.5) no↑') carries the implication that this freedom of movement is essential to having a life. This is an example of an extreme case formulation (Pomerantz, 1986; see Chapter 4, p. 57). In Chapter 4, this device was used as a way of upgrading the importance of Ellie's budgeting plan. However, here it is used by Darren in a quite different way to defend an argument by extreme claims. The 'if' raises the strong possibility that wheelchair users do *not* have a life, which is confirmed in his third turn: 'But can you tell me why not↑' (line 50). This three-part argumentative structure sounds very rhetorical, a strong way to emphasise the unfairness of his situation. Readers interested in argumentation and persuasion could look at Antaki (1994: 133). The implication is that there is no logical reason for Darren not having freedom of movement and therefore not having a life. Therefore, the fact that he does not have these rights must be due to other factors, other barriers. Together with his delivery to camera, these rhetorical strategies help Darren take a dominant position in these opening lines. Not only is he simply moving from his individual situation into a collective statement, but he is playing with the structure of the meeting and the argumentation it affords to achieve maximum effect.

Elaborating an argument

This is how extract 9.1 continues.

Extract 9.2

56.	Will	Darren Darren have you tried to write to your MP about it↑
57.	Dar	if I try and write to my MP (.) my mother does it (1) I don't
58.		bother (0.5) my mother does it (.) all
59.	Val	you don't bother your –↑
60.	Ian	MP
61.	Jun	his mother
62.	Val	your mum and dad would [do it↑
63.	Dar	[yeah yeah they look after me so I don't
64.		mind(1)

65.	Ang	that's worth doing isn't it↑ (1)
66.	Dar	worth doing↑
67.	Ang	yes it is worth doing if you keep on – if you keep on then
68.		they might do something about it for you
69.	Ian	yeah
70.	Dar	why – thank you (0.5) how do you mean though↑
71.	Ang	why don't you write to the – why don't you write to the prime
72.		minister and ask him for some help and advice and see if you
73.		can get some money for doing it right↑
74.	Dar	but if I write to the prime minister (.) =
75.	Ang	> you might get something out of it <
76.	Dar	= I'm just going to get my (0.5) letter I send to him (.) it's going to be
77.		ripped up and thrown away ( )
78.	Val	you think your letter would be ripped up and thrown away↑
79.	Ang	don't think [so
80.	Dar	[yeah
81.	Mar	not if you explain what you want
82.	Dar	but I cannot explain what I want↓ if I did (1) everything I (.)wanted
83.		like (1) can't have – any (evenings (.) colour ( ) a:::h (1) sorry (3)
84.		yeah I'm sorry ↓ a:::::hh ((June holds Darren's hand))
85.	Val	it's upsetting isn't it not being able to get out↑
86.	Dar	oh it is but you don't know do you – it's a pain in the butt
87.	Val	pain in the↑
88.	Joh	butt ((LF))

Although this is a longish sequence, with several different speakers, it is made up of the same types of two-part sequences familiar from other extracts in Part 1. Looking at the structure of this extract, there appear to be 10 sequences. A sequence is defined here as ending in a turn which could have closed down the conversation. However, many are longer than simple two-part sequences, with a third part (a 'good' or 'OK' or some response token or evaluation), and others consist of two follow-on sequences, so in fact four turns. Trying to account for the structure is sometimes a good way to start analysing an extract. It is also interesting to check through and see who is initiating each sequence and who is responding. In Table 9.1 the sequences are set out showing who delivered each 'part' of the sequence.

As Table 9.1 demonstrates, Darren only initiates four of the 11 sequences. At any end-of-sequence point, the whole extract and topic could have been terminated, yet he manages to keep

Table 9.1 Sequence structure of extracts 9.1 and 9.2 (showing first, second and third parts as 1,2,3)

44–9	Darren (1)	Mark (2)	Darren (1)	Mark (2)
50–2	Darren (1)	Mark (2)	Darren (3)	
53–5	Angela (1)	Ian (2)	Darren (3)	
56–8	William (1)	Darren (2)		
59–63	Val (1)	Ian (2a)	June (2b)	Val (1)	Darren (2)
65–70	Angela (1)	Darren (2)	Angela (1)	Ian (3)	Darren (2) →
70–3	→Darren (1)	Angela (2)		
74–4	Darren (1)	Angela (2)		
76–80	Darren (1)	Val (1)	Angela (2)	Darren (2)
81–4	Mark (1)	Darren (2)		
85–8	Val (1)	Darren (2)	Val (1)	John (2)

it going. How does he do this? For instance, at line 70, he responds to Angela with 'why – thank you', which could have been a final comment to round things off. However, he then keeps the argument going with another initiation 'how do you mean though↑'. At other points, he seems happy to allow others to initiate, and his responses can be heard not only as answers to their questions, but also as challenges to the force of what they are saying.

The formal structure of the meeting talk allows him to develop further his argumentation. At lines 76–7, he talks about what would happen to any letter he may write. It will be 'ripped up and thrown away', an exaggerated way of saying that there is no point in writing. When William, for instance, advises him in the fourth sequence to write to his MP, he responds that: 'if I try and write to my MP (.) my mother does it (1) I don't bother'. Each response he makes is a counter-argument to a suggestion of another member and this is what keeps the sequences flowing, since he provides slots for other members to come back with a fresh initiation. There seem to be some quite subtle judgements here on his part. As Darren keeps emphasising the colossal problem he faces, this also appears to keep the talk going, since no response entirely satisfies Darren's challenges and he moves to his final position at line 86: 'it's a pain in the butt'.

Exploring action together

So far, I have looked at Darren's speech as an example of strong, but individual, rhetoric. It has been observed how he uses the structure of the discussion to dominate and to place himself as the person who represents other wheelchair users. However, Darren is actually in a group situation, with other people present who arguably identify with him as people with intellectual disabilities. One therefore needs to look closely at what these other members do during Darren's speech. Extract 9.2 is full of joint work, and at line 56 it is William who introduces the solution of writing to an MP. This is an interesting suggestion, since it very concretely brings together personal action with political force. Following William's suggestion, Darren puts forward a whole string of reasons for not writing to his MP:

I try and write (line 57)
my mother does it (lines 57–8) – (twice)
I don't bother (lines 57–8)
they look after me (line 63)
I don't mind (lines 63–4)
if I write to the prime minister … I'm just going to get my letter I send to him it's going to be
    ripped up and thrown away (lines 74–7)
I cannot explain what I want (line 82)

All the phrases in which he places himself as subject are negative disclaimers ('I don't mind'; 'I don't bother') or are events in which he tries, but does not succeed, to do something. By contrast, he frames his mother and 'they' (who might include his father) as active and competent social actors, who 'do it all', even 'look after me'. Darren almost wallows in working up his identity as a cared-for person. The person who rips up and throws away his letter in lines 76–7 could be the prime minister, although the clause in which the ripping up occurs is in the passive format and so has no subject. Darren has very quickly stepped down from the strength of his previous rhetoric, and he now puts himself over as a passive, pathetic victim, dominated by his mother.

Angela and Mark, by contrast, use the following forms in their attempts to counter Darren's defeatism:

that's worth doing isn't it↑ (line 65)
it is worth doing (line 67)
if you keep on (line 67)
they might do something about it for you (line 68)
you write to the prime minister (line 71)
ask … and see if you can get some money for doing it right↑(line 72)
you might get something out of it (line 75)
explain what you want (line 81)

Their advice to Darren places him consistently in the role of active agent – someone who could achieve something by his actions. This portion of the discussion really seems to represent advocacy-in-action, with one or more self-advocates advising an individual about the best way of dealing with his (collective) problem. Solutions are being found from within the group, from the resources of the members themselves, and they are in effect engaging in verbal practices to *advocate for each other*. The work that Darren does in countering each suggestion has the effect of prolonging this flow of advocacy-in-action.

The sequence ends with Darren's 'a:::h' and 'sorry', his hesitation indicating how upset he is by the situation he is describing. He is comforted by June, who holds his hand. Like any social action, doing emotion can be analysed to see what effect it has on the interaction; the point is not to question the authenticity of the feeling, but simply to direct attention to its interactional consequences (Edwards, 2001). Darren's emotional hesitation, and the positioning of it within this extract, is interesting. It has the effect of terminating the flow of suggestions about what he could do, while it contrasts with his remark at line 86 ('pain in the butt'), which changes the mood yet again, with a smile and a choice of unexpected down-to-earth vocabulary. Darren immediately appears as a comedian, rising above his current plight. What is so interesting about this extract is the way in which several personal identities are created, all of which might lead to different forms of action. The identity of cared-for son leads to the action his parents might take in writing a letter for him. The identity of strong self-advocate leads to the action of the prime minister receiving his letter, but then tearing it up, while the identity of wheelchair user leads to the emotive suffering of inaction. Darren and the others are to some extent playing with the concept of taking action and exploring together what the possible consequences of certain actions might be.

Brian: A strong speaker

Having seen how members of self-advocacy groups can work jointly to help one person move towards political solutions, I turn now to an extract that has an equal claim to be considered self-advocacy talk, although it is largely an individual achievement. This extract was picked out by research group members (Mark, Angela, Ian and Harry) themselves as an example of 'strong speaking' and it occurred during the third visit undertaken by the research group. The meeting was held in the cafeteria section of a sports and leisure centre, and there were some 20–30 people present. Speaking up in this context was therefore quite an achievement.

Extract 9.3

57.	Bri	well (.) hh I think it's very very bad when-when you – when you
58.		label people you know and I don't like the term er mental
59.		handicap↓ [I prefer the term]
60.	Mar	[no::]
61.	Bri	learning difficulty my-myself [myself] only I

62.		don't like
63.	Har	[I quite agree]
64.	Bri	the term mental handicap cos I was – I was labelled myself some
65.		years ago until my mother spoke up for me↓ as a mentally defective
66.		but [we're not a]
67.	Ang	[what's that]↑
68.	Bri	mentally defective just because we're disabled you see
69.		disabled too↓ and as I say (.) disability is not inability you see
70.		[just
71.	Har	[( )]
72.	Bri	because we're disabled we're not <u>imbeciles</u> [you
73.	Mar	[no::
74.	Bri	see as some people so I think labels↓(.) labels can be pretty
75.		awful you know
76.	Mar	° no °
77.	Bri	very very awful this is why we phased out- phased out the
78.		spastics society where I work and called it scope↑ because it
79.		doesn't er put so much of a stigma on it [you see and where I
80.		work it's now called scope and it]
81.	Mar	[° stigma↑ that's what we talked
		about last week °] ((to Val))
82.	Bri	doesn't put so much of a stigma on it and we said that er er the
83.		spastics society had NOW been faded er faded into oblivion
84.		you know
85.	Mar	[yeah]
86.	Bri	[the spastics society] is no more so it's now scope because
87.		we found that (.) word s-spastics society put too much of a
88.		stigma on- on it you know↓ it had a stigma with it you know (0.5)
89.		unfortunately↑

Keeping the floor

The interview question which originally gave rise to Brian's speech in the extract above was a seemingly straightforward (but in fact rather complex) question about labelling. It will be explored in much more depth in Chapter 13, but for now, it is enough to know that the question was:

What do you think about people being labelled?

Several people have already spoken at the point when Brian takes the floor, and there has been some confusion and false starts from other members about what would constitute a good answer to the question. When Brian gets the floor at line 57 with a 'well' and a throat-clearing noise, this can be heard as an assertion of his right to clear up the confusion and give a definitive response. The first thing to note is thus his assertive strategy for gaining the floor in the first place.

Turning to the turn structure, it is noticeable that Brian has one long, overarching turn throughout this extract. When I first listened to the recording, it appeared as if Brian was the sole speaker, but on closer examination many intervening or overlapping remarks could be made out (lines 67, 71, 81). Brian is not simply performing a monologue: his audience is very active and supportive. How does he manage both to hold on to his turn and develop his own meanings, but also to keep his audience with him?

There are many other speakers who do short overlaps or interruptions. For instance, Angela's interjection 'what's that↑' (67) is seemingly ignored or simply not heard. Other interjections are broadly supportive of Brian's turn ('I quite agree' (line 63)), and so can be heard as encouragement for him to continue. However, there are many potential transition relevance places (see p. 40), where Brian appears to have reached the conclusion of what he is saying (for instance, at the end of line 69, and again at 75: 'labels can be pretty awful you know'). How, then, does Brian succeed in keeping his own speaking rights and not letting others take over? As Goodwin (1984) pointed out in relation to story-telling in family settings, there are patterns of non-verbal activity which support a speaker's extended turn in telling a story. The most obvious strategy Brian employs is the way he uses speed of delivery. The end of phrases, or units such as 'mental handicap' (lines 59 and 64) and 'disabled too' (line 69) are nearly all marked by a rapid move to the next phrase, without any pause whatsoever. This strategy removes the possibility that these will be heard as turn allocation points. By contrast, when he is in mid-phrase ('when-when you – when you' (line 57); 'I think labels↓(.) labels' (line 74)) he often repeats a word, or does slight hesitations, which slow down his speech slightly and have the effect of emphasising what he is saying. By contrast, if he hesitated at the end of the phrase, this would run the risk of another speaker getting in.

There are other possible devices for keeping the floor, and Brian also makes use of gaze direction, which can be seen in Figure 9.1. If a speaker turns their gaze away from the listeners at the completion points, or transition relevance places, then it is hard for someone else to come in. This strategy is used by different speakers on other occasions. Harry, for instance, often used gaze direction very effectively. He would glance round at his audience and engage individuals in short bursts of eye contact. All these are devices which enable a member to be in a position to deliver a long speech. They are prerequisites for public speaking, but they could not of themselves *constitute* strong self-advocacy talk. For this, it is important to examine more closely the identity work which threads through extract 9.3.

Moving from 'I' to 'we'

Brian introduces his speech by briefly, but strongly, stating his own opinion, both in general terms – 'I think it's very very bad when-when you – when you LABEL people' (line 57) – and

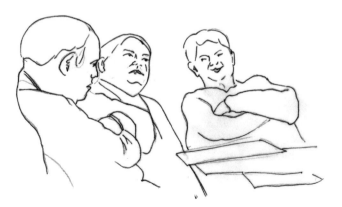

Figure 9.1   Keeping the floor by gazing upwards.

then in specific terms – 'and I don't like the term er mental handicap' (lines 58–9). This is very similar to what Darren did in extract 9.2 with 'I would like to say ... that we ... should be able to go out anywhere'. This type of opener is what Schegloff calls a pre-announcement (see p. 100, and Schegloff, 2007: 37–44), in which the speaker sets up his or her own stance towards the matter in question. It has the effect of setting up the frame for what he wants to say next – the listeners hear it in that context.

Brian then contrasts the label he is rejecting with the one he prefers, 'learning difficulty'. This gives a tight, logical structure to what he is putting over. He subsequently repeats the phrase verbatim: 'I don't like ... the term mental handicap' (lines 62–4), giving it strength and emphasis. This opening section is all framed as personal opinion, with the 'I' pronoun, and verbal forms such as: 'I think' (line 57), 'I don't like' (line 58) and 'I prefer' (line 59).

Following this strong opening, Brian then turns briefly to personal experience, which he uses very clearly as an example, a justification of his opinion relating to labels.

> I was labelled myself some
> years ago until my mother spoke up for me↓ as a mentally defective (lines 64–5)

At line 69, he moves from the personal to the general by quoting what sounds like a campaign slogan: *Disability is not inability*. He introduces it as his own insight, however, and there is no reason to believe that any of the other members would know it as a slogan. In fact, Brian takes care to personalise the slogan with the phrases 'as I say ... you see'. These could be heard as devices to draw the audience over to his point of view, and to put himself over as a good explainer. The final phase of his speech (from line 74 onwards) brings together the personal and the political, since Brian portrays himself as taking on a key role (along with others – 'we') in changing the very name of the Spastics Society to SCOPE.

The different phases of Brian's speech, moving from personal opinion, then personal experience, to general adage and then political action, are marked by his use of personal pronouns (the 'I' of the personal passages is replaced by 'we' when he reaches the stage of generalities). His final use of 'we' in connection with SCOPE links up with the earlier 'we': 'we're not a mentally defective just because we're disabled' (lines 66–8). In that first 'we' he had included himself in a group who could be called 'disabled', and it is this same group of people, including himself, who changed the name of the Spastics Society to SCOPE. Thus labelled people can be active agents, who can change things.

In addition to his use of pronouns, it is interesting to note Brian's portrayal of his own agency. He says, for instance, 'I think', 'I don't like', 'I prefer', 'we're not disabled', 'we said', 'we found'. Unlike Darren in extract 9.1, Brian consistently positions himself as a responsible *agent* rather than a passive recipient of others' actions. The only subject in which he is not included is 'my mother', who has a very brief role during a subordinate clause. In particular, he is clear about expressing his own opinion and referring to what he (and others) actually did: 'we phased out – where I work'.

Interestingly, he also uses verbs referring to verbal practices (talking and thinking) such as 'we said', 'we found'. The only absent subject is in the phrase: 'I was labelled myself'. The person or people who did the labelling are not present and are not specified. By their very absence they appear to pale into insignificance, by contrast with the firm action of Brian and those with whom he identifies. Through these precise strategies, Brian gives a view of himself as part of a political process, as actively able to change the view that society has of him. It is a masterful piece of rhetoric, and the audience responds very positively to him.

Doing social commentary

The following extract follows on immediately from the previous extract, and is included here just to illustrate a slightly different way of approaching the task of collective talk.

Extract 9.4

90.	Ang	excuse me what's that↑ I don't know what [stigma means↓
91.	Har	[disabled people
92.		(.) I THINK (.) is-is usually based (0.5) I think (.) the disabled people
93.		are the same people as are being labelled↑
94.		((Looks round → Angela, then back to whole group))
95.	?	yes
96.	Har	what I think what I think about this I think it is-I think it is wrong (.)
97.		anyone ANYONE in this group here could be dis- disabled (0.5)
98.		anyone
99.	?	mm
100.	Har	they come from- it's usually back there in Bristol where I live
101.		you know (0.5) I think to myself I think Bristol's a very big city and I
102.		think (.) there is people who label are usually- are usually in
103.		Bristol (.) an – and I said there again I think people who label people
104.		(.) there is nothing to la- laugh about because they have (0.5) – they
105.		are the same people as learning difficulty or people who are
106.		disabled (.) to me it is all the same↓ (1)

((throughout this speech, Harry has addressed the whole group, glancing round the group from time to time. Looks round towards camera and Angela, eyebrows slightly raised))

Angela has picked up on the word 'stigma' from Brian's long turn, and Harry then responds to her question. However, he does much more than a one-to-one response to Angela. In effect, he uses the opportunity to address the whole group, just as Brian did. Brian left unsaid the issue of who does the labelling, but Harry picks up this point and locates those who do the labelling as inhabitants of Bristol: 'there is people who label are usually- are usually in Bristol' (lines 102–3). Since Harry has drawn attention to the fact that he lives in Bristol, the implication here is that this story is based on his personal experience. He also specifies who could be described as 'disabled' ('anyone ANYONE in this group here could be disabled' (line 97)) and then makes a further attempt to clarify their identity and the identity of those who do the labelling: 'they are the same people as learning difficulty or people who are disabled' (lines 105–6). Harry appears to be making the point that people are basically equal, that everyone is a person.

His turn does the work of fleshing out the generalities of Brian's speech and giving it yet greater authority. Where Brian's strength was achieved through some technical language such as 'stigma' and the naming of national societies, Harry makes continued use of 'I think' (10 instances) and uses a slower pace of delivery than Brian's. He uses short phrases, pauses and glances around the group (e.g. line 94), all of which lend weight to his identity as a thoughtful social commentator, which is built both on the stylistic devices of a politician and also on his own foregrounded identity as someone who has experienced 'labelling'.

His comment 'there is nothing to laugh about' (line 104) is especially interesting. It is not clear whether he is commenting on people's tendency to laugh at people with intellectual disabilities or on the possibility that someone might laugh at his own speech right now. Whatever the case, it is clear how important it is for a self-advocate to be taken seriously. As was seen in earlier chapters (e.g. Chapter 3), people with intellectual disabilities are routinely disbelieved and not taken seriously. This is not something that can be taken for granted; self-advocacy talk gives people with intellectual disabilities an opportunity to defend their rights. They do this not just by the things they talk *about*, but as we have seen in all the examples so far, they do it by *how* they talk, and in particular by weaving together the personal and the political.

Roger: What does self-advocacy mean to members?

The final question that research group members asked in their focus group visits was 'What do you think self-advocacy is?' It would seem that this might be an obvious place to seek examples for the current chapter. However, not all talk *about* self-advocacy is self-advocacy talk. This question led to some very different responses, and as always these are embedded in local contexts.

Extract 9.5

1.	Rog	self-advocacy (0.5) i::::s (.) a special word (1)
2.		((pointing gesture with index finger of left hand))
3.		because the special word is (.) everybody is working
4.		together like a team (1) because we we do lots of
5.		advocacy↓ we does a lot of things (.) we go to self-advocacy
6.		groups↓ (.) we run groups↓ we does a lot of groups↓
7.		((finger gesture stops))
8.		but I'm finding is
9.		((folds arms))
10.		you work like a -we work hard↓ I'm thinking (0.5) if I didn't
11.		have that we wouldn't (.) have (.) a word
12.		((rounded gesture with both hands))

Roger's turn is very neatly constructed. He starts with the statement that self-advocacy is a special word, then he gives examples of what makes self-advocacy special in his experience, and finally comes back to a consideration of the word in line 11: 'if I didn't have that we wouldn't (.) have (.) a word'. He uses three-part rhetorical lists, in an even clearer way than Darren in extract 9.1 (see Antaki, 1994: 33) such as 'we go to self-advocacy groups; we run groups; we does a lot of groups' (lines 5–6). He is an extremely effective rhetorical speaker, just as Brian was in the previous extract, and through this he achieves his aim of working up collective ownership of the self-advocacy group.

As with Brian, it is interesting to look at how Roger uses pronouns. In his first turn he uses the following forms:

> Everybody ... we do ... we does ... we go ... we run ... we do ... I'm finding ... you work ...
> we work hard ... I'm thinking ... if I didn't have that ...we wouldn't have a word

The use of 'I' is contrasted with the 'we' of the group: 'I' is the person, himself, who is considering the issue and delivering his opinion, but self-advocacy is portrayed as a group, a 'we' activity. Roger builds up a group identity of effective social actors, by portraying the 'we' as a group who can achieve things:

we does a lot of things (line 5)
we go to self-advocacy groups (lines 5–6)
we run groups (line 6)

Roger effectively presents a group identity in which members are active, and the joint work he talks about is mirrored by the interaction they demonstrate. A bit later, he is urged by the supporter in his group (May) to go further, and he moves into the even more interesting territory of identity. This is how that same extract continues some six lines further on:

Extract 9.6

18.	May	what is self-advocacy↑(1)
19.	Rog	it's for learning difficulties
20.	May	um hm
21.	Rog	with um with special – special needs but I'm thinking is
22.		people (.) from outside ((*pointing gesture*)) can't go in
23.		can't come in
24.		((*circular hand movement*))
25.		we've got – all of us has got to be like- we said to some
26.		people we can't have people coming in↓ they've got to
27.		be the same (.) ((*circular hand movement again*))
28.	May	some big bosses tried to hijack and come in didn't
29.		they↑=
30.	Rog	= that's right so we kicked them out the door ((*LF*))
31.		because actually it's not – not very fair coming in and
32.		spoil (.) our (.)group↓ I'm thinking it's (.) OUR meeting
33.		and we run it like what we – we run it as↓
34.	Tra	thank you Roger

At line 18, May self-selects with her question 'what is self-advocacy↑'. She gets in here very quickly, with no pause between this and the previous turn. This question can thus be heard as implying that Roger's previous contribution may not have been quite on target. He immediately responds with 'it's for learning difficulties' (line 19), choosing to define self-advocacy not as an activity, but by a particular membership categorisation (Chapter 6, p. 87) of the people who take part in it.

From line 21 onwards, Roger goes on to give a story as an example of what this identity can mean. He refers to a particular occasion on which some other people came into their group who were not welcome. This is a particularly effective way of making salient the identity of 'learning difficulties': it is a prerequisite for ownership of the self-advocacy group. Instead of defining 'learning difficulties' as an impairment, Roger then contrasts it with 'people from outside' (line 22), the people who are not allowed to come into the group. May assists him with this contrast by specifying the outside people as 'some big bosses' (line 28) and even characterises their intention as trying to 'hijack' the meeting. Through this short piece of narrative, then, Roger and May together manage to give the strongest argument for foregrounding an identity as people with intellectual disabilities. It is by virtue of this identity that members own the self-advocacy group, and it is this that gives them their strength.

May's use of vocabulary could be drawing on various discourses. 'Hijack' is a metaphor from terrorism, but the words 'big bosses' sound very much more like a childish characterisation of adult, important people. In this context, however, it evokes laughter and so it comes over more as a shared joke. Just as Frank and Adam, in Chapter 6, used their shared past experiences to chat and to make jokes, so too do May and Roger. By using these words to describe the people who shouldn't have been in the meeting, May and Roger are effectively turning the tables on them. Whereas people with 'learning difficulties' are often treated as children, it is now the outsiders (the others) who are dealt with in childish language. Roger picks up the implication of May's words and carries on with the strong, bullish vocabulary 'we kicked them out the door', thus adding to the strength and power inherent in the 'learning difficulties' identity. Self-advocacy talk *belongs to* people with the label of 'learning difficulty' and it can only actually be defined as self-advocacy talk when it is done by them.

The salience and strength of this identity make it possible for Roger to reach his climax with 'it's OUR meeting and we run it like what we run it as' (lines 32–3). This is the clearest claim yet for the importance of interactional rights. Being in control of the process of self-advocacy (i.e. being in charge of the meeting) is the key to moving on to collective *action*. This is the crux of the matter, and all the extracts given in this chapter were in fact 'run like what we run it as'. It was people with the label of intellectual disabilities who took lead roles as questioners, discussants, rhetorical speakers and evaluators. Where the identity of intellectual disability is linked with these strong interactional rights, what emerges is something that sounds not just 'strong' in its content, but effective in the way it is structured.

Implications for practice

The implications of what has been analysed in this chapter are far-reaching and seem light years away from the talk that has gone on in previous chapters. People with intellectual disabilities no longer seem incapable, childlike or in need of support. This chapter has revealed them speaking up for themselves and standing up for their rights and those of others. They are capable of high rhetoric and strong argumentation. What has happened here? Are these simply different people from those who featured in the previous chapters? Or are they in a different context? In order to understand that context, I will summarise here what this chapter has shown about self-advocacy talk itself.

Brian and Harry both come over as individual, strong, rhetorical speakers. They both demonstrate how important it is to have assertive strategies to gain a turn, keep the floor and keep your audience with you. Both these speakers, as well as Darren and Roger, used rhetorical devices such as three-part lists and repetitions. The term 'rhetoric' can be used pejoratively (as in 'empty rhetoric') to mean that a speaker's words have no substance, but are used simply to gain effect. However, all talk is tied to its local situation of interaction and in these self-advocacy discussions a certain amount of rhetoric was often considered to be appropriate and effective. Members were being asked, in effect, to perform and rehearse their arguments in public (Silverman, 1973). Moreover, the public setting was a very particular one in which members purported to share the identity of 'self-advocate'. They were therefore able to draw on a shared interpretative repertoire (Wetherell, 1998) about rights, labelling and discrimination, which could be worked up into the verbal shorthand of a speech. Individual speech-making in self-advocacy is a useful resource.

Much of the analysis in this chapter was about the mechanisms that self-advocates used in order to move from individual self-advocacy into political or collective action, echoing many of the ethnographic examples Goodley (2000) gives in his study of the UK self-advocacy movement. However, the route from the personal to the collective was found to be a two-way street; members were interweaving the personal and the collective voice. Brian, for instance, moved between 'I' and 'we' and portrayed the changing of the name of the Spastics Society as part of his personal action. Darren, even more clearly in extracts 9.1 and 9.2, used the problems he faced personally as a wheelchair user to trigger discussion of possible individual and collective action. As Goodley (2003) observes, people with intellectual disabilities can and do also 'self-advocate' in their individual, everyday lives. What is happening here in more formal meetings, though, is that the personal issues to do with individual identity are worked up to form the backdrop to collective voice. Other analyses (Redley & Weinberg, 2007) have illustrated the problems and tensions that can occur when people with intellectual disabilities appear to be stalled at the level of individual story-telling. However, as seen in Harry's talk (extract 9.4), it is precisely this link between individual life experience and political talk which can produce a strong position.

In order to 'do self-advocacy talk', members need to bring with them their own issues and to be prepared to use these in the talk. This is the *self* in the self-advocacy and it is this element which one of the research group members referred to when he commented:

> And we've got to feel – we've got to be personal in our lives as well, to speak out. And you've got to say, I've spent my time in an institution, that sort of thing. You've got to really pour it out. You've got to be more open. (Self-advocacy discussion, 2001)

The aspects of self-advocacy talk described thus far have very general significance. They are not just a product of the 'Finding Out' project. Any research, or consultation, exercise (e.g. Fyson & Fox, 2008) would find these features very useful:

- An orderly meeting structure, where people take turns to speak.
- A few members who are prepared to deliver strong rhetoric.
- An expectation that personal stories of members' experience can be used within political talk.

Unlike the previous chapters in this book, Chapter 9 has not featured many 'supporter' voices. The role that supporters undoubtedly do play in formal self-advocacy contexts will be the topic of Chapter 10. However, the focus here is on the agency and rights of people with intellectual disabilities themselves, and it is important to understand those rights in order to support a self-advocacy group effectively. Many of the characterisations of self-advocacy talk here were to do with individuals portraying themselves as decisive social actors, rather than as passive recipients of others' actions. In extract 9.3, it was seen how active agency could be achieved through the precise use of verbal forms. In extract 9.2, members explored possible routes for action through the talk itself. Other members were feeding Darren with possible active roles, which he countered with the passive, cared-for identity he created for himself. It is the resourcefulness of the self-advocates themselves that marked these passages out as self-advocacy talk, and these three extracts would certainly not have been selected as strong self-advocacy talk if, for instance, supporters had been responding to members' complaints with suggestions of what they should do. It should be noted that resourcefulness is a marked feature of the talk precisely because of the backdrop of discourses in which people with intellectual disabilities are placed in passive, helpless roles, just as Darren indicated. It is this contrast that makes the talk challenging and makes it important for self-advocates to 'do resourcefulness'.

A final theme to emerge from this chapter is about self-advocacy as team work. In the final two extracts, the team work Roger talked about was reflected in the smooth team approach to producing the talk. Doing team work, as demonstrated in this example, was dependent on a background of shared knowledge (this was how May was able to support Roger in putting over his story about 'kicking out the bosses').

Darren's extract also demonstrated how self-advocates could produce and construct political action together, through interaction. Instead of dominating with one long turn, Darren demonstrated his interaction skills in bringing in other members and keeping the talk going by reinitiating sequences and producing verbal challenges. This led to interaction in which members were pushing Darren into considering possible actions, taking his own issues beyond the personal and well into the political. As Roger described, and Darren and others demonstrated, self-advocacy is actually about a 'we': the process of self-advocacy is about collective talk, and it is through talk that positions can be explored and change can be brought about.

It seems then that the key to understanding self-advocacy as a mechanism is the group, the collective. Inherent in this concept is an idea of belonging, and Roger expressed this very

eloquently in his description of his self-advocacy group. It is precisely the membership categorisation of 'learning difficulties' that enables self-advocates to be strong in taking ownership of
the interaction within their own group.

People who identify as self-advocates have rights within their own organisation to deal with
their own talk, to find their own solutions and to take ownership as a collective. It is these features
(which are features of the talk-in-interaction) which show how existing genres are being merged
and shaped within self-advocacy talk to produce:

> a socially ratified way of using language in connection with a particular type of social activity.
> (Fairclough, 1995: 14)

It is by embracing this newly formed genre of self-advocacy talk that self-advocates are creating
a strong challenge to the dominant orders of discourse relating to intellectual disability.

How conversation works: summary points

- All talk is 'naturally occurring', even if it is part of a group discussion or a meeting, as in this
  chapter. What matters is the analytical stance; in discourse analysis, the analyst is interested
  in the way matters are played out between participants (Holstein & Gubrium, 1997; van den
  Berg *et al.*, 2003b: 3–5).

- Turn allocation can be more complex in larger groups than in one-to-one situations, and it
  is useful to understand some of the strategies that can be used for keeping the floor. These
  include non-verbal devices, such as looking away at transition relevance places and slowing
  down or hesitating when in mid-sentence.

- The use of rhetorical devices is one of the strategies that construct 'self-advocacy talk' (see
  Antaki, 1994: 133). For instance, members may use pre-announcements (Schegloff, 2007:
  37–44) and people can be brought into the talk by virtue of specific, expert membership
  categories. An array of features like this which commonly occur together define self-advocacy
  talk as a particular 'genre' (Fairclough, 1995: 14).

Inclusive approaches communication: summary points

- Self-advocacy groups give people with intellectual disabilities a chance to discuss their *own*
  issues, on their own terms. People bring their own, real-life experiences and produce from
  this a collective voice and identity.
- The context of a peer support group enables people to develop their own strength, to explore
  their own arguments and their lives and purposes.
- Self-advocacy talk can only occur when people with intellectual disabilities are trusted to get
  on with it themselves, to be resourceful and to support each other. The supporter's role is
  therefore to understand this and to step back.
- Support can be given by other people with intellectual disabilities. That is what peer support
  is all about.

Chapter 10

Supporting People to Speak up in Group Situations

If self-advocacy, as was seen in the previous chapter, means people with intellectual disabilities owning and having control over their own talk, what role can a non-disabled supporter perform? Several of us (including myself) have played the role of non-disabled supporter, and we are aware that this role has long been a source of sensitivity and tension in the literature (Worrell, 1987; Dowson & Whittaker, 1993; Goodley, 1997; Iles, 1999). If people with the label 'intellectual disability' are to take up their own cause, how can this be done with and through non-disabled people who do not share their life experiences?

Having carried out voluntary tasks which could be termed 'support' in self-advocacy contexts, as well as tasks that were part of paid projects over the years, I want to preface this chapter with some generally appreciative comments. Those who are closest to the self-advocacy movement realise the way in which good support is essential to the operation of self-advocacy groups:

> It is not professional involvement per se that limits or enables self-advocacy but the nature of interventions made by supporters in groups. (Goodley, 2003: 123)

Goodley suggests that it is the underlying philosophy of self-advocacy supporters which matters. Those who are paid to be support workers in self-advocacy groups have an incredibly important, but sensitive, job to do. They need to operate efficiently in terms of back-up, information, arrangements, emotional support and myriad other things, while at the same time respecting absolutely the right of members to determine things for themselves. It is very hard to get this right, but the success of the self-advocacy movement across the globe depends on supporters' skills in this respect. In 2004, I was fortunate in being invited to organise a conference in Tokyo, with some colleagues, and we travelled with members of a self-advocacy group with whom I had previously worked. Visiting People First groups in Tokyo, I was struck by the similarity between the ethos in Japan and in the UK. Supporters were extremely busy, but essentially did not have a voice. They explained, they dealt with problems, they organised, but did all this in a way which helped the people with intellectual disabilities themselves 'own' the group.

Some (e.g. Redley & Weinberg, 2007) have critiqued the interventions of non-disabled supporters in formal consultation meetings, who carried out the task of summarising and speaking up on behalf of a person with intellectual disabilities. This of course can imply that the person with intellectual disabilities cannot speak up unaided. However, given that joint work is common

Disability and Discourse. Analysing Inclusive Conversation with People with Intellectual Disabilities, 1st edition. © Val Williams. Published 2011 by John Wiley & Sons, Ltd.

in routine, everyday, social activities, one would expect the more difficult tasks of public speaking also to require some support. That is what the current chapter explores.

In Chapter 9, extracts of self-advocacy talk were chosen where non-disabled supporters made only minimal contributions. However, their work is often more extensive. Sometimes this work occurs behind the scenes, in preparation meetings or sessions; at other times, there are interventions from support workers *in situ* in order to 'repair' the talk, sort out misunderstandings or simply prompt people. This chapter highlights particularly the verbal practices and arrangements which supporters draw on both in 'front stage' events such as research interviews, and in 'backstage' events such as group conversations.

Tracy and May: Rescue work in a self-advocacy group discussion

The following extract is taken from one of the research visits carried out in the 'Finding Out' project, where Mark (one of the research group members) asks one of the set research questions. This question is explored in more depth in Chapter 13, but here it is of interest because of the work done by May, the support worker for the host group. Tracy is one of the people in that group, and Mark is one of the research group members.

Extract 10.1

26.	Mar	the first question is (.) what do you think about people being
27.		labelled↑(5)
28.	May	you go ( ) first yeah↑
29.	Tra	mm
30.	May	tell them what you think about being labelled↑
31.	Tra	um (3) we're not allowed to use (.) those um um um (.) labels
32.	May	which are the labels you don't want people to use↑ which are the
33.		names you don't want people to use↑
34.	Tra	well I mean like um (.) um don't know exactly
35.	May	OK↓ do you know what labels are↑
36.	Tra	no I don't
37.	May	[OK]
38.	Mar	[do you] want me to explain↑
39.	May	yeah

As I have discussed throughout this book, the way in which turns are allocated is often important in a conversation, and the first noticeable thing in extract 10.1 (see also Table 10.1) is that Mark and May are the only two speakers to 'intervene' in the conversation, or to self-select (see Chapter 3, p. 38). Both May and Mark seem to have greater turn-taking rights than other speakers. It is Mark who starts, as would be expected. It is his agenda and he has the first turn, at line 26, by delivering one of the group's planned questions. This is an invitation to speak, but at this point, if one goes simply by what has been said, there is no clue as to who is invited to speak. There is a five-second pause after this question. It seems that no one is going to answer. Mark's turn as a first-pair part is an example of a near violation of the adjacency pair structure, as the expected second part does not happen. In other words, there is some **trouble in the talk** (or interactional trouble) here. (Readers who have not read Part 1 are advised that these terms are introduced and discussed on pp. 38–9; 42).

May's first turn, 'you go (…) first yeah↑' (line 28), can be heard as a kind of repair (Chapter 5, p. 73) – she is dealing with the trouble in the talk and breaks into the five-second pause in

Table 10.1 Structure of turns in extract 10.1

First part	Second part	What is happening here?
30. May: tell them what you think about being labelled↑	31. Tracy: um (3) we're not allowed to use (.) those um um um (.) labels	*Tracy attempts to answer Mark's question as rephrased by May – addressing the whole group. But she hesitates, pauses, seems unable to answer.*
32. May: which are the labels you don't want people to use↑ which are the names you don't want people to use↑	34. Tracy: well I mean like um (.) um don't know exactly	*Tracy responds directly to May, but hesitates again – admits she does not know.*
35. May: OK↓ do you know what labels are↑	36. Tracy: no I don't	*May diagnoses the cause of the hesitation by offering an analysis of what has caused Tracy's problem. Tracy agrees.*

order to do that. When Schegloff *et al.* (1977) first discussed 'repair', they particularly noticed how a speaker can use a repair turn to locate trouble in a previous utterance; this is very much what May does here. She does not offer an answer directly to Mark, but designs her turn to back up Mark's invitation to speak. This intervention could be glossed as: 'someone ought to speak, and it ought to be one of the four members from the interviewee group who says something here, so would someone like to have a go first?' The very fact that she does not answer Mark directly, but encourages the group members to do so, gives us a clue as to her identity and rights in that talk. She is not a group member and she recognises that the question was not directed towards her. There is thus a presumption underpinning this conversation, that self-advocacy members should speak for themselves.

The following section (lines 30–6) constitutes the response to Mark's original initiation, in which there are six turns comprising three adjacency pairs, all initiated by May. May's whole involvement in this sequence has a repair function, helping members to achieve an appropriate second part for Mark's initiation. The first strategy supporters seem to use, then, is simply to self-select at points of trouble in the talk so that they can offer some clarification and repair in order to assist self-advocacy group members to contribute to the talk.

Supporting understanding of being a self-advocate

Repair talk can be complex, and perhaps there is slightly more in extract 10.1 than simply getting Tracy to speak. In order to get at other important support strategies, I will first consider Tracy's 'we're not allowed to use (.) those um um um (.) labels' (line 31). Mark had used the formulation 'What do you think …?' in his original question, but Tracy constructs her answer with the passive voice, in 'we're not allowed to'. The grammatical choice she makes is significant, as is the vocabulary item 'allowed', implying that she and others are subject to rules set by others. In doing this, she effectively puts herself, and the others, in the 'we' category, in a passive position as recipients of instructions from an unnamed other source.

In the following turn, however, May ignores this formulation and reacts as though Tracy had used the preferred option of 'we/I don't want …', since she asks Tracy 'which are the labels you don't want people to use↑'. Either she had misheard or she finds Tracy's answer unacceptable in the present context, implying as it does that someone had laid down a rule about labels and about the language that is acceptable in their group. Tracy after all has some face to keep, as a self-advocate, a representative of a People First group and as an interviewee. May's question to Tracy, and indeed my analysis of it, reflects our shared understanding of an important aspect of self-advocacy, as a context in which members can and do decide things and speak for themselves (as in Chapter 9).

Following Tracy's first unhappy attempt at a response, May offers her what is in effect a supportive frame – both helping her to understand the original question and giving her a hint as to the kind of response that she should deliver. She goes from the general invitation ('tell them what you think') to a more specific strategy in which she asks a direct question of Tracy ('which are the labels/names?') and then to a diagnosis of the cause of the problem (do you know what labels are?). She seems to be following the general rule of first allowing as open a response as possible and then gradually narrowing things down when the more open invitations do not work. She rephrases the question twice in lines 32–3, using exactly the same frame but inserting first the word 'labels' and then the word 'names'.

> which are the labels you don't want people to use↑ which are the
> names you don't want people to use↑ (lines 32–3)

This is an enabling move, giving Tracy a double chance of understanding and checking at the same time that her misunderstanding was not due simply to an unfamiliarity with that particular vocabulary item: 'labels'. May supports Tracy to reformulate what she is saying by actually changing the question to which she should respond.

Despite this support, Tracy's response at line 34 is even more confused and fraught with hesitation. May's subsequent turn, 'do you know what labels are↑' for the first time acknowledges the fact that Tracy's answers are based on a failure to understand. Instead of responding to Tracy's contribution at face value, May moves back one level to enquire about the concepts on which Tracy's original answer was based. Tracy appears to find this much easier to answer and acknowledges that she does *not* understand.

What is implicit in May's work here is her recognition that Tracy's earlier attempts at answering Mark's question were based on misconceptions and as such were inadequate. May can advise Tracy on what counts as an adequate response and what constitutes a misunderstanding, and her right to do this is ratified by Tracy's acquiescent responses. Supporters are often the ones who spot the need for such repair work, and in doing so they determine what might or might not count as adequate. This notion of adequacy is closely linked, as seen in this example, to common understandings of what the self-advocacy organisation is, and in what membership category (see Chapter 6, p. 87) Tracy should be responding. As Sacks (1995) noted, membership categories are important in conversation because they bring with them a whole set of assumptions and background detail about the individual. However, they are not fixed in stone: this work about helping Tracy to shift into 'self-advocacy' membership is very subtle. In this particular case, it is Mark, another person with intellectual disabilities, who intervenes and offers the explanation. Mark and Tracy together are trying to find out what the problem is for Tracy and to repair the misunderstanding by a further attempt at an explanation. It is due to their joint work that the conversation proceeds in an orderly way. In this particular context (of a research interview), Mark's intervention at line 38 has great significance, since it supports the frame of 'research interview' and the interactional rights of people with intellectual disabilities to sort out their own misunderstanding and troubles.

Readers will recall from Chapter 3 an example with Brendan and Jack where a similar pattern emerged, with a supporter taking over a questioning and clarification role in order to encourage a member of his own group to speak. However, in that case the pattern of talk became quite oppressive, with Brendan seemingly being forced by his supporter to say something. It is interesting to see how differently the two examples turned out and what a fine line the supporter has to tread in getting it right. These issues will be further explored after a brief look at another example of supporter talk.

Alex and Fiona: Bringing someone in through a 'relevant membership category'

The following rather longer extract is taken from a two-hour research 'meeting' with a network of self-advocacy groups. It is the same meeting that featured in Chapter 9, with Brian's speech about changing the name of the Spastics Society to SCOPE. There were about 20 people sitting round tables in a room in a sports centre, and both questions and discussion were sometimes difficult to hear. This was a challenging situation for all those present and so it is not surprising that some support work occurred during the discussion. Two supporters of the self-advocacy groups were present, and again the present author was supporting the four members of the research group while also operating video and audio equipment.

Extract 10.2

568.	Fio	I don't know whether you want to ( ) I mean Alex
569.		do you [want to talk about it Alex↑]
570.	Chr	[I tell you who talked about it Fiona] Jane Jones used to be
571.		there
572.	Fio	yeah↑ yeah ↑
573.	Chr	( )
574.	Fio	go on then Alex ((*looking at Alex*))
575.	Alx	all these years I've been in Bay Hospital(1) er (1) the food wasn't very
576.		use to people (.) because - people were eating the same food and I I
577.		went and seen about it and I went I went I went to the (advocacy)
578.		meeting and I said this is not the right food for the residents to eat
579.		and I said – I asked them (0.5) er can we have different (1) er food to
580.		eat and they said- he said – they said they can't change it they
581.		couldn't change to er (.) you know the the same sort of food
582.	Fio	you got it changed in the end though didn't you Alex ↑ (.) it did
583.		change in the end
584.	Alx	° yes they did in the end↓ ° ((*Alex speaks quite quietly, everyone else is*
585.		*quiet. Stares ahead of him, sad expression.*))
586.	Fio	because you were in fact one of the founder members of Bay – of
587.		Bay's People First weren't you↑
588.	Alx	yes

This extract occurs after the second question from research group members: 'Have you been in any tricky situations, when you've been discriminated against?' There has already been some talk in answer to that question when a supporter, Fiona, starts to allocate a turn at the start of this extract, nominating Alex as next speaker. This seems to be exactly the same strategy as May used in extract 10.1, when she suggested that Tracy could answer Mark's question. However, contrary to Fiona's suggestion, Christine (another group member) then self-selects, not in order to respond, but to nominate a speaker called Jane Jones. Fiona simply acknowledges this, with 'yeah↑ yeah ↑' while persisting with her own selection of Alex at line 574 ('Go on then Alex').

What this does is in some respects to sideline Christine's contribution and to make it appear like an interruption. It could well be that Jane Jones is not present or that she has already spoken. Whatever the reasons for Fiona's persistence, that short exchange with Christine gives Fiona's selection a force it might not otherwise have had. It comes over as a deliberate opener for Alex, who then does have an extended turn starting at line 575.

Following Alex's long turn, the structure is slightly more complex, consisting as it does of a number of question–answer pairs (adjacency pairs) (Chapter 3, p. 39) between Fiona and Alex, in which Fiona appears to be prompting Alex to mention other aspects of his time in Bay Hospital. Throughout this sequence, Fiona consistently self-selects (lines 582, 586) and then selects Alex for next turn (Chapter 3, p. 38). In other words, after each of Alex's contributions, that part of the talk could have finished and another speaker might have been selected to talk next. However, Fiona's interventions effectively keep Alex in the frame.

Clearly, Fiona knows things about Alex that she feels are relevant to this discussion. The first thing is that 'you got it changed in the end' (i.e. he had been instrumental in changing the food arrangements in the hospital). Her second intervention, however, is even more explicit: 'because you were in fact one of the founder members of Bay – of Bay's People First weren't you↑'

What Fiona does here is to openly refer to a specific membership category, which Alex holds. He was one of the founder members of 'Bay's People First'. She is asking him to speak in that role or make that particular category relevant here in this talk. By doing this, she clearly signals to Alex (and others) that he has something to offer to this discussion. However, her invitation is first met with a simple 'yes', and then there is a break in the video due to a loudspeaker announcement in the centre where we were meeting. After the break and interruption, the discussion continues where it left off. Fiona at least has not lost her thread:

Extract 10.3

589.		Fio you were – you were also Alex if I recall – [( )]
590.		((*loudspeaker announcement*)) [centre assistant contact
591.		reception …]
592.		((*resumes*) am I right in thinking that you were the first resident of Bay
593.		Hospital ever to – ever to [change ward ever to actually get a
594.		change of ward at your own request
595.	Ang	[(((*from this point to end of extract, an overlapping whispered*
596.		*conversation takes place between Angela, Mark, Ian and Val*))]
597.	Alx	[yes] yes well um the last time I – I didn't like it ( ) because I didn't
598.		like the staff the way they were (.) you know what they were doing (2)
599.	Fio	yeah yeah (2)
600.	Alx	which wasn't very nice for people to do you know (.) mucking you
601.		about and (off) and all such as that
602.	Fio	you talk about discrimination but discrimination takes place within
603.		services doesn't it ↑

Fiona's lead-in for Alex at lines 592–4 is formulated with reference to a very specific achievement of Alex's. It is, in effect, an invitation to talk more about his role in the hospital and about the discrimination that went on there. At any event, this is how Alex hears it, as is evident by his next turn at line 597 when he mentions the reason why he changed ward and the conditions in the hospital. Similar invitations to talk are to be found elsewhere in the data. For instance, at one point in a different discussion, Mark brought Harry into the talk through shared knowledge of a problem he had experienced over a taxi journey. He turned to him and said, 'You've had something like that, haven't you?' The reader may also want to refer to Chapter 5, in which similar 'openers' and encouragement talk were highlighted in one-to-one social situations.

What Fiona is building on here, both in selecting Alex and encouraging him to continue, is shared knowledge of the fact that he would have something very relevant to say about discrimination. Just as May's work in extract 10.1 could be traced back to understandings about self-advocacy, so Fiona's here is firmly grounded in her understanding of Alex as former hospital resident, and as 'one of the founder members of … Bay's People First' (586–7). It is because of this shared knowledge that she is able to bring him in as a suitable respondent and support his rights to have a turn. Alex also builds on this shared knowledge, by referring to circumstances that he explicitly signals as having already shared with Fiona by a 'you know':

> I didn't like the staff the way they were (.) you know what they were doing
> (lines 597–8)

This use of shared knowledge and reference to other conversations is very common in the data. Not only is a member prompted to speak, he is also assured that what he has to say is important and relevant at this moment.

Engineering a sustained turn

One of the points of self-advocacy talk, as was explored in Chapter 9, is for members to speak at length, and so it is worth outlining briefly, across extracts 10.2 and 10.3, what is done by Alex himself and by Fiona to help Alex keep the floor. As with Brian in Chapter 9 (extract 9.3), the timing and sequencing of non-verbal acts are crucial. Video evidence during his long turn at line 575 reveals that Alex leans forward slightly, using his hands and arms in symmetrical gestures to emphasise his points. He also looks away from any one person during long stretches of his longer turns, especially during pauses. This has the effect of helping him to 'own' the pauses; no one interrupts during his long turn, even though there are several short pauses and self-repairs, 'I said – I asked', and a number of hesitations, 'er'. His quiet tone, noted in the transcription at lines 584–5, and his sad expression also appear to contribute to the dramatic effect of his talk and to his rights to speak.

However, Alex is also successful in this discussion because of what Fiona does. Having nominated Alex as speaker, she gives him her full attention (unfortunately there is not video evidence of this) and gives him feedback noises like 'yeah yeah' (599). This is followed by a two-second pause, and so the expectation is raised that Alex has more to say. Fiona orchestrates the waiting. Her acknowledgement operates not only as a confirmation of what he has said, but also as an encouragement for him to continue. It is the quality of her attention that underpins Alex's contribution.

Attributing expert status and linking with wider meanings

Not only is it the business of self-advocates to talk, but it is also important that their talk has weight and is taken seriously. Not only does Fiona invite Alex to speak, give him the floor and help him to sustain a long turn, she also signals to him that he is an 'expert'. The first way in which she does this is by achieving a tentative impression, with phrases like 'if I recall' (line 589) and 'am I right in thinking' (line 592). She promotes Alex's role as expert, due to his personal experience of the situation. This is echoed elsewhere in the data, for instance by Len and Sam in Chapter 5, who are talking about a football stadium. Len as a supporter played down his knowledge of the layout of the stadium and deferred to Sam's superior status as an expert. This strategy of downplaying your own expertise and simultaneously boosting someone else's rights as expert witness seems to be a central support strategy. It is reminiscent of the work that family members may do in using forgetfulness of detail to signal each other's respective rights to tell particular stories (Goodwin, 1984).

The second way Fiona attributes expert status is by the aspects of the Bay Hospital story that she chooses as worthy of mention. Each time she intervenes, she picks out an event that puts Alex in an active role:

you got it changed in the end (line 582)
you were in fact one of the founder members of Bay – of Bay's People First (lines 586–7)
you were the first resident of Bay Hospital ever … to get a change of ward at your own request (lines 593–4)

Fiona constructs the situation as one of institutional change. She takes aspects of what is being said by Alex and links them up with a wider argument. This strategy culminates in her final turn, when she shifts to an evaluative framework, to bring out the point and the relevance of Alex's story:

> you talk about discrimination but discrimination takes place within
> services doesn't it ↑ (lines 602–3)

This is perhaps occasioned by the immediately preceding turn and Alex's mention of the bad, indeed abusive, aspects of hospital life: 'mucking you about ( ) and all such as that'. However, it is equally possible to see this comment about discrimination as relating to the whole purpose of Alex's story. Throughout this extract, Fiona has been designing her turns to *enhance* and add to Alex's turns. In this last attempt, she succeeds in making Alex's story relevant to the overall purpose of the conversation, which was (roughly) 'to produce examples and further thinking about discrimination'.

In the present example, Fiona's remark is based on a whole package of shared assumptions. For instance, this is the first time that anyone has used the word 'services' in this meeting, and so there is an (unexplained) assumption here that:

a)   a hospital is an example of a service.

The very fact that 'discrimination within services' is worthy of mention rests on the assumption that:

b)   services are intended to help people, not discriminate against them.

Fiona then builds on Alex's talk, and makes the third assumption:

c)   this is an example of discrimination.

She is thus able to draw the conclusion that 'discrimination can take place within services', and because of assumption b) this is a shocking thing and worthy of mention. Her use of 'doesn't it↑' has the effect of drawing in her listeners to this argument with its implied answer 'yes'.

This knitting together of examples and wider meanings is clearly a powerful move, whether it is performed by a self-advocate or by a supporter, and has some resonance with what we know about teacher talk (Payne & Cuff, 1982; Stubbs, 1983). For instance, the teacher in a classroom situation nearly always takes on the right to dictate what is relevant to an overall plan, and indeed owns that agenda, even when using scaffolding techniques which are sensitive to the level of the learner, as in the present context (Geekie & Raban, 1994). Later chapters will explore how self-advocates can take on these functions for themselves. Indeed, to have full interactional rights in self-advocacy, participation and research, people with intellectual disabilities have to learn how to take control of the 'meta-functions' in talk; they too need to be able to determine what is relevant and appropriate, and to move into functions traditionally carried out by their supporters.

Angela and Val: Prompting reflective talk

Moving from 'frontstage' to 'backstage' events (see Goffman, 1959), I now turn the spotlight on my own work with the four research group members during the fortnightly sessions we held at the local People First office. Between 1997 and 2001, I met with them in a voluntary capacity as a research supporter, and was often involved in helping them to learn what they needed to do for their project. As with everyday encounters, supporters often have to 'perform in public' and to rescue or support various encounters. However, it is often preferable for the work to be done beforehand, so that people with intellectual disabilities are well prepared for the situations they encounter. Extract 10.4 is part of a conversation in which I am looking back with members over the interview visits they have already conducted. The occasion, however, becomes very much a preparation and in some ways a coaching of members about the importance of their identity as researchers.

Extract 10.4

1.	Val	so:o (1) really you- you've -you can look back and see all the different
2.		places you've been [to –
3.	Ian	[oh yeah↑↓
4.	Ang	you know I- I've got all the photographs in my
5.		photograph album at [home
6.	Val	[yeah
7.	Ang	and I take it up the Shrubbery and show it to people↓ (.)
8.	Val	mm
9.	Ang	and I'm quite proud of what I did (.)
10.	Val	mm hm
11.	Ang	and I take it home at – at Christmas↑ and I went up and
12.		show it to Uncle Rob and Jenny↑ (.)
13.	Val	mm hm↑(.)
14.	Ang	don't you↑and his girlfriend↑
15.	Val	yeah
16.	Ang	and it's quite – it's quite - you feel quite really important (.) I spoke to
17.		I it's in my (family) I showed it to Tony today↑ he's my boss↑ oh you
18.		<u>do</u> do a lot then Angela↓' (.) and he's quite you know – and (I was)
19.		telling Tony right↑ and he was quite – he was quite – he was quite
20.		impressed with what I do↑ (.)

Extract 10.4 opens (as the tape starts) with an introduction by the author as group supporter or facilitator. Essentially, line 1 is a suggestion – something that is intended to set the agenda for the talk that follows. However, I change the formulation of what I am saying as I speak; in the CA literature, this is called a **self-repair** (see Schegloff *et al.*, 1977).

> you've ... (presumably, 'done lots of visits') is changed to: 'you can look back and see all the different places you've been to' (lines 1–2)

This formulation makes the issue concrete. Instead of simply referring to the research interviews or visits, the remark has the effect of directing members' attention to the locations, 'the places you've been to', rather than the content of what they were doing there. As a prompt for some reflective talk about our research, it proves to be a very successful initiation.

Following my initial remark, the group members start talking enthusiastically. In particular, it is Angela who seizes the opportunity to reflect and discuss her reactions to the work, and she does this in a very personal way. In terms of sequence organisation, apart from the very first two-part sequence (I initiate at line 1 and Ian responds at line 3), the rest of the extract appears to be one overarching 'three-part sequence', consisting of an initiation, a response and an evaluation. From line 4 onwards, Angela's contributions constitute one extended turn in the form of a response to my initial suggestion that the group could 'look back and see all the different places they've been to'. The theme of locations is taken up by Angela, who then picks up the idea of 'look back' and introduces the photographs she has of the visits, referring to how she has shown them in three different locations: at home, the Shrubbery (a day centre) and at Uncle Rob's. The photographs perform a link role between the *places* we have visited and the *places* where they are shown to other people. Angela has picked up the purpose I had introduced, and the idea of the photos is an extremely potent tool for focusing both herself and other members.

Angela intersperses her contribution with a commentary about how she feels: 'I'm quite proud of what I did' (line 9); 'it's quite – you feel quite really important' (line 16). It is those feelings that provide the point of her story. Then she moves into a short narrative about her 'boss' and herself, using direct reported speech to bring to life what her boss had said: 'you do do a lot then Angela'. The vocabulary she uses, 'impressed', 'proud', 'important', together with the institutional identity given to Tony (the boss), all help to reveal what the story is about, which is identity. It is through showing her photos that Angela is enabled to feel proud, especially in a context where she would normally be the client at the day centre, someone who is not expected to do something important like research. Throughout this section, however, Angela does not use the word 'research'; no one does. What we are talking about is photos of 'the different places you've been to' and it is hard to tell, from Angela's description of the scenes from her life, whether her acquaintances were impressed with the range of places she had visited or whether more discussion had gone on about what the activity was at those places. It has to be said that the photos in question were mainly of other people and of our research meetings, rather than landscapes or tourist views of the places we'd visited. This was known to me (as I had taken the photos) and so provided an opportunity to take this scene-setting a bit further. Angela had given a golden opportunity for some identity work about research.

Shaping a researcher identity

The following short extract follows on immediately from the previous one. It is in this one where I start taking on a more didactic role, and I kick in with some more deliberate support talk.

Extract 10.5

21.	Val	right (.) cos um (1) you know you you've (.) you can <u>now</u> say –
22.	Ang	[achieved a lot
23.	Val	[when you say something↓- carry on
24.	Ang	I have achieved a lot (.)
25.	Val	mm hm
26.	Ang	too much
27.	Val→	((LF)) and you've got a view of what <u>other</u> people think [outside of
28.		Norton now

29.	Ian	[yeah
30.	Har	yeah
31.	Val	which (.) makes it much [more important
32.	Ian	[we could beat – we could beat ( )
33.		people outside
34.	Val	well it's not a matter of <u>beat</u>ing people is it↑=
35.	Ang	=it's not=
36.	Val	=it's just - it's just (.) finding <u>out</u> really what life is like for [other -]
37.	Ang	[when you think]
38.		about it (.) we have seen a few places haven't we↑
39.	Val	uh – huh(.) u-huh yes you [certainly have

In extract 10.4 there appeared to be one long sequence, delivered in short bursts, but led by Angela's initiations, while extract 10.5 is definitely led by me, not Angela. Embedded in this extract is a lengthy sequence (lines 21–31), which is started by my suggestion:

21.	Val	right (.) cos um (1) you know you you've (.) you can <u>now</u> say –

In a way, extract 10.5 is like a mirror image of extract 10.4, and it is noticeable how the support work done in extract 10.5 builds on the picture Angela has painted in the preceding talk.

Angela herself had just introduced the scenario, complete with reported speech, about speaking to her 'boss' and indeed to other people in her life about our visits:

I showed it to Tony today↑ he's my boss↑ 'oh you <u>do</u> do a lot then Angela↓'(.) and he's quite you know – and (I was) telling Tony right↑ and he was quite – he was quite – he was quite impressed with what I do↑ (.)

What I do at line 21 is to seize the opportunity of this scene and to probe for some further script: 'you can <u>now</u> say –'. Through pursuing the things people might say to others, it is possible to explore the kinds of meanings they might attribute to the research. None of this, it has to be said, was part of any plan or design during this particular session; it was simply an opportunistic move on the part of a research facilitator.

At lines 22–3, Angela and I overlap, and I give the floor to her with 'carry on', showing with my 'mm hm' at line 25 that I am paying attention to her words. Angela then repeats what she had said, 'achieved a lot', which was her response to 'you can now say'. In effect, she is completing the sentence, filling out the frame I had given her for her scripted talk. Her choice of what she wants to talk about in relation to the research is her own achievement and she uses an extreme formulation 'too much' at line 26, introducing self-humour (evidenced by my laughter at line 27). Immediately, however, I use this slot to move the talk on and in fact develop the script that Angela has suggested:

27.	Val→	((LF)) and you've got a view of what <u>other</u> people think [outside of
28.		Norton now

It is this turn which is perhaps the most interesting: I do not reject Angela's formulation of having achieved a lot, but I add to her potential script by referring to a version of what research actually is. Not only do they know what they think and can speak up for themselves, but also research should arguably give them a handle on what *other* people think – the people they have met on their research visits. The emphasis placed on 'other' is significant in this context.

Both Ian and Harry respond with a minimal 'yeah', and I conclude my very didactic contribution by orienting the group once more to the 'importance' of their work. It is the fact that research tells them about *other people's views* which makes it important and not just the fact that it gets them out and about on visits. Effectively, Angela's introduction of a dramatic, scripted scenario has enabled me to feed the group with the actual words and ideas they may need to understand and to explain their activity to others. This is a strong piece of preparation and coaching, albeit within a framework that has been freely provided by a group member.

Finally, the sequence started by Ian at line 32 is perhaps even more telling. Ian picks up the issue of finding out 'what other people think' and uses it as the basis for his next assertion: 'we could beat … people'. Immediately this is seized by me and challenged as being an inappropriate way of thinking about research. Supported by Angela, who echoes my 'it's not', I provide a strong challenge to Ian's idea about the competitive nature of research:

34.	Val	well it's not a matter of <u>beat</u>ing people is it↑=
35.	Ang	=it's not=
36.	Val	=it's just - it's just (.) finding <u>out</u> really what life is like for [other -]

What I do here is to contrast two formulations of research – highlighting the words 'beat' and 'finding *out*'. Evidently, this contrast strongly implies that it is not necessary to be competitive in order to find something out. In particular, the purpose of visiting other self-advocacy groups and asking them questions should not be to prove one's superiority to them, and the remark probably reflects my continued uncertainty about group members' motivations and ideas about themselves as researchers. Members are being supported to build ideas about the importance of what they have done. This work is about joint identity-building, and the actual support strategies used are entirely dependent on this joint work, using the contingencies of group members' own talk. This is a learning context and to a large extent I play the role of an educator. It could be said that I do at least the following things in extracts 10.4 and 10.5:

- structuring the session with boundary markers: right (.) cos um (1) you know you you've (.) you can <u>now say</u>
- focusing: 'you can look back and see all the different places you've been to'
- summing up: 'you've got a view of what other people think'
- defining what counts as the right way of speaking in this context: 'I don't think I want to answer that now'
- defining boundaries of relevance: 'it's not a matter of <u>beat</u>ing people is it↑

Implications for practice

A core activity for supporters in this chapter has been that of helping group members display their experience through talk. This chapter strikes at the heart of what it means to 'have a voice'. When people with intellectual disabilities participate in policy-making, attend meetings, represent each other or do research, there is always some concern about tokenism and competence. Chappell (2000), for instance, as well as Walmsley (2001) and other commentators on inclusive research, raise the tensions and issues inherent in the undertaking. Can we assume that people who by definition have cognitive impairments could manage the academic tasks involved in research? Evidently, the majority of people with intellectual disabilities will need support to take part in research, and so the activity is often referred to as 'participatory' research (Zarb, 1992).

Similarly, it has been noted that supporters of people with intellectual disabilities in other public and formal domains are often mistrusted or accused of speaking *for* the self-advocate. However, there have seldom been opportunities to look behind the scenes and to examine the social activities that take place in preparing people with intellectual disabilities. This chapter has provided rare evidence of what happens both front and backstage during self-advocacy encounters.

This chapter is not intended to imply that supporters are talking all the time or that they dominate conversations in self-advocacy groups. It ought to be noted that the extracts in this chapter were deliberately selected as places in which supporters spoke up and are not necessarily typical of supporters in general. From a quantitative analysis of data in the interviews for our project, for instance, supporters only had some 20% of turns. In selecting the extracts for this chapter, I was deliberately seeking examples where a supporter had several subsequent turns and where they did some work about relevance of the members' contributions and about interpretation.

Self-advocacy supporters often take up a particularly close stance in relation to the people with intellectual disabilities they support. Walmsley (2001), for instance, has described this role as 'non-disabled ally' and this seems to capture nicely the position the supporters in this chapter take; they are both allied to the group members, but distinct from them. One of their distinctive features is the dependence that other group members often demonstrate towards them. There are times in every visit when all talk appears to be directed towards the supporter, and they may have to deliberately avoid eye contact in order to redirect the talk to the members.

The first general task for supporters, then, is to ensure that people with intellectual disabilities can take the floor and express their views in public. In extract 10.1, this work was done by a very general 'opener' which offered the floor to an individual in the group. Support workers can also intervene and do repair work when people run into trouble. Troubles can happen, for instance, when people fail to answer and to play their part in a social exchange, as happened with Tracey. There can also be trouble due to lack of understanding, and when people do speak up, they may say things that are deemed to be inappropriate. The support worker in extract 10.1 took care of all the points in the conversation where Tracy had trouble and evidently saw it as her place to do this. She drew both on her knowledge of Tracy and on her general knowledge about the kinds of knowledge self-advocates should have.

In extract 10.2, likewise, a supporter was seen to perform significant facilitation work in ensuring that the group discussion ran smoothly. Like May, Fiona played a very strong part in the outcomes of the meeting. This extract illustrated how supporters can select speakers and make sure they keep the floor and are listened to by others. Further, Fiona used her knowledge of the history of self-advocacy in that region to point out the significance of what Alex might have to say, and she gave him (and the listeners) a strong message about the aspect of his identity that was relevant to this particular discussion: 'one of the founder members of Bay's People First'. Garland (2008) has noticed a very similar phenomenon, where an Irish language teacher conferred 'expert status' on one of her students due to her perception of him as a cultural insider. In the present context, having identified Alex as a hospital resident, Fiona was then able to do further identity work on Alex's behalf, by her prompt questions, to portray him as someone who was a founder member, a changer and a mover. All these moves meant that Alex did in fact have an extended opportunity to take the floor and to talk about his experience. Even then, though, the supporter did not leave it at that. She took it on herself to link what Alex said about his own experiences with wider meanings – in effect, she drew out the relevance of the issues he raised with the underlying purpose of the research group's original question about discrimination.

The identities oriented to by Fiona and Alex were to do with power relations within the hospital. They built up a picture that was part of their shared knowledge about hospitals, the abusive power wielded by staff on wards, and the even more powerful hospital management, who held meetings and ultimately had the power to change things such as food or wards. The powerlessness of the residents was contrasted with the fact that things could be changed, either by an individual or by group action. This was a very strong message and one that was reinforced by Fiona's final statement, with its background of assumptions about 'services that discriminate'. The strength of this final message, and of Fiona's final summary, was only possible because of the success Alex and Fiona had achieved in making the connection between Alex's situational identity as interviewee and his transportable identity as a founder member of a People First group. Self-advocacy supporters can therefore have important work to do in reinforcing the significance of what people with intellectual disabilities have to say.

The later examples in this chapter were slightly different, as they were from 'backstage' sessions for research group members. The analysis shows how I picked up elements of what members offered and used them as opportunities for teaching them about research. Extract 10.5 was a good example of how far supporters and members were in tune with each other's intentions, prepared to build on each other's leads and ready to collaboratively construct new meanings for research. The talk did not just belong to the supporter – we built that learning context jointly. For instance, Angela herself introduced the topic of the photos; she also started to talk about the scripts she used in discussing her achievements and she focused on her individual *pride* in something which others would find to be a surprising, unexpected activity for someone with an intellectual disability.

Both in public discussions and behind-the-scenes work, supporters need to be sensitive to the momentary changes that can take place in the talk. The same session could move from a 'learning' framework into a much looser frame, where people with intellectual disabilities could chat about the way in which they perceived their role. As other authors have shown (Antaki *et al.*, 2006), supporting self-advocates can be problematic. To a large extent, then, doing effective support talk is simply a matter of remaining sensitive to the possible directions in talk, and being open to take up new discourse and situational identities as matters unfold, at one point a tutor, at another a friend, and at yet another a group coordinator. Underlying this, though, is something much deeper – a recognition that it is the people with intellectual disabilities who 'own' the activity and not the non-disabled supporter. Supporting that ownership, as seen in this chapter, meant taking opportunities for prompting and support to allow people with intellectual disabilities to realise their own power. The theme of ownership of research will be taken up again in Chapter 12.

How conversation works: summary points

- As was seen in Chapter 5, repairs (ten Have, 1999: 116–19) can function as invitations or prompts to say something more (Sacks, 1995: 7). Self-repair (Schegloff *et al.*, 1977) can also serve this function. Repairs can perform many functions in talk (see Sacks, 1995, for early examples), and in this chapter it has been seen how repair talk can actually be part of an 'invitation' or a 'prompt'.

- Membership categorisation (Silverman, 1998: 74–97) is fundamental to the way talk works, as was seen in Chapter 6. By prompting, or reminding, someone about a particular category to which they belong, one speaker can encourage another speaker to talk.

- Getting a turn in talk is important, but also it is important in group situations to be able to keep the floor. Speakers have ways of doing this work themselves, for instance, by looking away at potential turn allocation points. However, other speakers can also help them, by giving them sustained attention, through gaze, smiling and short 'filler' remarks.

Inclusive approaches to communication: summary points

- Support talk in self-advocacy groups can be done by members or by paid supporters. They often do this in ways that build on their own knowledge about individuals, and about the purpose of the talk in general; for instance, they may suggest that a particular speaker takes the floor, because they know he or she has something relevant to say.
- Support for individual speakers can be in the form of prompts, which help people with intellectual disabilities to work out what might be relevant to say. Sometimes this kind of support can have far-reaching implications, because the supporter is effectively coaching the other person about the significance of their own experience.
- Behind the scenes in a research project, the supporter may feel free to take on a more didactic role. The particular style of support that seems to work well is very opportunistic and based around what the group members themselves want to talk about.
- A key role for anyone doing support talk, in self-advocacy or in inclusive research, is to help people with intellectual disabilities achieve a sense of ownership.

Chapter 11

Being Interviewers with the Label of 'Intellectual Disability'

Those who have read earlier chapters in this book will have noticed the huge contrast between the voices of people with intellectual disabilities in their private lives and their collective voice in self-advocacy contexts. Where previously they were ignored, forced to speak or encouraged to come into conversations through friendship and shared interests, the people in Chapters 9 and 10 are strong leaders of their own community, fighting the oppression faced by disabled people.

Chapters 11–13 focus on a related area – 'inclusive research' – which is a social activity that is even more contestable in the context of people with intellectual disabilities. As was seen in Chapter 4, people with the label 'intellectual disability' are often considered incompetent to manage their own lives and in need of support and advice in many everyday activities. How, then, could they actually do research, which arguably requires a high level of competence and skill? These matters have been discussed often within the literature on 'inclusive research' and are referred to in Chapter 1 (see in particular Walmsley, 2001, for an account of the arguments and critiques; and for practice-based examples, Williams, 1999; Walmsley & Johnson, 2003; Williams *et al.*, 2005). The emancipatory project of Oliver (1992) and other disabled academics can seem like a far cry from the ways in which people with intellectual disabilities become involved as 'researchers', and some academics would object to the use of the word 'research' in this context. However, people who were formerly the object of research studies can and do become actively involved in the process of doing research, as Steel (2005), Northway and Wheeler (2005) and contributors in Lowes and Hulatt (2005) testify.

Rather than reiterate the concerns and arguments in this area, this book makes no assumptions. As with any social activity, a 'research project' can be examined by analysis of the interactions that take place within it. Among the 'turns' to discourse in social research is the realisation that:

> The empirical data of social research are predominantly products of specific discursive practices.
> (van den Berg *et al.*, 2003a: 1)

This book adopts the same view and aims to examine this new type of inclusive research by studying the talk as it actually happened during the interview visits in the 'Finding Out' project.

Disability and Discourse. Analysing Inclusive Conversation with People with Intellectual Disabilities, 1st edition. © Val Williams. Published 2011 by John Wiley & Sons, Ltd.

The 'Finding Out' group members themselves often discussed the status of what they had done, reflecting on what research meant to them. For instance, one member commented on the hard work involved in research, despite the misconceptions of others:

> It's not actually a very easy job, people think, Oh it's easy, but it's not. You come home in the night time, and you're knackered. And people think you go to a meeting and you sit on your backside all the day, and that is crap. (Group discussion 5, 1999)

This was a small endeavour, which started at a point when I was between jobs, just before I arrived at the Norah Fry Research Centre where I still work. In my own development, therefore, it was and still is a pivotal point. Each activity in the project opened up to me a whole host of questions about research, and a central aim of this chapter is to consider how and to what extent these occasions constituted a new type of social activity and how far they drew on existing repertoires of research interviewing. As I shall explore in this chapter, members of the research group both rehearsed traditional patterns of communication in research interviews and made something new out of them. Traditionally, research encounters are set up by the researcher, and the interaction is therefore shaped and determined almost entirely by the agenda of the researcher (Silverman, 1973; van den Berg *et al.*, 2003a). In the inclusive research in this chapter, however, there are additional layers of peer identification and of open meaning-making which make the communication both rich and challenging.

Mark and Andrew: The interactional right to take control of an interview

As in previous chapters, it is worth looking in depth at an extended extract first to get a flavour of how these events unfolded. The first extract is from the fourth visit in the 'Finding Out' project to a small independent self-advocacy group. There were four people in the group being visited: Frances, Jenny, Andrew and Keith. Extract 11.1 follows on from a question about jobs, but as will be seen, it picks up on some unfinished business from the previous question about discrimination. The two questions under discussion here, in the written words of the group, were:

- Have you been in any tricky situations when you've been discriminated against?
- What work have you done?

Extract 11.1

646.	Mar	I want to go back to [Andrew (.) on that – on that thing
647.		((*leans forward looking directly at Andrew*))
648.	Fra	[and Mrs Potter wasn't [it↑ ((*LF*))
649.	Jen	[yeah
650.	Mar	were you <u>pressured</u>↑(0.5) =
651.	Kei	that was years ago wasn't it↑(*sits back in seat, smiles*))
652.	Mar	= did you feel that you were pressured against doing the job↑(1)
653.		((*leans forward towards Andrew*))
654.	And	e::r yeah I did feel pressured in – in one way yeah↓ because =
655.	Mar	mm
656.	And	= um they never give me the opportunity to prove what I
657.		could and couldn't <u>do</u> you see=
658.	Mar	oh right right↓

659.	And	= you know I was quite capable of looking after a group
660.		and giving them tasks to do↑=
661.	Mar	so -
662.	And	= it was left to one of the students there (.) and I felt I felt
663.		(.) very demoralised about it you know er very (.) <u>hurt</u> about it
664.		*((looks at Mark, but at 'hurt' turns to Sarah; hand gestures on 'tasks'*
665.		*and 'demoralised'))*
666.	Mar	so that was (.) you tu- (.) er ju- (.) this going back to question <u>two</u>
667.		again
668.	Several	*((LF))*
669.	Mar	really going back to question [two again because you are
670.	And	[yes
671.	Mar	saying that you were PRESsured by not (.) showing a person what you
672.		were doing↓ but you were <u>also</u> discriminated against it
673.	And	(is that right)↑
674.	Mar	yeah

As the members noted in their own discussion, taking control of the communication is part of being a researcher, and extract 11.1 gives a good example of how this occurs in action. It is Mark (one of the research group members) who clearly controls who will speak next. His rights in this respect are made more obvious by the fact that a sub-conversation is going on between Frances, Jenny and Keith at the opening of the extract, but despite this Mark makes a very deliberate selection of Andrew for next turn:

> Mar   I want to go back to Andrew (line 646)

The video reveals that at this point Mark was leaning forwards with his gaze directly on Andrew, slightly smiling and with both hands outstretched in front of him. In this context the continued talk between Frances, Jenny and Keith actually comes over as an interruption of *Mark*.

Mark's openers to Andrew at lines 650 and 652 continue, focusing on the issue of 'pressure', and he successfully hands the floor to Andrew to establish a dialogue. From that point on, Andrew and Mark have alternate turns, although Mark's turns are minimal: 'oh right right↓' (line 658); 'mm' (line 655). Andrew is effectively showcased as a respondent with a right to tell his story, and overlaps and interruptions in the rest of the extract do not cause trouble for members. On the contrary, they seem to lend a flow to the whole sequence, since they indicate that everyone is engaged and listening to each other.

At line 666, Mark starts to do more than simply keep the talk going with 'mm' or 'oh right'. He starts with 'so' at line 661, which is then interrupted, but he carries on to say:

> Mar   so that was (.) you tu- (.) er ju- (.) this going back to question <u>two</u>
>   again (lines 666–7)

This turn is very significant, since Mark is actually offering his own interpretation and evaluation of Andrew's response. Looking back to the start of this extract, I could now appreciate that his initiating remarks (lines 650 and 652) were not neutral invitations to speak; they were strongly suggestive of the way in which Andrew should frame his response: 'were you <u>pressured</u>↑'. The laughter at line 668 is perhaps an indication that members too feel that Mark has framed the whole sequence, almost to the point of setting it up.

In order to understand a bit more of what is going on here, it is useful to look at the wider context of talk, since that was what Mark was clearly referring to. Some 50 lines earlier, Andrew had said the following:

Extract 11.2

593.	And	well I was um I was a volunteer care worker for about (.) um for
594.		about three years up there (.) and um they never give me the
595.		opportunity to look after the group or help them out properly↑
596.		you know (.) the ones who wasn't able to do anything for
597.		themselves and um after about two years I got fed up with it –
598.		fed up with it because er it was a childish the staff were treating
599.		me like a child to start off with
600.		((*hand gesture on 'properly', then on 'childish'*))
601.	Fran	that's true

It now becomes evident that the job that Mark refers to in extract 11.1 is that of volunteer care worker, which Andrew had mentioned earlier. Although an initial analysis should be context-free in CA, I would acknowledge that my interpretation of Andrew's remarks does rely on some background knowledge, and so I will share that here. In day centres in the UK, as previously in long-stay hospitals, people with intellectual disabilities have always carried out jobs. Sometimes these jobs were seen as industrial or other forms of 'training', and people worked in workshops, very much as still happens in other countries in Europe. However, this was considered exploitative in the UK, so workshops were generally phased out through the 1980s and 1990s. Some people attending day centres, nevertheless, still wanted to see their attendance as 'work', and many of the more able clients were used to help out in a general sense with running the centre and helping with less able people. It is this type of role that Andrew is referring to in extracts 11.2, and this would be familiar to most members of the research group and the self-advocacy group they were visiting. This identification of a background argument relates to the idea of an **interpretative repertoire** in discursive psychology (Wetherell, 1998). As seen in previous chapters, it is the backdrop of knowledge which enables people to understand each other and to conduct their conversation without too many hiccups. By trying to unpick all this, the analyst can get behind what is observable on the recording and appreciate how it is situated in the wider social fabric – in this case, the social fabric of the intellectual disability world.

It can now be seen that there are links between extract 11.1 and 11.2, which Mark has recalled. He makes these quite explicit by referring back to what Andrew had said about his 'volunteer job' and queries the underlying meaning of it. In order to do this, he asks Andrew a question that is *not* part of the pre-set agenda of interview questions. The question 'did you feel that you were pressured against doing the job↑' (line 652) is one that he has made up, locally tailored to Andrew's earlier story. Mark here is taking on the classic functions of the interviewer, as described by Silverman (1973), which include the right to decide what will count as relevant to the research agenda. He effectively sidelines a conversation which is not at that point part of the research, he allocates turns and he establishes that this display of Andrew's experience is the business of the occasion. The ordinary resources of conversation are used in a very particular way to lend this event (at this point) definition as a research interview, and Mark's adoption of the interactional rights (see Chapter 5, p 73) of an interviewer are a key feature of the social activity of research. It will be noted how much more powerful these rights are by comparison with the conversation dead-ends which some of the participants in earlier chapters experienced in their everyday lives.

There are lots of short remarks in this extract, such as 'right, right' and 'yes' from Mark. Often referred to as gap fillers, they serve the purpose of encouraging the speaker to continue. Line 657, for instance, could have formed the end of Andrew's contribution, but Mark continues with a 'right right' in the following line, and Andrew continues with: 'you know I was quite capable of looking after a group' (line 659). Mark and Andrew achieve what may be called 'collaboration' or even collusion during this talk. Andrew appeals to Mark with phrases that imply Mark's agreement – 'you see' (line 657) and 'you know' (line 659) – and all this is matched by the use of gesture, both by Mark and Andrew. An example comes after line 663, where Andrew gestures with his hands towards his chest, thus appearing to illustrate and to emphasise his feelings. In all these ways, Andrew is the perfect interviewee! He is giving Mark precisely what was asked for, namely an example of being pressured.

Making sense of experience

While I have commented here on Mark's *competence* as an interviewer and the competence of others present in playing their roles as interviewees, it is interesting that the topic of the talk is also actually *about competence*. Andrew's whole case rests on the contrast between himself as someone who *could do* things, if given the chance, and the group whom he wanted to look after, who in fact needed to be given tasks to do. However, his bad feelings about this episode are based on the reported views of third parties, who had actually judged him *incompetent* to do the job he was doing. These third parties are referred to generally as 'they', and the blame is squarely put on their shoulders for being unfair to him and not allowing him to show 'what I could and couldn't do'.

His appeal to Mark at lines 659–60 should be heard in the light of his general argument about being treated unfairly. This is what he wants to get across to Mark – he is in fact someone 'quite capable' and he trusts that Mark will understand that. In the particular setting of the day centre, about which he was talking, this would give him the status of a member of staff rather than a client. It is interesting to see how he introduces the other social actors in this short narrative. The identity of the student is contrasted with his own, but he is referred to as 'one of the students there', not even worth bothering about as an individual. Our shared understanding of a student (in the context of a day centre) was someone who is only there for a few months (on a practical placement), someone who is temporary. The fact that such an unimportant person could be chosen for a job over Andrew himself is further argumentative justification of his hurt feelings.

When Mark evaluates this narrative (line 666 onwards) his logic is that people should be allowed to prove their capabilities. The point of Andrew's narrative depends on portrayal of a situation in which his competence has to be proved to powerful others, and Mark shares this frame of reference. The pressure consists of not 'showing a person what you were doing' (lines 671–2) and that, as Mark says, is a type of discrimination. The work that they both do to create Andrew's experience as 'discrimination' depends on the assumption that they have similar identities, similar experiences. If the final evaluation had been offered by me or by someone who did not share the identity of 'intellectual disability', it could not possibly have had the same force. Mark's argumentative structure is as follows:

- Andrew has a similar identity to his own.
- People like them can get pressured.
- One way of being pressured is that people don't let you show what you can do.
- Andrew is able to achieve things.
- People should be given a chance to 'prove themselves'.
- If they are not given this chance, that amounts to discrimination.
- This example will help everyone understand what we were trying to talk about by the word 'discrimination'.

This is peer research at its richest. It can be noted that the discursive work that Mark does (i.e. his discourse identity as interviewer and evaluator of experience) is in itself a demonstration of his competence. The tight interconnections between discourse and transportable identities (Zimmerman, 1998) can again be observed, as the local situation feeds into the wider issue of competence and incompetence.

Mark's move in eliciting this talk from Andrew, and then in relating it to the research question, reinforces what Silverman (1973) calls 'the scheduled nature' of the interaction. The research group members have the right to determine that schedule. It is also interesting to note that the video transcript shows Mark engaging in some quite tightly coordinated work with hand gesture and gaze. As Mark raises the issue of 'going back to question two', he is physically referring to the printed questions in front of him on the table, and he emphasises this by glancing down at the paperwork. After his two-handed gesture on 'pressured', he then places his right hand on the paper and leaves it there for the rest of his turn and Andrew's subsequent one, leaving only his left hand free for punctuation. It may well be that there is an institutional pattern to the gestures accompanying Mark's argumentation, as Argaman (2009: 531) noticed with regard to the 'embodied practices' which marked arguments in superior–subordinate relationships. In other words, Mark's use of gestures matches his newly acquired status as a researcher. In laying one hand on the printed questions, he performs a very authoritative expression of ownership of the research paperwork, with all that its printed status implies.

In other research visits as well, members of the research group (and those they visited) reflected openly about the meaning of the points they were raising. They questioned what 'discrimination' may mean and, as we shall see in Chapter 13, they often focused on the wider meanings behind issues of labelling. Thus their pre-scheduled research questions led very strongly to a form of talk in which, as Silverman pointed out, is about meaning making:

> In hearing interview-talk, then, surface appearances (the words used by the subject) are only important for the glimpses which they give of the patterns which purportedly underlie them. (Silverman, 1973: 33)

Most researchers would perhaps assume that they need to take away the 'data' and reflect on it later. What is perhaps slightly unusual in this inclusive research is the way in which this pattern is actively attended to in the talk. Although led by Mark-as-researcher, this task is performed out loud and is done, as it were, jointly with the audience. These are not traditional researchers who aim to factor themselves out of the data and simply record subjects' views. The analysis is collaboratively worked up *in situ*, and the category of discrimination is actively taking on a new and fuller shape during the course of the talk together. Some of the distinctiveness of research done by people with intellectual disabilities is starting to emerge.

Group or team work as researchers

One essential feature of doing interview talk seems to be the adoption of asymmetrical conversational rights, whereby interviewers are distinguished from interviewees, just as a chairperson is. The researcher/interviewer comes with predetermined questions, and in the present case, these questions were printed out on sheets of paper with symbols, so that they could take charge of asking them. In extract 11.1 Mark made use of the printed sheet to lend authority to his remarks. However, sticking rigidly to a printed list of questions would not necessarily be considered good interviewing practice. By contrast, consider the following:

Extract 11.3

424.	Tho	well it wasn't <u>in</u> the centre I <u>used</u> to work (.) I used to work on
425.		the electric board
426.	Ang	yeah what doing↑
427.	Tho	underground servicing (1)
428.	Ang	> that's interesting↑<
429.	Tho	yeah (2)

Although it might appear trivial, this extract is typical of ones in which members use ordinary conversational resources to take control of the direction of the interviews. In line 425 ('what doing↑') Angela encourages Thomas to say more, to give more detail, thus indicating that his response was relevant to the purpose. Line 427, 'that's interesting', is important here as it gives positive feedback to Thomas that he is on the right lines and that his experience is worth recounting in this context.

The researchers in these events presented themselves as a team. They brought off this team work, for instance, by supporting each other in either posing or explaining a question, and there were certainly plenty of instances where they jointly followed up a response. The following example is one of many similar ones.

Extract 11.4

216.	Ang	what do you do
217.	Har	yeah what you doing↑
218.	Mar	what is your job↑
219.	Jess	I goes to work ((*looks towards Harry*))
220.	Ang	what do you do when you get there↑=
221.	Har	= do you work in a factory or to a day centre↑
222.	Ang	a shop↑
223.	Jess	no I work in a canteen [washing up -
224.	Ang	[washing up↑
225.	Jess	yeah (2) not <u>washing</u> up um cleaning tables and taking meals
226.		out

Jess is responding here to a question about the work she does, but clearly the research group members want to get more out of her! Each time one of the group members (first Angela and Harry, then Mark at line 218, followed by Angela again and finally Harry at line 221) intervenes with a question, they produce a more explicit choice to guide Jess's answer:

- What is your job?
- What do you do when you get there?
- Do you work in a factory or to a day centre?
- Washing up?

There are many other instances where some complicated negotiations have to take place between team members about which question should be asked next, who is going to ask it and whether particular questions have already been answered.

At most points where there was trouble about the meaning or intention of particular words or phrases, it was research group members who were called upon to discuss exactly what they meant by a question. The only time that this rule was not observed was when a member of staff (supporter) from the interviewee group decided to try and help, and this was then heard and acknowledged as a usurping of the rights of the researchers. In the following extract, Jenny has just questioned what discrimination means. Mark is given the first opportunity of explaining, but when he appears to stumble, the supporter (Sarah) offers her help. However, the fact that she has to ask permission to do this work invokes Mark's privileged status:

Extract 11.5

397.	Mar	what it means Jenny is when people with a (.) learning difficulty
398.		like (0.5) can't (1) can't solve a problem (0.5) it feels that
399.		they're discriminated against (.) that's what it means (.) can
400.		anybody else explain↑

401.	Sar	can I give an example perhaps Mark↑ because um (.) I've
402.		been discriminated against because I've been a <u>wo</u>man in the
403.		past

The key point seems to be the conversational right to own and define what counts as knowledge. Perhaps more than anything else, it is that feature of the interaction which marks group members out as 'researchers'.

Blurring of the boundary between researcher and researched

The strict division into 'researcher' and 'researched' was not, however, always maintained. At times research group members were called upon to explain a question – to make it their own. During the course of one interview, for instance, Angela expands on the question about jobs by asking members the following:

Extract 11.6

205.	Ang	if you went – if you went to a training cent- if you went to the
206.		same place <u>every</u> day of the week would you get fed up (.) or
207.		would you rather go and do something different↑

This question has a nice apparent logic, as a two-part, alternative structure. However, it is clear on closer examination that it is not an open question, since the two alternatives given are essentially the same (1. going to the same place every day = getting fed up; 2. preferring to go and do something different). By posing the question, Angela is telling people quite clearly what her own view is and what sort of answer would be most acceptable to her. She is effectively offering her own experience and expert views as a person who has actually had experience of going to a training centre. In traditional research, that role belongs squarely to the research participants – those who are being interviewed. However, the whole point about doing inclusive research is that people *share* these experiences and it is their open reflection about their views and perceptions that is so interesting.

There are many other occasions on which the alignment into 'researcher' and 'researched' is breached. For instance, members of the research group sometimes give examples from their own experience, to clarify a question, thus breaking Silverman's (1973: 41) observation that 'the interviewer's questions imply that nothing need to be made available about his own views and experiences'.

Take, for instance, the following exchange:

Extract 11.7

96.	Har	no no one should be never on the streets at night↓ because
97.		someone some people (.) as I said↓ because this is what Jack
98.		Straw announced (.) no one should be never on the streets after
99.		midnight (1) nor even after ten o'clock at night (.) because I tell
100.		you this (.) some people can get attacked at night (0.5)
101.	Ste	do you- right
102.	Har	yeah because- (1)
103.	Ste	do you get like (3) do you think (1)
104.	Har	well sometimes one or (.) or supposing let's put it round this
105.		way supposing you went to work like I do by Wallcroft which is in

106.		Norton right↑ where I've got to go on the bus every day↑like the
107.		77 from Foster Road right over to Wallcroft
108.	Ang	do you catch that one Harry ↑
109.	Har	yeah Wallcroft you know

Prompted by a previous speaker's story about being attacked at night, Harry starts with a general proposition, backed up by the authority of the English government Home Secretary's words (lines 96–100). If he had left it at this, one could say that he was doing the same kind of work as Mark in extract 11.1 in exploring the general significance of an interviewee's contribution. Steve then self-selects, to get a turn (lines 101, 103), perhaps to further explore this significance, but he is hesitant and Harry comes back in with a personal story of his own journey to work, linking his experience and the interviewees' by the phrase: 'supposing you went to work like I do' (line 105). However, he does not reach the point where he might link his story with the business of being safe on the streets at night because Angela, another interviewer, interrupts him with 'do you catch that one Harry' (line 108), signalling her interest in the detail of bus routes. Note that these details would not be particularly relevant to the interviewee group. Has the point of the interview been lost at this juncture?

Rather than discount this as inexperience or bad interview practice, it would perhaps be more appropriate to consider such examples to be a central feature of the methods employed by this team. It is when all members share their experiences openly that the talk becomes richer and more conversation-like. This texture of ordinary conversation could be heard as a means to slow down the interview, to allow for repair and adjustment, and give interviewees time to reflect and to make their own responses richer. In addition, it is by making salient aspects of their personal (outside-the-context) identities that interviewers enable interviewees to make a judgement about their membership, and the relationship between aspects of interviewers' identity, as compared with their own. For instance, Harry's status as an independent bus user would have been of interest to interviewees, as they might then want to make salient aspects of their own independence. The blurring of boundaries can be seen to be an important resource, as the very activity of inclusive research depends on, and grows out of, a sharing of experience and identity between all parties.

Implications for practice

The practice implications in earlier chapters related to support work, while the implications of this and subsequent chapters are for those who seek to involve people with intellectual disabilities as interviewers in research projects. Research group members have consistently referred to the skills they developed in interviewing. They have even analysed those skills in order to present workshops at conferences and other events. The central skills referred to were:

- Listening.
- Following up what people say.
- Using body language appropriately.
- Getting the questions right.
- Relaxing the interviewee.

These skills are central aspects of producing good, rich, qualitative interview data for any researcher and not specific to research done by people with intellectual disabilities. Research group members embraced their discourse identities as respectful listeners with great enthusiasm, as was seen in the extracts in this chapter. Interviewees' contributions were taken seriously and respectfully, as members elaborated together on the meaning of what had been said. Interviewees, as Silverman (1973) observed, are accorded the status of experts in qualitative research interviews, and this was exactly what Mark and his fellow researchers achieved by the quality of their attention. As has been seen in this chapter, members of the research group also exercised considerable control over the unfolding occasion of the research interview, by:

- Choosing a next speaker.
- Orchestrating the talk (with a loaded question).
- Determining the sequence of knowledge that will be explored ('going back to question two').

In an extract such as 11.1, research group members appeared very similar to the powerful, controlling interviewer in Suchman and Jordan's (1990) description of the survey interviewer, who is trained not to allow deviations from the script.

Being an interviewer might therefore seem unremarkable, since it is drawing very heavily on models of traditional, qualitative interviewing. However, when one considers people with *intellectual disabilities* taking control of an interview in this way, it is both challenging and surprising. Indeed, controlling what will count as relevant knowledge is perhaps the most powerful act that members performed, since they were challenging the interactional rights they had been assigned (as incompetent, less-than-full members of society) and also the very discourses about them, formulated by powerful others. As seen in earlier chapters, and in Ochs and Taylor (1992) and Shakespeare (1998), they are often in conversations that are controlled by others. Therefore, the importance of being in charge of the agenda and of making their own rules for talk cannot be overestimated.

As this chapter shows, it is also possible to start distinguishing some of the hallmarks, or distinguishing features, of inclusive research carried out by people with intellectual disabilities. It is not accurate to consider this kind of activity as simply 'copying' traditional, academic research practice. It seemed that members were taking tools which had been made available to them and truly making them their own. The tools of a research interviewer were transformed in their hands.

Sharing a labelled identity

In most social research, the interviewer stands apart from the interviewee. The purpose of the occasion is to tap the views of the interviewee; the interviewer's own identity is irrelevant. In the present project, however, not only were the interviewees expected to be experts on their own experience, they were also expected to share that experience and to identify with the interviewers. This assumption of talking to your peers was part of the research group's purpose in setting up the interviews. This is explored further in Chapter 13. A constant task for all members was to address the questions:

- Who am I? i.e. What aspects of my identity should I be making relevant here?
- Who are you in relation to me? i.e. What aspects of identity do we have in common?

We have seen in this chapter some quite elaborate and detailed strategies for doing this identity work through the fine details of eye contact, hand gestures and body posture. Sharing of experiences was a two-way event, using conversational strategies for matching up the two sets of experiences: Mark often acknowledged a contribution by saying something like 'we found that in our group too'. In addition, research group members did not keep their personal experiences out of the discussion. Interviewees showed interest and involvement in the accounts given by interviewers of their own lives. Talking with peers was very different from talking with an objective, outside interviewer, and this sharing was what marked out inclusive research as different. The common experience of being labelled became a positive force for change, as discussed in Corbett (1991) and Corker (1999) in relation to disabled people more generally.

The interactional rights of interviewer and interviewee

In the traditional research interview, the rights to determine content and structure lie with the interviewer, whereas in the current project, these rights were often shared by both teams. On occasions interviewers stepped outside their discourse identity as interviewers to contribute their own views and experiences. A distinctive feature of this kind of research was its collaborative team work, and this joint approach extended across the boundaries of group adherence. In the main, it was the task of research group members to pose questions and not to answer them. However, on occasions they did answer as well. Similarly, it was not unheard of for interviewees to put a question to the researchers. Thus these interviews moved more towards the model favoured by some feminist researchers (Gluck & Patai, 1991) who seek to break down the traditional barriers between interviewer and interviewee.

I returned to the participating groups (i.e. those who had been interviewed) some two years after the original interviews to explain my PhD research, and was surprised by the fact that they all described their participation in those events as doing research. For them, there was no absolute distinction between researcher and researched, although by then the research group had produced the 'Finding Out' book. All the people included in that publication felt their contribution had been recognised. This assumption of collaborative enterprise was a revelation to me, and it continued into the mini-conferences which research group members held in March 2001. This joint ownership of research has continued in other inclusive projects I have been involved in since then, and I now think of it as an almost inevitable snowballing effect. Interviewees were as proud of the outcomes of the project as the research group members themselves and talked in terms of the research they would do next.

Working things out openly

Traditional interviewers are not only enacting research through their talk in the interview situation, but also in what goes on after the interview (Silverman, 1973). All talk in an interview is considered to be on the record, and the interviewer has the rights to take away the data (usually quite literally, on an audio recorder) and to mull over them – to listen, to transcribe, to analyse and to make meanings.

In a sense the interviewing team did have those rights. They were making both audio and video recordings, with my assistance, during the events, and they did go back over much of this material in order to write up their own articles and booklet. However, inclusive research was also somewhat distinctive in this respect. As observed in this chapter, a hallmark of the process was the way in which members openly explored interpretations together. The interviewees were also prepared to enter into that discussion and seemed to be genuinely engaged with the questions pursued.

A research agenda of challenge and change

Inclusive research can be characterised as research which involves strong feelings. Members chose to do research about issues that concerned them and their lives, not about something abstract and objective. It was highly 'subjective' research and could best be understood in the context of self-advocacy, where personal stories (the subjective) were used to develop solutions and support for each other. Self-advocates did research about matters which concern their own lives. For them, the issues that they chose to pursue were both important and practical. They wanted action and they saw research as part of that action, as Oliver (1992) did in his seminal paper on emancipatory research. Interestingly, I have shown in this chapter how the actual process of doing the research can be as much a part of the action as any product of the research findings. Indeed, there was little distinction in the current project between findings and process. It was by becoming researchers that members could change societal attitudes, in that they became more powerful and challenged others' expectations. By examining these research interviews, this challenge is witnessed at its source, actively forming itself through interaction.

How conversation works: summary points

- Turns at talk can be used in order to fulfil certain functions – to challenge, to ask questions or to praise someone, for instance. However, talk does not occur in isolation. Sometimes, there is a kind of orchestration with non-verbal body language alongside verbal language, and the precise timing and sequencing is crucial (see Goodwin, 1981, 1984; Heath, 1997).

- Some formal social activities, such as research, have rules and methodology books written about them. There are prescribed ways in which they *should* take place. However, this may not accord entirely with what actually happens. CA and other forms of discourse analysis enable the analyst to look closely at how social activities are constructed through communication. (For a discussion of the links between professional knowledge and CA, see Perakyla & Vehvilainen, 2003.)

- When people talk, they choose words and phrases that may refer to other conversations. By using words (like 'pressured' in the current chapter) they can make links between meanings and repertoires.

- There are some interactional rights which are associated strongly with more powerful roles in conversation, such as determining what is relevant to the talk. In this way, a CA analysis of the minutiae of talk can feed into an understanding of how power is enacted (see Wooffitt, 2005: 186–210).

Inclusive approaches to communication: summary points

- Accounts of inclusive research, from the inside, show that people with intellectual disabilities *can* be researchers in their own right.
- Applying 'standards' of social research to inclusive contexts is not always useful. When people with intellectual disabilities do research they are creating a new form of social activity based on peer identity. This is a rich form of research and has its own hallmarks and standards.
- In much inclusive research team work is important. It is also possible for people to share their own experiences with those whom they interview. That helps people to identify as peers.
- Research is about working out meanings, and researchers with intellectual disabilities may do this openly during a project. The insights they have stem from their own experience, and that is the basis for inclusive research.

Chapter 12

Behind the Scenes in Inclusive Research

'We are the artists of our lives'

Introduction

However much people with intellectual disabilities are given equal, friendly contexts for talk and offered opportunities to get turns in conversations, there are also other important prerequisites for having an equal voice in research. These are choice and autonomy, which are now also central to disability policy and practice. For instance, it was the policy paper 'Our Health, Our Care, Our Say' (DH, 2006b) which heralded the personalisation agenda in the UK, a title which speaks for itself. Moreover, autonomy is also embedded in UK *law* with the 2005 Mental Capacity Act, which explicitly endorses the 'presumption of capacity' for all individuals, whatever their label or diagnosis. The first guiding principle of the Act is that:

> A person must be assumed to have capacity unless it is established that he lacks capacity. (MCA, 2005: 2)

As outlined in Chapter 1, policy and legislation worldwide are premised on the idea of the basic underlying autonomy of all human beings (UN, 2007). However, as Chapter 4 in particular revealed, it is precisely that autonomy which is called into question by the label 'intellectual disability', which is premised on *incompetence*. One response to the tension between policy and practice appears to be the foregrounding of talk about autonomy, as was seen in Chapter 8. 'It's entirely up to you', the manager said to Charles, who wanted to make his own choice about where to hold his birthday party.

I have been keenly aware over the past 10 or more years that matters of autonomy are the key to including people with intellectual disabilities meaningfully in research (Williams *et al.*, 2005). As Abell *et al.* (2007) also explore in relation to their roles in another self-advocacy research group, it is vital that people with intellectual disabilities feel a sense of ownership if the research is to be truly 'inclusive'. However, many commentators would argue that the diagnosis of 'intellectual disability' means that people can simply not understand enough to be in control of their own research study. Research implies scholarship, thinking, complex planning and understanding, and so the terms 'intellectual disability' and 'research' do not sit happily together (Chappell, 2000).

Disability and Discourse. Analysing Inclusive Conversation with People with Intellectual Disabilities, 1st edition. © Val Williams. Published 2011 by John Wiley & Sons, Ltd.

In particular, there are frequently worries about what role the non-disabled researcher or supporter plays in inclusive research projects (Walmsley, 2001) and suspicions that the whole thing is a sham – with the non-disabled researcher actually making the decisions and using people with intellectual disabilities in tokenistic ways. Zarb (1992) suggested that research which was not initiated and controlled by disabled people would be better called 'participatory' rather than 'emancipatory' (Oliver, 1992; Mercer, 2002; Barnes, 2003), thus attributing to it in some respects a lower status. However, since then there has been some informed and transparent commentary about the role of non-disabled supporters in research (Chapman & McNulty, 2004), based on experience of a working relationship with self-advocate researchers. Chapman found that it was possible to work as a team, with different people having their own roles in that team, as I did. Barton (2005) also focuses on positive practice that will enable inclusive research to make a difference. In Tarleton *et al.* (2004) and Williams and England (2005), self-advocates who have worked on research projects explore with the author and colleagues the role of supporters. What is important is that the voices and autonomy of people with intellectual disabilities are both fostered and respected.

In order to look further into the matter of 'who owns the research' it is important to gain access to what really happens behind the scenes. Such access of course is rare. The rich data I have on tape or video were part of why I felt it was worthwhile to write this book! Based on my experience of social research in general, I would estimate that 90% of all research takes place in offices, sitting at computers, in meetings or in libraries. The public events (actually collecting data or talking about them) are the jewel in a much larger crown. In other chapters, I have included extracts which give a flavour of what happened behind the scenes in the 'Finding Out' project (see Chapter 6, extract 6.7; Chapter 10, extract 10.4). This current chapter explores in more depth the whole process of research and how people are involved at each stage, from planning to analysis. I am also allowing myself the freedom to range a little more widely and to use data from other projects, including a two-year project about direct payments called 'Journey to Independence' in which I worked with a team of three people with intellectual disabilities, who were employed as researchers by a self-advocacy group (Gramlich *et al.*, 2002).

The issue of autonomy is a central one, and the most subtle task for support work in this area is to ensure that people with intellectual disabilities 'own' the work in which they are engaged. As this chapter shows, this often involves some sensitive identity work, and is a developmental and gradual process. Moreover, I have been well aware that each of the inclusive projects I have worked in has been different, largely due to the different personalities and backgrounds of those in the team. If I were to write about any of these projects without access to recordings of our talk, I would probably portray them all in a very different way. In some ways, going back to what actually happened is an auto-ethnographic endeavour (where researchers look at themselves). That is what I will attempt here.

Planning research activities

The paradigm of emancipatory research (Oliver, 1992) brought with it the strong idea of research originating from, and being controlled by, disabled people. Therefore, concerns about issues of ownership were very much at the front of my mind when embarking on research with people with intellectual disabilities during the later 1990s. At that point, I had already facilitated several projects at a college of further education, in which people with intellectual disabilities had effectively done their own research about the history of hospitals where they had lived. It certainly seemed at that point that it was important that people with intellectual disabilities both understood and controlled the direction and meaning of what they were engaged in as researchers.

Therefore, it is not surprising that frequently there were moments in preparation talk during the project when the idea of ownership was highlighted.

Extract 12.1 is taken from a recording of a group session in the 'Finding Out' project, when all four members of the research group were present and talking with me. I saw myself as the supporter for the group and had brought written minutes of the previous session; at this point, these were being handed out to everyone in the group.

Extract 12.1

15.	Val	*((giving minutes out of last meeting))*
16.		right it's only Mark who's taken these minutes so far but just
17.		to look at that together↓ (0.5) we talked about (.) plans↑ (0.5)
18.	Ian	yeah
19.	Val	things you'd like to do↑
20.	Mar	what page is this on↑
21.	Val	on page three↑
22.	Ang	page three
23.	Mar	oh yeah (2) (I want to tell you something about that)
24.	Val	right (1) and (2) one of the things that you said on there was
25.		um (.) that you wanted to: (.) do su - well Mark said he
26.		wanted to do his <u>own</u> book
27.	Ang	he did
28.	Val	on research↓ and some of you said you'd like to actually learn
29.		more about research and perhaps write something as well (0.5)
30.		I mean there was lots of other things you said
31.	Ian	yeah
32.	Val	like (.) you'd like to travel (0.5) some of you would↑(1)
33.	Mar	((LF))
34.	Val	and you would like to get paid↑
35.	Har	yeah

My turn at line 16 is a framing remark, introduced by 'right' and accompanying the act of handing out the minutes. 'It's only Mark who's taken these minutes so far' refers to the fact that the minutes, though produced by me, were intended as a way for group members to keep control of what was said at each of their meetings. Therefore, while sounding very much like a teacher, I am picking out Mark as the person who had taken the minutes and thus modelling relevant aspects of a researcher's activity to the group. It is they who need to be active and take control. I then carry on with formal strategies for looking back at what group members themselves had said, thus placing the agency of all actions with members, rather than with me. The formulations in the next few lines are:

we talked (line 17)
you'd like to do (line 19)
you said (line 24)
you wanted to (line 25)
things you said (line 30)

There is a persistent use here of the second person plural (you) together with a verbal action ('you said'). I am literally quoting back to them their words by using the authority of the written minutes, and re-storying this as a research paradigm that comes from them. This strategy seems to be much stronger than a memory jogger. It is also about encouraging members to take owner-ship of what they had previously said and what they intend to do in the group:

well Mark said he wanted to do his <u>own</u> book (lines 25–6)
some of you said you'd like to actually learn more about research (lines 28–9)
you'd like to travel (line 32)
you would like to get paid ↑ (line 34)

The implication of all these planned actions is that the research group is *theirs*: it belongs to them and exists only because of their plans. The authority of the written minutes from the previous meeting gives to the supporter the power to refer to their previous agency, the ideas they had already expressed. Paradoxically, however, in the here-and-now of this current meeting, members appear far from active. The responses to all my suggestions are mainly confirmations, such as 'yeah' or 'he did', along with laughter at one point. It is definitely me who is making all the running here and pretty much taking control of the agenda.

Decisions during the conduct of research

Taking ownership of research is not just about planning and choosing what to do during the course of a project. In formal, funded projects the scope for making the type of decisions high-lighted in extract 12.1 is limited, since funded research has at least roughly to stick to a plan. However, decision-making is also important in the minutiae of how research is conducted.

Extract 12.2 is from a large group discussion during 'Skills for Support', where not only the two self-advocate researchers, but also five other people with intellectual disabilities, had a list of questions to ask their support workers. The previous work done during this meeting on the same day had centred on what made 'good support' and many examples had been given which highlighted control and autonomy; for instance, stories had been told of support workers who did not give people choices:

> Well, I lived in a residential home, being told what to do, what time to go to bed, when to get up in the morning, when to have your meals. It was basically – you felt like a robot, and I think that the attitude of the supporters in residential care is – they forget that you are people, they forget that you are a human being sometimes. (Focus group 1, 2005)

In other words, 'choice' is very much on the agenda and had been associated with being a person – being 'human' as it was phrased. Extract 12.2 occurs during the afternoon session, which is somewhat unusual in its set-up. Six or seven people with intellectual disabilities have been invited along with their support workers, and Kerrie Ford and Lisa Ponting are both in 'chairing' roles. They have compiled a list of written questions, and at the point of this extract they have given the opportunity for the people with intellectual disabilities present to put those questions for the support workers to answer. Thus all the people with intellectual disabilities have a ques-tion sheet in front of them and the discussion has been running fairly fluently for about 10 minutes when some trouble occurs.

Extract 12.2

76.	Jim	is it easy to work with all the people you support (0.5)
77.	Sam	where are we at the moment↑
78.	Ker	we've jumped [out of order
79.	Sam	[I'm a bit confused by er (.) where we are

80.	Ker	what does everybody think about that being out of order↑
81.	Lis	where are we cause I get confused ((*shows her paper to Val*))
82.	Val	they've just asked the one about this – ((*points to paper*)) there is
83.		some worry here that people are thinking that we should do the
84.		questions in order↓ and other people are thinking that it's OK to
85.		jump around (.) so can people say if they are worried↑ can you
86.		just raise your hand if you are worried jumping around the
87.		questions↑ ((*people raise hands*))
88.	Sam	to ME I get lost and I get confused↓
89.	Lis	you're not the only one↓ I do too
90.	Val	so Kerrie and Sam and Lisa are getting confused↓
91.		is it OK with people if we just stick to the order then↑
92.	voices	yeah yeah
93.	Val	but the next one Jim was number three
94.	Jim	oh yes
95.	Lis	sorry Jim (.) carry on
96.	Jim	what training have you had↑ and what training do you feel you
97.		need↑

Meetings such as this one are organised with very clear participation rights. In this case, the people with intellectual disabilities present are aligned as 'questioners', and that is marked by their question sheets (just as Mark used the question sheet in Chapter 11 in controlling the flow of the talk). All the others present in the room are aligned as people who could answer questions, except for me and two 'home group supporters' in the room (who remained silent). In the main, we do not intervene at all during the discussion, having no assigned role in asking or in answering questions.

Therefore, my lengthy intervention from line 82 is of interest as a marked event. Although he had been designated as the next speaker at line 76, Jim has chosen a question from the list which was not literally the next written question. This is what prompts the trouble that ensues from line 77, with the procedural interventions started by Sam: 'where are we at the moment↑'. Others present, including Kerrie and Lisa, then support him by explaining that the questions are not being asked in order, and Sam's next turn is an implied complaint, expressing the fact that he is 'confused'. Kerrie picks this up and appeals to everyone for an opinion. The issue now is not the answer to the original question; instead the talk has stepped back into a procedural framework, where the group is ostensibly deciding *how* to ask the questions.

At this point Lisa turns to me to ask me to point out which question has been asked, which I do. However, my subsequent remarks from line 83 are addressed to everyone in the room and can be heard as backing up Kerrie's question a few lines earlier:

> there is some worry here that people are thinking that we should do the questions in order↓ and other people are thinking that it's OK to jump around (.) so can people say if they are worried↑can you just raise your hand if you are worried jumping around the questions↑

This intervention highlights the contrast between two groups of people – those who are in favour of 'order' and those who favour being spontaneous and 'jumping around'. Because each participant has made his or her own decision, this has resulted in a split in the group and this is what I clarify for the whole room. What happens next is an appeal for a vote, and this is duly done in line 87. Thus the supporter task here is essentially to determine a quick, collective decision on how to proceed. In some circumstances, the rights of autonomy for one person with intellectual disabilities may conflict with the rights of another, and Lisa recognises this with her 'sorry' to Jim, who had asked the original question and now has to shift.

As a 'non-disabled' team member, I do not simply intervene and sort out the problem. By appealing to a group vote and by working jointly with others in the group (Kerrie with her group question and Lisa with her 'sorry' to Jim), I highlight the rights of all participants to decide for themselves on the best way to proceed. In this context, the exact nature of a supporter intervention can be very important. It is not just about telling people what to do, but also offering them a structure to take control of the social activity of research.

Doing analysis together

It is often considered too difficult for people with intellectual disabilities to get involved in analysis (Chappell, 2000; Richardson, 2002). Therefore, it may be of interest to have an insider's view of how this happened in the 'Skills for Support' study, where some of the sessions to overview the videos and discuss the analysis were recorded. The reader who has followed this project through the book will appreciate that my role was not that of a support worker. Instead, I was the principal researcher, working with the two self-advocate researchers as a team, which also included a research supporter and the personal assistant of one of the team members.

This set-up is relevant to how we worked on analysis in this project. First, the two co-researchers viewed each of the videos we had made. One or other of them was usually present during the filming as well. The purpose of the initial viewing was to choose key moments which were important to them, and they had accessible recording sheets where they could note these down, with their support workers.

Following that, I focused on their chosen extracts to do some transcription and formulate some analytic ideas. I then took those ideas back to the team to discuss. That was how the discussion in extract 12.3 took place.

At this point, we are discussing the video of Ellie and her budgeting (see Chapter 4) and have selected a short passage near the start of the recording, where the budgeting activity is just being started. Only Kerrie had been present at the recording, but both she and Lisa had seen this video before. During the section we viewed, Ellie was talking about several things – her holiday, her support worker's holiday, her shoelaces, and so on. The support worker, Jennie, for her part, was sitting with paper, pen and calculator, and was attempting to get started with the budgeting and shopping choices. At one point, she raised her pen and said 'right', effectively cutting off the former talk and starting on the shopping list talk. That is the action under discussion in the following talk in the research team. Lisa has said that this action was teacher-like and patronising, while Kerrie has countered by saying it is necessary to focus Ellie on the task. That is the point in our discussion when the following occurs:

Extract 12.3

15.	Val	do you think when people are chatting about social things like
16.		Ellie does at the beginning (.) it's part of being friendly and
17.		being relaxed with your support worker↑
18.	Lis	yes
19.	Ker	yea:h =
20.	Val	mm hm↑
21.	Ker	= but =
22.	Lis	= there again it depends↓ it depends who you - your
23.		support worker is
24.	Val	mm hm
25.	Ker	the house have always (.) have always said (.) to me
26.		there's a time and a place for something↓ (.)

27.	Val	mm hm↑
28.	Ker	[and if you -
29.	Lis	[have I got to sign here Val↑ ((*picking up a paper*))
30.	Val	yeah let's just leave it for a minute is that alright↑
31.		[put it up there]
32.	Ker	[if you er] are trying to concentrate on something then it's
33.		best to focus your mind on just that one thing otherwise (.) you
34.		might forget something or your brain might wander off
35.		[on something -
36.	Lis	[I agree with Kerry
37.	Val	yes and that's exactly what I did just now wasn't it ↑
38.	Lis	yes
39.	Ker	yeah
40.	Val	((LF))
41.	Lis	because you took my tea↑ [never mind
42.	Val	((LF voice)) [no not the tea the form
43.		I said let's leave that and do this now didn't I
44.	Lis	mm
45.	Val	and to my mind that's a bit what um the support worker is
46.		doing there (.) [but I thought it's really interesting -
47.	Ker	[yes but you do it er -
48.	Lis	you do it in such a way that -
49.	Ker	it's like an adult um er it was like um with Angela the
50.		example of this morning like I was telling you↓

Extract 12.3 starts with my turn at line 15, which is an opener designed in such a way to favour a preferred response of agreement (see Chapter 3, p. 39 for an explanation of 'preferred' and 'dispreferred' turns). The formulation or construction of my words is designed to suggest agreement and serves to move the conversation away from the actual pencil-waving and on to the topic of Ellie's social talk. Both Lisa and Kerrie give the preferred response of 'yes' at lines 18 and 19, but Kerrie immediately moves on with a 'but' and Lisa latches on to this 'but': together they frame a response that adds a condition to the proposition I had made about social talk:

> Lis   = there again it depends↓ it depends who you – your support worker is
>   (line 22)

It is hard to see from the text what the force of this remark might be, other than that it does the work of modifying their agreement: this is Lisa's follow-up to the 'but'. What actually happens is that Kerrie then comes in with her own modifier:

> Ker   the house have always (.) have always said (.) to me there's a time and a
>   place for something↓ (.) (line 25)

This turn is punctuated with slight pauses, maybe simply a strategy to keep the floor; however, the hesitancy also has the effect of marking Kerrie's contribution as a genuine account of her own experience, something she is remembering as she speaks. Her choice of the word 'house' signifies the staff who work in the house where she lives and is a shorthand form she often uses; here it comes over as an institutional word, something which perhaps highlights the right of the staff (the 'house') to determine what is right and wrong, and she gives us their words as direct speech: 'there's a time and a place for something'. Whatever the case, it certainly starts to touch on, and make salient, the institutional experience of Kerrie and Lisa but also of Ellie in the video they were watching.

In Kerrie's remark, citing as she does the direct speech of her staff members, there is a presumption that the staff dictate what can be talked about and what tasks should be done at different times. This is precisely the work which had been done by the support worker in the video, calling Ellie to focus on the task of writing the shopping list by waving her pen at her. Kerrie goes on, at lines 32–5, to position herself as agreeing with this strategy, backing up her argument with constructs about cognition ('concentrate', 'focus your mind', 'your brain might wander off'). By talking about the way her own mind works, she is starting to imply an insight into the minds of other people with intellectual disabilities, a very strong argument in this context, where we are basically analysing the support strategies of personal assistants from the point of view of people with intellectual disabilities.

However, just before we get to that point there has been an interruption sequence, from lines 29–31, initiated by Lisa who picks up a form which she had on her desk to show it to me. I deal with this by sidelining it – suggesting she leaves it – and thus marking it as an activity irrelevant to the present discussion. In our interaction we thus inadvertently mirror precisely the support strategy which is under discussion, the strategy of focusing people on the task at hand! There are therefore now three levels of interaction in which 'focusing' work is being displayed:

a)   The original video where we saw the support worker and Ellie.
b)   Kerrie's recounted experience of her support staff and herself.
c)   The current here-and-now interaction with Val and Lisa.

This coincidence does not go unnoticed (at any rate, not by me), and occasions the laughter and my explanation from line 37 onwards, turning the analytical perspective back on ourselves and particularly on my own work as a non-disabled colleague. Kerrie does the sensitive work of saving face for me by modifying my (implied) self-criticism and saying that the focusing had been done 'like an adult', something which had previously been agreed in our team as constituting good practice in support. The way in which my focusing work could have been said to be more 'adult-like' is not revealed and is probably irrelevant: Kerrie is simply providing a way of taking the spotlight off what has just happened and moving back to a previous example.

What does all this have to say about 'autonomy'? The question is whether Kerrie and Lisa, as researchers, could be said to be in control of the activity of analysis. It is clear in this particular project that everyone in the team had an important role to play. What we have seen here is a layered range of strategies (reported, viewed on video and enacted) to ensure that someone keeps to the matter in hand and that their attention does not stray. As Kerrie herself argues, this may sometimes be necessary and may not affect fundamentally the autonomy of the disabled person. However, in interactional terms, this 'focusing' work is a powerful move. Effectively, in each of the three layered examples it puts the agenda into the hands of the support worker and takes it away from the other participant. Instead of following Ellie's or Lisa's attempt to introduce a new social activity or sequence, the supporter in each case is pulling the conversation back to the original planned task.

My turn at lines 30–1, for instance, could come over as both teacher-like and/or patronising. There is no particular evidence one way or another about how it is taken in the interaction, apart from being the occasion of our mutual laughter later. Nevertheless, it has the effect of keeping the conversation focused on the video and on our analysis. The autonomy of both Kerrie and Lisa and myself at that point is determined and limited by the task we are undertaking, arguably a work task (we were all working in 'paid' time), and so I am concerned to get the balance right between getting the job done and supporting their moment-by-moment autonomy. Within this work context, autonomy evidently does not mean simply 'do as you choose'.

Reflecting on research

Strategies to support ownership of research are not limited to the work the present author has done. I am grateful to an MSc student for the following extract from a video recording of her work. It is taken from a recording of a different set of people with intellectual disabilities, who were meeting with a regional coordinator to discuss their involvement in a recent research study in the area. Annette, the coordinator, is standing in front of the group, flipchart pen in hand, asking questions to which various group members supply answers.

Extract 12.4

1.	Ann	who decides what research you want to do
2.	Jon	we do we should be↓the most important thing about
3.		research is deciding what you want to find out
4.	Ann	so that's people with learning difficulties (.)
5.		should be doing the research↑
6.	Dav	yes so they can find it out for themselves can't
7.		they↑instead of staff doing it for them they
8.		should do it
9.	Ann	((writes this up on chart))
10.	Jon	good tip for you↓ if you want the pen to work keep it warm
11.	Ann	so people with intellectual disabilities doing their
12.		own research↓ ((turns around to face group))
13.		so that's you being in control↑
14.	Voices	yeah

Although this seems on the face of it to be a very straightforward activity in which Annette is simply recording answers, in fact, she does far more than this. Where there is a response that has not yet been ratified as adequate by the questioner, CA sometimes calls this a candidate response (see Chapter 3, p. 43; Wooffitt, 2005: 176). This is what Jon does at line 2, where he gives a literal answer to Annette's question: 'we do we should be'. However, the second part of this turn is used by Jon to justify the importance of 'deciding what you want to find out'. In other words, Jon does some affirmation work here, pointing out that the question was a sound one.

Annette does not, however, immediately turn to the flipchart. She probes further, with her clarification question at lines 4–5. Where Jon had merely referred to 'we', Annette specifies what this 'we' might refer to in terms of the identity of 'learning difficulties'. Interestingly, although he agrees with this, Dave (another group member) then rephrases Jon's contribution and expands on it in the third-person plural ('they can do it'). At this point Annette seems to accept the response as adequate and turns to the flipchart to write up what members have said. However, she does not leave it there. She writes and speaks the words 'that's people with learning difficulties doing their own research', but then turns back to the group for a final confirmation in line 13: 'So that's you being in control↑'. Noticeably, two matters have been reformulated in this final confirmation. One is the pronoun, which has reverted to 'you', and the other is the introduction of the word 'control'. Research is seen as synonymous with control, and indeed the whole matter is personalised as 'you being in control'.

Through a series of exchanges, then, Annette has used clarifications to expand on information and to reformulate the way in which members have framed their involvement in deciding on research topics. This is now seen as a way of being in control and is also linked explicitly with group members ('you') in the membership category of 'people with learning difficulties'.

It would seem important, then, to take opportunities to reflect on research and to assist people with intellectual disabilities in verbalising their ideas about research. This happened in all the projects in this book. Here is an example from the 'Finding Out' project:

Extract 12.5

201.	Mar	you've got yah – but (.) I don't think you're going to get as much
202.		information from an MP than you are from a researcher↑ (1)
203.	She	hh hh
204.	Har	[what we should do is write a letter to Tony Blair
205.		and tell him -]
206.	Mar	see what I mean↑[the person who's got the most] – sorry Harry I
207.		interrupted you
208.	She	the person who's got the most – go on finish that sentence/
209.	Ang	power
210.	Mar	((LF))
211.	Ang	power
212.	Mar	((LF)) the person who's got the most
213.	Ian	power
214.	Ang	that's a good word isn't it↑
215.	She	((LF))
216.	Mar	no the person who's got the most - (1) inevitability about the er (.)
217.		about the:: (1) information we want the research (.) has got the
218.		most _right_ to interview other people↓ to _find_ out more research
219.		and _how_ it affects people
220.	She	who has got the most power then↑
221.	Mar	people with learning difficulties

The preceding discussion had been to do with politics, the government's 'Back to Work' policy and the much publicised cuts in disability benefits which had been in the news. These topics had been introduced by Harry, and all four members of the group were engaged in the conversation at this point. Mark then introduces his own visit to a Member of the European Parliament (MEP), and he moves on from this to contrast the two identities of MP (Member of Parliament) and researcher.

The supporter in this extract is Sheila, and I'd like to highlight her contributions, since they are very typical of other places in which supporters, including myself, intervene in discussions to prompt other people. At lines 204–6 there is an overlap between Harry and Mark, in which Mark cedes to Harry as next speaker. However, at line 208 Sheila invokes her prerogative to say who should speak next. She gives precedence to Mark, thereby setting off the sequence which leads to his formulation at line 221: 'people with learning difficulties'. By encouraging Mark to continue, Sheila implies that what he has to say might be important. Mark then takes over and builds up a fill-the-gap structure: he keeps his audience waiting for his key word. Angela guesses, then Ian; they both supply the word 'power' in Mark's frame. Throughout this sequence, it is evident that Sheila is still supporting the closure of his sentence by her continued attention. A large part of the role of the supporter is to supply this attention, as was seen with Fiona and Alex earlier in this chapter.

Mark chooses to reject the term 'power', although his turn at line 216 is actually powerful, since in it he expresses the central and important issue of who has the 'right' to do research. The fill-the-gap game invests the whole sequence with a light, jokey and self-congratulatory tone. A good deal of joint work is going on here. This is not just Mark's speech, but is being followed closely by at least Angela and Ian. Mark is continuing here with the identity work of being a researcher which has been so evidently a theme throughout the session. The vocabulary he chooses is both authoritative and draws on a discourse of rights: 'inevitability' (line 216), 'information' (line 217), 'right' (line 218). Sheila's final move (line 220) draws together Angela's and Ian's 'power' with what Mark has been saying. Without it, they would perhaps never have got to the formulation with which Mark concludes:

| She | who has got the most power then↑ |
| Mar | people with learning disabilities (lines 220–1) |

This passage is fascinating, because members are quite literally together building new possibilities for their own identities as people with 'learning difficulties' and as researchers. Sheila provides the supportive frame, but it is Mark who pulls together the two sets of meanings in one overarching clause:

| Mar | the person who's got the most … power … inevitability …_right_ … |
| | people with learning disabilities (lines 208–21) |

Having a 'learning disability' or an 'intellectual disability' is construed as an advantage, if you want to do research.

Public statements about research by people with intellectual disabilities

This chapter ends with some of the public statements and presentations made by people with intellectual disabilities who have done research in order to illustrate the kind of powerful talk that can occur at the end of a research project. These examples are taken from discussions or meetings when people had had at least two years' experience of research. The first example is from Lisa and Kerrie, and is taken from a video made after the end of the 'Skills for Support' project, when both the researchers with intellectual disabilities were talking on camera about the 'story of their research'. Extract 12.6 followed a summing-up question from me: 'What do you think people will say about our research in about one year's time?'

Extract 12.6

88.	Lis	I think in a year's time everyone will know what we've done
89.		and say 'well done' (.) but don't pat me on the back because I don't
90.		like it ↓
91.	Ker	I think if you want my view Valerie my hopes and dreams
92.		would be for other disabled people to remember that it was
93.		done by disabled people for disabled people and for PAs ((*personal*
94.		*assistants*)) and I hope that it will be remembered that disabled people
95.		aren't stupid they've got brains and that they can learn from it and
96.		that disabled people to have many opportunities and
97.		happiness and fulfilment of life
98.	Lis	what we do is to get better lives for people with learning
99.		disabilities so that people with learning disabilities can get
100.		better support (.) so if we don't get better support after all
101.		we've done what is the point of us doing our job↑ we've done
102.		all this and done our job now you have a go

There is considerable fluency in both Lisa's and Kerrie's contributions, although the turns taken by each are not linked in any sort of adjacency sequence: they are not responding to each other, but talking to camera on an individual basis. All this shows that both researchers show considerable awareness of the potentially public nature of this occasion, although the actual participants are only the author, the camera and one of the support workers from the project.

Both Kerrie and Lisa choose ways of framing their relationship to the research as autonomous actors, who 'own' the project and its outcomes. For instance, Lisa uses the plural first-person 'we', which emphasises ownership: 'we've done'; 'what we do'; 'us doing our job'; 'we've done all this'; 'our job'. Kerrie moreover chooses to describe the project not only as their work, but also as their work 'as disabled people':

> my hopes and dreams would be for other disabled people to remember that
> it was done by disabled people for disabled people (lines 91–3)

The selection of vocabulary such as 'hopes and dreams' (line 91) has a ring of public speaking to it and signals a neat rhetorical structure with its three-part mention of 'disabled people'. Interestingly, Lisa also rejects, in a joke-like fashion, the possibility that someone might 'pat me on the back' for her achievement. This could be heard as a reference to the type of patronising support and encouragement which we had looked at in our research and which warns her that her research work could be seen simply as an individual achievement. As she goes on to say, she explicitly contrasts this individual model of achievement with the wider goals of the research itself:

> what we do is to get better lives for people with learning disabilities
> (lines 98–9)

The importance of the research is thus highlighted by Lisa not as a matter of individual skill, but as a matter of public good. Quite explicitly, Lisa and Kerrie are drawing on a repertoire of ownership and achievement, but also linking this with their identity as disabled people in common with 'other disabled people'. This is quite a different repertoire from that which relates to achievement, when people with intellectual disabilities seek approval for what they have done, as Angela did in Chapter 10 with her statements about showing the photos of their research to other people and feeling 'quite important'.

Similar issues were very important in 'Journey to Independence' in which the three self-advocate researchers themselves had a 'journey' to accomplish. A large part of this was the need to become more aware of the potential significance of their research and their own identity in being part of that research (see Williams *et al.*, 2005). Stacey (in Gramlich *et al.*, 2002) made a statement in discussion at the end of the project, which appears in the final report:

Having a learning difficulty is not something to be ashamed about. I am proud of who I am. If I resented it, then I would be a wreck. Some people may think that people with learning difficulties cannot be researchers, but we know that we can do it. In a lot of research, we are the exhibits. But now we are not just part of the picture – we are the artists of our lives. (Gramlich *et al.*, 2002: 120)

Like Kerrie's statement on video, this is carefully crafted with some fine rhetorical work, including the metaphor I have frequently cited, contrasting the position of being 'just part of the picture' with being 'the artists of our lives'. The issue of 'having a learning difficulty' is connected with the research process and is seen not only as an advantage here, but also as a necessary prerequisite for doing this type of research. It is not a matter of 'resentment' but of 'pride'.

Implications for practice

This chapter has focused on how people with intellectual disabilities go about doing research, and in particular how they take ownership and control of the process of the work. The reason for the self-advocacy researchers being there is to some extent linked both with their identity as people with intellectual disabilities and with their status as autonomous social actors. In other words, these activities are predicated on the fact that people with intellectual disabilities can and do 'speak up for themselves' and that their ideas and decisions belong to them.

What readers have seen in this chapter will not surprise those who are used to supporting people with intellectual disabilities in these activities. The talk that goes on, mainly behind the scenes, is often specifically designed to help people understand the significance of what they are doing. For instance, in talking with the research group members in the 'Finding Out' project, I was very opportunistic. Instead of just telling the members what to do, I was careful to frame their involvement in a project that was theirs. I used the device of minute-taking to record their previous statements and remind them of their decisions, ensuring that the talk became about 'your project' and 'your idea', rather than the supporter's own idea. Similarly in extract 12.5 the technique of expansion was used in order to take a response from people with intellectual disabilities and to associate it with further meanings, including the idea of 'taking control'.

Ownership is the key theme in this chapter; people with intellectual disabilities are in a strong position as researchers, but only when they frame the work as their *own*, something which they have been in control of. This does not necessarily mean that they need to claim to have done every part of the work. Indeed, in the video made by Kerrie and Lisa at the end of 'Skills for Support', they go on to talk about all the roles in the team and how good the team work was in that project. Ownership implies something deeper, that the research in question can be assumed to *represent* the voices of people with intellectual disabilities, that they have acted in their own right and that they have in some way led the research.

All decisions, to some extent, are made *with* others – they are social events (Jenkinson, 1993). Therefore, it is not surprising that this is also true in research. This chapter has added to the analysis of what could be called autonomy and how it was achieved. On the one hand, in public arenas it was about publicly 'owning' the work and performing, often in quite rhetorical mode. However, this public face of research was backed up by detailed interactional work, during which people with intellectual disabilities explored the significance of their own roles.

Employees cannot simply decide what they want on a moment-by-moment basis. When people with intellectual disabilities are employed as researchers, a balance therefore has to be achieved between getting the job done and being in control of every decision. In Williams *et al.* (2005) I have written about this in relation to another project, where we established visual systems for people to choose their work task. The fact is that in any work there are tasks which need to be done, and so it is important to establish systems for everyone to have a choice, but within the constraints of the overall agenda of work. Current tasks can be suggested by any of the team members, not just the supporter. In 'Skills for Support' we tried many systems for writing out tasks, creating wall displays with stickers and task sheets, so that team members could have a choice of jobs to do when they came into work.

People without intellectual disabilities who have some kind of supportive role in projects, including myself, often engage in work that could be described as 'educative'. The talk presented and analysed in this chapter is certainly predicated on a developmental model in which research-ers with intellectual disabilities gradually learn not only the technical tasks of doing research, but also their own place and potential strength. This is actually the learning of 'self-determination' in action.

The tensions are clear; to the extent that the supporter is positioned as an 'educator', the researchers with intellectual disabilities then become 'students' or 'learners'. It is true that people involved in a research project often refer back to it as something which showcases their 'achievements' or their learning and progress. It becomes, then, an individual accomplishment rather than a collective enterprise, a point that was made clear in the opening statements by Lisa and Kerrie. Even more worryingly, if supporters have to coach and educate people about their role and how to frame their involvement, then it is hard to reconcile this with autonomy. This chapter has shown how these matters were dealt with in the ebb and flow of naturally occurring interaction, talk in which each party drew on the contributions of the other and created frameworks for the next contribution. Not only did those labelled 'supporters' deliberately work up an idea of ownership, but people with intellectual disabilities themselves took the lead in these conversations, as Mark did in extract 12.5. All these matters, then, are achieved in interaction; autonomy and ownership are both constructs and can be talked into being during the course of a project.

A large part of the talk analysed in this chapter has focused on identities and on the relevant aspects of identity for research. As Stacey (Gramlich *et al.*, 2002) so fluently realised, it is the identity of 'having a intellectual disability' that is so fundamental to his power in taking part in research. In fact, it was his 'ticket'. If he did not have an intellectual disability, he would not be there, and by combining that identity with that of being a researcher he achieved, as Mark explains in extract 12.5, a position of power. In interaction with supporters, I have shown how the behind-the-scenes talk in research can help people with intellectual disabilities to work out which aspects of their own identity matter, in that particular context. As the next, final data chapter explores, identity work is also very important in carrying out inclusive research and could in many ways be singled out as a hallmark of that type of research.

How conversation works: summary points

- What people say often refers to other things that have been said on other occasions, or indeed to written texts. These links are sometimes referred to as intertextuality (Fairclough, 2001: 233). Analysing intertextual links can reveal the richly layered nature of talk.

- Following Goffman (1959) it is possible to contrast 'frontstage' with 'backstage' events. However, this distinction is not absolute: the public nature of talk is constructed by speakers through vocabulary choices, rhetorical structures, and so on.

- The use of objects in a communication event can have strong implications. For instance, paperwork plays a role in meetings, when speakers refer to what is written or use the paperwork as part of their communication.

Inclusive approaches to communication: summary points

- In inclusive research it is vital to build in time to have discussions with the whole team about the significance of the research and about the roles played by each person.
- Different support styles are necessary at different times. For instance, it is important to be able just to give 'back-up' when needed; at other times, supporters are more proactive.
- As researchers with intellectual disabilities grow in confidence and in their ownership and autonomy in research, it is important that the supporter notices and is able to step back. This is essentially about relinquishing power.

Chapter 13

Talk about Labelling and Identity

This final data chapter is the one that brings it all together. If readers read this chapter first they will have missed a lot, yet I trust they will still get a holistic picture of the achievements and issues in inclusive research. This chapter follows through in depth the first, and perhaps the most delicate, of the questions in the 'Finding Out' project:

What do you think about people being labelled?

This was a particularly interesting question, as it was central to the research group's initial interests in labelling (see Beart *et al.*, 2005, and the discussion of this issue in Chapter 1, pp. 4–7). It will be recalled that the group members objected to labels, and in particular did not accept that they should have the label 'learning difficulty'. When they asked about these things in interviews, the question frequently caused particular tension. As I explore in this chapter, this was largely about how people related the objective question about 'labelling' to their own identity. In Baker's words, it left respondents free to explore 'how and as a member of which categories' (1997: 131) they should speak. Therefore, an additional reason for following through this question is to explore how the group members actually managed their own identity issues in the context of pursuing research *about* identity.

The four members of the research group in the 'Finding Out' project thought carefully about the way they wished to word this first question. Their list of questions came from their own lives and this first one was absolutely central to their interests. Thus the actual writing of the question was also an event that gave meat for analysis; it occurred during a preparation session, which was itself recorded and transcribed. As I explore in the first section, the writing of the question was far from straightforward and the positions taken by members evolved according to the chance events that happened during that conversation. In CA terms, it was 'locally managed'. The chapter then examines the first time this question was used in a research visit, when there was immediately some trouble in the talk. Breakdowns of understanding can often be revealing! In this case, I became interested in how membership categorisation related to the issue of how people talked about their identities and their view of others' identities. Their talk about themselves and their views on labelling appeared to be deeply intermeshed with how they saw each other.

Disability and Discourse. Analysing Inclusive Conversation with People with Intellectual Disabilities, 1st edition. © Val Williams. Published 2011 by John Wiley & Sons, Ltd.

Preparing the research question

The first question to be explored in this chapter is about labelling, and so I shall start by situating the term 'labelling' in the group's own discursive history. The first extracts are from one of the first taped sessions which took place shortly after one group member, Angela, had attended a conference with me about disability research, where the issue of disability pride had been discussed with her by some of the authors who later contributed to the book *Disability Discourse* (Corker & French, 1999). The first extract I consider occurred very shortly after the tape recorder was switched on and after Angela had been asking other members what they thought about the issue of labelling.

Extract 13.1

27.	Val	do you want to say what you think Angela↑
28.	Ang	what me↑
29.	Val	yes
30.	Ang	> I don't think – I think it's horrible< why have people got to be
31.		labelled anyway↓ why can't people just be called their own names↑
32.	Mar	mm
33.	Val	yeah and that's what you said at the meeting wasn't it↑ at the
34.		conference↑
35.	Ang	yeah ((*sighs*))
36.	Val	right that's very good (.)
		((*Some talk missing here about asking people at college, then college courses and qualifications. Then I start again by self-selecting*))
62.	Val	but there were some people that Angela and I met at that
63.		conference who actually um <u>want</u> to be <u>called</u> disabled (.) they've chosen that
64.		label themselves
65.	Ang	they have
66.	Val	themselves (.) um
67.	Mar	why ↑ why have they done that↑
68.	Ian	why have they done it↑
69.	Val	because (.)
70.	Ang	° I don't know °
71.	Val	<u>they</u> feel that society is unfair to them and things are <u>wrong</u>
72.		so they want to fight to make things better same as you do
73.	Mar	[uuh]
74.	Ian	[oh yeah]
75.	Val	but they think they're actually stronger by uniting [and] actually using
76.		the label to say this is who we are [( )] this is what's happening to us
77.	Ian	[uuh]
78.	Har	[uuh](1)
79.	Mar	I think that's a very strong point (0.5)

This extract sounds like a mutually supportive conversation in which we are all inviting others to speak and backing their comments up with 'good' and 'strong point'. However, on closer inspection we are actually exchanging some rather conflicting views on labelling. I want here to focus particularly on the content of Angela's turn at lines 30–1, and my own argument at lines 62–76. Angela starts with a self-correction: instead of 'I don't think', she switches to 'I think it's horrible'.

Ang   I don't think – I think it's horrible why have people got to be labelled
                 anyway↓ why can't people just be called their own names↑ (lines 30–1)

Angela self-repairs in this turn (see Jefferson, 1974; Schegloff *et al.*, 1977, for overviews of the functions of repair turns). Here she effectively **upgrades** her opening comment into a strong statement of her own feelings, which prepares her audience for what is to follow and gives them a clue as to how to hear it. She then goes on to use a two-part structure: 'why have people got to be labelled anyway↓', followed by 'why can't people just be called their own names↑'. This is very neat, and Angela marks the two parts by a falling intonation pattern, followed by a rising one. Everything she does is aimed at persuading her audience of the self-evident truth of her statement. It is interesting also to note her choice of passive voice in 'why have people got to be labelled'. The deleted subject has the effect of making the act of labelling appear endemic. The labelling is an enforced situation, something that is imposed. By contrast, people's 'proper names' are offered as the natural, obvious alternative. Angela's position on labelling is expressed as a personal, emotional argument. She strongly connects what she is saying with her own feelings ('I think it's horrible').

The task I face during this conversation is tricky. While not wishing to undermine Angela's right to express her view, I do eventually propose a totally opposing viewpoint about labelling. However, had I done it in my own voice, this would have been a strong personal attack on Angela. Instead, I explain this position about disabled people's views through the voices of people we had met at the conference and talk about their opinions as if they were not necessarily my own. Nevertheless, there are strong elements of persuasion in what I say. It is interesting to contrast the vocabulary choices I make in lines 62–72 with Angela's earlier ones. Where she uses passive voice and deleted subject, I start mentioning the people at the conference as active social agents who make their own choices:

some people ... <u>want</u> to be <u>called</u> disabled (lines 63)
they've chosen ... themselves (lines 63–4)
they feel (line 71)
they want to fight (line 72)
they think (line 75)

I also use the device of quoting direct speech, giving a flavour of what these disabled people might say: 'this is who we are [( )] this is what is happening to us' (line 76). All these are per-suasive devices. No wonder, then, that Mark concedes that this is a very strong point. The dis-abled people who have chosen their own label are contrasted with Angela and her colleagues, who feel that they have 'been labelled' by others. This is the core of the difference between their two positions: it is the very right to choose your own identity category which is at stake.

The discourse of labelling, on which Angela draws, is not new. As indicated in Chapter 1, this was the starting point for the research group. By asking about *people being labelled*, they were posing a question steeped in assumptions about lack of choice, self-determination and human dignity. This is why the counter-argument of the people at the conference could not persuade them. Although those people did indeed have a strong point, it seemed to the group members illogical to embrace a label that had been imposed by others. As argued in Chapter 1, labelling is not a neutral term. By choosing this way of expressing themselves, group members are resisting the dominant discourse or diagnosis of 'intellectual disability' and belittling attempts to assign identity to them. The word 'labelled' foregrounds the socially constructed nature of identity. It implies that the identity referred to is impermanent, detached from the person beneath the label. Labelling was, for group members, a word steeped in that repertoire of resistance.

Writing the first research question: 'a delicate object'

I now pick up the talk at a point slightly further on in the same session, when we are starting to write up a list of the group's research questions.

Extract 13.2

141.	Val	right so the first one – what was that question then Angela↑ what do
142.		people↑ *((standing at flipchart, turns to look at group members))*
143.	Ang	what – what does your friend think about horrible things↑
144.	Val	what do you think about – (3) *((writing on flipchart))* well if you
145.		asked somebody what do you think about horrible things↑do you
146.		think they'd understand↑
147.	Ang	wa – what do your friends think about YOU being called na- you know
148.		being labelled and being called nasty things you know-[being sworn at
149.	Val	[wa-wa what do
150.		you think about – me↑ personally↑ or people like me being labelled↑
151.	Ang	no your friends↓[like students you go round with [your colleagues you
152.	Val	[yes [yes
153.	Ang	go round with your workmates whatever you call them do they like
154.		you being called horrible names↑ what do they think about it↑
155.	Val	so people like me you're going to say when you're talking to folk
156.		are you↑
157.	Ang	no students(1) colleagues
158.	Mar	what you mean like at college↑[(the friends you've got)]
159.	Ang	[yes yeah yeah] your
160.		colleagues like students
161.	Val	so I'll just put people for the minute shall I↑ people being labelled↑
162.	Ang	your best friend↓ what do they think about you – (1)
163.	Val	OK (.) are there other things =
164.	Har	= well maybe I mean – that could be something like people with
165.		learning difficulties
166.	Ang	° [don't like that word] °
167.	Mar	[yeah]
168.	Ian	don't Harry don't keep on about it↓ I don't like it

For the most part, this is a fairly straightforward sequence of adjacency pairs (see Chapter 3, p. 39), with me doing a first part and Angela a second part on each occasion. However, that is probably the only respect in which this extract could be termed straightforward.

After what had been quite a lengthy discussion about labelling, what I am clearly trying to do is to turn the group members' ideas into a written interview question. One of the ways I do this is to stand up in order to write what they were saying on the flipchart, adopting what could be seen as an authoritative physical position. What I am seeking is a direct question, which could subsequently be addressed to the potential interviewees, and I give them the frame for this with: 'what do you think about – ' (line 144). I am essentially asking the group members to project into the situation of the future interview and say now what they will say later.

Angela, however, persists in the indirect formulation with 'what does your friend think↑' (143). This is what seems to create the confusion. Throughout this exchange, Angela is referring to the people who will be interviewed ('your friends, your colleagues, students') while I am trying to establish the actual form of the question to be posed. In line 150, when I start getting specific about the object of the labelling ('people like me↑'), Angela challenges again, referring to 'your friends, like students'. It is this challenge that leads to the dropping of the modifier (like me) and to the final form of the question at line 161. We achieve a fabulous pronoun and grammatical muddle, both bent on different purposes.

In itself this is not so interesting, except for the pedagogical points that could be made: why didn't I take time to explain to Angela that what I was doing was writing a question? However, through our display of mutual misunderstanding, what we end up with is a very ambiguous question, which is written up on the flipchart as:

What do you think about people being labelled?

Its ambiguity fits well with the frame which Angela provided for the relationship between interviewer and interviewee. She seems to be foreseeing an opportunity for talk with someone (a friend) who is likely to identify with her in terms of the kind of issues she is facing. Therefore, the entire presupposition is that there is a sharing of membership between questioner and respondent in the future interviews.

There is also evidence from that first group session that delicacy is a quite conscious and deliberate intention in phrasing the question. In the last part of the extract above, when Harry tries to introduce the word explicitly, he is shouted down by the others. Use of the term 'learning difficulties' is actually heard as offensive and the very mention of the words is seen as an embarrassment, even within the confines of our own group. If a word is heard as abusive or insulting, then the very utterance of it can have catastrophic effects, as suggested by Rapley *et al.* (1998), who cite some of Todd and Shearn's (1995) data, where very bald, direct questions could certainly have been heard as downright rude:

> J: Does your boyfriend have a mental handicap?
> K: I don't know. I don't know him that well. I know him from school, but not that well.
> (Todd & Shearn, 1995: 21)

The research group members effectively decide to talk about labelling without using the word 'learning difficulty', which Angela declares elsewhere that she wants to 'boycott'. Their reasoning is quite clearly to do with sensitivity to the way in which they are going to be heard, and Mark makes this explicit in his reaction to another proposed question later in the same session:

Extract 13.3

234.	Val	do you ever get bullied or made fun of something like that↑
235.	Mar	I don't think
236.	Ang	I do I do
237.	Mar	I don't think it's a good question myself
238.	Ang	I do
239.	Mar	I tell you for why it's not a very good question one it might offend the
240.		person you ask the question to (0.5) and two it might give people bad
241.		reactions↓ it – it might cause an upset between the person you're
242.		asking the question to and also who's asking the question ( )
243.	Val	yes it's certainly worth thinking about those things

In this case, group members are thinking through how another possible question 'do you ever get bullied or made fun of' (234) may be heard by those whom they are about to interview. The question carries a strong implication that the respondent is in a category of people who are likely to be bullied or made fun of, and so is, in effect, a reference to that same membership category of person with 'learning difficulties'. That second question became in its final version:

Have you been in any tricky situations when you've been discriminated against?'

The research group members judge they would not like to hear the term 'learning difficulties' or have any implication that they are in that category. That is why they choose not to use it in their interview question. This is not only about 'doing discretion' (Silverman, 1997) but also about foreseeing the need to do discretion. This is a remarkable achievement for these first-time researchers. As will be seen, the resulting ambiguity of the first question leaves participants free to interpret in their own way what was intended, leading to some very rich data. A more restrictive question may well have been interpreted as rude or as a stimulus for stereotyped reactions.

Who is being labelled? Posing the question to other people

So, did this careful preparation pay off? Extract 13.4 is from the first of the research visits and includes the very first time that the labelling question was posed. However, despite all the careful preparation, their plan to be sensitive was immediately upset and challenged

Extract 13.4

81.	Mar	we're going to ask (.) um (.) yourself what you think of the questions
82.		we thought↓ the first one (1) what do you think about people being
83.		labelled↓ that's to – that to all of you
84.		((Mark looks round at everyone + smile + sweeping hand gesture))
85.	Jon	[well -
86.	Dar	[what – sorry ( ) you go
87.	Jon	in what sort of way↑ labelled in what sort of way↑
88.	Mar	er -what do you think about people being labelled
89.		being um like being – umm (.) like – like with a learning difficulty
90.	Wil	like – like – like us you mean↑
91.	Mar	no like – like learning disa- disability
92.	Wil	o::h
93.	Jon	people –dis – (0.5) I think it's not- it's not very- not very-very-
94.		very meaning – meaningful↓ but it was what- it was what was deci-
95.		decided (.) I can't remember who decided – who decided to – to use
96.		this one was it HM her majesty's government decided this one to be- to
97.		be standardised was it↑ ((eye gaze to Mark)) (1.5)
98.	Mar	ummmm ((looks down)) (2)
99.	Dar	you don't need to know that↓ ((looking to John))
100.	She	( ) we do-
101.	Mar	I think (.) we (0.5)
102.	Wil	we've gone off the wrong track now haven't we↑
103.	Mar	yeah we have actually↓
104.		((General noises)) uuh
105.	Jon	I think it's a bit of a cruel one don't you because it doesn't – it

106.		does- it makes- it makes the people feel – it makes their problem wo-
107.		worse the learning difficulty it doesn't break down the- down the –
108.		down the bar- the barriers it makes it – makes it bigger doesn't it
109.		learning difficulty↑ ((looking to Mark))
110.	Mar	yeah it makes it – it affects a lot of people with a disability
111.		we found that in the group ourselves
112.	Har	mm yes
113.	Mar	especially when it comes to day centres ↓ colleges↓ and (.) other
114.		places that people go ((looks round at everyone + hand gestures))

The discussion above was held in a dining room area within a day centre. A group of some 11 people are sitting round a table with Mark at the head; the other research group members are interspersed with the host group. Mark is visually the focus, with others directing their gaze towards him, and he has the most turns (8 out of 18), starting with his open invitation for someone to answer the first research question. He makes this quite explicit with: 'that's to – that to all of you' (83) with his hand gesture and smile. This was quite an exciting moment for all of us, since it was the first test of the group's preparation as a research group, the very first focus group we had arranged.

Immediately, though, there is some confusion about who should take up the response slot, with both Darren and Jon starting to ask for clarification. Darren defers to Jon with 'you go' (86), thus indicating that they have equal rights to be next speaker. Mark is then selected to do another turn and repeat his question (line 88), which again is met with a request for clarification (line 90), and he responds at line 91. Finally, it is Jon who takes up the main response slot at lines 93–7. There is also some hesitancy about the flow of the turn structure, for example the 1.5-second pause at line 97 and a long 'mmmm' by Mark and interruptions at lines 98–100, which give a sense of interactional trouble. However, on the whole the turn structure corresponds to what one would expect in a research interview or focus group (see Silverman, 1973; Baker, 1997), an event set up deliberately to get interview respondents to talk. Mark does assume the role of interviewer, with his shorter turns and questions (first parts), while Jon, Darren and William are all playing the part of respondents, and producing second parts, with the final third part doing the business of an evaluation, and delivered by Mark at line 110 (see Chapter 3, p. 39 for a discussion of what is meant by 'part', and Chapter 5, p. 71, for an introduction of the notion of 'third part').

What is happening here? Following the initial posing of the labelling question, a strong expectation is built up that the next turn will constitute a response. That would be the preferred option. However, Mark's question is met instead with a request for clarification, delivered jointly by Darren and Jon: 'labelled in what sort of way↑' (87).

This request is not just a general one, like 'what do you mean?'. Jon is asking quite specifically what label is referred to, and Mark clearly has some problems now, as he had deliberately set out *not* to use the words 'learning difficulty'. That could certainly account for his trouble in lines 88–9, which are filled with hesitation and stumbles.

Although Mark manages to repair the original question by specifying 'like with a learning difficulty' (line 89), he then plunges into even deeper water! In order to grasp what is happening here, the notion of 'recipient design' is useful. For instance, van de Mieroop (2008) analyses how speakers representing commercial companies construct their company identity through devices such as metaphors. As people construct their own 'we' identity in certain precise ways, this projects the other (or paired) identity onto the audience:

'Recipient design' is a central notion in communication and also for identity construction. The idea of integrating the perspective of the recipients in the analyses has been demonstrated here to be of great importance for a fuller insight into the way identities are meaningfully constructed. (van de Mieroop, 2008: 507)

The group had expressly thought through the possibility of people taking this question to refer to themselves, and the very next utterance fulfils their fears by getting straight to the nub of the identity issue: 'like – like – like us you mean↑' (90). William appears to be asking: 'Are we the object or the subject here?' Are they expected to give their views about something or to consider that they are the object being discussed – or are both things true? This is just like Baker (1982), in which adolescents are being interviewed by a young researcher and needed to know whether they were being asked to speak 'as young people' to another young person. In four words, William raises the whole issue of membership categorisation, looking for an answer to the question: 'as a member of which category should I be speaking?'.

An attempt to repair the talk

What Mark does is to negate what Jon has said with a 'no' and then to shift the focus from who is being talked about to the actual words in the label: 'like – like learning disa- disability' (91). This distances the term 'learning disability' from the current situation. It appears to have the interactional effect of depersonalising the issue and this is what occasions Jon's first response (line 93 onwards), in which he takes up the invitation to discuss the 'issue of learning disability'. This discussion, it should be noted, took place shortly after the term 'learning disability' had been adopted officially as the preferred term by the UK government, and Jon was clearly aware of this. In this response he starts to make lexical choices that both depersonalise, using actors like 'HM – her majesty's government' (line 96), and words that give a professional feel to the debate: 'standardised' (line 97). The subject deletion ('it was what was decided': lines 94–5) gives a more professional, even ironic, air to the talk. Instead of taking offence and perhaps reacting emotionally, Jon offers a response that starts to set out terms of an argument that exists independently of his own assigned identity. The issue moves from one in which people need to discuss their own membership categorisation, to one in which they are reflecting on the way in which very high-level forces in society are imposing, or standardising, the use of language.

However, this response is clearly not what Mark had expected to hear. Instead of giving an acceptance or thanks after Jon's response, Mark is non-committal with his: 'ummm' (line 98). Possibly, he is still rather thrown by the unexpected turn of events. Video evidence shows Mark breaking gaze with Jon immediately after the tag 'was it↑'. Dropping his face, and his mouth, he looks down and remains like that for a good two-second pause, and then also during the subsequent talk. Whatever the intent, his lack of response has the effect of indicating to the group that Jon's response was not adequate, and this leads to the very interesting sub-sequence.

99.	Dar	you don't need to know that↓ (*(to John)*)
100.	She	( ) we do-
101.	Mar	I think (.) we (0.5)
102.	Wil	we've gone off the wrong track now haven't we↑
103.	Mar	yeah we have actually↓

This is a kind of evaluative meta-sequence concerning the process of 'what we are doing' – it is talk about talk. It starts with two interrupted fragments, and then a meta-comment from William on the course of the present talk: 'we've gone off the wrong track now haven't we↑' (line 102). The tag question 'haven't we↑' opens a very strong expectation of a slot to be filled by a confirmation, and Mark provides this at line 103. Although this is still fraught with hesitancy and confusion, there is at least now some agreement that they are indeed on the wrong track. Note that it is Mark (a research group member), Darren and William (host group members) who work this out together. They are all sharing responsibility for sorting out what kind of conversation they should be having.

Getting back on track: body language matters

It is interesting to note how the use of 'we' and 'us' starts creeping in. First, William asks 'like us you mean?'. It is not clear at this point whether the 'us' is William and his friends in the day centre group. However, the possibility is that it includes everyone in the room. All that we can be sure of is that he counts himself as part of a category of 'us' and offers the possibility that this 'us' could be seen as a group of people who are labelled as having a learning difficulty. By the point at which they are trying to sort out what to say next, William says 'we have gone off the track' and this is met by Mark's 'yes we have actually'. The 'we' now refers to both the research group members and those they are visiting. The choice of the word 'we' and its reflection by each subsequent speaker serves to underline the commonality of membership – not as people with 'learning difficulties', but as members of the current situation, as people who are building up an interview context together. It turns out that the issue of who is included in 'we' is vital to moving forward the whole question of labelling.

It is clear here how one thing follows from another. Somehow the 'we' of line 103 gives the context for Jon's second response ('candidate response') at line 105:

105.	Jon	I think it's a bit of a cruel one don't you because it doesn't – it
106.		does- it makes- it makes the people feel – it makes their problem wo-
107.		worse the learning difficulty it doesn't break down the- down the –
108.		down the bar- the barriers it makes it – makes it bigger doesn't it
109.		learning difficulty↑ *((looking to Mark))*

He chooses some interesting vocabulary, framing this response, as he did the previous one, with an 'I think', which draws attention to his identity as a respondent rather than as a labelled person. The choice of the word 'cruel' is strong, bringing with it the possibility that one person (or group of people) is engaging in cruel actions towards another group. The designated people, though, again are unspecified ('the people'). However, Jon's second response gives a reasoned argument for the choice of one term over another, and it does some contrast work to show that 'it' (intellectual disability) is both 'cruel' and 'makes their problem worse', while the other term (learning difficulty) is not such a problem. The metaphor 'doesn't break down the barriers' brings the argument about labelling into the frame of other social barriers that are faced by disabled people, and this interpretation could be what occasions Mark's final positive evaluation of Jon's response.

Mar	yeah it makes it – it affects a lot of people with a disability
	we found that in the group ourselves (lines 110–11)

What seems to be happening here is that Jon and Mark are suddenly 'on the same wavelength' – they recognise that they are talking about the same issues and in fact that they share the same issues, the same identity.

This interpretation is backed by some interesting video evidence. At the beginning of this fragment, Jon can be seen coming back in with his second turn. As can be seen in Figure 13.1,

Figure 13.1　Jon challenges, with arms folded.

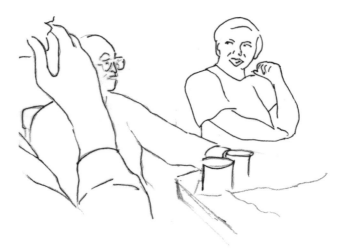

Figure 13.2　Mutual eye gaze, open body language: making a connection.

he folds his arms and engages Mark in a very definite gaze, simultaneously with the start of his 'I think'. Up to this point, Mark's body language has been one of avoidance (he puts his hand to his nose, strokes his face, then holds his mouth, while looking down). Jon carries on, however, with what he wants to say and his gaze direction is mostly towards Mark, sometimes glancing away. He appears to be monitoring his audience and his facial expression remains set in a serious mode with slightly raised eyebrows.

It is at the word 'people' that things seem to change, as can be seen in Figure 13.2. Mark does a definite look towards Jon and Jon then starts to unfold his arms, with one arm ready to gesture. He looks away shortly after Mark looks towards him, but then re-establishes gaze at about the word 'learning difficulty'. Through the whole of the next nine seconds or so of Jon's turn, Mark is looking down at the table and his papers, with his hand over his mouth, while Jon keeps him in his gaze and carries on with what he wants to say. Why doesn't Jon give up? What keeps him going and how do they achieve joint sense-making in the end?

What I ended up focusing on was a very short (two-second) burst of events that took place at or around the word 'barriers'. At this precise point, Mark can be seen to shake his head slightly and Jon immediately becomes a little more animated in his facial expression (a slight twinkling of his eyes?) which might be understandable as a sign he is becoming more engaged with the interaction. He moves his left arm up from the elbow, with a definite finger movement. This seems like the start of a pointing gesture. It could well be that these very slight movements on each side are occasioned by each other, or even by the sense of the word 'barriers'. Mark's head shake could have been interpreted, for instance, as an acceptance that barriers are dreadful and so are relevant to the present conversation, or simply that he is listening, and Jon's raising of his hand could be seen as a renewed confidence that his contribution is being accepted. Whatever the case, at the end of Jon's turn ('bigger doesn't it learning difficulty↑'), he does a slight eyebrow raise, like a glance, and then a slight nod as he finishes what he is saying. Together with the rising tone of his voice, the whole tone becomes definitely more confident. Jon appears to be signalling that he feels all right about what he has said and that he is now 'on the right track'.

There is a definite feeling of collaboration, then, as the turn passes to Mark, who looks up, takes his hand off his face and makes an open hand gesture. With a slight smile towards Jon, he embarks on his evaluative turn. All these things appear like markers that things are now all right and that Jon's achievement is recognised. Jon himself sits back, with his arms folded, and smiles slightly.

I have gone through this micro-segment in detail to show how video evidence can sometimes back up interpretation of the talk in a compelling way. Achieving collaboration is done by some very fine and detailed body work. Both Mark and Jon are as finely tuned to each other's non-verbal activity as to the sense of what each is saying. It is interesting how such a very small head gesture on Mark's part can occasion this. He has power to arbitrate on relevance, and this is immediately picked up by Jon, who appears to be more pleased by successfully accomplishing his turn than outraged by being labelled as someone with an intellectual disability.

Sharing identity

This extract has warranted some lengthy analysis, but I would still like to give some final thoughts about Mark's evaluation turn at line 110. First, he validates what Jon has said by confirming the general truth of the issue ('it affects a lot of people with a disability') and then turns back to the personal: 'we found that in the group ourselves' (line 111). His choice of 'we', as well as the definite article 'the', indicates that the group is in fact the group here present, while 'found' relates this to another context of talk that had taken place in that group. He effectively makes Jon's contribution relevant to these other context(s) and to other possible locations – 'day centres ↓ colleges↓ and (.) other places that people go'.

Mark's speech could be heard as an admission that research group members also faced these problems in day centres and colleges and so had discussed them from a personal point of view. It is by virtue of this admission that the two groups, represented at this point by Jon and Mark, can relax in the knowledge that they share some aspects of identity, and this is shown by Jon's more confident body movements and Mark's hand gestures at the end of line 114. It will be recalled that one of the researchers' aims was to establish a relationship of friendship, or a peer relationship, between interviewer and interviewee. Perhaps this is now happening.

With this final turn, Mark is doing two things. First, he is treating Jon's responses as appropriate in the context of the research interview. Second, however, he is also widening the context to his own group and to other people with a disability, in other locations. By doing this, Mark is including himself and his fellow group members in the same category as the interviewees: they are all people who have to face social oppression. The business of doing research is intricately bound up here with the topic under discussion, and both come together in an affirmation that they have the right to define themselves.

Implications for practice

Sometimes the views of people in the self-advocacy movement about labelling are seen as problematic (Walmsley, 2001). By contrast to people with intellectual disabilities, disabled people who subscribe to the social model of disability often express pride in their own identity and value the act of identifying as disabled, since this is a part of their political commitment to change:

> In the act of coming out (as disabled) we are changing the meaning of disability … The personal becomes political, and coming out becomes a political, collective commitment as well as a change in personal identity. (Swain & Cameron, 1999: 77)

In some respects, however, this chapter shows how the discourse of labelling did become such a 'political' tool in the hands of the research group members and their research participants. It was this discourse of resistance that enabled Jon to talk disparagingly of the government's standardisation of the label 'intellectual disability'. This is part of a model of disability that is particularly associated with people with intellectual disabilities in the self-advocacy movement; labelling is seen as a kind of oppression, caused by others' attitudes and actions, and is positioned as a social barrier. Like Rapley *et al.* (1998) this chapter has shown how talk about identity is a sensitive matter, and

> A person with an intellectual disability can, like any other, avow or disavow such an identity according to the demands of the situation in which they find themselves. (Rapley *et al.*, 1998: 807)

This chapter has examined talk in two different, but related contexts – the interview visits and the sessions – and it has revealed some of the links between these two events. The talk on identity issues in the interviews was not simply part of casual talk between self-advocates, it was carefully rehearsed and prepared in the session. In addition, the analysis of preparation talk has shown how closely the initial purpose of the question, and of the whole activity of questioning, was linked with group members' own concerns. Angela wanted to compare her experience of troubles with that of the people she would encounter on the visits, and that is what they accomplished. What is also remarkable is how well all four of the group members collaborated on this purpose. On that very first visit, the group members put themselves over as a united team, intent on their purpose of comparing their views with those of their peers.

On future occasions, when analysing and writing, group members commented frequently on how the same question could be heard differently at each interview. They became very aware of the wording of the questions, and there were some suggestions for changing the first question to make it clearer. However, I feel now (and argued the point with them at the time) that this analysis has demonstrated quite clearly how the ambiguity of the question led to some very rich talk. A balder, more open question would have been less interesting, as Rapley *et al.* (1998) found in reanalysing Todd and Shearn's (1995) data. The openness of reference meant that membership categories were not given, so interviewees had to establish their own interpretations. It was precisely the freedom of the wording that led to William's 'like us you mean?' in that first visit.

What can be concluded from this small example, then, is that preparation for research does matter. Moreover, it can also be seen how my own contributions to the phrasing of the question were vital, since I was guiding them in the very task they had to do. However, it was the people with intellectual disabilities themselves, the research group members, who did the important and sensitive task of thinking ahead. They wanted to ask a question that related to their own concerns, but without causing offence. They therefore realised that wording matters. When supporting a group like this, what I learnt about was trust; unless I had trusted them to be skilled researchers, none of this would have happened.

This chapter has also deepened understanding of some of the defining features of inclusive research, by looking in detail at how they are worked out in the course of the labelling question. The advantage of an inclusive research design is often seen as the peer–peer identification in the research interview, leading participants to be more open and natural in their talk. This chapter supported that view. It revealed how important collaboration is in the interview situation and how it can be achieved by fine details, such as small movements or facial expressions. Achieving such collaboration was not, however, just a learnable, rote performance; it could work out differently on each occasion. Sharing of identity had to be worked at, just as in Baker (1982), and respondents were not only considering their own position in relation to other social actors that are invoked in their accounts, but also in relation to the person who has asked them the question. Their primary interest was not only 'who am I?', but also 'who are you?', and both had to be jointly constructed.

How conversation works: summary points

- Membership categorisation is a vital tool in all conversation. In order to know how to interpret another person's talk, we need to know 'in what category' he or she is talking, and also in what category we should respond. Trouble in the talk (ten Have, 1999: 116–19) can be linked with breakdowns in understanding of membership categories.

- In many situations, when things run smoothly, matters about identity and membership categorisation are shared and understood. When they are not, there can be interesting breakdowns in communication (or trouble), which lead to repair work. All of this provides meat for the analyst, since it reveals, or displays, how participants are understanding or misunderstanding each other.

- The very fine detail of body language that is visible in video data (Heath, 1997; Kendon, 2004) can be very revealing when exploring sensitive matters. People get clues from each other about how the other person is understanding things. The timing and coordination of gaze, gesture and facial expression can therefore give the analyst clues as to how to interpret what is going on.

Approaches to inclusive communication: summary points

- Inclusive research is not just about the public events; it needs careful preparation behind the scenes.
- People with intellectual disabilities can be sensitive researchers, when they are trusted to get on with it and think things through for themselves. Their own interpretation of issues such

as labelling is the basis for them conducting their own research and their decisions have to be respected within inclusive projects.
- Talking about identity matters is a very sensitive business, and people have a right to define themselves and to decide for themselves how to talk about their identity. Communication in different situations, led by self-advocates and researchers, will enable people to develop and defend their own positions about labelling.

Chapter 14

Reflections on Doing Analysis

Two aims originally gave life to this book. One was to speak directly to practitioners, as well as colleagues with intellectual disabilities themselves, by taking a detailed look at interactions in which people with intellectual disabilities are involved; the second was to interest researchers and students by demonstrating how conversation analysis works and can be done in an inclusive way, leading to practical outcomes. These twin aims are reflected in the summary points highlighted at the end of each chapter. These two final chapters mirror the first two, in order to reflect further on what this book has revealed about communication involving people with intellectual disabilities, and also about the process of analysis itself. However, what I propose to do is to reverse the order of the first two chapters, turning first to the issues of interest to students or others who are interested in CA as a practical tool, and then, in the final chapter, to consider what this book can offer to the wider issues of power, identity and competence in supporting people with intellectual disabilities. Those more interested in the practical and social outcomes of the work described in these pages may wish to turn straight to Chapter 15.

The analysis done in this book was eclectic. Although it drew on CA, it was done with some practical goals in mind and it also strove to include people with intellectual disabilities in as many ways as possible. Therefore, what I have to say in this chapter should be read in the light of texts which will give the reader a clear understanding of the more 'pure' CA approach (ten Have, 1999; Wooffitt, 2005). However, there is no doubt that the approach to analysis taken in this book is significantly different from conventional, grounded analysis of interview data (Silverman, 2005: Chapter 8; Charmaz, 2006).

The present chapter offers an opportunity to consider the methodology, and in particular to reflect on my own experience as a qualitative researcher, in using the tools of CA, in order to apply that methodology in inclusive contexts with people with intellectual disabilities. I start with observations grouped under the different stages of a discursive project, namely data collection, transcription and analysis. Since this book is principally for those who may not have any experience of discourse work, part of my aim is to discuss my own experiences of the practicalities of collecting and analysing data. Some of this was quite distinctive, since I was carrying out research alongside researchers with intellectual disabilities; however, much of what I have to say here is simply about the experiential process of doing discursive research.

The central section of this chapter turns to some more general considerations about what a discourse approach can offer to social research and attempts to engage with some of the debates in discourse analysis, about the pure and applied nature of CA. Like many CA enthusiasts, I have

Disability and Discourse. Analysing Inclusive Conversation with People with Intellectual Disabilities,
1st edition. © Val Williams. Published 2011 by John Wiley & Sons, Ltd.

considerable experience with other forms of social research and continue to carry out qualitative research in a non-discursive tradition. This experience forms the basis for contrasting and commenting on the relative merits of a CA approach. The final section offers some reflections on the direction of travel for inclusive research more generally, research that involves people with intellectual disabilities in many different roles, and concludes with an attempt to bring together all the methodological strands which have threaded through the book. This final section is therefore specifically about the difference it makes to carry out discourse analysis in an inclusive way.

Data collection

The point of departure for CA, as for any other research methodology, is data collection. As was noted in Chapter 2, this is where CA's distinctiveness starts, since the goal is to record and analyse the social activities that happen all around us, without any intervention from the researcher (Sacks, 1995; ten Have, 1999: 33; Wooffitt, 2005: 41). This is generally referred to as 'naturally occurring' data. As discussed in Chapter 2, however, there have been some debates and concerns recently about this concept: if the researcher is recording conversations where the participants *know* that the researcher, or even just the recording device, is present, to what extent can these be 'naturally occurring'? Speer (2002) offers an authoritative view on this topic, claiming that all social action is done for some kind of audience. What is important is the way this is accounted for in the analysis – the researcher effectively has to include his or her own contributions as matters for analysis.

The recordings that provide the data in the current book were collected in diverse ways. For a fuller account of both of the main research projects, see the summary points at the end of Chapter 1 (pp. 18–19). In the 'Finding Out' project, keeping a tape recorder on during all the group sessions was merely a matter of expediency, based on a hunch that it might be useful later. The recordings were made before I had even heard of CA. From the point of view of members of the research group, who became the focus of the analysis, the recordings were originally made for their own purposes and with their own direction. Particularly when the group ventured out to interview other people with intellectual disabilities, their goal was to record what had gone on so that they could look back and then write down their own ideas. They did in fact do this and produced an accessible booklet, 'Finding Out' (Palmer *et al.*, 1999b), and a published book chapter (Palmer *et al.*, 1999a).

By contrast, 'Skills for Support' was planned and executed as a national-level, fully funded research study into personal assistance skills. Despite the concerns of discourse analysts (e.g. Potter, 2003) about mixed methodology designs, the plan for 'Skills for Support' included a survey, as well as an interview stage. It was only in the final stage that we attempted to collect video data and to analyse it. This type of design certainly makes it easier to obtain funding, but it also had advantages in building up to the video collection in a staged way. Note that critics of mixed designs often focus on analytical issues, which I deal with below. There is no *a priori* reason why a research team cannot collect data in a range of ways during the course of a project, with the possibility of quite distinct methods of analysis (Hammersley, 2003; Heritage & Clayman, 2010: 280–2). Silverman (2005), for instance, points out the dangers of researchers adhering strictly to different camps; every researcher has to think for him or herself about the ways in which methodological tools fit their own purposes:

> I view many such dichotomies (between quantitative and qualitative methods) in social science as highly dangerous. At best, they are pedagogic devices for students to obtain a first grip on a difficult field – they help us to learn the jargon. At worst, they are excuses for not thinking,

which assemble groups of researchers into 'armed camps', unwilling to learn from one another. (Silverman, 2005: 8)

One of the outcomes of our design was that it was relatively easy to obtain the video material, since potential participants in videos generally had already had contact with the project through the survey and/or interviews. Even more important, the active involvement of people with intellectual disabilities as researchers certainly helped here tremendously, in particular in facilitating processes of consent. Information and consent processes all have to have ethical approval in the UK, and have been further refined and clarified under the Mental Capacity Act 2005; in 'Skills for Support' we had full, accessible information sheets about the project, and were careful not to exercise any coercion when approaching individuals. People volunteered to take part in videos, following information sessions or after the group interviews. However, the active involvement of two people with intellectual disabilities in the research team helped overcome the usual divide between research participants and researchers. Potential participants in the research signed up to the videos, often with a sense of ownership and enthusiasm for the project. Several of them in fact stayed in touch and subsequently took part in the production of the training pack (Ponting *et al.*, 2010) and were extremely proud of their achievements.

When we reached the stage of video data collection, we carried out pre-visits to discuss the purpose of the project with all those who had consented to take part in videos. We asked people with intellectual disabilities and their support staff to show us what they normally did together. Thus in gross terms, the activities to be included on the videos were pre-planned. For instance, a particular couple might say that they normally sat down and talked together, before doing some domestic chores in the house; another couple might say that they often went shopping or to leisure activities. We knew in advance roughly what was on the 'agenda' of each couple we recorded.

In both projects, it is impossible, of course, to determine exactly whether a particular stretch of talk would have happened in the same way if the camcorder had not been present. In 'Finding Out', within the focus group interviews, the nature of the social activity was a public, on-the-record event, and so the recording equipment simply added to the gravitas of the occasion. No doubt the presence of a video camera does encourage speech-making and some of the self-advocacy talk that occurred may have been less well formed without a video camera. Nevertheless, the features of communication that emerged from analysis are very generic ones, about the ways in which people talk in group self-advocacy and research settings, and accord very well with the points made in discussion by self-advocates themselves. In 'Skills for Support', the final versions of videos were all sent to participants. On two occasions, we were able to talk with them after the event and they confirmed that the interactions captured on video were 'natural' in the sense of being typical and not set up or staged. Nevertheless, we recognised that there is a sense in which we all perform our social activities, and the analysis was not attempting to get at the 'typicality' of particular strategies, but merely to unpick patterns of talk that appeared to work well in empowering people with intellectual disabilities.

Selection and transcription of data

Having collected the data, the analyst then transcribes. Generally, the advice is to transcribe everything in a 'rough' way to start with:

> Transcribing recordings gives the analyst a 'feel' for what has been recorded, it helps to highlight phenomena that may be later considered in detail. (ten Have, 1999: 33)

That is exactly what was done in both projects with all the video and audio data. One interesting observation from the 'Finding Out' project, where I had audio and video data of the focus group interviews, was how much more useful the video recordings were for comprehension of what was going on. There were many occasions on which I simply could not hear something, which was subsequently clarified from the video.

In 'Skills for Support', we engaged in a far more concerted and organised attempt to include the co-researchers in the business of analysis, and both Lisa and Kerrie watched the videos, armed with an accessible recording sheet I devised for them. Their task was essentially to pick out the bits they thought were interesting and to say a word or two about why that was. For instance, they picked out an extract where someone with high support needs was being rolled over by her support worker to have her sling put on for lifting. They thought this was interesting because it showed how the person in question started responding and making noises, while the support worker herself was very vocal in talking and describing what she was doing.

Once extracts or stretches of talk have been selected as potentially interesting, the more detailed transcription starts (Psathas & Anderson, 1990; ten Have, 1999: 75–98) with the analyst having to go back and forwards over small portions of tape in order to clarify exactly how long pauses were, how much hesitation there is, and so on. As the authors above have noted, transcription can never be a straightforward rendering of a recording, but brings with it multiple layers of decisions about how much detail to transcribe and what is relevant to the purpose (Ochs, 1979). Transcribing may seem like a thankless task at times. However, that level of detail is needed to inform a good CA analysis, and it was also often the repeated listenings and viewings which gave rise to analytical insights. In addition, the use of video gives the possibility of observing and transcribing the non-verbal features of talk, and various systems for notating these features were tried during the course of both projects (see also Goodwin, 1981, 2007; Heath, 1997). In the current book, there has not always been room to explore these in depth, but on many occasions the analysis hinged on precise placement of non-verbal features, such as eye gaze, body posture or smiles.

Analysis

Before discussing the type of analysis represented in this book, I should make it clear that the great advantage of naturally occurring data is that they can be analysed and presented afresh in many different stages of a project. In 'Finding Out', the research group members themselves analysed their video data in their own way, as mentioned above. This bore very little overall resemblance to the detailed analysis of inclusive research presented in my PhD thesis (Williams, 2002). In 'Skills for Support', as a two-year, funded team project, attempts at analysis were coordinated by me as the lead researcher. Nevertheless, the analysis in Part 1 is not identical to the analysis of the team, as they presented it for instance on their training DVD (Ponting *et al.*, 2010). Similarly Part 2 does not simply represent a summary of the 'Finding Out' project and its outputs. Nevertheless, in both projects, the mutual nature of analysis had a profound effect on the stance taken to data selection and to the analysis itself, as will be explored further below. In 'Skills for Support', this was made explicit by the five themes under which the data were organised and which originated from the researchers with intellectual disabilities. These were: respect; choices; friendliness; giving good advice; and support to speak up.

CA as an analytical method is highly structured in its approach. I adhered roughly to the four steps outlined by ten Have (1999: 101–23) and started with turn structure, turn allocation and selection of next speaker, progressing to the repair work done during an extract, giving a sense of how fluent or troubled the talk was. It is only as a final point that the analyst looks at the choices made by each speaker within their turns and how these are constructed. It was found consistently that this type of discipline in analysis paid off and brought with it insights that a less systematic approach might have missed. For instance, throughout this book, the reader will have noticed comments about the way in which turns were organised, the points at which one speaker selected another or kept the floor during their own turn. All these are the bread-and-butter of CA, and existing insights about this 'machinery' of talk (Sacks, 1995; Schegloff, 2007) were able to inform the analysis of how talk worked in everyday life and in formal contexts for people with intellectual disabilities. For instance, it is only by taking into account the powerful structure of the two-part adjacency sequence that it becomes obvious how people with intellectual disabilities are often taking up 'second parts' rather than 'first parts'. Conversely, it becomes even more important to analyse how Colin, for instance, produces second parts for the non-verbal person he supports (Ben) in Chapter 4, thus highlighting his contribution as an active initiator.

Having done the structured, disciplined analysis of an extract, however, there is not always something interesting to say about it. This is where the analyst has to switch from grounded 'noticing' based on a particular extract to some type of analytical insight about the pattern of talk emerging. For every extract presented in this book, there are several others that did not yield that insight and so are not included; indeed, the reader could argue that not all the analysis given here is 'insightful'. Doing analysis, it was found, is very much like baking a cake, as the same ingredients and a similar recipe can produce two very different cakes.

Some of the tools I found particularly useful in making the jump from technical description to a deeper analysis included broader analytical concepts, which helped to explain (rather than simply characterise) what was happening in the communication. Here, Wetherell's (1998) idea about interpretative repertoires was extremely useful. As an analytic tool, it offers a way to get behind what is actually said and show how that is linked with wider streams of thought and argumentation in society at large. In attempting to interpret what is going on in the data, the analyst is primarily interested in the way in which members themselves make sense of it. The aim is to uncover their own interpretative devices, since, as Antaki (1988: 12) pointed out: 'much of what is said is only sensible against a background of silently agreed knowledge'. Wetherell (1998) used the term interpretative repertoire to show how the positions Aaron, the young man in her example, takes up can be referred to repertoires available to him:

> An interpretative repertoire is a culturally familiar and habitual line of argument comprised of recognisable themes, common places and tropes … (Wetherell, 1998: 400)

Repertoires are not only a speaker's resource; a useful strategy in my analysis was to ask how a listener was able to understand what was said. The analyst can get at that 'background of silently agreed knowledge' by unpicking the ways in which recipients of the talk display their understanding. As Rapley (2004) noted, there is compelling evidence that intellectual disability in particular draws on a discourse which provides a seemingly authoritative background of arguments and justifications for ways of talk. There are examples of this mutual understanding in every extract in this book, from Chapter 3 onwards, where Barry, Naomi and Barry's carers shared a repertoire in which people with intellectual disabilities are assumed to need support in order to apply for work. That is why they all colluded in silencing any 'false' information given by Barry and in foregrounding his experience in voluntary placements.

The field of identity studies (Antaki *et al.*, 1998b; de Fina *et al.*, 2006) also gave me a very useful handle on extending my analysis beyond the here-and-now. It was generally instructive to step back from the conversation once I had technically described what was going on and ask: 'How do I know who is talking?' This simple question often led me to realise that things tend to be differently arranged in conversations with people with intellectual disabilities and would

perhaps not happen in the same way in my own life. This helped me to see that seeking praise
from a support worker when sorting out what clothes to wear (Chapter 8) was somewhat 'odd',
and that the identity of 'intellectual disability' is deeply embedded in these discursive practices.
Based on an analysis of turn structure in the CA style, it was often possible to link what was
happening in the here-and-now of talk with wider identities. Here the three-level approach to
identity proposed by Zimmerman (1998) was very useful. Taking up a turn in a conversation
(a discourse identity) can contribute to a new situational identity, and this in turn can add to
the 'transportable' identity of an individual.

In 'Skills for Support' I had the advantage of being able to take my own analytic insights back
to my two colleagues with intellectual disabilities in the team, who had direct experience of the
issues we were analysing and often had an excellent handle on what was important in each
extract. My experience was that even quite technical and abstract matters often had real direct
relevance for my co-researchers. An example of a joint analysis session was given in Chapter 12
(extract 12.3), in which Kerrie Ford and Lisa Ponting showed sensitivity to the importance of a
'didactic' style of support. Their views were formed through close attention to the data (in that
case, the way in which a support worker focused a person on the task at hand by a gesture with
her pencil), but also through reflection on their own life experience. The great thing about this
type of analysis is that the data are there and are presented in a fairly full form to the reader. It
is for each reader to decide whether or not they agree with the analytical points made, and the
transcript in the text may give rise to further analysis. It is hoped that readers of this book will
feel free also to exercise their own analytic insight.

The distinctive stance of discourse analysis

At the same time as exploring CA in the wider context of discourse, I have been continuously
involved since 1997 in other forms of qualitative research and analysis, and more recently in
teaching about those methodologies and advising research students. I have also acknowledged
above that 'Skills for Support', for instance, had essentially a 'staged' design, with different
methods at each stage. This can be controversial among discourse analysts. As Potter (2003)
argues, discourse analysis is best thought of as an 'approach', one that acknowledges the centrality
of communication and focuses on the analysis of communication as an activity, rather than
simply analysing the outcomes and underlying content of what people say. I have therefore found
it interesting to reflect on what I have found to be distinctive about a discursive approach and
how the process and outcomes compare with other forms of analysis.

In terms of data collection, as Edwards (2003) suggests, the vast majority of qualitative
research involves going to people whose lives are concerned with the issue in question and asking
them about their experiences. Whether this happens through surveys, interviews (structured,
semi-structured or 'in depth') or focus groups, essentially the quest in conventional psychology
(and sociology) interviews is that the analyst is trying to see through the interview data to some
reality beyond. Discursive approaches re-situate the issue as one to do with talk. CA, in common
with ethnography, takes the approach that some research questions can be better answered by
observing what is going on at first hand.

The contrast between the two approaches was very clear to me when conducting research
which employed different types of data collection and analysis at each phase. The research question was about the skills support workers needed in order to give good support to people with
intellectual disabilities. At the interview phase, we asked service users and their support workers
about their experiences, and the vast majority expressed their satisfaction with one-to-one
support, especially under a direct payments arrangement. People said that this type of

arrangement put them in control of their lives, and they reflected movingly on the difference between that and former experiences of residential care. Nearly all our respondents said that now they were direct payments users, they were in control. However, it was only when we observed and recorded events as they happened that we were able to flesh out the general statements about 'control' and disentangle the processes by which this was achieved and the fine nuances of how support can work. This does not mean that the discourse analysis invalidated the findings of previous stages. In effect, the different stages of this study were examining different phenomena, and the analytic focus and reporting of each different stage of the research were totally distinct. As Potter argues:

> The power and broad relevance of DA comes from the centrality of discourse. Discourse is the vital medium for action. It is the medium through which versions of the world are constructed and produced as pressing or ignorable. (Potter, 2003: 491)

Generally, compared with other qualitative methods, CA is more detailed, looks at small segments of data and makes no claims to generality of the strategies or patterns observed. Despite this tight, fine-grained focus, however, Heritage and Clayman (2010) and Heritage *et al.* (2007) have recently argued that the evidence base for the frequency of phenomena in CA can in some cases be strengthened by quantitative methods. Conversely, over the past 10 years, I have been involved in several other qualitative research studies which would have benefited from at least an element of naturally occurring data collection and analysis. For instance, a study about the further education experiences of young people with intellectual disabilities (Everitt & Williams, 2007) revealed that one of the students' issues was about the use of a joint common room in the college and how they felt excluded by other students. To find out more about how that occurred and try to understand how to change the situation, it would have been very useful to record and analyse the interactions between student groups.

What, then, are the distinctive features of the stance taken in this book towards analysis? One of the key themes mentioned in Chapter 2 is the ethnomethodological stance (Garfinkel, 1967), where the analyst stands back from what she or he is observing in an attempt to see things afresh. Prior assumptions have to be thrown out, and in CA these can include the assumptions about who is who in a conversation, about particular institutional roles or about the social activity going on. As far as possible, that approach has guided my own analysis, as it does for the analysts in van den Berg *et al.* (2003b). Among the 'turns' to a discourse view of social research is the realisation that social research is itself a discursive practice.

> The empirical data of social research are predominantly products of specific discursive practices. (van den Berg *et al.*, 2003a: 1)

Thus in the 'Finding Out' project, I did not assume that what was taking place actually *was* an inclusive research project, 'owned' by the people with intellectual disabilities involved. Instead, on each occasion I sat down with a piece of data or a video extract, the essential question was 'What is going on here?' In explaining this to people with intellectual disabilities, I have always used a clip-art drawing of a spaceman landing on earth, and I ask: 'What would someone from outer space make of this event?'

Further, that approach allowed me as analyst to collect observable evidence about how the participants actually understood each other without my assumptions taking over. Compared with other approaches I have undertaken to describing inclusive research (Williams & England, 2005; Williams *et al.*, 2005), this was very different. So often, writers and researchers (and I include myself here) start from a theory or idea about what is important and then use examples from their experience in an attempt to illustrate that theory. In that vein, the literature about inclusive research starts from concepts of power and ideas about emancipation, and undeniably those theories have been extremely important in helping me and other academic researchers to think about what is important in developing our work with people with intellectual disabilities. However, CA takes the opposite approach, starting by trying at least to forget the prior theorisation of experience while focusing on what is actually happening in the here-and-now. Many qualitative researchers (e.g. Charmaz, 2006, in the context of grounded theory) lay claim to ideas about social constructionism, as opposed to a positivist stance to reality. As Hammersley (2003: 763) points out, though, CA goes further down the social constructionist route, by offering a methodology to analyse *how* social activities are constructed by talk.

Examples of this contrast between analytic methodologies have been evident through many of the research studies with which I have been involved in recent years. Some parents of young people with intellectual disabilities, for instance, talked in one study (Williams & Heslop, 2005) about the lack of responsiveness of mental health services and the fact that their child had to become quite aggressive before they got any useful reaction from official services. The young people themselves talked about trust and how important it was to get to know the person supporting them. All of these findings are valid. They arise from a grounded analysis of what participants talked about in interviews, essentially giving the analyst a window on their own experience and perception of events. However, a discourse analysis would aim to look more closely at how 'trust', for instance, is constructed in talk, and maybe also analyse the processes by which a service provider interacts with a family, exploring how that process is socially constructed by all parties. All social action happens in the ebb-and-flow of real-life situations, and it is by studying those as they happen that the analyst can make discoveries about the *how* questions of social life.

Critics of the CA approach sometimes assume that it is only concerned with the technical details of conversation and is not a good methodology for handling the broader issues of power and the conceptual issues underpinning theories of social life. However, in common with Wooffitt (2005: 186–210), that has not been my experience. Instead, CA has offered me a way to move from particular, contextually-bound conversations towards a systematic understanding of how power is constructed in everyday life. In that respect, some readers may find that my approach has more in common with wider forms of discourse analysis or even critical discourse analysis (Fairclough, 1995). Hammersley (2003), for instance, claims that change and facilitation of change is a general feature of some discourse analysis approaches:

> The mission of some discourse analysts is constantly to remind readers of this fact (that the world can always be constructed differently), and thereby to facilitate the process of change. (Hammersley, 2003: 757)

In 'Skills for Support' it was possible to analyse how talk could enact power structures by unequal distribution of turn-taking rights. The overriding difference between the turn structure in conversations in Chapter 3 and in Chapter 9 encapsulates for me the difference between the everyday life and the public experiences of people with intellectual disabilities today.

In summary, then, having conducted both discourse-related and other research studies in a qualitative tradition, I would argue that a discourse approach does the following well:

- It gives the researcher a way of returning to the basics and, when well applied, it is a relatively objective, rigorous way of looking at social life. Although many would argue that the researcher's viewpoint can never be eliminated, CA at least offers a disciplined way to take into account and analyse one's own prior assumptions.
- Discourse analysis, like ethnography, puts the researcher directly into contact with a segment of social life, something that can be observed, recorded and analysed in its own right. By

contrast, other forms of qualitative research depend on the words and views of someone recounting an event or an experience, and so at best can only be second-hand.

- Discourse analysis avoids the trap of falling into a positivist way of analysing material, where a truth is assumed to exist because a lot of people talk about it.
- Applied or institutional CA offers the reader a deeper understanding of how activities in social life occur. Different areas of communication may draw on the same set of practices, the same machinery of talk, but these can be used in distinct ways to achieve various social goals.
- This type of applied CA also provides a way of exploring the institutional arrangements by which society functions, and thereby looking in detail at the way power is enacted; by understanding these things, we can at least start to change them.

Over and above all of these issues, I must reiterate the fact that a discourse approach, involving video interaction analysis, is not an obscure or difficult thing to do. It is something which certainly has its accessible and familiar side, and where it is possible to include people with intellectual disabilities and others, and through which people can learn practical lessons about their own interactions.

To CA or not to CA?

This section ends with a disclaimer and then a counter-claim about CA. First, CA cannot do everything, and clearly if the goal is to find out about widespread experiences for instances of a phenomenon, then CA findings need to be followed by quantitative and statistical designs (Heritage & Clayman, 2010: 280–2). While this is an exciting new perspective on mixed design, others argue that the focus given by CA (and discourse analysis generally) 'cannot tell us all there is to know about human social life' (Hammersley, 2003: 773). Often, too, the goals in research are pragmatic and a researcher has to take an approach that will offer a ready handle on the realities that people experience so that the research findings can inform policy.

However, what I would want to counter is the common assumption that discourse analysis, and particularly CA, is 'only about conversation'; critics would argue that the world cannot be changed by changing communication. Hopefully, I trust that it is clear by now that although CA is about talk, the type of inclusive approach carried out in this book does not start and finish there. Researchers and policy-makers have to analyse and argue for structural changes that change the material circumstances of people's lives, but the tools of CA can have an important role in helping to understand how those changes will happen.

Perhaps the best way of illustrating this is to consider an example of a structural change that has made a big difference to the life experience of disabled people – the change brought about in the UK by direct payments (DH, 1996; Leece & Bornat, 2006), where service users are offered a cash payment instead of a directly provided service. This change happened, arguably, through talk: it was through the direct involvement and campaigning of disabled people themselves that the ideas behind direct payments became heard and were incorporated into policy (Zarb & Nadash, 1994). All of that involved social actions; however, the shift in policy which was then formalised in the Community Care and Direct Payments Act 1996 was more than talk – it became law.

Thus talk was translated into law, which in turn was put into action, and it was the ability to receive direct payments which put disabled people, potentially, into a new and different relationship with their support staff. It was direct payments that gave them new opportunities for interactions which were very differently arranged in terms of institutional power. In turn, these can be analysed, as they were in the 'Skills for Support' project in this book. One can appreciate how tightly talk and action are intertwined, and it is the privilege of analysis to be able to untangle some of this action and help to reveal how wider issues of power, status and change are embedded in social encounters.

Carrying out discourse analysis in an inclusive way

If discourse analysis is an exciting and relevant approach in qualitative research, then it can only get better by doing it in the context of an inclusive project with people with intellectual disabilities as co-researchers. The two main projects on which this book draws involved people with intellectual disabilities in very different ways, particularly in relation to CA. Effectively, the analysis of the 'Finding Out' project is *about* inclusive research and aims to describe it analytically as a social activity. 'Skills for Support', by contrast, opened the door to people with intellectual disabilities to be co-analysts of video data. They helped to plan and collect data, and it was their views that guided analysis. Therefore, this final section addresses questions about inclusive methodologies in research, and what has been revealed by this book.

What is 'research'?

Throughout all the projects which have featured in this book, one of my constant reflections has been on the status of the activity undertaken. Is it really 'research', and indeed, what does make any activity into research? These are open questions and are salutary to ask, since they enable me and other academics to reflect more openly on the activities we are undertaking in *any* research project. Of course, there is no particular reason why someone should require a PhD to have an answer to the question 'what is research?'. In common parlance, research is something which belongs to everyone and on which all citizens can have their own ideas.

Over the years, in training sessions with people with intellectual disabilities, the words 'finding out' have often been used as a way to encapsulate what research actually is. However, part of the power of research is precisely the power to define what *should* be found out, and that was largely what Oliver's (1992) emancipatory project was all about. In that sense, the 'Finding Out' project represented a far clearer example of emancipatory research, in which people with intellectual disabilities really did decide for themselves what they wanted to pursue, unconstrained by funders' expectations. Nevertheless, there were many points during the journey of that particular project where my own view of research jarred with what I could see happening; for instance, how could people really be doing 'research' if they wanted to express their own strong views, based on their prior experience? Over the course of the analysis, however, I realised that what we were doing in that project (and in similar ones) was actually reformulating what research could be, when it is in the hands of people with intellectual disabilities. The following remarks should therefore be read in that light. There are no assumptions here that people with intellectual disabilities can simply 'do research' in the sense that an academic researcher does it. However, they do imply that everyone has the right to create their own knowledge, in their own way, and to have support to do that.

The hallmarks of inclusive research

In traditional research, the researcher and the researched live in different worlds, coming together only for the purposes of 'data collection' and interacting according to the unwritten rules of a research interview. The interviewer poses questions, the participant answers. Further, most social research is done by academic researchers and is about people who in one way or another constitute an oppressed or minority group.

By contrast, inclusive research or emancipatory research (Oliver, 1992) is premised on peer interaction. This is, at least in principle, research 'from within'. In 'Finding Out', the research group members took on powerful roles as 'interviewers' and I showed in Chapter 11, for example, how Mark used the privilege of the research questions to keep the agenda in his own hands. However, there was also a sense in which the distinction between researcher and researched became blurred. Part of the technique of research group members was to share personal experiences within the interview context to a far greater extent than most traditional researchers, and meanings were discussed 'in public', as was discussed in Chapter 11. Often, the analysis was performed out loud and *in situ*. This necessarily meant involving the interviewees in that process, as well as the interviewers. For instance, if a member of the interviewee team did not agree with an evaluation or summary, they could say so. Equally, interviewees also took responsibility for procedural aspects of the interview at times, as was seen in Chapter 13.

Peer identity, like any form of identity, is not a given. Different contexts of social interaction give us all the opportunity to make salient various aspects of our identity, and to a large extent we respond to the nature of the occasion and to our particular purposes within that occasion (Antaki & Widdicombe, 1998b: Chapter 1). Members of the research group in 'Finding Out' were no different. However, it is apparent that the research was built on a measure of identification between researcher and researched. Collaboration was something that had to be worked at, and Chapter 13 started to uncover some strategies for doing this. Quite often this occurred through the fine details of body language, as was seen in Chapter 11, or the devices of adding an appeal such as 'isn't it?' to the end of a turn.

Doing identity work is not simply about making salient certain aspects of one's 'transportable identity' or talking about who you think you are. It is also about the distribution of interactional rights. Throughout this book, I have pointed out the tight and dynamic links between the discourse, situational and transportable identities of members (Zimmerman, 1998). In other words, by assuming the right to ask questions and give evaluative comments, members were taking up certain discourse identities. These led to a construction of them as research interviewers, a construction which both surprised and challenged all participants, since it conflicted with other aspects of their transportable identities.

It is hard to discuss the nature of research talk within the 'Finding Out' project without putting it within the framework of People First, or self-advocacy, talk. One of the outcomes of the analysis was that this type of research is not accidentally situated within a self-advocacy context. There are features that essentially link it to that context and mean it would not work without it. In Chapter 9, it was seen how individual stories of personal experience were often the springboard for self-advocacy members to move into political or collective action and how this process of talk was jointly accomplished, with members supporting each other. There was a discourse here of self-reliance, with an emphasis on solving problems for yourself. All these features were also a bedrock for the research process, where both interviewers and interviewees could explore their situations together, on the assumption that they were capable of reaching their own conclusions.

Both self-advocacy and research talk, in this context, are predicated on strong feelings, and to that extent this type of research had a campaigning edge to it. Members did not set out on a neutral search for some objective truth, nor were they doing academic research for its own sake, but recognised that they wanted to change aspects of their own lives and the way that they were treated. There was, therefore, a sense in which collaboration between researcher and researched was also an essential part of the process. The interviews were occasions for both parties to establish some kind of common cause, as was illustrated clearly in Chapter 13. It is hard to imagine that this project would have been successful, had the researchers pursued questions that did not fully engage them.

Finally, the 'Finding Out' project and the interactions which constituted it were jointly constructed with support from people who were non-disabled. Some writers therefore (Zarb, 1992; Chappell, 2000) might place it within the category of *participatory research*, in opposition to *emancipatory research*. However, all novice researchers have a right to some support, and it was not surprising that the researchers in the research group in 'Finding Out' needed practical and organisational support in order to accomplish their goals. The essential question that emerged from all this was: 'Did the members themselves have control over the content of the research?' Just as disabled activists (Morris, 1993) have long argued that independence does not mean doing everything for yourself, in the same vein research does not necessarily mean taking all the steps in isolation. On the contrary, the analysis presented in this book proposes that the very ownership of the research process has to be supported. Perhaps the most subtle, but necessary, task for the research supporter, as was revealed in Chapter 12, is to find ways of enabling members to appreciate the significance of what they are doing as researchers.

New developments in inclusive research

This book was written in 2008–9, and is based largely on two sources of data, one of which was some 10 years old at the time of writing. That time-lag is largely because of the difficulties in obtaining funding for CA work, compounded by the restricted sources of funding for social research generally. Additionally, inclusive research inevitably poses yet more problems for funders. Because working inclusively is always bound to take longer and require support and resources, the expense of inclusive research proposals can be prohibitive. Nevertheless, during the first decade of the twenty-first century there have been several attempts to work inclusively with people with intellectual disabilities as researchers, and the author and colleagues have been involved in several of these projects. Service-user research in general is now promoted by official funders in the UK, such as the Department of Health, and by government funders of higher education. There is also a much wider international movement of service-user-led research, where people with intellectual disabilities are increasingly having a voice; for instance, my colleagues Walmsley and Johnson (2003) draw on examples from Australia, and Johnson has also worked on inclusive projects with a network of service users in Ireland.

All the research reported in this book was exclusively about people with the label 'intellectual disability'; therefore, there is a sense in which the research itself mirrors the assumption that these people are in a different, special position when compared with other disabled people. While there may be some basis to believe this is so, nevertheless inclusive research can enable us to challenge some of these categories and assumptions about impairments. An anecdote from the 'Journey to Independence' project in 2000–2 (Gramlich *et al.*, 2002) may be revealing. Three researchers with intellectual disabilities were involved in that project, and had both a supporter and a research supporter who accompanied them on their interview visits. On one occasion, the team arrived to carry out an interview with a well-respected disabled activist at a Centre for Independent Living. The interaction could not have been less like an interview! The person being interviewed started by posing the questions, not answering them, and asked the researchers with intellectual disabilities whether they knew about the social model of disability. When they expressed some doubts, he proceeded to tell them all about it. While this interaction can be seen in a positive light, with disabled people sharing their ideas and theories about disability, the interactional rights of the team members actually to 'do research' were infringed. Further, in conversation after the event it became apparent that the three people with intellectual disabilities did not see their interviewee as a disabled person. To them, being disabled was tantamount to being restricted in outlook and power. Therefore, despite the evidence of his wheelchair, they failed to identify the man they had spoken with as a person with a disability.

This incident gave me food for thought at the time. I thought that there was not much chance of identification or inclusion within the disabled people's movement if people with intellectual disabilities do not recognise themselves as peers with other disabled people. However, in the years since that project, there have been other important ways in which disabled people have started to explore both the differences caused by different impairments and the commonalities that unite them. Thomas (2004), for instance, has argued that the social model of disability cannot and should not ignore the embodied experience of impairment, while people with intellectual disabilities, for their part, have started to carry out more joint work with other disabled people – work in which they do have a voice. In 2009, ideas about social barriers are relatively well understood among many people with intellectual disabilities, and their own contributions to disability theory have also started to be explored (Goodley, 2003).

Turning back to the current book, 'Skills for Support' also brought people with intellectual disabilities and other disabled people together. It took place within a disabled people's organisation, and that context was vital for the power and success of the project. Throughout its two-year course, the two people with intellectual disabilities in the project team were supervised and managed by a disabled person who did not have an intellectual disability. This enabled them to share ideas, discuss ways in which the organisation itself should change to accommodate their needs and learn from each other. One of the key issues for people with intellectual disabilities in being included in a disabled people's organisation was that they needed information to be made accessible to them, and the team published a practitioner article about that aspect of their work (Williams *et al.*, 2006).

At the same time as the growth of disabled people's research generally, during the past 10 years the research carried out by members of self-advocacy organisations (exclusively for people with intellectual disabilities) has also blossomed. Several organisations in the UK, such as Carlisle People First (Townson *et al.*, 2004) and Dorset People First, have been involved in exciting action research projects, led by people with intellectual disabilities with support from their own paid staff. Some of these have taken advantage of the MSc course offered in Bristol in order to increase their own skills in managing inclusive research. It would seem natural and right that the voices of people with intellectual disabilities can become stronger in this way, nurtured by the context and culture of self-advocacy. There are therefore still many different ways in which inclusive research is developing, and it remains important to take account of the wider context and setting for each project. I would contend that both generic disability contexts and self-advocacy contexts can contribute towards the power of people with intellectual disabilities.

The role relationships within a research project can be configured in many ways; however, they remain an important bedrock on which the research process is built and must remain solid and self-reflective. For instance, the relationship between the 'academy' and the world of service-users has come into the spotlight over the last 10 years, with commentators often expressing concern that partnerships of academics and self-advocacy organisations may only give tokenistic powers to people with intellectual disabilities. During that period, however, UK research has seen some very important partnerships, with self-advocates (Central England People First), for instance, working together with a nationally recognised academic, Eric Emerson, to contribute towards a national survey of people with intellectual disabilities (Emerson *et al.*, 2005). In the work represented in this book, the roles of academic/supporter/person with intellectual disabilities were configured differently in each project. In 'Skills for Support' the author was no longer described as a 'research supporter', but as a colleague – in fact, as the lead researcher. In that context, the differentiated team approach worked well in enabling each member of the team to have a voice in research matters and to discuss issues on an equal basis. However, as has been shown in this book, the devil is in the detail – giving empowering support is not something that just 'happens', whatever the job title may imply.

Inclusive analysis for change

The central, and essential, part of any research is the analysis, since it is through this that the researcher exerts his or her real power over the knowledge that has been created. If inclusive research is to have any real power, it is vital to reflect on how analysis can be done in these contexts.

'Skills for Support' was set up in a strikingly different way from 'Finding Out', which originated from a small group of people with intellectual disabilities who wanted to do their own project, and was virtually unfunded research throughout its existence. By contrast, as explained in Chapter 1, 'Skills for Support' was a research study of national scope for which funding was obtained by my own academic institution, the Norah Fry Research Centre, working in partnership with a disabled people's organisation. Therefore, the plan for the research and the methodology were already set when the self-advocate researchers joined the team. However, their own involvement in the 'video stage' of the project was still very much open to development. There were certainly no prescribed models of practice to build on.

What we actually did as a team is described in some of the papers from that project (Williams *et al.*, 2009a, 2009b, 2009c) and is also evidenced in the practical training resource pack that was produced (Ponting *et al.*, 2010), with a DVD showing Kerrie Ford and Lisa Ponting discussing extracts from the research. On the DVD, they are very much 'in control' of their insights about the data and discuss them openly. They are, frankly, impressive. What follows presents, in a nutshell, how we got to that final point of the resource pack, during the course of our two-year project. At the risk of repeating information, here is an outline of the different stages of our work:

a) The two self-advocate researchers in the project were directly involved in setting up encounters and meetings with other people with intellectual disabilities, and as a team we visited several sites in the UK in order to interview people with intellectual disabilities and their support workers.

b) Following those visits, we arranged video visits with a smaller sample, who consented to those visits. Kerrie or Lisa accompanied me on roughly half of the video visits and helped to make the videos.

c) All the videos were brought back to the team, and an accessible sheet was devised for the self-advocate researchers to look through each of the videos and pick out the clips that interested them. They did this over a period of time, with support from their support worker. At the same time, I got on with some rough transcription.

d) During this period, we had many discussions about what we had found out and what was emerging from the research. It was at that point that five main 'themes' emerged, which both Kerrie and Lisa felt were important for good support. These were therefore based on their own experience, their interviews, discussions in a focus group and on the videos they had seen so far. The five themes were: respect; choices; being friendly; giving advice; support to speak up. The organisation of our discussions, analysis and subsequent resource pack was led by the five themes.

e) The clips identified from the videos by Kerrie and Lisa, along with others that I felt fitted well with one or more of the five themes, were chosen for detailed transcription and analysis. I carried this transcription out myself, at first separately from the team.

f)   A final stage involved taking the analysis back to the team and discussing some of the points raised with Kerrie and Lisa. For instance, the discussion given in Chapter 12 about data analysis came from that period.

Some readers may wonder whether Kerrie and Lisa were in fact 'typical' of other people with intellectual disabilities, although this typicality never seems to be a problem for other social researchers. For instance, no one asks if I, as a university research fellow, am typical of the people I am researching. In response to these concerns, I would argue that Kerrie and Lisa were not typical, since (despite significant intellectual impairments) both had a gift for the fine detail that is necessary in CA-type analysis and were able to benefit and respond to research training. However, the point about their central role in the project was not that they had particular skills, but rather that they brought to the research their everyday experience of being treated 'as a person with intellectual disabilities'. The talk that we analysed, the videos we watched and the interactions we observed were riveting for them, because they were about matters that also occurred in their own lives. For them, it was far more than an academic exercise. When we talked about people with intellectual disabilities being patronised, for instance, they could relate to this as part of the problem they experienced on a daily basis.

Working with participants on their own data

Throughout this chapter, I have spoken about analysis as a way of working alongside researchers who represent the participant population (i.e., the people in the videos). However, there is another sense in which discourse work can be inclusive, in that it can return to the actual people in the data to ask them about their own contributions. In a sense, this was what happened in the 'Finding Out' project, since the research group members were also participants in the data. In 'Skills for Support', attempts were also made to return to original participants, to show them the videos and to discuss points with them. This was done as part of group work with a small number of individuals who came together regularly during the 'Skills for Support' project and contributed to other aspects of the resource pack at the end of the project (Ponting *et al.*, 2010). In both projects, one of the remarkable observations was that participants felt they owned the research and many actively wanted to be part of the final products. Several of the participants in 'Skills for Support' were able to come to the launch of the resource pack in March 2010 and were proud of their contributions.

The question arises, given this to-and-fro with participants, whether there can always be agreement about the meaning and analytical points in the data. My short answer would be no. Further, it is very hard to stand back from something in which you have taken part and to comment meaningfully on someone else's analytical observations. However, I am not contending that this is impossible, and I would certainly be interested to carry out further work with participants about their own data. Rather than directly contributing to analysis, participants' comments were always valuable in challenging and redirecting lines of enquiry. Two examples will be mentioned briefly, both from the 'Skills for Support' project.

On one occasion, a video of a person with intellectual disabilities and his support worker arriving at a railway station was shown to the participants, and they commented that this was 'just like anyone else' arriving at a railway station. They felt that they came over completely as friends and that no one would have known that one of them was paid as a support worker to the other. This comment led me (and the team) to explore further what it means to be friendly and how people manage their actions in order to come over as 'ordinary'. While we may have had differing observations about the analysis of the actual video, the participants' concerns became central in the direction of our own analytical interests.

On another occasion, a video made with a support worker and a person who did not use words (Colin and Ben in the present book) was shown back immediately to the couple, after returning from a shopping trip with them. My notes on the discussion afterwards include the following:

> Colin says the shopping trip needs to happen 'in one flow'. You cannot stop, hesitate, go back, or make any mistakes with the shopping. That would upset it. (AH3, Colin comments)

The support worker also pointed out that he often hung back during a shopping trip, and this was evident in the video. He said he liked to keep a distance as it encouraged Ben to take action for himself. In subsequent analysis of different video footage with this pair, these insights were very useful, since it was evident how Colin both stepped back from Ben, but also prepared him by enabling him to think ahead about his activities. Interestingly, the same video provoked quite different reactions from discussion with a group of people with intellectual disabilities, who felt initially that the support worker was being very 'bossy' with Ben in preparing him, asking him questions and keeping him on track with the shopping. An insider view can thus be very different, and give different insights, from the view of outsiders. However, after all this participation, it is up to the analyst to use evidence from the data in drawing analytic conclusions about what is going on in any extract. The difference in the 'Skills for Support' project was that the analyst was not just myself, as an academic researcher, but included two researchers with intellectual disabilities.

Inclusive research and discourse analysis do not often come together in the same project, but from the experience here, it would seem that some of the CA tools have a lot to offer to inclusive methodologies. Using video is an accessible way to keep the data fresh and to be able to review and make sense of what was found out. It is also a wonderful tool to use, in order to create training materials (Ponting *et al.*, 2010) and to offer something back both to practitioners and to people with learning disabilities.

Final remarks

If discourse analysis has something to offer inclusive methodologies, what does inclusion have to offer a discourse approach? My first observation would be a practical one, that the inclusion of researchers with intellectual disabilities opened doors to our project that would have perhaps remained closed otherwise. It was far easier for Lisa and Kerrie to find participants for videos than it would have been for a non-disabled researcher working on their own. When it comes to analysis, there are of course dangers. Doing CA requires the ability to see things afresh, to notice detail and to abandon prior assumptions. All these are hard for anyone to learn and so it is not to be expected that people with intellectual disabilities will necessarily be able to manage all the mechanics of analysis without a good deal of support. The analysis in some of our academic papers, and indeed in this book, is based on Kerrie and Lisa's ideas, but elaborated and worked up by myself. The kind of team work that we adopted involved an explicit recognition that members of the team took on different roles, and the role that I had was that of lead researcher and analyst.

Based on my experience of carrying out discourse analysis in an inclusive way, I would conclude that it is both significant and vital that inclusion is addressed within discourse work. Without direct involvement, the collection of video data for research purposes could resemble early anthropological investigations carried out on some remote tribe; the connection between the researcher and the researched is non-existent, and the power dynamic between them is re-enacted by the process of the research itself, in which the researcher collects, analyses and profits from the outputs of the research. By contrast, if one is interested in analysing institutional power imbalances, and strategies for creating equalising talk, then the analysis becomes far stronger and grounded when done with people who identify with the oppressed group. The team approach with people with intellectual disabilities in 'Skills for Support' gave me a chance to check the analysis, revisit data and discuss it in the context of the lived experience of the self-advocate researchers. Quite simply, the inclusion of people with intellectual disabilities made for better and more useful research.

The final, but important, recommendation for future action in the field of inclusive research generally is to engage in a more open process of communication between all parties involved in inclusive research and its development. It seems a nonsense to conduct exclusive debate about inclusive research, with those who are at the heart of the process not able to participate on an equal basis. What is needed is more action from self-advocates as well as academic or practitioner researchers, to commit to a real exchange of views in such a way that all parties can learn from the research that has already been carried out by and with people with intellectual disabilities. It goes without saying that people with intellectual disabilities also have a responsibility within this dialogue. If members of the self-advocacy movement do not want to engage with non-disabled people, then the dialogue cannot occur. This book has shown how all communication is at least a two-sided affair, with each person's turn in talk building on the local context, on what has just been said and understood between all parties. Building more opportunities for empowering research, just like opportunities for empowering personal support, will therefore rely on opportunities for more 'equal' conversations. Members of the People First movement and the growing community of self-advocacy researchers need to work out for themselves whether and in what ways they wish to develop their ideas, with or without the support of academic researchers, supporters and others in the disabled people's movement.

Chapter 15

Reflections on Change

Conversation analysis wisely always leaves theorising until the end; for if you start with firm notions of what you mean by big questions such as power, then the 'data' become merely an illustration of your own arguments (Schegloff, 1998, 1999a & b). Instead, CA tries to be theory-blind and to start from the fine detail of what actually happens in the talk, looking for evidence of how people have understood each other in real situations. I have tried to do the same. It is now the moment to sit back to summarise some of the points in the book and to offer some further speculation about what it all means. Nothing can equal the real data, the conversations and encounters with people with intellectual disabilities which have formed the backbone of each chapter. Therefore, this final chapter should not be read as a substitute for the book as a whole. The voices of people with intellectual disabilities have run through this book and are central to its very existence – it is people with intellectual disabilities and their talk that bring this book to life.

The first section of this chapter reflects on what the analysis in this book has to say about the larger social themes which both underpin and arise from the data – the themes of power, identity and competence. All of these, in many respects, thread through the book and emerge from the analysis in each chapter. This final chapter offers a chance to look at them afresh and to reflect on the findings in the light of questions raised in Chapter 1. These were questions about what it means to have an 'intellectual disability', about competence and incompetence, autonomy as a human right and the critiques of tokenism which are levelled at people with intellectual disabilities who organise into collectives.

The second section turns to the practices of those who interact with people with intellectual disabilities and draws together the issues, learning and practice implications of the conversations analysed in the various chapters of this book. It offers a chance to think about what lessons can be learnt, both for the practices of those involved directly in support work and also for policy-makers and for people with intellectual disabilities and their families who are involved with the 'personalisation' agenda (DH, 2006b, 2008). If disabled people are meant to be more in control of their lives, then a close look at their lived encounters should have something to say about how that policy direction can be envisaged and achieved.

The chapter concludes with the overarching theme of change and considers some of the ways forward that will include people with intellectual disabilities.

Disability and Discourse. Analysing Inclusive Conversation with People with Intellectual Disabilities, 1st edition. © Val Williams. Published 2011 by John Wiley & Sons, Ltd.

Power, identity and competence

A prominent slogan of the disabled people's movement over the past 30 years has been 'Nothing about us without us', a slogan which is precisely about the conversational rights we all share. It is seen as particularly important for disabled people to have a voice in matters that concern them, due to their historical exclusion from disability debates (see Campbell & Oliver, 1996; Shakespeare, 2006: 9–28, for historical overviews). Conversations about disability have traditionally been carried out without any input from disabled people themselves, and so disabled people have naturally demanded the right to take part in that talk, indeed to have a leading voice. The messages from this book take this a step further by revealing how important it is for power to be equalised within conversations. For people with intellectual disabilities, even when they are present and included in conversation, they may still have unequal rights. The slogan could be rewritten here as: 'Nothing about us without us having equal rights in the conversation'. What this book has attempted to do is to unpick what this may mean in practice and how 'equality' is done. However, in order to do that, it is essential first to acknowledge some of the wider influences which pull people into various positions in talk and what has been added to understanding of those underpinning social discourses.

Competence

My starting point was that communication is an opportunity: people can and do construct afresh what is happening between them, by getting together and talking through something (Sarbin & Kitsuse, 1994):

> Although both intersubjectivity and reciprocity are foundational to social interaction, they are by no means static or taken-for-granted. Rather, they are continuously negotiated and co-constructed during ongoing social interactions … (Schiffrin, 2006: 107)

However, as the conversations in these pages were analysed, it became apparent that speakers were not totally free agents, as their talk was shaped by understandings of how the world works. Discourse shapes new meanings but also draws on old ones (Antaki & Widdicombe, 1998a). This is simply the way communication works – we all draw on a vast range of shared understanding in order to communicate successfully at all, for we would soon come to a standstill if we had to explain and explore every minute detail during ordinary conversation. Luckily for the analyst, it turns out that analysis of participants' own understandings of each other provides a key, a way to get into what lies behind the talk: through unravelling some of that shared backdrop of knowledge, it is possible to work out and say something about issues that are wider than the here-and-now contingencies of each conversation.

In Chapter 14 (p. 203) I commented on the specific usefulness of the concept of 'interpretative repertoire' in analysis (Wetherell, 1998). This is a participant's resource, but it is also a resource for the analyst to step back from what is being said and link it with what lies behind the talk.

One of the opening questions raised in this book concerned the definition of 'intellectual disability' and the concerns among people with the label of intellectual disability about their label (Beart *et al.*, 2005). The repertoire of intellectual disability (learning disability in the UK) relies on notions of what competence is; people are defined as having an intellectual disability because they are not managing aspects of their lives independently (DH, 2001). The repertoire of 'intellectual disability' has been a constant backdrop to each chapter in this book. Having looked in detail at conversation involving people with that label, has this added anything to understandings about competence?

The best way may be to consider some examples. In Chapter 7, for instance, when Charles was discussing his party arrangements with his service manager, there was an assumption underlying that discussion, on which both parties drew, that it was to Charles' advantage to hire a hall at the least possible cost and that he would not be able to afford a commercial price. That might be the case, of course, with anyone who wanted to arrange a party. However, as the conversation continued, it became more and more like an advice-giving session, drawing on the identity of an incompetent individual who could not work out what would be to his best advantage. Similar examples can be found in almost every chapter: for instance, the communication between Ellie and Jenny about budgeting activities in Chapter 4 drew on an explicit plan for budgeting which was arranged for Ellie and which both parties referred to in the discussion. Underlying that was an assumption that Ellie was a person who needed such a plan, that the plan was part of a service arrangement with her and that Jenny's job was to help her implement that plan. It was with reference to that repertoire that Ellie and Jenny were able to justify their behaviour to the camera crew.

It is often instructive to stand back from a conversation and ask whether it would have happened in the same way with someone who did not have the label 'intellectual disability'. Because I know a fair amount about the world of Intellectual Disability, my own understandings of what is going on can also be treated as part of the data, as in an ethnographic approach (Rawlings, 1988; Atkinson & Hammersley, 2007: 4). What I found very useful was the back-step, not just to describe what I think is going on, but then to stop and ask myself 'how do I know?'.

In common with Antaki *et al.* (2007a, 2007b) and Rapley (2004), I found that, particularly in Part 1, much of the talk was premised on the *incompetence* of the person with intellectual disabilities. As was pointed out, this is not just something which support workers 'do' to the people they support; the repertoire of incompetence was something people with intellectual disabilities themselves appeared to buy into and was evident at many points – for instance, when people sought praise from their support workers for small choices or achievements in Chapter 7, or when information offered by the individual with intellectual disabilities was disbelieved, as in Chapter 3.

However, the analysis has shown how talk draws on a wider discourse than simply that of 'incompetence'. There are many other specific features of the Intellectual Disability world, together with special forms of reasoning and behaviour that go on within it, and these are all an important part of the background knowledge on which nearly all speakers in this book drew: a world in which the idea of 'protection' dominates, in which institutions have existed, people have activities and day centres provided for them and in which they have staff who work for them. Small details in the talk can sometimes reveal the ways in which all parties are drawing on this understanding, which to them is unremarkable. The two men who were talking about football in Chapter 6 seemed to find it quite routine that footballers would visit the person with intellectual disabilities 'at work' (a shorthand for 'day centre', upgrading the idea of day centre activities into employment). Angela and I also drew on knowledge about similar places when Angela was going through the conversations she would have in showing her photos to people she knew. These people were staff in her day centre, as well as her residential home, and we shared an expectation that it would be part of their job to be interested in what Angela had done in the research project! A final example is from Chapter 12 (extract 12.3), where a researcher with intellectual disabilities spoke about her 'house' as an animate agent: 'My house always says to me'. Where people live is closely bound up (or in this turn of phrase, identical) with the staff who are paid to support people, which can make it appear that living is impossible without an 'animated' household of staff.

These findings chime closely with the work of Antaki and his colleagues. For instance, Antaki *et al.* (2007a) show how proposing an activity to a person with intellectual disabilities is often done by emphasising the social aspects of that activity. This practice buys into and is built on an unspoken assumption that social contact is what matters above any rational decision about what the actual activity might imply. Further, Antaki *et al.* (2007b) notice that conversations about friendships in a residential home draw strongly on a repertoire of incompetence:

> In effect, the staff treated the residents as having an identity impaired in its powers of basic social discrimination. They are treated as being unable to tell who their friends are, and being in need of having to count care staff among them. (Antaki *et al.*, 2007b: 13)

While Antaki's data were from residential care contexts, the new forms of personalised support for direct payments users are intended to be more 'empowering'. The people in Part 1 were nearly all employers of their own support staff, for instance, and people in Part 2 were members of self-advocacy or research groups, conducting their own affairs. One would hope that these contexts would hold out a promise of something new and challenging. Even in these contexts, therefore, it is interesting to note how strong the reliance on shared knowledge about intellectual disability is. Where are there glimmers of a new repertoire, or even of a competing one?

One new and emergent repertoire is that of being an employer. Many of the people in Part 1 employed their own staff (Leece & Bornat, 2006) and one would expect a repertoire in which support staff are 'answerable' to their employer, where they want to please or to earn praise for their activities, or where they at least want reassurance that they are doing their job correctly. In fact, this type of repertoire was not often visible in the talk in this book; there were occasions when someone such as Frank in Chapter 1 (extract 1.1) or Ruth in Chapter 7 (extract 7.11) gave an instruction or some feedback to their support worker. It was interesting to observe how support staff tended to shift into a position of highlighting their personal identity as soon as people with intellectual disabilities stepped into the identity of 'employer'. However, these were rare instances and were remarkable because they stood out from the majority of the talk. It would be interesting to collect further data, once personalisation (DH, 2008) has had a greater effect in the UK, or to collect comparative data from other countries where personalisation has developed, perhaps in different ways, such as Sweden or the USA.

The discourse of employment has the potential, certainly, to challenge the very way society thinks about intellectual disability. As employers of their own staff, it would be expected that people with intellectual disabilities, in the ordinary run of their conversations, will start to perform different social actions such as praising or evaluating their support staff's performance. These are not what we have come to expect or associate with the category of 'intellectual disability', and so the performance of these actions in conversation literally means taking on new interactional rights. It is by doing new things with talk that people with intellectual disabilities will actually become the bosses of their staff. As with all social activities, being a direct payments employer is 'socially constructed', and the current book has shown how this can occur in the ebb-and-flow of real talk between one or more people. 'Skills for Support' produced a resource pack with a DVD (Ponting *et al.*, 2010) which is intended to support the process of change through enabling people with intellectual disabilities to take part in supporting and training their own personal assistants. This does not mean that people with intellectual disabilities will suddenly become 'competent'. As Williams and Holman (2006) argue in relation to direct payments, it is possible to be in control of staff while having the support needed to maintain that control. The dichotomy between autonomy and protection which is highlighted in recent literature (Fyson, 2009) could be challenged by a new repertoire, to do with being an employer.

What about Part 2 and the issues about collective voice? One would expect there to be stronger competing repertoires there perhaps (Goodley, 2003). For instance, in Chapter 11, Mark and Andrew explored the notion of competence quite explicitly and reached a joint conclusion that it does matter. They stated clearly that they wanted to be treated as 'competent' and that being treated in a way that prevented that competence was in fact discrimination. Their very act of discussing these issues, or posing their own questions and seeking their own theory, was one that reinforced their competence and autonomy at that point, and so it was interesting to see how the actual discourse situation fed into a new repertoire of 'competence'.

Doing ordinary

It was pointed out in Chapter 1 that institutionality is not only the historical background for people with intellectual disabilities, it is also something that permeates the way people are talked about and talked with (Watson, 2003; Welshman & Walmsley, 2006). This is a type of discourse in which support workers have institutionally powerful roles and can dictate what should happen in the lives of the people they support.

In the conversations in this book, however, efforts were clearly being made by all parties to achieve relationships which were more open, friendly and equal, and these were explored particularly in Chapters 5–8. Looking back at the issues that emerged from those chapters, it is clear that there are possible ways of behaving and interacting which imply a more 'personalised' relationship, one that steps out of the institutionality of the Intellectual Disability world (Williams *et al.*, 2009b). What this book has revealed is far more of the detail about what it means to 'do ordinary', rather than to behave in an institutional way. For instance, speakers could draw explicitly on a repertoire of friendship, one in which shared interests and experiences could be explored; they could also draw on a repertoire of autonomy, as was seen in Chapter 7. Much of this entailed breaking down and blurring the boundaries that exist between people's assumed roles; when the support worker mentions aspects of her personal life, or when the research group members challenge their supporter to talk about her own affairs, something is shifting in the dynamics of the relationship between people.

However, on all these occasions, it was very hard to ignore the 'incompetence' on which so much of the talk depended. In Chapter 7 (extract 7.8) Neil was worried about his own competence to handle his friend's drinking behaviour without a member of the support staff present, and in Chapter 8 (extract 8.2) Rachel felt she had to fill in and account for the fact that Alice had not responded adequately to a casual remark from a passer-by. What can be concluded is that people are very easily drawn back into the assumptions underpinning the world of intellectual disability. The repertoire of incompetence exerts a very strong magnetic pull.

Being an expert

Finally, another repertoire to be aware of, particularly in a collective context, is that of 'the expert', something which did not compete with the discourse of intellectual disability, but rather drew on it. For instance, it was noticeable how Fiona in Chapter 10 (extract 10.2) drew on a repertoire of 'expertise' rather than competence by deliberately bringing Alex into the discussion. He was an expert, precisely because he had insider knowledge about living in the local hospital, and moreover he had led complaints and campaigns about the treatment in that hospital. There were also instances where it could be seen that people demonstrated their understanding of each other by drawing on repertoires of 'expertise' or resilience. One of the most salient examples of this was in Chapter 13, where the analysis showed how people *had to* recognise and call on a peer-support repertoire in order to move forward with the research question and articulate their own ideas. It was only in the context of peer support that this was possible, and once people realised that they shared the label of 'learning disability' with the interviewers, they could become more 'competent' in saying what they felt.

What can be concluded about repertoires of 'competence' and 'incompetence'? First, it should be emphasised that this discussion is not about 'making people competent' by assuming that they are. As was discussed in the opening chapter, assumptions of incompetence are not an idle form of oppression, perpetrated on one group of people by another. If the individual were totally competent, then the logic would indicate that supporters would no longer be needed. It would seem, however, from the data in this book that there is a strong link between the context of the talk and repertoires of competence. In other words, when supporting someone on a one-to-one basis to manage their life, it is hard to avoid the more traditional discourses of intellectual disability, and much of the talk gets drawn back into shared assumptions and knowledge about that world. However, there are competing repertoires which challenge, and have the potential to reshape, that assumption of incompetence. If someone employs their own support staff, then it should be recognised in the conduct of their relationship that they can both be 'in control' but also have support where they need it. Independent living, as disabled writers have claimed (ODI, 2008), is about that element of control and not about being able to do things on one's own.

What the analysis in this book has shown is that being an expert actually complements being a person with an intellectual disability. It is not just the non-disabled support workers, but all the speakers, who have responsibility for the introduction of these newer repertoires. New types of talk, like old ones, will have to be jointly reconstructed. As Mark noticed in Chapter 12 (extract 12.5), being a person with an intellectual disability is not just about *being incompetent,* it is also about having power and through the identity of 'intellectual disability' people can realise that power.

Power

The three themes of competence, identity and power are intimately linked. However, the point of separating them in this discussion is that they represent different ways of looking at the data. While (in)competence was explored as part of a strong interpretative repertoire underpinning the talk, I was interested in power as it was manifested in the ways in which talk was accomplished, the positions that people took up as they conversed with each other and how the turns in a conversation were distributed. The idea of interactional rights was mentioned in Chapter 2, and was explained further in the light of the analysis in Chapter 5. Those analysts involved in institutional CA (Drew & Heritage, 1992; Heritage & Clayman, 2010) have built their discipline on noticing and analysing who has power in conversations. What they have particularly noticed is that these things are unequally distributed among individuals, according to their institutional position in the conversation. As was stated in Chapter 5, it is a powerful thing to have the interactional right to ask the question, to initiate and then to evaluate whether something is 'right' or appropriate. Conversely, it is a less powerful position to be the respondent and to be speaking on someone else's terms and with someone else's prompts.

So, what has been noticed in the current book? Were interactional rights equally distributed among participants? The first data chapter (Chapter 3) highlighted some routine interactional problems related to turn-taking itself. Barry (in extracts 3.1 and 3.2) had some grave difficulties in getting his turn in the conversation and had to adopt strong turn-taking strategies in order to avoid being usurped by his carers. This is an extreme form of infringement of conversational rights, but certainly one that will be well known to people who have experience of being with someone with an intellectual disability.

However, the idea of 'interactional rights' is slightly more subtle than simply being silenced. It is about the kinds of things that people do in conversations. For instance, it was noticed in Part 1 that the prerogative of praising another person, or acknowledging their achievement, fell routinely to the support worker. When support workers did this bit of interactional work, it was not remarkable: people in the conversation accepted it as natural, for instance, when Beth in Chapter 7 (extract 7.4) said that Penny's socks were the right colour or when Jenny in Chapter 4 (extract 4.2) praised Ellie's achievement in managing her budget. Similarly, the work of encouraging or eliciting talk was frequently accomplished by the support worker. When Kathy intervened in Chapter 3 (extract 3.4) to help elicit an answer from Brendan, this was unusual and remarkable precisely because Kathy was not a support worker. Therefore, in analytic terms, the roles of support worker and person with intellectual disabilities could be outlined through the functions normally associated with those roles in everyday talk. It will not have escaped the reader's notice that this distribution of rights is not an even, equal one. Arguably, the more powerful functions in talk were those the support worker routinely took on. To reiterate, defining functions of support talk included:

- Filling third-turn slots with an evaluation, some praise or an acknowledgement.
- Opening a conversation and encouraging the other person to contribute.
- Defining what was happening in the talk, and what counted as relevant.

Questions of power were raised in Chapter 1, particularly in respect of the relationship between people with intellectual disabilities and supporters. The type of analysis presented in this book is potentially useful, since it is through becoming aware of inequalities in talk, I would argue, that there is a possibility at least of changing them. I am thus happy to be counted as one of the discourse analysts mentioned by Hammersley (2003: 757) who are interested in analysis which will feed into change (see Chapter 14, p. 206).

Were there occasions when people with intellectual disabilities, for instance, took on the rights more ordinarily associated with their support staff? Kathy in Chapter 3, as I have noted, did the unusual thing of stepping into a 'support' role in the conversation with Brendan. However, other individuals in the course of their dealings with their support workers occasionally made similar leaps. In Chapter 6, for instance, it is remarkable that the conversation between Frank and Simon only proceeded so smoothly because they both understood that Frank had the right to define what was happening. It will be recalled how Simon started making a joke, but drew back when he noticed that Frank was not laughing. Frank also did some work around evaluating his support worker and giving him positive feedback at the end of the coffee-making episode: 'You're not bad mate'. These may seem like small things in a conversation, yet they are vital in indicating the start of a new, more equal relationship.

By becoming aware of the functions of talk, perhaps it is possible for support workers to deliberately step back from the 'power' associated with their role. By the same token, people with intellectual disabilities could take responsibility for being 'the boss' by taking on more of these functions and rights. It is possible for both the person with intellectual disabilities and the support worker to start rearranging the power balance at the centre of their relationship.

There were some large differences and contrasts between the everyday talk in Part 1 and the collective talk in Part 2. As Goodley points out:

> There is a danger of romanticizing the 'autonomy' of self-advocates if we ignore their day-to-day experiences of oppression. (Goodley, 2003: 127)

Every time I moved between Chapter 8 and Chapter 9, the wide gulf struck me afresh. In order to understand more accurately what this contrast consists of, the concept of 'interactional rights' was again helpful. Self-advocacy (Goodley, 1997, 2000) is a social activity which is defined by participants taking back their interactional rights as full members, and a detailed textual analysis of talk revealed to me exactly how interactional rights are distributed. In Chapters 9–13, people with intellectual disabilities were defining who they were, asking questions of each other and solving their own problems. These are the social activities that constitute 'power'. Nowhere is this more true than within the process of research. In becoming 'researchers', Mark and his colleagues took on a far more powerful range of interactional rights than the people in Part 1. They were able to:

- Ask their own questions.
- Organise discussions.
- Decide on who should speak next.
- Say whether particular answers counted as relevant.

All this is powerful work and challenges the expectations that are held about a person with intellectual disabilities. It is interesting to reflect on what it takes to make these changes. Clearly, the responsibility lies with the researchers with intellectual disabilities themselves. It is not something that can be simply engineered by calling a project 'inclusive', or even by paying people with intellectual disabilities to be researchers.

Another of the tensions and questions with which this book opened was the issue of support within self-advocacy, participation (Redley & Weinberg, 2007) and in research (Chappell, 2000). In inclusive projects there are often people who are there as supporters, as non-disabled researchers or as colleagues of the researchers with intellectual disabilities. Similarly, in a self-advocacy group, Chapter 10 explored the role played by supporters employed by self-advocates. In order that the researchers do take on more powerful interactional rights, it is essential that they prepare for these situations, but also that they are not usurped by others. An interesting example occurred in Chapter 11 (extract 11.5), when a support worker in one of the focus groups offered to help by exploring the meaning of 'discrimination'.

397.	Sar	can I give an example perhaps Mark↑ because um (.) I've
398.		been discriminated against because I've been a <u>wo</u>man in the
399.		past

Although she was not a member of the group being interviewed, nevertheless this was an interesting intervention since she felt she had to ask Mark for permission in order to speak at all. The potential power of her contribution was hard to disentangle from her role within the group. Her introduction of the idea of 'gender discrimination' could have been taken as a powerful move to redefine the concept Mark was asking about. However, what was important was to look at how it was actually taken in the group. In fact, the sequel to this extract was simply an acknowledgement by Mark, and then a request for others to speak. Sidelining a potential contribution is a subtle, and very powerful, move on the part of anyone in a conversation; the fact that it was done by a researcher with an intellectual disability is a key example of the way in which power can be redistributed in talk.

Supporters had important roles to play, as was seen in several chapters. In order to get into the discussion, to remember what is needed in a particular context of talk and to express and realise their own power, people with intellectual disabilities worked jointly with supporters. All that is public work. However, when research simply looks at data from public events, it would seem that only half the picture is obtained. In the current book, supporters were seen backstage, doing work that was geared to the development of ownership and autonomy on the part of the self-advocates. This book has unpicked some of the ways this joint work can happen, especially the ways in which power can be redistributed between supporter and person with intellectual disabilities.

Identity issues: the links between the personal and the public

The issues of power, I found, were best delineated by the things that speakers actually did in their talk, while the issue of competence could be seen as a backdrop, or repertoire, of assumed knowledge on which people drew in their talk. Identity matters, in some ways, cut across all these distinctions. Identity work is done not only when someone speaks about themselves, but also in the way categories are used in talk. When someone speaks in the role of a support worker or a chairperson, for instance, then that brings with it a bundle of assumptions about what to expect from that person. This is known as membership categorisation, and again, this is a very general feature about how talk works, and was one of the first contributions of CA (Sacks, 1995; Silverman, 1998).

Some of the questions raised about identity at the start of this book were to do with identification: how do people in this book relate to the label they have been assigned and how can a rejection of that label sit alongside a collective identity? It will be recalled that part of the backstage discussion featured in Chapter 13 turned particularly on the ways in which the labelling discourse of people with intellectual disabilities differed from that of disabled people who founded the social model (Corker & French, 1999).

In the final chapters of this book in particular, the analysis has drawn closely on the multi-layered nature of identity work, as Zimmerman (1998) suggested, and seemed to be a very apt way of looking at the data I had. Identity is constantly shifting and being used in different contexts, as Johnson (2003) observes in her study of teacher identities:

> Identities shift and change according to the conversational resources available at particular points in time. (Johnson, 2003: 231)

As in the current work, Johnson sees the connection between a construction of identity within talk, and a wider, ideological identity framework.

These connections were visible throughout the current book; for instance, research group members in Part 2 openly reflected on their lives as people with 'learning difficulties' and about their feelings about being labelled. It was this tension which literally created something new for their identity record. They were not simply becoming researchers in the sense in which I might, by entering an already established field. They were creating the identities into which they were stepping, as researchers with 'learning difficulties'. The analysis added to the arguments about whether it is possible to be both a person with 'learning difficulties' and a researcher. In fact, it was not only possible, but for this kind of research it was necessary. The common experience of being labelled became a positive tool for change, as Gramlich *et al.* (2002: see Chapter 12) subsequently reflected. This type of positive identity move was made, however, only after experience, talk and support. What this book has revealed is how these matters can shift through the processes of interaction.

Becoming a researcher creates a powerful identity, both for groups and individuals. However, an identity issue which became very salient for me was the tension between personal and public life: that leap from individual to collective voice. People with intellectual disabilities who stand on public platforms are often criticised for 'not being typical' of others, or of not in fact being people with an intellectual disability. It is assumed that they could not operate in such a coherent and powerful way if they 'really' had an intellectual disability. Conversely, in these projects, people with intellectual disabilities, once they stepped down from the public platform, frequently went home to a situation where they were disempowered. Assumptions about their incapacity and childlike status again kicked in. There were some sharp disjunctions here between the different levels of identity which have been highlighted in this book. The identity of 'public speaker' was built on the micro-level identities taken up in the flow of the talk. People with intellectual disabilities literally stepped into the role of researcher, or self-advocate, by virtue of the way in which they controlled the talk. However, this new persona, or identity, did not necessarily move with them back into their private life. A self-advocate sometimes had to pack up their public life and leave it in the care of others while they stepped back into the 'everyday' reality, which was built on quite different identity assumptions.

One small example will suffice. On one occasion during the course of 'Skills for Support', the team had taken part in a training workshop and had presented some of the data and emerging findings about the research on a conference platform. Before the end of their presentation, a taxi driver had arrived to take one of them home. He was anxious to leave, and although the presentation was completed, the researcher in question was whisked away immediately afterwards, and back to her persona as a person with intellectual disabilities. I went with her to the car and witnessed the taxi driver calling her 'Little Miss Riding Hood', and asking her 'Did you enjoy yourself then, had a good time?'. His tone of voice can well be imagined by others in the field of Intellectual Disability.

Clearly, the practical implication of all this is that those who support people with intellectual disabilities in their day-to-day lives can learn a lot from public or self-advocacy contexts. The reverse is probably also true. In addition to emphasising the importance of constructing new contexts of talk, this book has shown how intimately the two arenas are linked. The work done by supporters in Part 1 was often mirrored quite precisely by strategies used in supporting people to speak up in Part 2. For instance, bringing someone into a conversation or a discussion by referring to some shared point of knowledge is a key strategy, in both private and in public life (Williams *et al.*, 2009a). People with intellectual disabilities, as well, use strategies in talk to link their private with their public lives. For instance, when Darren (Chapter 9) was arguing for the rights of wheelchair users, he did not do this in the abstract but drew directly on his own experiences as a wheelchair user and referred to the social context of his own life, including his family. The analysis showed how expertly he moved between the personal and the political, and it was precisely this move that gave power to the public statements of people with intellectual disabilities. It may be felt that personal life talk is considered to detract from people's status as public participants – a tension raised in Chapter 1. However, the current analysis has demonstrated not only that it is possible to weave both together, but that it is necessary. It is by bringing their own lives to the public meeting, or to the research project, that people with intellectual disabilities exert power. This is policy-making based on individual life experience, and the paradox of being a person with intellectual disabilities is precisely realised in the quotation in Chapter 12:

> Having a learning difficulty is not something to be ashamed about. I am proud of who I am. If I resented it, then I would be a wreck. (Gramlich *et al.*, 2002: 120)

It is the 'intellectual disability' label that gives people like Gramlich and other self-advocates their power. By bringing their own life into the picture, they are able to make the real links between the rhetoric of public policy and the private realities of being a person with intellectual disabilities.

Doing personalised support

Throughout this book, I have shown people with intellectual disabilities in some quite routine and ordinary interactions with others, as well as on important public platforms where they are speaking up for their rights. Part of the goal of pursuing this analysis was the practice-related aim of learning about *how* to manage those interactions, for people with intellectual disabilities and for those who talk with them. Although the following sections are about 'support talk', this can, of course, be done by people with intellectual disabilities themselves or by those who are paid to help them. Simply because this is 'support talk' does not mean that it is the sole prerogative of non-disabled supporters. In the following remarks, I have deliberately related each topic to personalised support at an individual level, as well as to the task of supporting people with intellectual disabilities in collective situations. There are many missed links between these two arenas, and it is hoped that this book will contribute towards mutual, joint learning across those boundaries.

It is instructive first to remember the policy context in which 'Skills for Support', in particular, was carried out. As outlined in Chapter 1, this is the policy of 'personalisation', and the key features are:

- Statements that disabled and older people have a right to be included in a society which takes account of differences, and values them positively.
- An assumption that disabled people will fight for these goals on their own behalf, and that it is important therefore that they have a voice.
- That 'choice and control' are the underpinning and defining features of independent living, and that these can be achieved *with the support* needed by each individual.

However, as Shakespeare (2006) points out, good care and support are individual matters and not just about a move towards greater autonomy for the service user. Therefore, the lessons learnt from the extracts in this book do not just apply to situations where someone is employing a personal assistant. A personalised system should allow everyone to have a greater choice about *how* they want their care to be delivered:

> Equality, autonomy, independence and flexibility should be fostered within more traditional caring relationships. (Shakespeare, 2006: 152)

All of us have choices in how we talk and how we relate to each other. This is no different for people with intellectual disabilities or for those who converse with them. The problem is however, as outlined above, that these communications can easily get pulled back into the straitjacket of institutionalised talk, where the non-disabled person assumes that they have to take control. The following sections therefore aim to summarise some of the overarching communication strategies that might lead to more personalised encounters.

Turns at talk

In Part 1, there were scenes in which people with intellectual disabilities had to fight to have a voice. Although there was only one example of someone with an intellectual disability really being sidelined and excluded from a conversation, this will doubtless resonate with many people with intellectual disabilities and those who work with them. I also showed how easy it is for people to be disbelieved, not taken seriously, and how sometimes people can be forced into speaking when they want to remain silent. This is where concepts of turn-taking and turn-selection can become more than simply analytical tools. They are the backbone of CA, but they are also the backbone of understanding how to start making changes for and with people with intellectual disabilities. For instance, the supporter Naomi in Chapter 3 at least tried to make sure Barry had a voice by turning towards him, indicating that he should take the next turn, and by showing in her face that she was listening to him. Barry himself was clearly aware that he had to jump in quickly if he was going to have a say. One of the lessons about turn-taking related to transition relevance places, which were the places at which a turn could be concluded. When taking part in a conversation where someone is clearly being excluded, it is important to notice these points and (as it were) to 'hold them open'. It is sometimes too easy to jump in and have a say. It is only when the other person stops and waits that someone with an intellectual disability may have a chance to come into the conversation at all.

Part 2 featured self-advocacy talk, where people with intellectual disabilities spoke up and took the floor on their own terms. As was shown in Chapters 10 and 12 in particular, communication in a meeting is often done jointly. People who become public speakers will do so because others recognise their right to speak, and in fact may prompt or create slots for them to have their say. Simply by being aware of how turn structure works in a larger meeting or discussion will mean that one can offer the floor to a particular speaker and effectively prompt them. Like the CA analyst, someone taking part in a debate or a meeting can be sensitive to potential turn-allocation points, when a previous speaker has come to the end of what they have to say, and can sometimes offer another person the right to have the floor.

Reliable witnesses

In Chapter 3, I discussed a tension faced by the support worker between believing what the person with intellectual disabilities says and ensuring its accuracy. It would seem that sometimes people with intellectual disabilities get 'put through the mill', and higher standards of accuracy may be demanded of them because of worries about their incompetence as reliable witnesses. In a more positive vein, during self-advocacy discussions, Chapters 10 and 12 showed how support talk could actually encourage someone to speak up about their own experiences, so that the person came over not only as a reliable witness, but as an expert. When Fiona encouraged Alex in Chapter 10 to talk about his experience as a hospital resident, she framed his contribution with respect, reminding him and others that Alex had an important story to tell. Chapter 5 also showed how Sam, a football enthusiast, was reminded by his support worker that he 'had met a lot of the players' and asked about details relating to his expertise in football.

Attributing expertise to someone has a lot to do with understanding membership categorisation. Category membership brings with it a whole bundle of ideas, themes and background to talk about, and so will put the person with intellectual disabilities in new shoes, opening up a new range of speaking opportunities. The business of being a reliable witness and how this is achieved is followed up in Williams (2005).

Giving and receiving advice

Giving advice and guidance is always going to be a key part of a support worker's job. That is often why they are there in the first place. However, in Chapter 4, I explored how important it is to give this guidance *on the terms* of the person with intellectual disabilities. Some of this involves what has been called 'meta-talk' – talking *about* the talk. One practical way is to make sure, if possible, that people understand what support they need and that they are in control of that plan. That is what Ellie had achieved in Chapter 4, with her very fine understanding of how her routine of budgeting matched her needs as a person with autism. In Williams *et al.* (2009b) this theme is developed further under the heading given by one of the participants in 'Skills for Support', who put it like this: 'I do like the subtle touch'.

In self-advocacy and research contexts, the advice function of the support worker is perhaps even more salient. For instance, all new researchers will need advice, mentoring and guidance, and so learning the skills of research is not unique to people with intellectual disabilities who take up that role. Nevertheless, there are power implications to giving advice, and the work done by an educator often puts that person in a powerful position. For instance, in Chapter 10 (extracts 10.3 and 10.4) I was seen carrying out the functions of an educator, effectively defining what was relevant and acceptable about the skills of being a researcher. Perhaps the same principle applies here as in everyday life: giving this advice and guidance can be most effective if it is done on the terms of the person with intellectual disabilities, picking up on their own interests and what they have to say about things. Angela's photos and her description of how she showed them to others helped me to be opportunistic in shaping the discussion and using it for the purposes of learning more about research.

Timing and sensitivity to context

Much of good support is about timing. Sensitivity to the needs of the person with intellectual disabilities sometimes means that time has to be given for someone to talk through their own issues so that they really 'own' things. Rushed advice can often come over as bossy. However, as Chapter 4 showed, with Colin and Ben, good timing can also mean being quick off the mark and reacting fast so that risks are avoided. Again, there is a parallel here between the way CA is done and the way good support can work. CA does not categorise types of utterances, nor does it offer a cookbook approach to analysis. That is because it recognises that all utterances are embedded in a tight sequence of talk and are produced and understood in the light of the fine detail of what has gone before. This can include body language and mutual interpretation of an utterance, and it can certainly encompass individual differences. That is all true of good support too, since communicating with people with intellectual disabilities is all about knowing the individual, attending to issues of timing in what is going on in the here-and-now and becoming skilled at fitting in one's own contribution to that micro-context.

Opening up conversations

As discussed in this chapter, it is often very easy to be pulled into ways of interacting that emphasise the incompetence of the person with intellectual disabilities. However, it is possible to become more aware of this and remind people that they *can* think for themselves and make their own choice. The central chapters in this book are all concerned broadly with ways in which support workers could move away from institutional talk and they have tried to define what would constitute a more 'ordinary' way of interacting.

How do people successfully open up communication channels? For a start, in 'ordinary' conversation speakers generally have equal rights in talk, and so it becomes problematic if a support worker is doing most of the talking and the person with intellectual disabilities plays only a minimal role. However, it must be remembered that many people with intellectual disabilities do of course have practical difficulties in verbal language and so their ability to take a full role in the conversation may be limited. What can then be done by both parties to make the talk more 'equal'? In Chapter 5, some of the strategies for opening up talk were explored, and it was seen how follow-up questions often worked much better than simple open questions alone. In Chapter 6, I looked at ways of keeping a social conversation going, which involved drawing on shared interests, topics that people knew they had mentioned before or activities they had actually experienced together.

It is also salutary to remember how easy it is to slip into a situation where the support worker is hounding the person with intellectual disabilities, forcing them to talk, as Brendan was in Chapter 3. This is not equal, or 'ordinary', talk between adults, but resembles more what may happen in adult–child talk (Ochs & Taylor, 1992). Therefore, a more equal and less institutional conversation will only happen if someone really listens and follows up what the person with intellectual disabilities wants to say. This implies good personal knowledge of the individual, and it was precisely that knowledge which Kathy brought to bear with her friend Brendan in Chapter 3.

Sharing interests and blurring boundaries

A method we all use when we want to get talking is to find something in common with the person we are talking to. As support workers get to know the person with intellectual disabilities better, they will have a wealth of shared experience to which they can refer in conversation. It is far easier for anyone to talk with a person who knows and shares what has gone on in their lives, since they do not have to start from scratch and explain things. Again, this is something that is true for all of us (for instance, an incident at work can lose its humour when recounted at home, since family members do not share the context and background). However, the principle of 'sharing' has a particular resonance in the context of supporting people with intellectual disabilities, since their staff members have often felt they had to maintain a professional distance. In this book I have tried to show how being friendly can imply stepping out of that professional role at times and blurring the boundaries between being a support worker and being an ordinary individual with one's own life. That can also happen in research or learning contexts, as was apparent in Chapter 6 (extract 6.7), and on that occasion it was most definitely the people with intellectual disabilities who pushed the boundaries into the personal arena. They effectively used a set-up interview practice session to pursue their own interests in finding out more about what I was doing outside the group.

These matters still raise concerns in the professions associated with Intellectual Disability. That is perhaps because they are misunderstood. For instance, blurring the professional boundary does not mean that a support worker should conduct the business of their own private life while doing their job. Disabled people who are looking at issues about the relationship with their PA (Patel & Pridmore, 2010) are very clear that making private calls on a mobile phone while at work is *not* acceptable. By contrast, the type of friendliness witnessed in this book consisted of a relaxed sharing of interests, a willingness to show other sides of one's own personality and the skills to be open about those in talk. On that basis, people like Frank in Chapter 6 can get to know their support worker as a person in their own right, and this in itself can oil the wheels of conversation. When two people get on together and have something in common, then they can even share jokes and enjoy their chats while they are doing practical tasks together such as making a cup of coffee. Readers who would like more detail on the issue of building conversation on past shared experience are referred to Williams *et al.* (2009a), which explores particularly how important it is to have (in the words of Kerrie Ford, one of the co-researchers in 'Skills for Support') a 'bit of common ground'.

Attention to body language

Through each of the chapters about everyday life interactions, and about more formal self-advocacy interactions too, body language was seen to be very important as part of the overall communication. Again, there is a congruence here between the toolbox of the CA analyst and the toolbox of someone engaging in conversation. In some forms of CA, the analyst pays close attention to the exact placement of particular gestures, eye gaze or body posture (see e.g. Goodwin, 2007). People with intellectual disabilities and their support workers also need to become sensitised to how their body language contributes to the interaction. People can show through their body language that they are friendly by smiling and relaxing together. It is also possible, as was seen in Chapter 6, to identify as people who share an ordinary interest by the way you dress, stand and behave. When I saw two people sharing a drink and leaning against the kitchen cupboard while chatting about football, I did not think of an institutional relationship. This was much more like 'equality'.

However, one of the key and sensitive tasks in relating to people in this book was attentiveness. In group settings where people were speaking up, the support worker's job was often simply to listen. In Chapter 10, for instance, I flagged up how a support worker could show they were attentive and concentrated on listening, which helped Alex to speak up and make a sustained contribution to the discussion. This was not simply an auditory activity, but entailed watching, sustained eye contact and showing interest through facial expressions.

We are all attentive to each other in ordinary conversation, and mostly this attentiveness does not reach the level of conscious awareness. However, the CA analyst will only have evidence of what is going on through the ways in which people demonstrate that they are understanding each other, and this understanding is based on an implicit rule-book of knowledge about how social interaction works. This is not specialist knowledge, but simply something that most people share in order to operate in the social world and is acquired early in life. As Wooffitt explains: 'the way we design our turns unavoidably displays the kind of inferences we are making' (2005: 33). When I talk about support workers listening and being sensitive to their conversational partner, I am therefore not talking about anything 'special' to the role of the support worker. Nevertheless, I am assuming that attentiveness includes an implicit understanding of the way in which conversation works on a turn-by-turn basis, and the implications for the other speaker on this particular occasion.

Examples of this type of attentiveness are given throughout the book. For instance, in Chapter 6 Adam was very clearly attending to the way in which Frank took his joke. This led him to stop his incipient laughter and to deal with the matter in hand in a more serious way, which was what Frank had indicated at that point. The business of being attentive can become even more skilled when the other conversational partner uses forms of communication which are different or limited. In Chapter 4, for instance, Colin responded to Ben's signs by expanding quite considerably on the possible meanings that Ben might be intending. In that context, and with his knowledge of Ben's topics of conversation, Colin watched Ben's face carefully and was able to produce a two-way conversation in which Ben himself was the initiator and Colin the respondent.

Three-way encounters

Both in everyday life and in self-advocacy meetings and research, people with intellectual disabilities meet others with whom they may communicate. The supporter is often there as a third party, a 'shadow' as some PAs have expressed it:

> Being a personal assistant is a bit like being a shadow in as much as you have to learn to move with your client while not blocking the sun from their face. Your job is not to 'steal their thunder' but rather to allow them to build the confidence that they need to live their lives the way they want to. (Clayton, 2006: 138)

However, as some of the talk in this book has shown, that role may also include encouraging successful communication, interpreting for the person with intellectual disabilities, giving them time to respond or enabling them to carry out a social task, such as paying for something.

In Chapter 8, it was seen how this type of public, three-way support can easily go wrong. It is all too common for the support worker to become the focus of attention or to answer *for* the person with intellectual disabilities. Therefore, stepping back is often the key to providing good support in this situation. Moreover, there may be occasions when the support worker will have to deflect an attempt to speak directly to him or herself, indicating that the person with intellectual disabilities should be addressed. This also happens in group situations, in meetings and certainly in inclusive research, although it is hard to capture examples of it on video. Nevertheless, the support worker played a very different role in public events, where she was practically silent, compared to sessions behind the scenes. Being able to step back in public is often dependent on intricate preparation work, and this happens also in everyday life. A good example of preparation work was done in Chapter 8, for instance, by Colin preparing Ben to pay his money in the youth club.

People who may have very limited verbal language can also be supported to take a part in 'public' life, to meet and greet neighbours and friends (as Ben did in Chapter 8) and to have a story to tell. One of the interesting strategies observed in this book was where support workers acted almost as ventriloquists, telling the story for the person with intellectual disabilities and literally narrating his or her life. Although this may be considered something one would do for a young child or a baby, nevertheless supporters used that practice to enable people with intellectual disabilities to have a role in the story of their own life. At times, they can become the 'voice' for the person they support.

Support to take control

A central task for support talk, and one that runs through nearly all the chapters, is that of facilitating, or enabling, a person to take charge of some action or idea. This is where we get to the heart of the sensitive business of being an 'empowering' support worker. It is often said that people cannot be empowered, but have to take power for themselves. Nevertheless, with the idea of personalisation (DH, 2008: see Chapter 1) comes the notion that support workers should be enabling the person they support to be in control of their life. If the disabled person is to all intents and purposes *already* in control, then the support worker may simply have to work to the rules and ideas of their disabled employer. However, in our videos there was only one occasion where a person with intellectual disabilities was heard to ask or tell their support worker to do something. Most people with intellectual disabilities, it can be safely assumed, will still need encouragement to take up the role of 'being the boss'.

Does this book add anything to our knowledge of how this type of facilitation can be successfully achieved? Looking at the business of choices, for instance, is an interesting case. Support workers are often told that they should enable people with intellectual disabilities to make their own choices, and indeed the importance of doing this in a person-centred way, with accessible information, is underlined in the Mental Capacity Act 2005. In Chapter 7, it was seen how this can turn out in practice. Like other conversations in this book, those concerning choices were two-way interactions. Therefore, when Brian expressed his own stance towards the business of buying (or not buying) DVDs, his support worker, Emma, merely supported his own choice by coming in with a joke about the number of DVDs Brian had bought. However, when someone is about to make what seems to be an unwise choice, the matter is not so easy. This was the case with Charles, in the long extract in Chapter 7. His choice to hold a party in a leisure centre was going to be much more expensive and possibly more inconvenient than taking up the offer of a party organised by the service he worked for. Charles was strong enough about his autonomy to listen to the manager talking about the pros and cons, and then make up his own mind later. As his manager said, 'It's entirely up to you'. Many people with intellectual disabilities, though, in the same situation would be swayed by the arguments of their support staff.

Making a single decision is a social activity and, on a larger scale, so is being in control of one's life – all this is about interactional work. What the conversations in this book show more than anything is how these things are done jointly. Therefore, when people with intellectual disabilities, for instance, want to do research, their decisions about that research can be discussed with others. That is the point of the supporter's role in Chapters 12 and 13. What was explored there is how that support can be achieved without the supporter 'taking over'. Some of this is about actually making explicit the question of ownership. Just as I encouraged the research group members to discuss their own role in the research in Chapter 12, in the same way Beth reminded Penny in Chapter 8 that it was 'her choice'.

In the ebb and flow of real-life talk, stepping back can be achieved in different ways. One way is simply to hesitate and not jump into a conversation too soon. That is what May essentially was doing in Chapter 10, as she supported Tracy to speak and then helped to analyse the cause of the trouble for Tracy in responding to Mark's question. At other times, stepping back can be physical as in Chapter 8, when Michael was checking into a hotel and his support worker, Teresa, walked through the door of the hotel after him, thereby enabling him to take control of the encounter. Stepping back can also imply something more general about relinquishing some of the more powerful roles in conversation, and this perhaps will only happen as people with intellectual disabilities take on a wider range of more powerful interactional rights, thus becoming self-advocates, researchers and employers of their own staff.

Implications for change

My central aim in writing this book was to draw together insights arising from analysis of interactions in different settings that included people with intellectual disabilities; in Chapter 1, I expressed the wish that 'those interactions can be carried out on a basis of equality'. It is time now to offer some reflections on the ways in which understanding of interaction can actually change the state of affairs for people with intellectual disabilities.

There is a practical and obvious sense in which all those who are involved in support work can learn about communication by reading and reflecting on the extracts in this book and also (and perhaps more importantly) by observing and thinking about their own interactions. This practical goal was also reflected in the training materials produced by 'Skills for Support' (Ponting *et al.*, 2010), which aim to provide a resource for people with intellectual disabilities to train their own support staff. It is precisely that 'twist' – i.e. people with intellectual disabilities moving into training roles – that gives the strongest clue to how change may happen. When people with intellectual disabilities become active agents for change, they themselves will enable interactions to be carried out on a basis of greater equality. As this book has consistently emphasised, however, this move into becoming an 'active agent' also needs support, and the subtlety of providing that support has been explored in every chapter. In the various models of inclusive research summarised at the end of Chapter 14, team work and partnership were key themes. The support people with intellectual disabilities need in order to become researchers should also be 'empowering', so that people can take up independent roles as active political campaigners and researchers by being in control of their own support. Autonomy is a universal human right, as was discussed at the start of this book. However, autonomy is generally achieved in collaboration with others; it is the control over that relationship which is at the heart of achieving autonomy, as it is also for other groups such as older people with dementia (Boyle, 2008). That is also the meaning of independence enshrined in the disabled people's movement and in the UK Independent Living Review (ODI, 2008), and it is the same concept which underpins the relationship between the collective movement of people with intellectual disabilities and their support structures.

The two parts of this book, moving from individual voice to collective voice, revealed some striking differences. There are strong accounts in the literature from individuals who have shown resilience and strength in their own lives (Goodley, 2000), often with the support of families (Souza & Ramcharan, 1997). However, this book has shown that the powerful identity achieved on collective platforms by self-advocates was seldom carried over into their personal life, and the people in Part 1 therefore seemed to be in a strikingly different position from those in Part 2. Simply by exploring these differences and unpicking the communication events in both arenas, it is hoped that change can occur. Routine support in everyday life would certainly be different if it were carried out in collective, self-advocacy contexts. Research itself is a tool for change, and inclusive research quite specifically has a campaigning edge to it. However, in order to effect changes at the micro-level of communication encounters, perhaps support workers and personal assistants themselves need to be 'empowered' to take roles in research and to work alongside the people with intellectual disabilities they support. No one can be expected to adopt and embrace change without a corresponding position of power and understanding.

Finally, it is worth spelling out the implications of these findings for policy, both in the UK and in other countries where personalisation and participation are on the agenda. In the English Learning Disability strategy (DH, 2001), as was seen in Chapter 1, the arenas of individual and collective voice are often linked, as if they were part of a continuum of participation. This book has shown that this link cannot simply be assumed, but has to be worked at. If people with intellectual disabilities are expected to bring their private, lived experience to the table of commissioners and policy-makers, then there should be more connections forged between their experience in public and their lives at home. Private life, of course, must remain private. However, one of the practical ways of communicating across these two arenas would be to enable supporters to work in more holistic ways, accompanying and providing individual support to people with intellectual disabilities in their public lives. This already happens with personal assistance support for some people with physical impairments (Patel *et al.*, 2010) and indeed with some people with intellectual disabilities, and could be a useful way forward in envisaging personal assistance for the people in this book.

Personalisation has been considered a win-win policy in the UK, enabling cuts in congregate services alongside personalised support for individuals on their own terms (Duffy, 2007; Daly & Roebuck, 2008). However, researchers have also pointed out the dangers of social isolation and the risks personalisation may pose to people with intellectual disabilities (Fyson, 2009). This book has shown how some of those matters are played out at the micro-level of interaction, but it also points out how important it is to understand that personalisation does not mean leaving people to fend for themselves, without any support. On the contrary, the messages in this book are about co-production of a personalised support service, in everyday communication, in self-advocacy and in research. That means that supporters are still necessary, but that more attention needs to be paid to the ways in which they will learn the new skills of a non-institutionalised way of working, in which power is more equally distributed. Alongside workforce strategies for support workers, there needs to be attention to support and training for people with intellectual disabilities themselves, so that they can learn the skills needed to become employers of their own staff. Possible contexts for that learning have been glimpsed in this book in the conversations that take place in self-advocacy groups and in research projects.

If personalisation could be seen as a risky policy, one of the risks will be that opportunities for collective participation may be undermined with the closure of group services, such as day centres. Part 2, along with other literature (Goodley, 2003) and direct statements by self-advocates (Gramlich *et al.*, 2002), has added weight to the arguments for continued funding for collective, user-led movements of disabled people. In particular, people with intellectual disabilities need to have their own place to develop their collective voice, as was seen in Chapter 9, whether this is with other disabled people or separately. This is not an argument for the continuation of oppressive forms of day service. Nevertheless, it is essential that people with intellectual disabilities continue to be able to communicate their ideas, as they do in their own self-advocacy organisations, in the company of people they identify with. If they are not enabled to do this, then personalisation will eclipse participation.

A final few words

This book will end with three aspirations. First, I hope that the present book has made a contribution by showing how CA is done and how it can be put to useful ends, so that more researchers are encouraged to have a go. Second, inclusive research is presented and explored as an evolving and exciting power base, which can help us all to understand how change will happen. I trust that inclusion in research will continue to develop in self-advocacy groups, in academia and in the disabled people's movement generally. The third wish is the most important of all. It is hoped that members of the self-advocacy movement, as well as those who just want to go shopping with their support worker, will continue to realise the power of talk to change their own lives.

Appendix

Transcription Conventions

The transcription conventions used in the extracts in this book are based on the standard CA conventions (see Wooffitt, 2005, pp. 211–12). The general attempt is to transcribe what is heard and observed without recourse to grammatical conventions (full stops) and so on. Those would be pre-empting the analysis. However, there are occasions in the text where it seemed sensible to use conventions such as capitals for proper names, so that the extract was more readable.

Line numbers	These relate to the original transcript from which each extract is taken
Underlined word	Something that is emphasised or stressed, compared with the surrounding speech
CAPITAL LETTERS	Something that is louder than surrounding speech
↑	Upward intonation pattern
↓	Downward intonation pattern
(0.4)	Numbers in brackets refer to length of pauses (with 1 = 1 sec)
(.)	Very short pause, under 0.1 sec
( )	Something that cannot be heard or interpreted clearly
(( ))	Double brackets are used around anything that is not verbal language
((italics))	Are used to describe what people are doing, who they are looking at, and so on
LF	Laughter
[ ]	Square brackets indicate overlapping speech
=	Equal sign indicates that one turn follows on from the previous one without any gap
° °	Speech that is softer than the surrounding speech
> <	Speech that is noticeably faster than surrounding speech
:::	Elongation of vowel sound

Non-verbal actions are marked in this book simply by words in brackets, to show the place where they occurred. A finer-grained and more sophisticated system for marking non-verbal features is illustrated in Kendon, 2004.

Disability and Discourse. Analysing Inclusive Conversation with People with Intellectual Disabilities,
1st edition. © Val Williams. Published 2011 by John Wiley & Sons, Ltd.

References

Abbott, D. & Howarth, J. (2007) Still off-limits? Staff views on supporting gay, lesbian and bisexual people with intellectual disabilities to develop sexual and intimate relationships, *Journal of Applied Research in Intellectual Disabilities*, 20(2): 116–126.

Abbott, S. & McConkey, R. (2006) The barriers to social inclusion as perceived by people with intellectual disabilities. *Journal of Intellectual Disabilities*, 10(3): 275–287.

Abell, S., Ashmore, J., Beart, S., *et al.* (2007) Including everyone in research: The Burton Street Research Group. *British Journal of Learning Disabilities*, 35(2): 121–124.

American Association on Intellectual and Developmental Disabilities (2010) *Intellectual Disability: Definition, Classification and Systems of Support*, 11th edition, bookstore.aaidd.org/BookDetail. aspx?bid=97.

Antaki, C. (1994) *Explaining and Arguing: The Social Organization of Accounts*. London: Sage.

Antaki, C. (1988) Explanations, communication and social cognition (pp. 1–14), in C. Antaki (Ed.) *Analysing Everyday Explanation*. London: Sage.

Antaki, C. (2002) Personalised revision of 'failed' questions. *Discourse and Society*, 4(4): 411–428.

Antaki, C., Finlay, W. M. L., Sheridan, E., Jingree, T. & Walton, C. (2006) Producing decisions in a self-advocacy group for people with an intellectual disability: two contrasting facilitator styles. *Mental Retardation*, 44: 322–343.

Antaki, C., Finlay, W. M. L. & Walton, C. (2007b) 'The staff are your friends': conflicts between institutional discourse and practice. *British Journal of Social Psychology*, 46: 1–18.

Antaki, C., Finlay, W. & Walton, C. (2007c) Conversational shaping: staff members' solicitation of talk from people with an intellectual impairment. *Qualitative Health Research*, 17(10): 1403–1414.

Antaki, C., Finlay, W. M. L., Walton, C. & Pate, L. (2008) Offering choice to people with an intellectual impairment: an interactional study. *Journal of Intellectual Disability Research*, 52: 1165–1175.

Antaki, C., Walton, C. & Finlay, W. (2007a) How proposing an activity to a person with an intellectual disability can imply a limited identity. *Discourse and Society*, 18(4): 393–410.

Antaki, C. & Widdicombe, S. (1998a) Identity as an achievement and as a tool (pp. 1–14), in C. Antaki & S. Widdicombe (Eds.) *Identities in Talk*. London: Sage.

Antaki, C. & Widdicombe, S. (Eds.) (1998b) *Identities in Talk*. London: Sage.

Antaki, C., Young, N. & Finlay, M. (2002) Shaping clients' answers: departures from neutrality in care-staff interviews with people with a learning disability. *Disability and Society*, 17(4): 435–455.

Disability and Discourse. Analysing Inclusive Conversation with People with Intellectual Disabilities, 1st edition. © Val Williams. Published 2011 by John Wiley & Sons, Ltd.

Argaman, E. (2009) Arguing within an institutional hierarchy: how argumentative talk and interlocutors' embodied practices preserve a superior–subordinate relationship. *Discourse Studies*, *11*(5): 515–542.

Arminen, I. (2000) On the context sensitivity of institutional interaction. *Discourse and Society*, *11*(4): 435–458.

Armstrong, D. (2002) The politics of self-advocacy and people with learning difficulties. *Policy and Politics*, *30*(3): 333–345.

Aspis, S. (1999) What they don't tell disabled people with learning difficulties (pp. 173–182), in M. Corker & S. French (Eds.) *Disability Discourse*. Buckingham: Open University Press.

Atkinson, P. & Hammersley, M. (2007) *Ethnography: Principles in Practice*, 3rd edition. Abingdon: Routledge.

Atkinson, J. & Heritage, J. (Eds.) (1984) *Structures of Social Action: Studies in Conversation Analysis*. Cambridge: Cambridge University Press.

Atkinson, P. & Heritage, J. (1992) *Talk at Work*. Cambridge: Cambridge University Press.

Baker, C. (1982) Adolescent–adult talk as a practical interpretive problem (pp. 104–125), in G. Payne & E. Cuff (Eds.) *Doing Teaching: The Practical Management of Classrooms*. London: Batsford Academic and Educational.

Baker, C. (1997) Membership categorization and interview accounts (pp. 130–143), in D. Silverman (Ed.) *Qualitative Research: Theory, Method and Practice*. London: Sage.

Baker, P. A. (2007) Individual and service factors affecting deinstitutionalization and community use of people with intellectual disabilities. *Journal of Applied Research in Intellectual Disabilities*, *20*: 105–115.

Bakhtin, M. (1986) *Speech Genres and Other Late Essays*. Austin, TX: Texas University Press.

Barnes, C. (2003) What a difference a decade makes: reflections on doing 'emancipatory' disability research. *Disability and Society*, *18*(1): 3–17.

Barnes, C. & Mercer, G. (1997) Breaking the mould? An introduction to doing disability research (pp. 1–14), in C. Barnes & G. Mercer (Eds.) *Doing Disability Research*. Leeds: The Disability Press.

Barnes, C. & Mercer, G. (Eds.) (2007) *Disability Policy and Practice: Applying the Social Model of Disability*. Leeds: The Disability Press.

Barnes, M. (2002) Bringing difference into deliberation? Disabled people, survivors and local governance. *Policy and Politics*, *30*: 319–331.

Barton, L. (2004) The disability movement: some observations (pp. 285–290), in J. Swain, S. French, C. Barnes & C. Thomas (Eds.) *Disabling Barriers – Enabling Environments*, 2nd edition. London: Sage.

Barton, L. (2005) Emancipatory research and disabled people: some observations and questions. *Educational Review*, *57*(3): 317–327.

Beart, S., Hardy, G. & Buchan, L. (2005) How people with intellectual disabilities view their social identity: a review of the literature. *Journal of Applied Research in Intellectual Disabilities*, *18*(1): 47–56.

Beresford, P. (2001) Service users, social policy and the future of welfare. *Critical Social Policy*, *21*(469), November: 494–512.

Beyer, S., Grove, B., Schneider, J., *et al.* (2004) *Working Lives: The Role of Day Centres in Supporting People with Learning Disabilities into Employment*. The Department for Work and Pensions, Report 203.

Billig, M. (1999) Whose terms? Whose ordinariness? Rhetoric and ideology in CA. *Discourse and Society 10*(4): 543–582.

Bloor, M. (1997) Addressing social problems through qualitative research (pp. 231–238), in D. Silverman (Ed.) *Qualitative Research: Theory, Method and Practice*. London: Sage.

Boyle, G. (2008) Autonomy in long-term care: a need, a right or a luxury? *Disability and Society*, *23*(4): 299–310.

Bryman, A. (2008) *Social Research Methods*, 3rd edition. Oxford: Oxford University Press.

Campbell, J. & Oliver, M. (1996) *Disability Politics: Understanding Our Past, Changing our Future*. London: Routledge.

Chapman, R. & McNulty, N. (2004) Building bridges? The role of research support in self-advocacy. *British Journal of Learning Disabilities, 32*: 77–85.

Chappell, A. (2000) Emergence of participatory methodology in learning difficulty research: understanding the context. *British Journal of Learning Disabilities, 28*: 38–43.

Charmaz, K. (2006) *Constructing Grounded Theory: A Practical Guide through Qualitative Analysis*. London: Sage.

Chomsky, N. (1966) *Aspects of the Theory of Syntax*. The Hague: Mouton.

Clark, C. & Pinch, T. (1988) Micro-sociology and micro-economics (pp. 117–141), in N. Fielding (Ed.) *Actions and Structure: Research Methods and Social Theory*. London: Sage.

Clayton, A. (2006) The professional shadow: a personal assistant's account (pp. 137–138), in J. Leece & J. Bornat (Eds.) *Developments in Direct Payments*. Bristol: Policy Press.

Cole, A., Williams, V. *et al.* (2006) *Having a Good Day? Report of a Survey of Community-based Day Ppportunities for Adults with Learning Disabilities*. London: SCIE.

Concannon, L (2005) *Planning for Life: Involving Adults with Learning Disabilities in Service Planning*. Oxford: Routledge.

Corbett, J. (1991) So, who wants to be normal? *Disability, Handicap and Society, 6*(3): 259–260.

Corker, M. (1999) New disability discourse, the principle of optimization and social change (pp. 183–191), in M. Corker & S. French (Eds.) *Disability Discourse*. Buckingham: Open University Press.

Corker, M. & French, S. (Eds.) (1999) *Disability Discourse*. Buckingham: Open University Press.

Coulson, S. (2007) Person-centred planning as co-production (pp. 105–118), in S. Hunter & P. Ritchie, *Co-production and Personalisation in Social Care: Changing Relationships in the Provision of Social Care*. London: Jessica Kingsley.

Craig, J., Craig, F., Withers, P., Hatton, C. & Limb, K. (2002) Identity conflict in people with intellectual disabilities: what role do service-providers play in mediating stigma? *Journal of Applied Research in Intellectual Disabilities, 15*(1): 61–72.

Daly, G. & Roebuck, A. (2008) Gaining independence: an evaluation of service users' accounts of the individual budgets pilot. *Journal of Integrated Care, 16*(3): 17–25.

Davies, C. & Jenkins, R. (1997) 'She has different fits to me': how people with learning difficulties see themselves. *Disability and Society, 12*(1): 95–109.

de Fina, A., Schiffrin, D. & Bamberg, M. (2006) Introduction (pp. 1–23), in A. De Fina, D. Schiffrin & M. Bamberg (Eds.) *Discourse and Identity: Studies in Interactional Sociolinguistics*, 23. Cambridge: Cambridge University Press.

Department for Constitutional Affairs (2007) *Mental Capacity Act 2005 Code of Practice*. London: The Stationery Office.

Department of Health (1996) *Community Care (Direct Payments) Act 1996: Elizabeth II. Chapter 30*. London: The Stationery Office.

Department of Health (2001) *Valuing People: A New Strategy for Learning Disability for the 21st Century*. London: Department of Health.

Department of Health (2006a) *Let Me In: I'm a Researcher. A Report by the Department of Health Learning Difficulties Research Team*. London: Department of Health. www.dh.gov.uk/en/Publicationsandstatistics/Publications/PublicationsPolicyAndGuidance/DH_4132916.

Department of Health (2006b) *Our Health, Our Care, Our Say*. London: Department of Health.

Department of Health (2008a) *Putting People First*. London: Department of Health.

Department of Health (2008b) *Transforming social care*. Local Authority Circular. www.dh.gov.uk/en/Publicationsandstatistics/Lettersandcirculars/LocalAuthorityCirculars/DH_081934.

Department of Health (2009) *Valuing People Now: A New Three-Year Strategy for People with Learning Disabilities. 'Making it Happen for Everyone'*. London: Department of Health.

Disability Rights Commission (2002) *Disability Rights Statement*. www.officefordisability.gov.uk/working/independent-living. Accessed 21 March 2010.

Dore, J. (1977) Children's illocutionary acts (pp. 227–238), in R. Freedle (Ed.) *Discourse, Comprehension and Production*. Norwood, NJ: Ablex.

Dowse, L. (2009) 'Some people are never going to be able to do that'. Challenges for people with intellectual disability in the 21st century. *Disability and Society*, 24(5): 571–584.

Dowson, S. & Whittaker, A. (1993) *On One Side: The Role of the Advisor in Supporting People with Learning Difficulties in Self Advocacy Groups*. London: Values into Action.

Drew, P. & Heritage, J. (1992) *Talk at Work: Interaction in Institutional Settings*. Cambridge: Cambridge University Press.

Duffy, S. (2007) Care management and self-directed support. *Journal of Integrated Care*, 15(5): 3–14.

Dybwad, G. & Bersani, H. (Eds.) (1996) *New Voices: Self Advocacy by People with Learning Disabilities*. Cambridge, MA: Brookline Books.

Eayrs, C., Ellis, N. & Jones, R. (1993) Which label? An investigation into the effects of terminology on public perceptions of and attitudes towards people with learning difficulties. *Disability, Handicap and Society*, 8(2): 117–127.

Edge, J. (2001) *Who's in Control? Decision-making by People with Learning Difficulties Who Have High Support Needs*. London: Values into Action.

Edwards, D. (2001) Emotion (pp. 236–246), in M. Wetherell, S. Taylor & S. Yates (Eds.) *Discourse Theory and Practice*. London: Sage.

Edwards, D. (2003) Analysing racial discourse: the discursive psychology of mind–world relationships (pp. 31–48), in H. van den Berg, M. Wetherell & H. Houtkoop-Steenstra (Eds.) *Analysing Race Talk: Multidisciplinary Approaches to the Interview*. Cambridge: Cambridge University Press.

Edwards, D. (2005) Discursive psychology (pp. 257–273), in K. L. Fitch & R. E. Sanders (Eds.) *Handbook of Language and Social Interaction*. New York: Lawrence Erlbaum.

Emerson, E., Malam, S., Davies, I., & Spencer, K. (2005) *Adults with Learning Difficulties in England 2003/4: Full Report*. NHS Health and Social Care Information Centre.

Emerson, E. & Robertson, J. (2008) *Commissioning Person-Centred, Cost-Effective Local Support for People with Learning Disabilities*. SCIE Adult Services Knowledge Review 20. www.scie.org.uk.

Everitt, G. & Williams, V. (2007) Have your say about college. A report on FE provision for young people with learning disabilities in Somerset. www.bristol.ac.uk/norahfry.

Fairclough, N. (1989) *Language and Power*. London: Longman.

Fairclough, N. (1992) *Discourse and Social Change in Society*. London: Polity Press/Oxford: Blackwell.

Fairclough, N. (1995) *Critical Discourse Analysis: The Critical Study of Language*. London and New York: Longman.

Fairclough, N. (2001) The discourse of New Labour: critical discourse analysis (pp. 229–266), in M. Wetherell, S. Taylor & S. Yates (Eds.) *Discourse as Data: A Guide for Analysis*. London: Sage.

Fairclough, N. & Wodak, R. (1997) Critical discourse analysis (pp. 258–284), in T. Van Dijk (Ed.) *Discourse as Social Interaction*. London: Sage.

Felce D., Lowe K. & Jones E. (2002) Staff activity in supported housing services. *Journal of Applied Research in Intellectual Disabilities*, 15: 388–403.

Finkelstein, V. (2004) Representing disability (pp. 13–20), in J. Swain, S. French, C. Barnes & C. Thomas (Eds.) *Disabling Barriers – Enabling Environments*, 2nd edition. London: Sage.

Finlay, M. & Lyons, E. (1998) Social identity and people with learning difficulties: implications for self-advocacy groups. *Disability and Society*, 13(1): 37–51.

Finlay, W. M. L., Antaki, C., Walton, C. & Stribling, P. (2008a) The dilemma for staff in 'playing a game' with people with a profound intellectual disability. *Sociology of Health and Illness*, 30: 531–549.

Finlay, W. M. L., Antaki, C. & Walton, C. (2008b) Saying no to the staff: an analysis of refusals in a home for people with severe communication difficulties. *Sociology of Health and Illness*, 30: 55–75.

Finlay, W. M. L., Walton, C. & Antaki, C. (2008c) Promoting choice and control in residential services for people with learning disabilities. *Disability and Society, 23*: 349–360.

Forrester-Jones, R., Carpenter, J., *et al.* (2006) The social networks of people with intellectual disability living in the community 12 years after resettlement from long-stay hospitals. *Journal of Applied Research in Intellectual Disabilities, 19*(4): 285–295.

Frawley, P. (2008) *Participation in Government Disability Advisory Bodies: An Intellectual Disability Perspective*. Report for the Department of Human Services – Disability Services. Melbourne: LaTrobe University.

Frederickson, N. & Cline, T. (2002) Learning difficulties (pp. 231–260), in N. Frederickson & T. Cline, (Eds.) *Special Educational Needs: Inclusion and Diversity*. Maidenhead: Open University Press.

French, S. (1999) Controversial issues: critical perspectives (pp. 81–89), in J. Swain & S. French (Eds.) *Therapy and Learning Difficulties: Advocacy, Participation and Partnership*. Oxford: Butterworth-Heinemann.

Fyson, R. (2009) Independence and learning disabilities: why we must also recognise vulnerability. *Journal of Integrated Care, 17*(1): 3–8.

Fyson, L. & Fox, L. (2008) *The Role and Effectiveness of Learning Disability Partnership Boards*. Nottingham: International Centre for Public and Social Policy.

Garfinkel, H. (1967) *Studies in Ethnomethodology*. Englewood Cliffs, NJ: Prentice-Hall.

Garland, J. N. (2008) The importance of being Irish: national identity, cultural authenticity, and linguistic authority in an Irish language class in the United States. *Pragmatics, 18*(2): 253–276.

Geekie, P. & Raban, B. (1994) Language learning at home and school (pp. 153–80), in C. Gallaway & B. Richards (Eds.) *Input and Interaction in Language Acquisition*. Cambridge: Cambridge University Press.

Georgakopoulou, A. (2006) Small and large identities in narrative (inter) action (pp. 48–82), in A. de Fina, D. Schiffrin & M. Bamberg (Eds.) *Discourse and Identity*. Cambridge: Cambridge University Press.

Gergen, K. (2001) Self-narration in social life (pp. 247–260), in M. Wetherell, S. Taylor & S. Yates (Eds.) *Discourse Theory and Practice*. London: Sage.

Gillman, M., Heyman, B. & Swain, J. (2000) What's in a name? The implications of diagnosis for people with learning difficulties and their family carers. *Disability and Society, 15*(3): 389–409.

Glaser, B. (1992) *Basics of Grounded Theory Analysis*. Mill Valley, CA: Sociology Press.

Gluck, S. & Patai, D. (1991) *Women's Words: The Feminist Practice of Oral History*. London: Routledge.

Goffman, E. (1959) *The Presentation of Self in Everyday Life*. New York: Doubleday Anchor.

Goodley, D. (1997) Locating self-advocacy in models of disability: understanding disability in the support of self-advocates with learning difficulties. *Disability and Society, 12*(3): 367–379.

Goodley, D. (2000) *Self Advocacy in the Lives of People with Learning Difficulties*. Buckingham: Open University Press.

Goodley, D. (2001) 'Learning difficulties', the social model of disability and impairment: challenging epistemologies. *Disability and Society 16*(2): 207–231.

Goodley, D. (2003) Against a politics of victimisation: disability culture and self-advocates with learning difficulties (pp. 105–130), in S. Riddell & N. Watson (Eds.) *Disability, Culture and Identity*. Edinburgh: Pearson Education.

Goodwin, C. (1981) *Conversational Organization: Interaction between Speakers and Hearers*. New York: Academic Press.

Goodwin, C. (1984) Notes on story structure and the organisation of participation (pp. 225–246), in J. Atkinson & J. Heritage (Eds.) *Structures of Social Action: Studies in Conversation Analysis*. Cambridge: Cambridge University Press.

Goodwin, C. (2007) Participation, stance and affect in the organization of activities. *Discourse and Society, 18*(1): 53–73.

Gramlich, S., McBride, G., Snelham, N. & Myers, B. with Williams, V. & Simons, K. (2002) *Journey to Independence: What Self Advocates Tell Us about Direct Payments*. Kidderminster: BILD.

Gramlich, S., Snelham, N. & McBride, G. (2000) Our journey into the unknown. *Community Living*, October/November: 9–10.

Grant, G., Goward, P., Richardson, M. & Ramcharan, P. (2005) *Learning Disability: A Life Cycle Approach to Valuing People*. Buckingham: Open University Press.

Hall, L. & Hewson, S. (2006) The community links of a sample of people with intellectual disabilities. *Journal of Applied Research in Intellectual Disabilities, 19*: 204–207.

Hammersley, M. (2003) Conversation analysis and discourse analysis: methods or paradigms? *Discourse and Society*, 14(6): 751–781.

Heath, C. (1997) The analysis of activities in face to face interaction using video (pp. 183–200), in D. Silverman (Ed.) *Qualitative Research: Theory, Method and Practice*. London: Sage.

Heritage, J. (1984) A change of state token and aspects of its sequential placement (pp. 299–345), in J. M. Atkinson & J. Heritage (Eds.) *Structures of Social Action: Studies in Conversation Analysis*. Cambridge: Cambridge University Press.

Heritage, J. (1997) Conversation analysis and institutional talk: analysing data (pp. 161–182), in D. Silverman (Ed.) *Qualitative Research: Theory, Method and Practice*. London: Sage.

Heritage, J. & Clayman, S. (2010) *Talk in Action: Interactions, Identities, and Institutions*. Chichester: Wiley-Blackwell.

Heritage, J., Robinson, J., Elliott, M., Beckett, M. & Wilkes, M. (2007) Reducing patients' unmet concerns: the difference one word can make. *Journal of General Internal Medicine, 22*: 1429–1433.

Holstein, J. & Gubrium, J. (1997) Active interviewing (pp. 113–129), in D. Silverman (Ed.) *Qualitative Research: Theory, Method and Practice*. London: Sage.

Hutchby, I. (2002) Resisting the incitement to talk in child counselling: aspects of the utterance 'I don't know'. *Discourse and Society*, 4(2): 147–168.

Iles, I. (1999) Navigating paradox: reflections on facilitating self-advocacy for people with learning difficulties. *Journal of Learning Disabilities for Nursing, Health and Social Care*, 3(3): 163–167.

Jefferson, G. (1974) Error correction as an international resource. *Language in Society, 2*: 181–199.

Jefferson, G. (1979) A technique for inviting laughter and its subsequent acceptance/declination (pp. 79–96), in G. Psathas (Ed.) *Everyday Language: Studies in Ethnomethodology*. New York: Irvington.

Jenkinson, J. (1993) Who shall decide? The relevance of theory and research to decision-making by people with an intellectual disability. *Disability, Handicap and Society*, 8(4): 361–375.

Jepson, M. (2008) Who decides? Using the Mental Capacity Act to support people. *Learning Disability Today, 8*: 20–25.

Jepson, M. (in preparation) Who decides? The Mental Capacity Act and everyday decisions for people with learning disabilities. PhD thesis to be submitted to the University of Bristol.

Jingree, T., Finlay, M. & Antaki, C. (2006) Empowering words, disempowering actions: an analysis of interactions between staff members and people with learning disabilities in residents' meetings. *Journal of Intellectual Disability Research, 50*: 212–226.

Johnson, G. C. (2003) The discursive construction of teacher identities in a research interview (pp. 188–212), in A. de Fina, D. Schiffrin & M. Bamberg (Eds.) *Discourse and Identity*. Cambridge: Cambridge University Press.

Johnson, K., Hillier, L., Harrison, L. & Frawley, P. (2001) *People with Intellectual Disabilities Living Safer Sexual Lives*. Melbourne: Latrobe University.

Johnson, K. & Traustadottir, R. (2005) *Deinstitutionalization and People with Intellectual Disabilities*. London: Jessica Kingsley.

Johnson, K. & Walmsley, J. with Wolfe, M. (2010) *People with Intellectual Disabilities: Towards a Good Life?* Bristol: Policy Press.

Kendon, A. (1983) Gesture and speech: how they interact (pp. 13–47), in J. Wiemann & R. Harrison (Eds.) *Nonverbal Interaction*. London: Sage.

Kendon, A. (1990) *Conducting Interaction: Patterns of Behaviour in Focused Encounters*. Cambridge: Cambridge University Press.

Kendon, A. (2004) Gesture and speech in semantic interaction (pp 158–175), in A. Kendon (Ed.) *Gesture: Visible Action as Utterance.* Cambridge: Cambridge University Press.

Leece, J. & Bornat, J. (Eds.) (2006) *Developments in Direct Payments.* Bristol: Policy Press.

Lowes, L. & Hulatt, I. (2005) *Involving Service Users in Health and Social Care Research.* London: Routledge.

Mansell, J., Elliott, T., Beadle-Brown, J. Ashman, B. & Macdonald, S. (2002) Engagement in meaningful activity and 'active support' of people with intellectual disabilities in residential care. *Research in Developmental Disabilities, 23*: 342–352.

March, J., Steingold, B. & Justice, S. with P. Mitchell (1997) Follow the Yellow Brick Road! People with learning difficulties as co-researchers. *British Journal of Learning Disabilities, 25*: 77–80.

McClimens, A. (1999) Participatory research with people who have a learning difficulty: journeys without a map. *Journal of Learning Disabilities for Nursing, Health and Social Care, 3*(4): 219–228.

McHoul, A. & Grace, W. (1993) *A Foucault Primer: Discourse, Power and the Subject.* Melbourne: Melbourne University Press.

Mean, L. (2002) Identity and discursive practice: doing gender on the football pitch. *Discourse and Society, 12*(6): 789–817.

Meininger, H. (2006) Narrating, writing, reading: life story work as an aid to (self) advocacy. *British Journal of Learning Disabilities, 34*(3): 181–188.

Mental Capacity Act (England and Wales) (2005) London: The Stationery Office.

Mercer, G. (2002) Emancipatory disability research (pp. 228–249), in C. Barnes, M. Oliver & L. Barton (Eds.) *Disability Studies Today.* Cambridge: Polity Press.

Morris, J. (1993) *Independent Lives.* London: Macmillan.

Myers, G. (1998) Displaying opinions: topics and disagreement in focus groups. *Language in Society, 27*: 85–111.

Myron, R., Gillespie, S., Swift, P. & Williamson, T. (2008) *Whose Decision? Preparation for and Implementation of the Mental Capacity Act in Statutory and Non-statutory Services in England and Wales.* London: Mental Health Foundation.

Newcomb, A. F. & Bagwell, C. L. (1995) 'Children's friendship relations: a meta-analytic review', *Psychological Bulletin, 117*: 306–347.

Northway, R. & Wheeler, P. (2005) Working together to undertake research (pp. 199–208), in L. Lowes & I. Hulatt (Eds.) *Involving Service Users in Health and Social Care Research.* London: Routledge.

Nunkoosing, K. (2000) Constructing learning disability: consequences for men and women with learning disabilities. *Journal of Learning Disabilities, 4*(1): 49–62.

Ochs, E. (1979) Transcription as theory (pp. 43–72), in E. Ochs & B. Schieffelin (Eds.) *Developmental Pragmatics.* New York: Academic Press.

Ochs, E. & Taylor, C. (1992) Family narrative as political activity. *Discourse and Society, 3*(3): 301–340.

Office for Disability Issues (2008) *Independent Living: A Cross-Government Strategy about Independent Living for Disabled People.* London: ODI.

Oliver, M. (1990) *The Politics of Disablement.* London: Macmillan.

Oliver, M. (1992) Changing the social relations of research production? *Disability, Handicap and Society, 7*(2): 101–114.

Oliver, M. (1996) *Understanding Disability.* Basingstoke: Macmillan.

Oliver, M. (1997) Emancipatory research: realistic goal or impossible dream? (pp. 15–31), in C. Barnes & G. Mercer (Eds.) *Doing Disability Research.* Leeds: The Disability Press.

Oliver, M. (2004) If I had a hammer (pp. 1–12), in J. Swain, S. French, C. Barnes & C. Thomas (Eds.) *Disabling Barriers – Enabling Environments,* 2nd edition. London: Sage.

Palmer, N., Peacock, C., Turner, F. & Vasey, B. (1999a) Telling people what you think (pp. 33–46), in J. Swain & S. French (Eds.) *Therapy and Learning Difficulties: Advocacy, Participation and Partnership*. Oxford: Butterworth-Heinemann.

Palmer, N., Peacock, C., Turner, F. & Vasey, B. (1999b) *Finding Out*. Unpublished report of a research project, available from val.williams@bristol.ac.uk.

Palmer, N. & Turner, F. (1998) Self advocacy: doing our own research. *Royal College of Speech and Language Therapy Bulletin*, August: 12–13.

Patel, R. & Pridmore, A. (2010) *A Successful Working Relationship*. London: Skills for Care.

Payne, G. & Cuff, E. (Eds.) (1982) *Doing Teaching: The Practical Management of Classrooms*. London: Batsford Academic and Educational.

People First website (2009) www.peoplefirstltd.com. Accessed March 2010.

Perakyla, A. & Vehvilainen, S. (2003) Conversation analysis and the professional stocks of interactional knowledge. *Discourse and Society*, 14(6): 727–750.

Perry, J. (2004) Hate crime against people with learning difficulties: the role of the Crime and Disorder Act. *Journal of Adult Protection*, 6(1): 27–34.

Pine, J. (1994) Language of primary caregivers (pp. 15–37), in C. Gallaway & B. Richards (Eds.) *Input and Interaction in Language Acquisition*. Cambridge: Cambridge University Press.

Pomerantz, A. (1986) Extreme case formulations: a way of legitimizing claims. *Human Studies*, 9: 219–229.

Pomerantz, A. & Fehr, B. (1997) Conversation analysis (pp. 64–91), in T. van Dijk (Ed.) *Discourse as Social Interaction*. London: Sage.

Ponting, L., Ford, K., Williams, V., Rudge, P. & Francis, A. (2010) *Training Personal Assistants*. Brighton: Pavilion Publishing.

Potter, J. (2003) Discursive psychology: between method and paradigm. *Discourse and Society*, 14(6): 783–794.

Prime Minister's Strategy Unit (2005) *Improving the Life Chances of Disabled People*. www.strategy.gov.uk/downloads/work_areas/disability/disability_report/pdf/disability.pdf.

Psathas, G. & Anderson, T. (1990) The 'practices' of transcription in conversation analysis. *Semiotica*, 78: 75–99.

Rao, S. (2006) Parameters of normality and cultural constructions of 'mental retardation': perspectives of Bengali families. *Disability and Society*, 21(2): 159–178.

Rapley, M. (2004) *The Social Construction of Intellectual Disability*. Cambridge: Cambridge University Press.

Rapley, M., Kiernan, P. & Antaki, C. (1998) Invisible to themselves or negotiating identity? The interactional management of 'being intellectually disabled'. *Disability and Society*, 13(5): 807–827.

Rawlings, B. (1988) Local knowledge: the analysis of transcribed audio materials for organizational ethnography. *Studies in Qualitative Methodology*, 1: 157–177.

Redley, M. (2009) Understanding the social exclusion and stalled welfare of citizens with learning disabilities. *Disability and Society*, 24(4): 489–501.

Redley, M. & Weinberg, D. (2007) Learning disability and the limits of liberal citizenship: interactional impediments to political empowerment. *Sociology of Health and Illness*, 29(5): 1–20.

Richardson, M. (2002) Involving people in the analysis: listening, reflecting, discounting nothing. *Journal of Learning Disabilities*, 6(1): 47–60.

Rioux, M. & Bach, M. (Eds.) (1994) *Disability is not Measles: New Research Paradigms in Disability*. Toronto: Roehrer Institute.

Roberts, C. & Sarangi, S. (2005) Theme-oriented discourse analysis of medical encounters. *Medical Education*, 39: 632–640.

Robertson, J., Emerson, E., Gregory, N., *et al.* (2001) Social networks of people with mental retardation in residential settings. *Mental Retardation*, 39: 201–214.

Rodgers, J. (1999) Trying to get it right: undertaking research involving people with learning difficulties. *Disability and Society, 14*: 421–434.

Ryoo, H.-K. (2005) Achieving friendly interactions: a study of service encounters between Korean shopkeepers and African-American customers. *Discourse and Society, 16*(1): 79–105.

Sacks, H. (1984) Notes on methodology (pp. 21–27), in P. Atkinson & J. Heritage (Eds.) *Structures of Social Action: Studies in Conversation Analysis*. Cambridge: Cambridge University Press.

Sacks, H. (1995) *Lectures on Conversation*, vols I and II. G. Jefferson & E. E. Schegloff (Eds.). Oxford and Cambridge, MA: Blackwell.

Sacks, H., Schegloff, E. & Jefferson, G. (1974) A simplest systematics for the organization of turn-taking in conversation. *Language, 50*(4): 696–735.

Sarangi, S. (2003) Institutional, professional and lifeworld frames in interview talk (pp. 64–84), in H. van den Berg, M. Wetherell and H. Houtkoop (Eds.) *Analysing Race Talk: Multidisciplinary Approaches to the Interview*. Cambridge: Cambridge University Press.

Sarangi, S. & Roberts, C. (1999) The dynamics of interactional and institutional orders in work-related settings. Introduction in S. Sarangi & C. Roberts (Eds.) *Talk, Work and Institutional Order: Discourse in Medical, Mediation and Management Settings*. Berlin: Mouton de Gruyter.

Sarbin, T. & Kitsuse, J. (1994) A prologue to constructing the social (pp. 1–16), in T. Sarbin & J. Kitsuse (Eds.) *Constructing the Social*. London: Sage.

Schegloff, E. (1968) Sequencing in conversational openings. *American Anthropologist, 70*(6): 1075–1095.

Schegloff, E. (1992) On talk and its institutional occasions (pp. 101–136), in P. Drew & J. Heritage (Eds.) *Talk at Work*. Cambridge: Cambridge University Press.

Schegloff, E. (1998) Reply to Wetherell. *Discourse and Society, 9*(3): 413–416.

Schegloff, E. (1999a) 'Schegloff's texts' as 'Billig's data'. A critical reply. *Discourse and Society, 10*(4): 558–572.

Schegloff, E. (1999b) Naivety vs. sophistication or discipline v. self indulgence: a rejoinder to Billig. *Discourse and Society, 10*(4): 577–582.

Schegloff, E. (2007) *Sequence Organization in Interaction: A Primer in Conversation Analysis*, 1. Cambridge: Cambridge University Press.

Schegloff, E., Jefferson, G. & Sacks, H. (1977) The preference for self-correction in the organisation of repair in conversation. *Language, 53*: 361–382. Reproduced in G. Psathas (Ed.) *Interactional Competence*. Washington, DC: University Press of America, 1977.

Schegloff, E. & Sacks, H. (1973) Opening up closings. *Semiotica, 7*: 289–327.

Schelly, D. (2008) Problems associated with choice and quality of life for an individual with intellectual disability: a personal assistant's reflexive ethnography. *Disability and Society, 23*(7): 719–732.

Schiffrin, D. (2006) From linguistic reference to social reality (pp. 103–134), in A. de Fina, D. Schiffrin & M. Bamberg (Eds.) *Discourse and Identity*. Cambridge: Cambridge University Press.

Searle, J. R. (1969) *Speech Acts*. Cambridge: Cambridge University Press.

Shakespeare, P. (1998) *Aspects of Confused Speech: A Study of Verbal Interaction Between Confused and Normal Speakers*. Hillsdale, NJ: Lawrence Erlbaum.

Shakespeare, T. (2006) *Disability Rights and Wrongs*. London: Routledge.

Sigelman, C. K., Budd, E. C., Spanhel, C. L. & Schoenrock, C. J. (1981) When in doubt, say yes: acquiescence in interviews with mentally retarded persons. *Mental Retardation, 19*: 53–58.

Silverman, D. (1973) Interview talk: bringing off a research instrument. *Sociology, 7*(1): 31–48.

Silverman, D. (1997) *Discourses of Counselling: HIV Counselling as Social Interaction*. London: Sage.

Silverman, D. (1998) *Harvey Sacks: Social Science and Conversation Analysis*. Cambridge: Polity Press.

Silverman, D. (1999) Warriors or collaborators: reworking methodological considerations in the study of institutional interaction (pp. 401–425), in S. Sarangi & C. Roberts (Eds.) *Talk, Work and Institutional Order*. The Hague: Mouton de Gruyter.

Silverman, D. (2005) *Doing Qualitative Research*, 2nd edition. London: Sage.

Simpson, M. (1995) The sociology of 'competence' in services. *Social Work and Social Sciences Review*, 6(2): 85–97.

Simpson, M. (1999) Bodies, brains and behaviour: the return of the three stooges in learning disability (pp. 148–156), in M. Corker & S. French (Eds.) *Disability Discourse*. Buckingham: Open University Press.

Skills for Support Team (2008) *A New Type of Support: Final Report of the 'Skills for Support' Project*. www.bristol.ac.uk/norahfry.

Smith, J. A., Flowers, P. & Larkin, M. (2009) *Interpretative Phenomenological Analysis: Theory Method and Research*. London: Sage.

Souza, A. with Ramcharam, P. (1997) Everything you ever wanted to know about Down's Syndrome, but never bothered to ask (pp. 3–14), in P. Ramcharan, G. Roberts, G. Grant & J. Borland (Eds.) *Empowerment in Everyday Life: Learning Disability*. London: Jessica Kingsley.

Speer, S. (2002) 'Natural' and 'contrived' data: a sustainable distinction? *Discourse Studies*, 4: 511–520.

Stalker, K. (1998) Some ethical and methodological issues in research with people with learning difficulties. *Disability and Society*, 13(1): 5–19.

Steel, R. (2005) Actively involving marginalized and vulnerable people in research (pp. 18–29), in L. Lowes & I. Hulatt (Eds.) *Involving Service Users in Health and Social Care Research*. London: Routledge.

Stubbs, M. (1983) *Discourse Analysis: The Sociolinguistic Analysis of Natural Language*. Oxford: Blackwell.

Suchman, L. & Jordan, B. (1990) Interactional troubles in face-to-face survey interviews. *Journal of the American Statistical Association*, 85(409): 232–241.

Sutcliffe, J. & Simons, K. (1994) *Self Advocacy and Adults with Learning Difficulties*. Leicester: National Institute of Adult Continuing Education.

Swain, J. (1995) Constructing participatory research: in principle and in practice (pp. 75–93), in P. Clough & L. Barton (Eds.) *Making Difficulties: Research and the Construction of SEN*. London: Paul Chapman.

Swain, J. & Cameron, C. (1999) Unless otherwise stated: discourses of labelling and identity in coming out (pp. 68–78), in M. Corker & S. French (Eds.) *Disability Discourse*. Buckingham: Open University Press.

Swift, P. (2008) Understanding the Mental Capacity Act. *Care Management Matters*, July/August.

Swift, P. & Mattingly, M. (2008) *A Life in the Community: An Action Research Project Promoting Citizenship for People with High Support Needs*. London: Foundation for People with Learning Disabilities.

Tarleton, B., Williams, V., Palmer, N. & Gramlich, S. (2004) 'An equal relationship?' People with learning difficulties getting involved in research (pp. 73–90), in M. Smyth & E. Williamson (Eds.) *Researchers and Their 'Subjects': Ethics, Power, Knowledge and Consent*. Bristol: Policy Press.

Taylor, S. (2001) Locating and conducting discourse analytic research (pp. 5–48), in M. Wetherell, S. Taylor & S. Yates (Eds.) *Discourse as Data: A Guide for Analysis*. London: Sage.

ten Have, P. (1999) *Doing Conversation Analysis: A Practical Guide*. London: Sage.

Thomas, C. (2004) How is disability understood? An examination sociological approaches. *Disability and Society*, 19: 569–583.

Tideman, M. (2005) Conquering life. The experiences of the first integrated generation (pp. 211–221), in K. Johnson & R. Traustadottir (Eds.) *Deinstitutionalization and People with Intellectual Disabilities*. London: Jessica Kingsley.

Todd, S. & Shearn, J. (1995) *Family Secrets and Dilemmas of Status: Parental Management of the Disclosure of 'Learning Disability'*. Cardiff: Welsh Centre for Learning Disabilities, Applied Research Unit.

Todd, S. & Shearn, J. (1997) Family dilemmas and secrets: parents' disclosure of information to their adult offspring with learning disabilities. *Disability and Society*, *12*(3): 341–366.

Townsley, R., Ward, L., Abbott, D. & Williams, V. (2009) *The Implementation of Policies Supporting Independent Living for Disabled People in Europe: Synthesis Report*. Utrecht: Academy Network of European Disability Experts.

Townson, L., Macauley, S., Harkness, E., *et al.* (2004) We are all in the same boat: doing 'people-led research'. *British Journal of Learning Disabilities*, *32*(2): 72–76.

United Nations (2007) *United Nations Convention on the Rights of Persons with Disabilities*. Geneva: UN.

van de Mieroop, D. (2008) Co-constructing identities in speeches: how the construction of an 'other' identity is defining for the 'self' identity and vice versa. *Pragmatics*, *18*(3): 491–509.

van den Berg, H., Wetherell, M. & Houtkoop-Steenstra, H. (2003a) Introduction (pp. 1–10), in H. van den Berg, M. Wetherell & H. Houtkoop-Steenstra (Eds.) *Analysing Race Talk: Multidisciplinary Approaches to the Interview*. Cambridge: Cambridge University Press.

van den Berg, H., Wetherell, M. & Houtkoop-Steenstra, H. (Eds.) (2003b) *Analysing Race Talk: Multidisciplinary Approaches to the Interview*. Cambridge: Cambridge University Press.

van Dijk, T. (1997a) The study of discourse (pp. 1–34), in T. van Dijk (Ed.) *Discourse as Structure and Process*. London: Sage.

van Dijk, T. (1997b) *Discourse as Social Interaction*. London: Sage.

van Dijk, T. (2001) Principles of critical discourse analysis (pp. 300–317), in M. Wetherell, S. Taylor & S. Yates (Eds.) *Discourse Theory and Practice: A Reader*. London: Sage.

Vygotsky, L. S. (1987) Thinking and speech (pp. 39–285), in L. S. Vygotsky, *Collected Works* (vol. 1, pp. 39–285). Eds. R. Rieber & A. Carton; Trans. N. Minick. New York: Plenum. (First published 1934, 1960.)

Walmsley, J. (2001) Normalisation, emancipatory research and inclusive research in learning disability. *Disability and Society*, *16*(2): 187–205.

Walmsley, J. & Johnson, K. (2003) *Inclusive Research with People with Learning Disabilities: Past, Present and Future*. London and New York: Jessica Kingsley.

Ward, L. & Simons, K. (1998) Practising partnership: involving people with learning difficulties in research. *British Journal of Learning Disabilities*, *26*: 128–131.

Watson, N. (2003) Daily denials: the routinisation of oppression and resistance (pp. 34–52), in S. Riddell & N. Watson (Eds.) *Disability, Culture and Identity*. Edinburgh: Pearson Education.

Welshman, J. & Walmsley, J. (Eds.) (2006) *Community Care in Perspective: Care, Control and Citizenship*. Basingstoke: Palgrave Macmillan.

Wetherell, M. (1998) Positioning and interpretative repertoires: conversation analysis and post-structuralism in dialogue. *Discourse and Society*, *9*(3): 387–412.

Wetherell, M. & Potter, J. (1992) *Mapping the Language of Racism*. New York: Harvester Wheatsheaf.

Wetherell, M., Taylor, S. & Yates, S. (2001a) *Discourse Theory and Practice*. London: Sage.

Wetherell, M., Taylor, S. & Yates, S. (2001b) *Discourse as Data*. London: Sage.

Williams, V. (1999) Researching together. *British Journal of Learning Disabilities*, *27*: 48–51.

Williams, V. (2002) Being researchers with the label of learning difficulty: an analysis of talk in a project carried out by a self-advocacy research group. Unpublished PhD thesis: Open University, School of Health and Social Welfare.

Williams, V. (2005) 'Did you solve it yourself?': evaluation of narratives of self-identity by people with learning disabilities. *Communication and Medicine*, *2*(1): 77–89.

Williams, V. & England, M. (2005) Supporting people with learning difficulties to do their own research (pp. 30–40), in L. Lowes & I. Hulatt (Eds.) *Involving Service Users in Health and Social Care Research*. Abingdon: Routledge.

Williams, V. with Ford, K., Ponting, L., Rudge, P. & Francis, A. (2006) Including people with learning difficulties. *Learning Disability Today*, *6*(3): 10–16.

Williams, V. & Heslop, P. (2005) Mental health support needs of people with a learning difficulty: a medical or a social model? *Disability and Society, 20*(3): 231–245.

Williams, V. & Holman, A. (2006) Direct payments and autonomy: issues for people with learning difficulties (pp. 65–78), in J. Leece & J. Bornat (Eds.) *Developments in Direct Payments*. Bristol: Policy Press.

Williams, V., Marriott, A. & Townsley, R. (2008) *Shaping our Future: A Scoping and Consultation Exercise to Determine Research Priorities in Learning Disability For The Next Ten Years*. Report for the National Coordinating Centre for NHS Service Delivery and Organisation RandD (NCCSDO).

Williams, V., Ponting, L., Ford, K. & Rudge, P. (2009a) 'A bit of common ground': personalisation and the use of shared knowledge in interactions between people with learning disabilities and their personal assistants. *Discourse Studies, 11*(5): 607–624.

Williams, V., Ponting, L., Ford, K. & Rudge, P. (2009b) 'I do like the subtle touch': interactions between people with learning disabilities and their personal assistants. *Disability and Society, 24*(7): 815–828.

Williams, V., Ponting, L., Ford, K. & Rudge, P. (2009c) Skills for support: personal assistants and people with learning disabilities. *British Journal of Learning Disabilities, 38*: 59–67.

Williams, V., Simons, K. & Swindon People First Research Team (2005) More researching together. *British Journal of Learning Disabilities, 32*: 1–9.

Wooffitt, R. (2001) Raising the dead: reported speech in medium–sitter interaction. *Discourse Studies, 3*(3): 351–374.

Wooffitt, R. (2005) *Conversation Analysis and Discourse Analysis: A Comparative and Critical Introduction*. London: Sage.

Worrell, B. (1987) Walking the fine line: the people first advisor. *Entourage, 2*(2): 30–35.

Zarb, G. (1992) On the road to Damascus: first steps towards changing the social relations of research production. *Disability, Handicap and Society, 7*: 125–138.

Zarb, G. & Nadash, P. (1994) *Cashing in on Independence: Comparing the Costs and Benefits of Cash and Services*. London: British Council of Disabled People.

Zimmerman, D. (1998) Identity, context and interaction (pp. 87–106), in C. Antaki & S. Widdicombe (Eds.) *Identities in Talk*. London: Sage.

Index